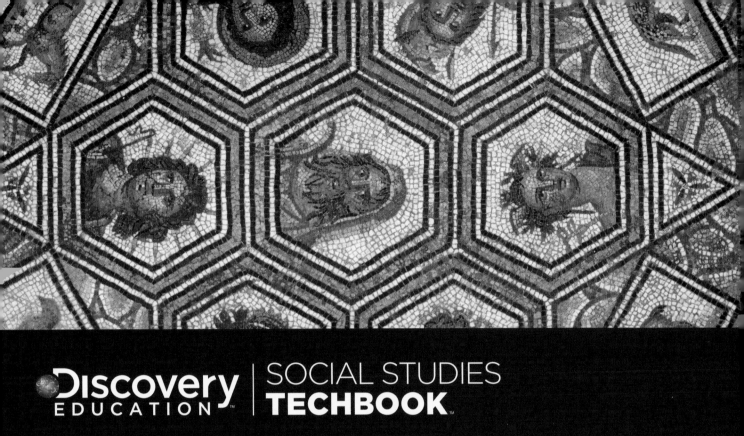

# Medieval and Early Modern World History
## California Edition
## Core Text Companion

**Sign in to Social Studies Techbook
at www.DiscoveryEducation.com**

ISBN 13: 978-1-68220-432-0

Library of Congress Cataloging-in-Publication Data available upon request from the Library of Congress.

Printed in the United States of America.

1 2 3 4 5 6 7 8 9 10

**800-323-9084**
One Discovery Place, Silver Spring, Maryland 20910
©2018 Discovery Education. All rights reserved.

# Table of Contents

## UNIT 1 | Empire, Belief, and Power

### CHAPTER 1 | Connecting the World

**CONCEPT**

*How did the regions of the world interact around 300 CE?*

### CHAPTER 2 | The Roman Republic and Empire

**CONCEPTS**

*How did geography and trade routes impact the growth of Rome?*

*Was the Roman Republic democratic?*

*How did Rome's transition from Republic to Empire impact its citizens?*

*How did the spread of Roman culture influence life throughout the Empire?*

*Why did Rome decline and fall?*

### CHAPTER 3 | Medieval Europe

**CONCEPTS**

*How did Christianity develop?*

*How did Christianity become the world's largest religion?*

*How did power and social class impact life in medieval Europe?*

*How did the Black Death spark social, political, and economic change throughout Europe?*

Dear Student,

You are about to experience social studies like you never have before! In this class, you'll be using Social Studies Techbook™—a comprehensive, digital social studies program developed by the educators and designers at Discovery Education. Social Studies Techbook is full of Explorations, videos, Hands-On Activities, reading passages, animations, and more. These resources will help you experience history, geography, economics, and civics. They will help you develop the ability to apply facts and ideas from the past and present to shape your community, nation, and world in the future. Social Studies Techbook allows you to work at your own pace to investigate meaningful social studies questions. You'll even be able to monitor your progress in real time using the Student Learning Dashboard.

*The Core Text Companion* is a print resource that accompanies the digital Social Studies Techbook. With this companion, you have access to Social Studies Techbook's core text—the key ideas and details about each social studies concept—even when you do not have access to a device or the Internet. You can use this resource to explore important ideas, make connections to the digital content, and develop your own understanding of social studies topics.

This print resource is organized by concept and includes the following:

- LESSON OVERVIEW: What's it all about? An introduction, Essential Question, Lesson Objectives, and key vocabulary will help you prepare for each social studies concept.

- ENGAGE: What do you already know? Follow a link to uncover your prior knowledge about each concept.

- EXPLORE: What information is contained in the concept? The Explore pages include core text and images to help you address each concept's Essential Question.

- CHECK FOR UNDERSTANDING: What did you learn as you read the concept? How would you respond to the Essential Question?

Throughout this resource, you'll find QR codes that take you to the corresponding online section of Social Studies Techbook for that concept. For instance, the QR code in the Explore section provides a direct link to the Explore tab and its content. Once you are inside Techbook, you'll have access to maps, interactive explorations, and other digital resources to help you investigate each concept's most important ideas.

Enjoy this voyage into the exciting world of social studies!

Sincerely,

The Discovery Education Social Studies Team

Dear Parent/Guardian,

This year, your student will be using Social Studies Techbook™, a comprehensive, digital social studies program developed by the educators and designers at Discovery Education. Social Studies Techbook is an innovative program that brings history, geography, economics, and civics to life. In class, students experience dynamic content, interactive investigations, videos, primary source documents, maps, and other resources that support high-quality social studies instruction.

As a print resource accompanying the digital Social Studies Techbook, *The Core Text Companion* allows students to explore the core Techbook content when the Internet is not available. Students are encouraged to use this resource to read about key concepts, think about the past, understand the present, and shape the future. Each concept online has five tabs: Engage, Explore, Explain, Elaborate, and Evaluate. *The Core Text Companion* includes the following:

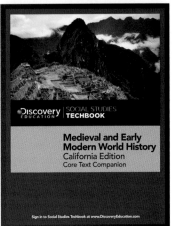

- LESSON OVERVIEW: Students preview a concept's Essential Question, Lesson Objectives, and key vocabulary to help them make connections to social studies content.

- ENGAGE: Students activate their prior knowledge of a concept's essential ideas and begin making connections to the Essential Question.

- EXPLORE: Students deepen their understanding of the concept by exploring the Core Text to address an Essential Question.

- CHECK FOR UNDERSTANDING: These links provide students with opportunities to directly address the concept's Essential Question and demonstrate what they have learned.

Within this resource, you'll find QR codes that take you and your student to a corresponding section of Social Studies Techbook. Once in Techbook, students will have access to the Core Interactive Text of each concept, as well as thousands of resources and activities that build deep conceptual scientific understanding. Additionally, tools and features such as the Interactive Glossary and text-to-speech functionality allow Social Studies Techbook to target learning for students of a variety of abilities.

To use the QR codes, you'll need a QR reader. Readers are available for phones, tablets, laptops, desktops, and virtually any device in between. Most use the device's camera, but there are some that scan documents that are on your screen. Download a free QR reader in the App Store or Google Play. To access Social Studies Techbook resources, follow these steps:

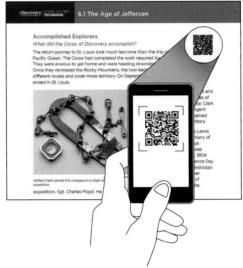

1. Open the QR code reader on your device.

2. Hold your device so the QR code is visible within your device's screen. One of two things will happen:

   • The device may automatically scan the code; or,

   • The device will scan the code when you press a button, similar to taking a picture.

3. Once scanned, the QR code will direct you to a page or resource on the Internet.

4. For resources in Social Studies Techbook, you'll need to sign in with your student's username and password the first time you access a QR code. After that, you won't need to sign in again, unless you sign out or remain inactive for too long.

Scan this QR code to access a video that provides a deeper introduction to Social Studies Techbook:

We encourage you to support your student in using the online interactive materials in Social Studies Techbook, as well as the core text and questions in *The Core Text Companion*. Together, may you and your student enjoy a fantastic year of social studies!

Sincerely,

The Discovery Education Social Studies Team

# Social Studies Techbook and *Core Text Companion*: Introduction and Guide

## How to Use Discovery Education Social Studies Techbook

Discovery Education Social Studies Techbook is a complete digital basal resource designed to engage students in history, geography, economics, and civics. Discovery Education Social Studies Techbook provides teachers with powerful tools for engagement, inquiry, exploration, and evaluation. Unlike a textbook copied into digital format, Discovery Education Social Studies Techbook uses a variety of digital resources, including video, audio, text, and interactive and hands-on experiences, to provide engaging content while meeting the needs of students with different learning styles.

From any browser, navigate to www.DiscoveryEducation.com. Input the username and password that were provided to you.

### Course Page

Upon sign in, you will land on the course page. On this page, you'll find links to curriculum standards, the Techbook Atlas, the Interactive Glossary, and Reviewer Materials.

The course page allows you to navigate the content contained within each course and provides quick links to helpful information. From this page, you can access all of a course's units, chapters, and concepts.

### Concept Pages: The 5Es

The concept structure is set up to accommodate the 5E Instructional Model, with recommended resources for each of the 5Es: Engage, Explore, Explain, Elaborate, and Evaluate. Both students and

teachers can access the resources for instruction and assessment from the concept page by clicking on each E tab. On any tab, Teacher mode can be turned on or off.

## ENGAGE

In Engage, students first encounter and identify an instructional task. They make connections between past and present learning experiences and lay the organizational groundwork for the activities ahead by considering a question, a problem, a surprising event, or an interesting perspective. Engage activities conclude with the introduction of a compelling Essential Question that brings meaning to instruction and can serve as the basis for student inquiry.

## EXPLORE

Explore is embedded with resources that support student inquiry. The Core Interactive Text (CIT) provides students with secondary text, video segments, images, maps, infographics, and more—all of which students can analyze to compile evidence that addresses the Essential Question. The teacher acts as a facilitator, providing materials and guiding the students' focus. The students' inquiry process drives the instruction during exploration.

## EXPLAIN

In Explain, students begin to assemble the information that they have been gathering into a more concrete, communicable form. Social Studies Explanations facilitate students' reflections on the Essential Question and also provide students with a means for reporting and evaluating evidence. Students are also encouraged to put these explanations into their own words and demonstrate understanding in various modalities.

## ELABORATE

Elaborate includes both interactive and primary-source-based activities that pose investigation questions and include sources for addressing these questions. Elaborate also features a Source Library that includes primary and secondary sources that can form the basis of teacher- or student-created inquiry.

## EVALUATE

Evaluate offers flashcards for concept review as well as assessment opportunities. The Evaluate stage should be an ongoing process that occurs throughout the lesson, providing for student practice assessment as well as formal assessment as the learning occurs. Brief and extended constructed response items assess students' ability to analyze a variety of source materials and require students to construct and defend arguments with sound evidence.

Students can review concepts with practice assessments graded in real time. When students answer a question incorrectly, they will have the chance to explore remedial resources on the topic. In the teacher view, teachers can also assign a constructed response item or create their own assessment.

## What Is the Discovery Education *Core Text Companion*?

Online, the Core Interactive Text (CIT) serves as a student pathway through each concept. *The Core Text Companion* is designed to work with Techbook and includes the core text, images, and captions from each concept's Explore section. When a device or an Internet connection is not available, students can still access key information, consider Essential Questions, view primary source images, and glean information needed to complete online activities.

### LESSON OVERVIEW

For each concept, students will first encounter a Lesson Overview, which briefly introduces the concept's focus, lists key vocabulary terms, and previews the concept's Essential Question and Lesson Objectives. Students can scan the QR code on this page to connect directly to the digital version.

### ENGAGE

In Engage, a compelling question encourages students to link their prior knowledge of the topic or related topics. A QR code links to the online Engage activity, and the Essential Question sets the stage for exploration of the concept.

### EXPLORE

In Explore, the full Core Interactive Text guides students through key events and ideas in history and highlights visual resources and captions that help them make connections to the text. A QR code at the beginning of each section connects students to the appropriate Explore section online, where they can supplement their reading with multimedia resources and Hands-On Activities. Other QR codes throughout Explore connect students to additional interactive and primary source-based activities

### CONSIDER THE ESSENTIAL QUESTION / CHECK FOR UNDERSTANDING

The first box at the end of each concept brings students back to the Essential Question and provides a QR code to the Social Studies Explanation online. The second box at the end of each concept checks students' comprehension by posing a constructed response question. The QR code in this box links to a constructed response item within the digital Techbook.

# 1.1 The World in 300 CE

photo: Getty Images

# LESSON OVERVIEW

## Introduction

In this concept, you will learn about the ways in which the kingdoms and empires of the ancient world shared goods, ideas, and knowledge.

## Essential Question

How did the regions of the world interact around 300 CE?

## Lesson Objectives

By the end of this lesson, you should be able to:

- Describe the economic and cultural connections between civilizations across Afro-Eurasia.

- Describe the early cultures of the Americas.

- Analyze the continuity and change in life outside of major kingdoms.

## Key Vocabulary
Which terms do you already know?

- ☐ Aksum
- ☐ Alexander the Great
- ☐ Andes
- ☐ aqueduct
- ☐ Ashoka
- ☐ Buddhism
- ☐ bureaucracy
- ☐ Chandragupta
- ☐ cultural diffusion
- ☐ Emperor Wu Di
- ☐ empire
- ☐ Gupta Empire
- ☐ Han dynasty
- ☐ Huns
- ☐ Jainism
- ☐ Liu Bang
- ☐ maize
- ☐ Mayans
- ☐ Oceania
- ☐ pastoral
- ☐ Persia
- ☐ Roman Empire
- ☐ Silk Road

# ENGAGE

**Lions in Rome? Visit Engage to learn more.**

## Essential Question

How did the regions of the world interact around 300 CE?

---

# EXPLORE

## Empires Connect Regions

*How did large empires create cultural unity and encourage cultural diffusion across regions?*

During the first centuries of the Common Era, many of the people living in Eurasia lived under the domain of a large empire. During this time, the Romans controlled much of Europe, the Persians held power of Southwest Asia, the Gupta dynasty grew in South Asia, and the Han unified China. Each of these empires had a different political structure, and each exercised a different level of control over the daily lives of the people living under its rule.

However, inside each of these empires, the rulers spread their common language. They encouraged worship of the state religions or belief systems. Trade inside the empire brought goods from one corner of the region to another, and minor cities were linked to great capitals. The empires traded with and fought wars against the smaller kingdoms at their edges. They also traded with, and fought against, one another.

Outside of these great empires, smaller kingdoms developed complex societies and left behind cultures that would continue to grow and flourish.

### Rome Rules Europe

The Roman Empire began as a small city-state in what is now Italy. During the last centuries before the Common Era and the first centuries of the Common Era, it expanded its borders. By 200 CE, it included almost all of modern-day Europe, parts of North Africa, and much of Southwest Asia.

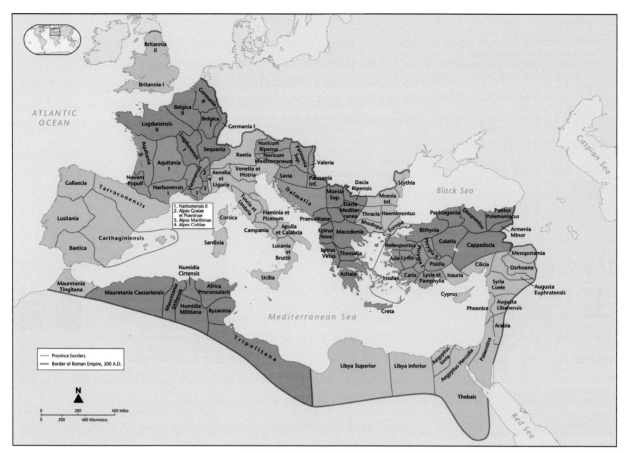

*The Roman Empire included all of the land surrounding the Mediterranean Sea.*

Although Roman officials took charge of conquered provinces, the majority of the population was left alone. Usually, they maintained their local language, religions, and traditions. The Romans often studied their conquered territories to find valuable innovations. By borrowing from other cultures, Rome made advancements in science, medicine, law, government, architecture, and warfare.

The people that the Romans conquered were also influenced by Roman culture. Latin, the Roman language, was the official language of government and of trade. As the Roman Empire spread, Latin became used in more places. In fact, many of the languages of Europe today—including French, Spanish, Italian, Portuguese, and Romanian—come from local variations of Latin that developed during the Roman Empire.

Architecture was another strong Roman influence that extended throughout the empire. Romans constructed government buildings and the homes of the elite ruling class using a distinct style. Roman engineers also developed indoor plumbing, fast-drying cement, and aqueducts.

A network of carefully built roads connected the empire. This made it easier for Roman rulers to send troops to stop revolts in a region. The roads also made it easier to communicate and trade across the empire. Food and agricultural supplies from all over the empire could be transported to Rome or other major cities. The central government controlled trade tightly, collecting taxes and monitoring the amount of each good. Many goods had to be stamped by the government indicating their origin, manufacturing, and even quality.

Starting in 300 CE, Rome began to struggle with increasing internal conflicts and outside invaders, weakening the empire. Meanwhile, great empires were expanding to the east.

## The Persian Empires

*How did the Persian empires shape the region's culture?*

In 550 BCE, a powerful new empire arose in Persia (modern-day Iran). The Achaemenid Empire stretched all the way west to the Mediterranean Sea and all the way east to the Indian subcontinent. It spread the old Persian language, which evolved into modern Farsi, and Zoroastrianism, an early monotheistic faith. Inside the empire, artistic and cultural influences blended to create a strong cultural legacy.

While it was defeated by Alexander the Great 200 years later, the Achaemenid Empire was the first of several important empires centered in Persia. These empires shaped the political, economic, and cultural structure of western Asia.

### Parthian Empire

When Alexander the Great died, his vast territory was divided among several of his generals. Seleucid I inherited Syria, Mesopotamia, and Iran. He established his own dynastic rule, a rule that passed from father to son. Around 240 BCE, the Seleucids were overthrown by a group from northeastern Iran that established the Parthian dynasty.

Early in the Parthian era, the empire continued to promote Greek culture throughout the region. However, over time, the Parthian Empire became more distinctly Persian. The Parthians resisted several Roman invasions.

The Parthian Empire was decentralized, and by the 100s CE, there were frequent conflicts between nobles and military leaders inside the empire. At times, there were even multiple kings claiming power at the same time. Rulers of a small state in southern Iran eventually gained power, and by the mid-to-late 200s CE, the Sasanian dynasty ruled the Persian Empire.

### Sasanian Empire

Unlike the Parthians, the Sasanian rulers centralized power, making all officials directly responsible to the throne. This led to a much stronger government and less political instability. It also better equipped the Sasanians to protect against their aggressive neighbors, allowing the rulers to focus on issues other than defense.

photo: Getty Images

*A fire altar from the Sasanian Empire, located in present-day Iran.*

The state in the Sasanian Empire greatly valued art and scholarship. Persian art experienced a renaissance and grandiose structures were built throughout the empire. Metalworking and other arts achieved a new level of sophistication.

The rise of Islam in Arabia and the increasing instability of its neighbors ultimately led to the downfall of the Sasanian Empire. The Sasanians were defeated in 642 CE by Arab forces united under an Islamic empire.

## Empire in India

*How did the Indian economy and culture flourish during the Gupta Empire?*

South Asia—a region that includes modern Afghanistan, Bangladesh, Bhutan, the Maldives, Nepal, India, Pakistan, and Sri Lanka—has a long history. This region is sometimes called the subcontinent because it is separated from the rest of Asia by the Indian Ocean and tall mountain ranges. Early civilizations in South Asia sprang up in the valley of the Indus River. These early civilizations produced well-planned cities and traded across Asia, but they declined around 1900 BCE.

Between 1500 and 500 BCE, new ideas began to develop in South Asia. Most historians believe that speakers of an Indo-European language that would eventually become

photo: Getty Images

*Postage stamp showing Ashoka pillars found everywhere in India.*

Sanskrit migrated into South Asia from modern-day Iran. These migrants mixed with the local population and, over time, developed an oral religious tradition. These traditions were recorded in four texts called the Vedas, which would become the foundation of modern Hinduism. Later, Buddhism and Jainism also emerged as important religions.

In the late 200s and early 300s BCE, the Mauryan Empire unified much of the region under a single, powerful ruler. The empire's most famous ruler, Ashoka, became a devout Buddhist after years as a warrior. He marked his rule with public projects and helped spread Buddhism throughout South Asia and beyond. After Ashoka's rule ended, the empire began to split.

## A Golden Age

In the first few centuries of the Common Era, India was divided into many provinces with unstable rule and continuing conflicts. In 320 CE, one of these provincial powers—the Gupta Empire—rose to control all of India.

Many of the Gupta kings were very invested in education and the arts, and they gave liberally to schools, hospitals, and other charities. The arts and sciences flourished. Hinduism became the state religion, and many great works of Hindu literature were written during the time. Indian scholars made advancements in astronomy, astrology, and medicine. There were also major advancements in mathematics, including geometry, trigonometry, and the creation of the decimal system of notation.

What set the Gupta Empire apart from other empires was that the rulers promoted education not just among royalty, but the people at large. People were encouraged to learn Sanskrit, read literature, paint pictures, and learn music.

Near the end of the 400s CE, the empire began to struggle. It lacked effective leadership, and the centralized empire began to fragment. Still, Gupta rule had created a more unified cultural identity across South Asia.

## The Han Dynasty Unites the East

### *What were the cultural values of the Han dynasty?*

In East Asia, early river civilizations flourished around the Huang He (Yellow) River valley and spread to the Yangzi River valley beginning in the 1700s BCE. While varied dynasties and states flourished in the region, China was unified by a powerful emperor named Shi Huangdi around 221 BCE. Huangdi centralized power, began major construction projects, and forcibly relocated thousands of peasants. The modern name China is a reference to Huangdi's Qin (pronounced "Chin") Empire.

In 206 BCE, Liu Bang, a minor official in the Qin Empire, led a revolt overthrowing the corrupt and repressive government and seizing power. He established the Han dynasty. The Han dynasty was the second major Chinese dynasty and became the longest lasting: over 400 years. At its peak, the Han Empire included all of modern-day China, northern Vietnam, Inner Mongolia, southern Manchuria, and most of Korea.

The Han government was highly centralized and supported by an extensive bureaucracy. Promotion within the bureaucracy was based primarily on merit rather than birth or lineage. Rule was based on Confucian ideology, which focused on moderation, virtue, and filial piety.

The rulers also loved music and art, leading to the development of new techniques and styles. While little of the architecture from that time is still standing, the Han created house models and painted pictures of buildings on the tiles of tombs. Engineers in the Han dynasty developed pulleys and wheelbarrows for moving goods. They also figured out how to harness both water and air to power simple machines.

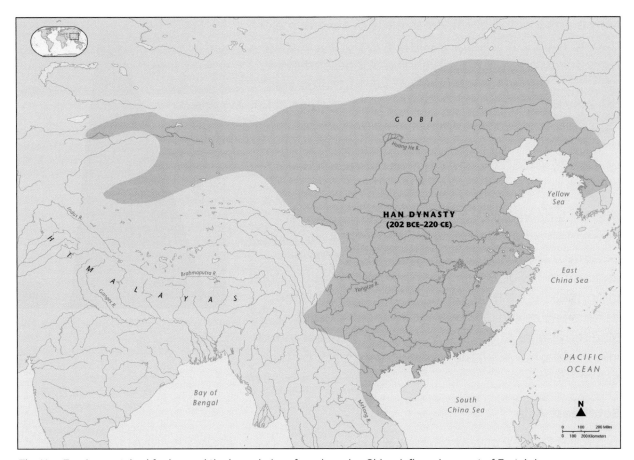

*The Han Empire stretched far beyond the boundaries of modern-day China, influencing most of East Asia.*

The art and inventions of the Han dynasty spread throughout the east and beyond along the Silk Road, an extensive trade route. As a result, trade began between China and the Mediterranean.

Around 100 CE, the dynastic line began to destabilize. Emperors died young or died without a son to take their place. By 220 CE, conflicts over the throne inside the highest levels of power ended the empire. China dissolved into warring states and would not be reunited for 350 years.

The legacy of the Han dynasty lived on. It shaped culture in the East much like Rome did in the West.

## Kingdoms of Trade
*What role did trade play in the development of smaller kingdoms throughout the Middle East, Africa, and Asia?*

### East Africa

Two major trading powers arose in East Africa. The first was the city of Meroë. While it was part of the larger Kingdom of Kush, Meroë was so wealthy that it is often considered a kingdom in its own right. Recently, archaeologists in modern-day Sudan have excavated the ruins of Meroë. They have found a large and complex city with grand boulevards, intricate temples, and well-preserved pyramids.

Meroë was located at the crossroads of several major trading routes. It built its wealth on exports, sending ivory, hardwoods, iron tools and weapons, and even elephants throughout the ancient world. Meroë was the only kingdom in Africa to develop a written language. However, historians have been unable to decipher it, so little is known about the inner workings of the city. In 330 CE, the city was conquered by another rising regional power: the Aksumites.

Aksum, a powerful kingdom in northern Ethiopia, developed alongside Meroë. However, the two quickly became rivals, vying for control of trade. After it conquered Meroë, Aksum became the greatest market in northeastern Africa. Aksumite merchants traded as far away as Alexandria, Arabia, and the eastern Mediterranean. At its peak, Aksum's empire extended into Arabia; however, they were pushed back by the rise of Islam.

photo: Getty Images
*A stone obelisk at Axum (or Aksum) in northern Ethiopia.*

## Southeast Asia

The political structure of Southeast Asia developed very differently from most of the ancient world. Rather than one or two dominant kingdoms, many individual courts, called *mandalas*, exerted control over the rings of territory that surrounded them. They garnered power through a balance of alliances, flow of trade, and labor. Mandalas existed at important places for major trade routes: in the major river valleys and at areas where sea traffic would land on shore.

The largest mandala uncovered so far is Oc Eo in southern Vietnam. Oc Eo was a port settlement that was connected to other settlements by canals up to 60 miles long. Evidence shows that it was a rich marketplace, where items were traded from as far as Rome and inner Asia. Craftsmen at Oc Eo also manufactured their own trade goods such as jewelry and pottery. Unfortunately, there is no record of the government structure or information about the people who lived there.

photo: Getty Images
*Why do you think natural resources such as this frankincense tree were so important to the Arabian empires?*

## Arabia

While Rome controlled parts of northern Arabia, southern Arabia was dominated by several overlapping kingdoms such as Ma'in, Saba, and Hadharamaut. These kingdoms were all wealthy due to their agriculture and trade. Arabian marketplaces were filled with items from around the ancient world.

However, the most valuable items were the spices they grew and sold. Frankincense and myrrh were prized in all of the major empires. The kingdoms also controlled the most valuable trade routes. This, however, led to much conflict between the various kingdoms and prevented any one kingdom from becoming the most powerful for very long.

While these kingdoms were not as large or powerful as Rome, China, or India, they played a key role in the economic and cultural exchange of the ancient world.

The large empires of Europe, Asia, and Africa were far-flung, but historical evidence shows they were interconnected. Archaeologists have unearthed Roman coins in Egypt and Indian metalworking in China. How did these goods travel such long distances? There were trade networks that connected these empires. In addition, there was a network of smaller kingdoms that built their wealth and power on trade.

## The Silk Road

*How did the Silk Road foster connections between ancient civilizations?*

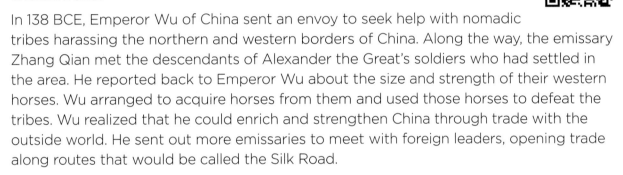

In 138 BCE, Emperor Wu of China sent an envoy to seek help with nomadic tribes harassing the northern and western borders of China. Along the way, the emissary Zhang Qian met the descendants of Alexander the Great's soldiers who had settled in the area. He reported back to Emperor Wu about the size and strength of their western horses. Wu arranged to acquire horses from them and used those horses to defeat the tribes. Wu realized that he could enrich and strengthen China through trade with the outside world. He sent out more emissaries to meet with foreign leaders, opening trade along routes that would be called the Silk Road.

### Persian Royal Road

Emperor Wu was not the first leader to understand the value of trade. The Achaemenid Empire established the Persian Royal Road, which ran from northern Persia to the Mediterranean Sea in Asia Minor (modern-day Turkey). Like the Roman roads, the Royal Road was officially used for moving troops and for the empire's postal system. Traders took advantage of the road, too. Over time, the addition of smaller side roads expanded the Royal Road all the way into the Indian subcontinent, across Mesopotamia, and into Egypt.

### Many Trade Routes in One

The Silk Road was not actually a single road, but a large network of trade routes with the Persian Royal Road as one of the central arteries. It took several centuries for it to reach its true size, but by 300 CE, the Silk Road stretched from China through India, Asia Minor (Turkey), up through Mesopotamia to Egypt, the African continent, Greece, Rome, and Britain.

Each major civilization played a different role. China initiated the road and provided the most sought-after commodity: silk. The Parthians controlled most of the routes because they were concentrated in Parthian-controlled Mesopotamia. Rome became the primary consumer, especially of China's silk.

Trade increased the power of the nomadic tribes along the routes. They became the primary merchants, amassing wealth and building new cities. Few traders traveled the whole road. Instead, traders had small routes between towns where they sold their goods to traders with different routes and bought new goods to take back. Each trader increased the price of a good in order to earn a profit. As a result, goods traded on the Silk Road were quite expensive. The farther away a good started, the more expensive it became.

Many goods traveled along the Silk Road. There were raw materials such as jade, silver, and iron from China; food such as olives, olive oil, and wine from the Mediterranean; spices from Arabia; coins from Rome; ivory from East Africa; tin from Southeast Asia; and cotton from India. Paper and gunpowder traveled from China, becoming essential resources throughout the East and West. China was also the source of the most desired product in Egypt, Greece, and Rome: silk. All of these goods are luxury goods, and the cost of travel and intermediaries made them more expensive, meaning that the people who directly took part in the Silk Road were often wealthy.

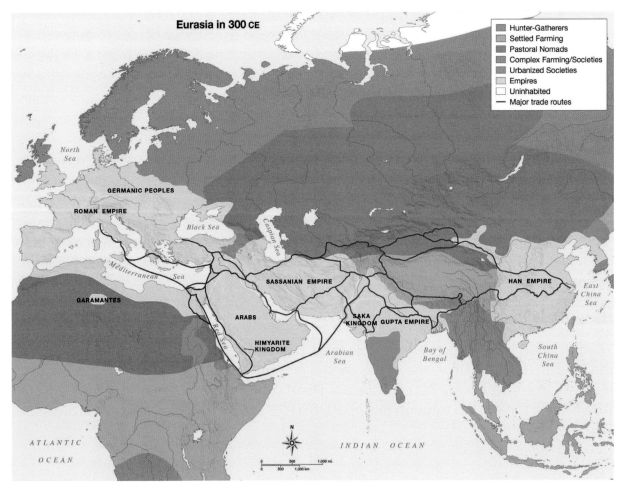

*Extensive trade routes connected the major kingdoms of the ancient world.*

## Ideas Travel with Trade

That most luxury consumers were wealthy does not mean, however, that the rest of the people were unaffected. Art, religion, philosophy, technology, language, science, and architecture all moved across civilizations along these trade routes. For example, by 300 CE, Buddhism was on the decline in India, but it traveled along trade routes to East Asia, where it flourished. Christianity traveled to Europe and East Africa. The mathematical advancements of India spread to Asia and Europe. Diseases also moved freely along the road. The bubonic plague, which began in Constantinople, swept through western Asia and Europe along the routes of the Silk Road.

Although they were impacted by the cultural exchange of the Silk Road, most people at the time did not know it. Only the wealthy interacted with the trade network directly, and most of them only knew their local trader or merchant. For many people living in the ancient world, their ties were very local. While the leaders

**Explore this resource and create a proposal to establish trade and cultural ties with another region in 200 CE.**

of the major civilizations were aware of the different kingdoms, they rarely, if ever, interacted directly. Although more connected than ever before, the world in 300 CE was still very large.

## A Pre-Columbian Metropolis

*How did Teotihuacan shape the culture of Mesoamerica?*

In 375 CE, in central Mexico, there was a city of nearly 200,000 people. Its city center, which is laid out in a grid structure designed to follow the path of the sun, was 8 square miles wide and filled with thousands of apartment compounds, each housing multiple families. At its center, there was a massive 2-mile long boulevard marked by three pyramid complexes, the largest of which was 200 feet tall and 730 feet on each side. This was the city of Teotihuacan.

To support this enormous population, the farmers of Mesoamerica, or modern Mexico and Central America, used new techniques to grow maize, or corn. Around 100 CE, farmers began to plant maize in chinampas, floating gardens built above marshlands. These gardens required less effort to tend than the grains grown in Eurasia and could be harvested several times a year.

*photo: Getty Images*

*These Aztec floating gardens were a later variation of the chinampas of central Mexico.*

Teotihuacan was at least as large—if not larger—than its counterparts in Europe and Asia, its power extending over most of central Mexico. The fingerprints of Teotihuacan culture appear throughout Mesoamerica and as far south as Guatemala.

The leaders of Teotihuacan controlled the nearby obsidian deposits that they used to manufacture spear and dart heads. For other groups in central Mexico, the only way to get the superior obsidian heads was to obtain them from Teotihuacan. These weapons became the basis of a vibrant trading economy that extended throughout central Mexico.

Archaeological evidence shows that a wide range of goods were traded in Teotihuacan, including salt, exotic feathers and shells, cotton from the Pacific Coast, and cacao from the Gulf of Mexico. There is also evidence of textile manufacturing and craft production within the city. The city's wealth allowed for the development of a rich cultural life, including massive temples, intricate art, and religious statues. Many of the religious symbols depicted in Teotihuacan have been found in the ruins of later civilizations.

While we know Teotihuacan's power came to an end around 600 CE, the cause is still a mystery. What we do know is that around this time, artwork and religious sculptures were destroyed, and the major buildings were intentionally burnt. Was it done by invaders, or by a rebellion from within? These are the questions historians and archaeologists are still trying to answer.

## Central and South America

### *How did the environment shape the American cultures?*

Teotihuacan was one of the world's largest cities, but in the early centuries of the Common Era, two other major population centers were developing: the Maya of Central America and the early peoples of South America.

### The Mayan City-States

In 200 CE, around the same time that Teotihuacan began to grow into a major power, another major civilization began to rise in Mesoamerica. The Maya occupied an area covering southern Mexico, Guatemala, and northern Belize.

Unlike many other empires, the Mayan civilization was highly decentralized. Historians estimate there were 40 cities at the peak of the civilization in about 900 CE, each with 5,000 to 50,000 residents. Each city was the center of its own independent state ruled by its own king, much like the mandalas of Southeast Asia. Each king controlled the production and distribution of resources in his city and surrounding areas. As a result, conflict was frequent. Cities often attacked each other, taking captives who were then tortured, mutilated, or sacrificed.

The strength of the Mayan Empire came from its stable and plentiful food base. The Mayans used advanced irrigation to water plants and terracing techniques to retain soil in the hot, dry climate. In many areas of the Yucatan Peninsula, aboveground freshwater is scarce, so the Maya carefully collected rainwater and drew water from sinkholes, which the Spanish later called *cenotes*. The Maya raised productive crops of maize (corn), beans, and squash.

The Yucatan Peninsula is largely made up of limestone, which the Maya used to create monumental temples and pyramids. They also carved elaborate sculptures. The Maya developed a written language, used complex mathematical concepts, and developed an accurate calendar to govern agricultural cycles and religious rituals. The civilization flourished until the 900s CE, when the major cities began to decline. However, many people in the Yucatan region can still trace their lineage and language back to the ancient Maya.

## The Andes

Far from the valleys of Mesoamerica, the Andes Mountains were home to several thriving civilizations. Two of these in particular had an impact that reached far beyond their own borders: Moche and Tiwanaku.

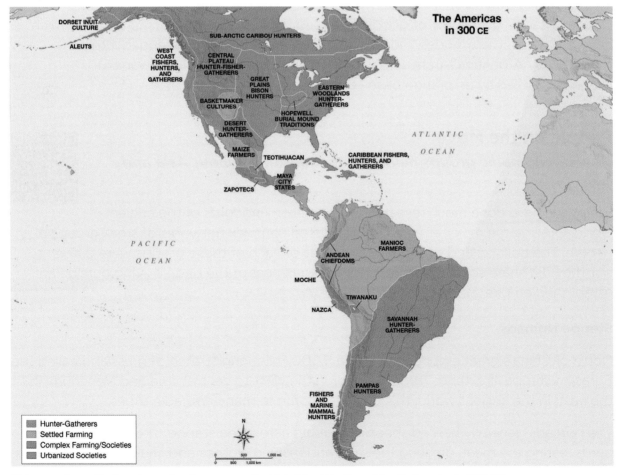

*This map shows the locations of various groups that inhabited North and South America in 300 CE.*

The Moche civilization began to emerge around 100 CE along the northern coast and valleys of ancient Peru. Rather than a unified empire, Moche was really a loose confederation of two different but related linguistic groups. The Moche accumulated wealth and power by conquering other territories and quickly became the most powerful civilization in the region. The Moche groups developed incredibly sophisticated and complex art and architecture. Archaeologists have found sculptures, pottery vessels from molds, gold headdresses, turquoise and silver jewelry, textiles, knives, copper bowls and drinking vessels, and realistic portrait pots that archaeologists believe were made to look like real people

Tiwanaku was located near Lake Titicaca in modern-day Bolivia. It was nearly 13,000 feet above sea level, making it one of the highest cities in human history. Tiwanaku began in the 200s CE and expanded dramatically around 375 CE, reaching its peak between 500 and 1000 CE. At that point, the city, laid out in a grid, occupied more than two square miles. Individual homes arranged around common courtyards covered the city. Outside of the city center, dykes and aqueducts directed water from Lake Titicaca through canals that ran along raised beds growing tubers and quinoa. Historians estimate this advanced irrigation system helped support a population of 30,000 to 70,000 people.

The Tiwanaku thrived on a very active and extensive trade network. Large llama caravans carrying a variety of goods traversed the large and dispersed empire, which covered the southern Andes, modern-day Peru and Chile, and extended into modern-day Argentina. Archaeologists have found the distinctive Tiwanaku pottery—marked by an orange base—throughout this area.

## People on the Move

*How did nomadic groups help spread ideas throughout Asia and Africa?*

Historians have done much research on the major kingdoms of the ancient world. Outside the major empires, there existed complex networks of small groups of people. The political and economic structures of each of these groups were different, but they did share some characteristics. In Asia, most of the people living outside an established empire were nomads.

### Steppe Nomads

North of China's great empires, there is a 5,000-mile-long stretch of grassland called the Eurasian steppe. It extends from Hungary in the west to central Asia and Manchuria in the east. In the ancient world, this area was home to many nomadic tribes.

The nomads generally herded sheep and goats across the steppe. They lived off their herds, eating the meat, drinking the milk, and making clothes and shelter from the hides and fur. They relied on horses to carry supplies and help them to cross rough terrain such as mountains.

*An illustration of Attila the Hun.*

photo: Getty Images

Because their herds were always in need of grass, these nomads moved frequently, which brought them into frequent contact with each other and gave them knowledge of a vast range of territory. Although mountains divide the steppe, nomads moved freely and interacted across the entirety of the grasslands. While they generally moved in small family groups, in some seasons they came together in much larger numbers, sharing information and kinship.

These nomadic tribes have a reputation as fierce fighters. Nomadic raids were common. Nomads sometimes raided settlements to get more resources; they could only transport small amounts of food and other necessities. Other times, they raided to obtain treasure for their leaders because possessions were a primary way of demonstrating rank.

Nomads also, at times, formed a large war confederacy, exerting their dominance over other nomadic groups and invading their homes. For example, one confederacy called the Huns started in Russia and moved into the Hungarian plain, raiding settlements in the Balkans, Italy, and Gaul. They were widely feared but dissolved suddenly after the death of their last major leader, Attila. The Huns and other nomadic confederacies also continuously threatened the borders of China and the Parthian and Sasanian Empires.

## Saharan Nomads

Several nomadic cultures developed in the Sahara Desert and the Sahel. The loss of grass and green space over centuries forced the people of western Africa to constantly move to find food and water. Most of these groups stayed in relatively small areas until the domestication of the camel. Camels allowed them to travel much longer distances through the desert. These nomadic groups developed into traders, bringing goods overland from the west to the east of the continent.

Historians used to believe that these nomadic groups were less developed than the people living in the settled empires. Early historians called these groups "barbarians" in comparison to the "civilized" kingdoms. However, new research shows that this was not the case. The nomadic tribes were just as developed and complex as their settled neighbors. In fact, the kingdoms nearby acquired many of the innovations of civilization from the nomads. For example, historians now know that nomads developed chariots, learned how to domesticate horses, and developed sophisticated ways to manipulate bronze. Little is known of these groups because they left no written records.

# Migrations

## *How did migrations impact populations around the world?*

For nomads, movement was a pattern of their daily lives. However, they were not the only groups on the move. Many groups living outside the empires moved more gradually from region to region, propelled by both environmental and political factors.

### Germanic Tribes

Past the northern border of the Roman Empire were a number of communities known collectively as the Germanic tribes. These tribes lived in large settlements and relied on agriculture. Although they shared many characteristics, the tribes generally remained independent of one another in individual chiefdoms led by their own bloodline or chosen leaders. They typically settled in areas with enough resources to maintain a relatively large population. They often cleared forests to make more room for their fields. However, they also frequently exhausted the resources of the area in which they settled and therefore had to migrate to a new area.

This continuous migration caused a great deal of conflict, particularly with Rome. Germanic tribes frequently migrated into what Rome considered its territory, leading to fighting and war. As a result, some Germanic tribes, such as the Goths and the Franks, formed partnerships for the sole purpose of fighting Rome.

### Bantu

The Bantu-speaking people lived in Nigeria for centuries, but around 100 CE, they began moving south and east. Historians are not sure what caused this initial move, but once they started, they did not stop. The Bantu were pastoral, meaning they relied on land for the grazing of sheep and goats, and they planted agriculture. The Bantu traveled all the way to central Africa, where they settled. However, central Africa is a plateau with thin topsoil and limited groundwater. Like the Germanic tribes, they exhausted the land and had to spread farther to support the population.

The Bantu continued to move south and east across the continent, encountering and absorbing other groups. Through their migrations, they shaped culture throughout central Africa.

### Polynesians

The Polynesian people populated the islands of Oceania. Historians have several theories about their migration methods, but most agree that they came from the Malay Archipelago (modern-day Malaysia) sometime between 3000 and 1000 BCE.

The first evidence of a culture on the islands is the Lapita culture. The Lapita appear to have been an explorer culture because they spread throughout Oceania, seemingly propelled only by their curiosity. When they would arrive on a new island, some would stay and establish villages while others continued on. However, they did not lose contact with each other and slowly built an interconnected culture across the islands of West Polynesia.

Approximately a thousand years later, the Polynesians, descendants of the Lapita, struck out once again. The islands of the east were more spread out, so the migration was much slower, and the cultures that developed in East Polynesia were more isolated from each other. Unlike the Bantu, the Polynesians moved onto uninhabited islands and so did not encounter other groups. However, while each island developed its own unique traditions, they maintained the core aspects of Polynesian culture.

## Hunter-Gatherers

In areas of greater abundance, groups did not have to develop ways to cultivate plants or herd animals. These groups are known as hunter-gatherers, who depended on wild foods for their subsistence. In a typical hunter-gatherer culture, the men hunted for game or fished, and the women and children gathered nuts, berries, and plants.

Hunter-gatherer cultures required large areas of land, so they could only exist where populations were relatively low. They rarely had permanent settlements, only in places where food was especially abundant. Instead, they traveled in small family groups like nomads, sometimes meeting up in larger groups in the winter season.

Hunter-gathering groups existed across the globe in 300 CE from Oceania to South Africa to North and South America. In Australia, the Aboriginal peoples moved from place to place hunting game or fishing along the coast. Similarly, the majority of tribes throughout North and South America in 300 CE were hunter-gatherers. Some, like those on the Great Plains, were required to move around a great deal, following the buffalo. Others, like those in the Pacific Northwest, had enough food to mostly stay in one location.

As you can see from the many civilizations discussed in this concept, the world in 300 CE was a mix of interaction and isolation. The lives and cultures of people across the globe would both change and remain the same as they began to trade, share ideas, and fight with their neighbors.

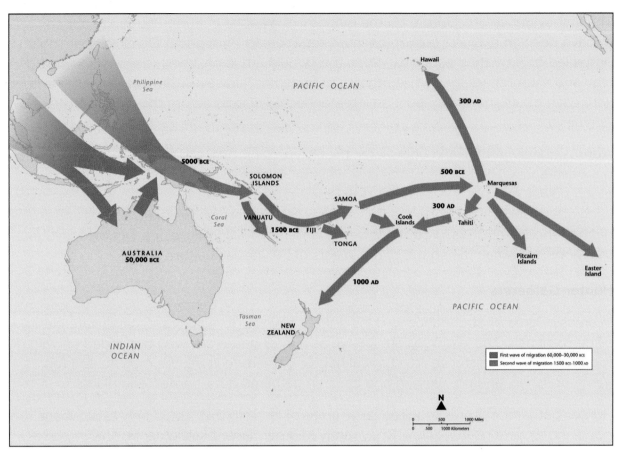

*This map shows how people migrated to Australia and New Zealand from nearby islands.*

## Consider the Essential Question:

How did the regions of the world interact around 300 CE?

Go online to complete the Social Studies Explanation.

## Check for Understanding:

Many of the kingdoms that existed around 300 CE valued science, art, and learning. Describe one innovation from a particular civilization. How did this advancement affect other regions?

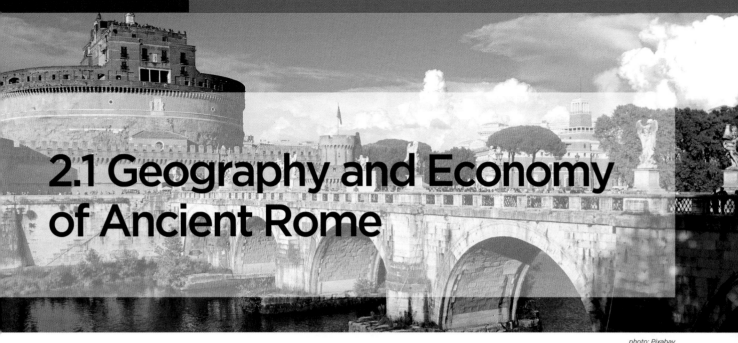

# 2.1 Geography and Economy of Ancient Rome

photo: Pixabay

# LESSON OVERVIEW

## Introduction

In this concept, you will learn where the Roman Empire was located and how it expanded through conquest and trade.

## Essential Question

How did geography and trade routes impact the growth of Rome?

## Lesson Objectives

By the end of this lesson, you should be able to:

- Locate ancient Rome and its important cities and rivers on a historical and a modern map.

- Connect ancient Rome's location and its expansion through conquest and trade.

- Analyze the impact of coined money and roads on trade inside the Roman Empire.

## Key Vocabulary
Which terms do you already know?

- ☐ Aachen
- ☐ agriculture
- ☐ Alps
- ☐ Apennine Mountains
- ☐ barter
- ☐ climate
- ☐ climate region
- ☐ ecosystem
- ☐ empire
- ☐ Forum
- ☐ Gaul
- ☐ George Washington
- ☐ Great Britain
- ☐ Italy
- ☐ latitude
- ☐ Latium
- ☐ longitude
- ☐ markets
- ☐ Mediterranean Sea
- ☐ North Africa
- ☐ peninsula
- ☐ Remus
- ☐ Roman Empire
- ☐ Rome
- ☐ Romulus
- ☐ Spain
- ☐ Tiber River

 **SOCIAL STUDIES TECHBOOK**

How did geography and trade routes impact the growth of Rome?

# ENGAGE

**How can roads build an empire? Visit Engage to learn more.**

## Essential Question

How did geography and trade routes impact the growth of Rome?

# EXPLORE

## The Founding of Rome

*Where was ancient Rome?*

At its height, the Roman Empire was one of the largest and most prosperous empires in the world. It lasted for approximately 1,000 years. However, this powerful empire had simple beginnings.

Historians have determined that Rome began as a collection of small towns located on seven hills near the shore of the Tiber River in Italy around 753 BCE. Rome is located in the center of modern-day Italy on a peninsula, which is a piece of land surrounded by water on three sides. This peninsula stretches into the Mediterranean Sea.

photo: Getty Images

*Map of the Roman Empire around 300 CE.*

These early towns were influenced by the nearby Greeks. The townspeople lived in houses that had stone foundations, as the Greek houses did. They used an alphabet that was adapted from the Greek alphabet. They adopted Greek history, education, and philosophy. Their religion was also based on the Greeks' religion because they believed in similar gods and goddesses.

Over time, the towns joined together to form the city of Rome. In 509 BCE, the Roman Republic formed, and the city eventually became the political center of a large empire that at its height extended from Great Britain to Spain and from North Africa to Southwest Asia. This means that at its peak, the Roman Empire spanned from 60° to 20° latitude north and from 10° longitude west to 50° longitude east.

## Natural Benefits

*What benefits did Rome's location provide the city and its inhabitants?*

Rome's location offered several advantages. One of the advantages provided by the Italian Peninsula was the protection offered by the hills and mountains found throughout the region.

Two major mountain chains found in Italy had a significant impact on the development of ancient Rome. The Alps, Europe's highest mountains, separated the Italian Peninsula from the rest of the continent. The Apennine Mountains run north to south along the length of the Italian Peninsula. The Apennine Mountains made it difficult for people to cross from one side of the peninsula to the other. These two mountain chains helped protect Rome from outside attacks. The seven hills of Rome were also used to protect the city.

*photo: Getty Images*

*The Sella Pass in the Dolomites, present-day Italy. What does the image suggest about the history of the Roman Empire?*

*photo: Getty Images*

*This stone carving depicts workers tending the fields in ancient Rome.*

The climate of central Italy, where the city of Rome was located, also helped the people of Rome. The region had mild, rainy winters and hot, dry summers. This climate made it possible for the region to develop a strong agricultural base. The mild climate enabled Romans to grow wheat, grapes, and olives and build a consistent food supply. This food supply supported the people and allowed Rome to prosper.

While the climate made yearlong farming possible, Rome was also strengthened by close access to water. The growing agricultural system was aided by the presence of the nearby Tiber River. Along with supporting Rome's farmers, the Tiber River provided several other benefits to ancient Rome.

## The Importance of Rome's Waterways
### *How did Rome's geography help it prosper?*

Like many other ancient civilizations, the agricultural system of ancient Rome was supported by the presence of a major river. The Tiber provided a reliable source of freshwater, which the Romans used for irrigating their farms, as well as drinking water for humans and animals. However, unlike many other civilizations, Rome did not develop in the river's delta.

photo: Getty Images

*The Tiber provided a source of freshwater to Romans and was also an important route for trade and transportation.*

Instead, Rome developed about 15 miles from where the Tiber River empties into the Mediterranean Sea. This distance provided Rome with additional protection, because invaders had to move inland from the coast to reach the city. However, Rome was still close enough to the sea that Romans were able to use the river as an easy access point to the Mediterranean.

Rome's location on the Italian Peninsula, and its closeness to the Tiber River, provided access to trade routes on the Mediterranean Sea. As a result, trade was an important part of life in ancient Rome. Rome developed several trade routes throughout the Mediterranean Sea and established trade with other civilizations throughout the Eastern Hemisphere, especially the Greeks. Through this trade, the Romans continued to adapt Greek culture and technology. Later, the Roman armies used these same routes to conquer large amounts of territory and expand the empire along the Mediterranean.

As more trade moved through Rome, merchants gained power and wealth. One famous merchant, Marcus Gavius Apicius, used his wealth to travel the world looking for rare foods for enormous feasts. A cookbook of his recipes became legendary, but he eventually bankrupted himself with his lavish parties. Trade created opportunities for lower-class Romans to become rich. An early Roman law did not allow senators, who were usually wealthy and politically powerful Romans, to own ships for trading. While many senators ignored the law, it showed that merchants were sometimes regarded as less respectable than Romans whose wealth came from their large land holdings.

As the empire continued to expand, it became difficult for farmers in Rome to produce enough food to meet the demand of the growing population. Wheat was imported from North Africa, and olive oil was imported from Spain. The need to provide enough for its people meant that trade became increasingly important throughout the empire.

## Roman Roads and Bridges

*How did Roman roads and bridges impact the economy?*

As Romans fought and conquered new territories on and beyond the Italian Peninsula, they built paved roads that connected those territories back to Rome. The phrase "all roads lead to Rome" reflects the historical fact that Roman roads connected the capital of the empire to most of the distant territories that they conquered.

photo: Library of Congress
*Many Roman roads, such as this one in Jordan, were built so well that parts of them still exist today.*

The strength of Roman engineering is reflected in the construction of these roads. The roads were built of several different layers, and the top layers were often paved. The Romans also built drainage ditches along the sides of the roads to prevent water from damaging them. Rome's work is so enduring that some parts of this original road system still exist today in Europe and the Middle East.

In addition to roads, Romans built a network of bridges to create a land-based connection between the city and its territories across rivers and other bodies of water. These bridges were built out of stone and as a result were strong and durable. Many of the bridges included arches. This element of design helped to make the bridges strong, and also allowed boats to move in the water underneath the bridges.

Many of Rome's major construction projects, such as its roads, were built by soldiers. The roads were a priority for Rome's military because it was important for troops to be able to move quickly and easily transport supplies from one part of the empire to another. However, traders,

**Explore this interactive to learn more about how Rome's transportation system helped its economy.**

messengers, and others also benefited from these roads. Traders were able to bring spices, jewelry, furs, perfume, and food from North Africa, Asia, and Europe, so people all over the empire could buy goods they might not otherwise have had. Tax collectors also traveled on these roads, bringing wealth and resources from conquered territories back to rulers in Rome. Rome's elaborate system of roads and bridges helped make it possible for the Romans to hold together their large empire for a long time.

## Rome's Monetary System

*What effect did the Roman monetary system have on Rome's economy?*

Another accomplishment that helped the empire's trade-based economy was the development of metal coins. Romans were not the first people to create or use coins. In fact, early in their history, Romans used the same names for money that ancient Greeks had used. Although the Lydians, inhabitants of what is now modern-day Turkey, had first introduced the coin, by the third century BCE, the Romans had enhanced the usage of coins for money.

The Romans made coins out of gold, silver, and other metals. The coins were worth different amounts based on the different metals from which they were made. The Romans had several different denominations of coins. Like today, coins were given a monetary value that was guaranteed by the government.

Having a common monetary system throughout the empire made trade much easier and more efficient. Because the value of coins was agreed upon, it was easier to determine what price should be paid for goods. Coins were also easy to carry, which was important in larger empires such as the Roman Empire. The coins also played a role in showing the culture of ancient Rome.

## The History of Money

*What is the cultural and historical significance of Roman coins?*

In addition to the important role Rome's monetary system played in its economy, it reflected elements of Roman culture. Coins usually had images of either the ruler or the mint where the coins were made imprinted on them. Putting pictures of rulers on coins was important in a time when many people did not know how to read. Coin images allowed people to determine a coin's worth as well as recognize the authority of the ruler. The images gave the appearance of an emperor being like the gods. Additionally, coins often depicted images of Roman gods and goddesses or important events.

photo: Getty Images

*A sampling of Roman coins.*

Archaeologists have found Roman coins throughout Europe. Today, when scholars examine Roman coins, they are able to learn about the people who ruled the empire and the deities that the Romans worshipped. The fact that these coins have been found far from Rome shows how much the Romans were able to expand their trade network based on their control of Mediterranean trade routes.

The expansion of the Roman Empire was influenced by its geography. Rome's location allowed for successful agriculture, which allowed the city to grow. It also provided the Romans with easy access to trade routes, which enabled the city to meet the demands of its growing population. Rome's location helped to protect it from outside forces while providing access to the sea that allowed for travel and conquest. Because of the location of ancient Rome, a collection of small towns was able to grow into a major city, and eventually become a powerful empire.

**Consider the Essential Question:**

How did geography and trade routes impact the growth of Rome?

Go online to complete the Social Studies Explanation.

**Check for Understanding:**

How did ancient Rome design and construct its roads? What aspects of ancient Roman civilization depended on its roads?

# 2.2 Roman Origins and Early Political Structures

photo: Getty Images

## LESSON OVERVIEW

### Introduction

In this concept, you will explore how the Roman government changed over time to become more fair and democratic.

### Essential Question

Was the Roman Republic democratic?

### Lesson Objectives

By the end of this lesson, you should be able to:

- Trace the roots of Roman civilization to the contributions of Etruscans and Greek colonists.

- Analyze the political structure in ancient Rome and the democratic concepts developed in the region (separation of powers, representative government); compare with the democracies of Athens and of modern states.

- Describe the role of the Punic Wars in the growth of the Roman Empire.

## Key Vocabulary
Which terms do you already know?

| | |
|---|---|
| ☐ Aeneas | ☐ Octavian |
| ☐ Alps | ☐ oligarchy |
| ☐ assembly | ☐ Pantheon |
| ☐ bicameral | ☐ patrician |
| ☐ Carthage | ☐ peninsula |
| ☐ census | ☐ plebian |
| ☐ Cincinnatus | ☐ Punic Wars |
| ☐ citizen | ☐ Remus |
| ☐ code of law | ☐ representative |
| ☐ Commodus | ☐ representative government |
| ☐ Constantine | |
| ☐ consul | ☐ republic |
| ☐ democracy | ☐ Roman Empire |
| ☐ dictator | ☐ Roman Republic |
| ☐ Diocletian | ☐ Roman Senate |
| ☐ Emperor Augustus | ☐ Rome |
| ☐ Etruscans | ☐ Romulus |
| ☐ Europe | ☐ Senate |
| ☐ Forum | ☐ Sicily |
| ☐ Gaul | ☐ slavery |
| ☐ gladiator | ☐ slaves |
| ☐ Goths | ☐ social class |
| ☐ Hannibal | ☐ Spain |
| ☐ Italy | ☐ Tiber River |
| ☐ Julius Caesar | ☐ tribune |
| ☐ jury | ☐ Twelve Tables |
| ☐ Latium | ☐ Zama |
| ☐ Mediterranean Sea | |

## ENGAGE

**Why are written laws important? Visit Engage to learn more.**

### Essential Question

Was the Roman Republic democratic?

## EXPLORE

### The Roots of Roman Civilization

*How did the Roman civilization begin?*

Historians today do not know the full early history of Rome, but they do know some details. Historians agree that Rome began as a small collection of towns along the banks of the Tiber River in the center of the Italian Peninsula. Other stories about the founding of Rome come from the Romans themselves.

*Romulus and Remus.*

photo: Getty Images

According to the legends and stories written by Roman historians and poets, the founding of Rome began with Aeneas, a hero of the Trojan War. The Roman writer Virgil described this story in an epic poem called the *Aeneid*. According to the poem, after Troy was destroyed, Aeneas left the city and settled in central Italy. He lived among the people who had already settled in this area, known as the Latins. The Latins provided Aeneas with input on their style of government and taught him their namesake language, Latin, which later became the empire's official language. He married the daughter of the king, and his descendants eventually became rulers of the region. Two of Aeneas's descendants, the twins Romulus and Remus, were abandoned at birth and rescued and raised by a she-wolf. As an adult, Romulus returned to the place where he had been rescued as a baby. There, he built a city and named it Rome.

This legend of Rome's founding ties the ancestry of Romulus and Remus to the Greek hero Aeneas. This is one of many ties between the history of Rome and the history of Greece. The ancient Romans greatly admired the ancient Greeks. Roman cultural and political life was heavily influenced by the Greeks, and by the Greek colonists who had settled on the Italian Peninsula. The Romans adopted and adapted aspects of Greek religion and political philosophy. They were also influenced by a group of people called the Etruscans, who had already settled this area of Italy.

## The Etruscans

### What role did the Etruscans play in Roman history?

Based on the legend of the *Aeneid*, Romulus became the first of seven kings of Rome who ruled from the city's founding in 753 BCE until 509 BCE. Because of a lack of archaeological evidence from this time period, not much is known about the rule of many of these monarchs. During this time, Rome came under the control of the Etruscans, another group of people who lived in central Italy, in the late seventh century BCE. Like the Romans, the Etruscans had been influenced by Greeks who had colonized Italy before Rome was founded.

The Etruscans made important contributions to Roman life. Under the Etruscan rulers, the city's marshes were drained and several large temples were built. The Roman Forum, the city's central meeting place, was also expanded during the rule of the Etruscans. It is likely that the Romans adopted their alphabet, numerals, and other aspects of art and dress (including the toga) from the

photo: Library of Congress

*Ruins of the Roman Forum.*

Etruscans. The Etruscans had been influenced by many Greek religious practices, and Romans adopted these practices, as well as many of the deities, from both the Greeks and the Etruscans.

The last of the Etruscan kings, a ruler named Tarquinius Superbus, ruled Rome from 534 BCE to 509 BCE. He is believed to have been a harsh ruler whom the Romans resented. A group of Romans rebelled against Tarquinius and expelled the Etruscan king around 509 BCE. With no king in control, the Romans needed to establish a new form of government.

## The Roman Republic

*What form of government was established after the king was removed from power?*

After Tarquinius Superbus was removed from power, the Roman people needed a new form of government. In approximately 509 BCE, the Romans established a republic. A republic is a form of government in which people elect their leaders. Rome was not a democracy as we know it today, however, because not all of the people were allowed to participate fully in the new government.

Roman society consisted of three social classes. These classes were the patricians, the plebeians, and the slaves. The patricians consisted of priests, government officials, and wealthy landowners and were considered upper class. The plebeians were common people, such as artisans, laborers, and farmers. Slaves were usually people who were captured in war, and they had no role in government.

Plebeians could vote in the early Roman Republic, but only the patricians could hold office. The plebeians resented this, so in 494 BCE, they threatened to create a new city with its own government. This action forced the patricians to agree to change Rome's government. Over the course of

**Explore this interactive to learn about different perspectives on the Roman Republic.**

about 200 years, the plebeians fought and won the right to take part in many aspects of the government. The plebeians' political fight for equal rights in government was called the Conflict of the Orders.

## Roman Government

*What was Rome's political structure?*

The Roman Republic consisted of three parts: the magistrates, the Senate, and the assembly. The magistrates were 20 elected officials who ruled for one year. The magistrates performed many duties, acting as judges, tax collectors, and urban planners. The two highest magistrates were called consuls. A consul was the most powerful political position in Rome. The consuls issued laws and led the army. To prevent one person from becoming too powerful, each consul could veto the decisions of the other. Additionally, consuls, like the other magistrates, only served for one year. In the early stage of the republic, only patricians could be elected as consuls. After 367 BCE, however, at least one consul had to be a plebeian.

One of the strongest supporters of Rome's political structure was Cicero, a Roman statesman and consul. Cicero argued for the importance of a republic that shared power among many people. He thought it was dangerous for any one person to gain too much power. He prevented an aristocrat named Catiline from overthrowing Rome by force. That made Cicero very popular among Romans, who believed he had saved the republic.

The second part of the government was the Roman Senate. The Roman Senate was made up of 300 men, who at first were only selected from the patrician class. Senators were elected and held their offices for life. Initially, the Senate's only job was to advise the consuls, but over time, it gained power, eventually becoming the most important part of the government and making decisions about laws, foreign policy, and finance.

photo: Getty Images

*Painting of Cicero in the Roman Senate, accusing Catiline of betrayal.*

The third part of the government was the assembly, which protected the rights of the plebeians. The plebeians had an assembly, or lawmaking body, of their own called the Council of the Plebs. This assembly could elect 10 officials, called tribunes, or tribunes of the plebs. The tribunes had the power to veto the actions of the consuls or the Senate. The veto power meant that this group of tribunes had the ability to limit what the Senate and the consuls could do, which made them very powerful.

## Principles of Democracy

*What democratic principles were present in the government of ancient Rome?*

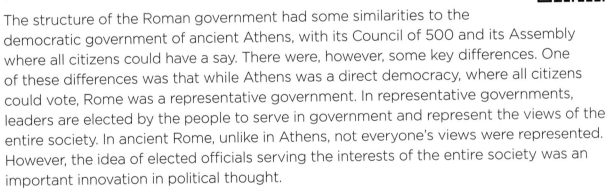

The structure of the Roman government had some similarities to the democratic government of ancient Athens, with its Council of 500 and its Assembly where all citizens could have a say. There were, however, some key differences. One of these differences was that while Athens was a direct democracy, where all citizens could vote, Rome was a representative government. In representative governments, leaders are elected by the people to serve in government and represent the views of the entire society. In ancient Rome, unlike in Athens, not everyone's views were represented. However, the idea of elected officials serving the interests of the entire society was an important innovation in political thought.

Another principle of the Roman Republic that impacted later governments was the separation of power. Separation of power means that no one person, group, or branch of government has all the power. This idea was central to the creation of the U.S. government. The U.S. government is separated into three branches—the legislative, executive, and judicial branches—each with its own powers and responsibilities. Although Rome's government did not have the same structure as the U.S. government today, it also divided the responsibility of governing among three different political groups: the magistrates and consuls, the Senate, and the People's assembly.

## A Time for Strong Leadership

Although the Romans were wary of one person obtaining too much power, they believed that in times of crisis, having a dictator, or one ruler with total control over the government, was a more effective form of leadership. Because of this, the Senate had the ability to appoint a dictator to serve for a period of six months during wars or other times of crisis. In 458 BCE, the Senate chose a Roman named Cincinnatus as dictator during a time of war. Cincinnatus quickly led Rome to victory and then immediately resigned as dictator, even though his six-month term was not over. To Romans, Cincinnatus was the ideal politician because he used his power to help Rome, rather than for his own personal gain.

photo: Getty Images

*Painting of Cincinnatus receiving the Roman Senate.*

The Romans believed that Cincinnatus demonstrated the ideal of citizenship. The idea of Roman citizenship was that citizens were expected to serve their country in exchange for protection by the government. The responsibilities of citizenship were different for different people. Some were selected to take part in the government, while others were expected to serve in the military. The idea of citizenship was important to other civilizations, such as the ancient Greeks, and remains an important concept today. The United States still strongly promotes the idea of citizenship, and its citizens are expected to serve their country in a variety of ways, including voting, paying taxes, and serving on juries.

Another democratic principle that was part of the Roman government was a written code of laws. Early in the republic, laws were not written down, and only the patricians who made the laws knew what they were. The plebeians objected to this, feeling that they would not be treated fairly unless the laws were written down. They protested and eventually forced the patricians to agree to a set of written laws. In 451 and 450 BCE, Rome's first written laws were produced on 12 bronze tablets, or tables. These laws, which came to be known as the Law of the Twelve Tables, were displayed in the Roman Forum for everyone to see. Written law remains important today throughout the world.

## The Punic Wars

### What effect did the Punic Wars have on Rome?

As Rome's government grew stronger, so did its military. The Roman Republic forced the lands it conquered to provide it with military forces. Its territory became so large that the republic could call on nearly 800,000 soldiers from its many lands.

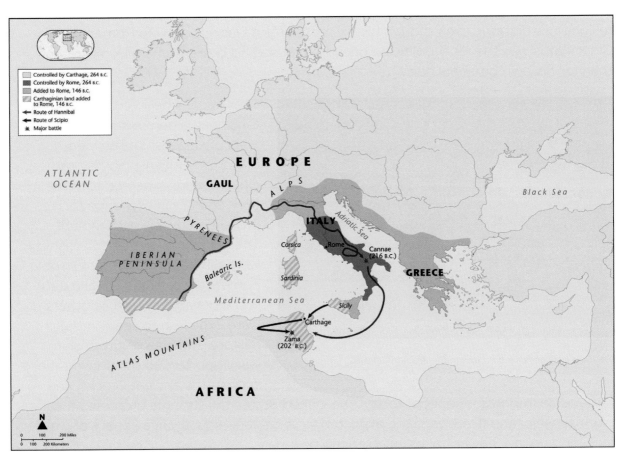

*Map of the battles during the Punic Wars.*

The armies of the Roman Republic used new kinds of armor and tactics. Soldiers protected themselves with shields called scutums, which were two large pieces of wood glued together and fitted with iron. The wealthier and more experienced soldiers wore large coats of armor. In battle, the soldiers arranged themselves in a checkerboard pattern, forming many small groups of soldiers with empty square spaces in between. This allowed the soldiers to move around more easily than if they were all in one large group.

For approximately two centuries after the Roman Republic was formed, Rome expanded its territory by conquering other small states throughout the Italian Peninsula. In 264 BCE, Rome looked to expand its territory beyond the Italian Peninsula. Rome hoped to gain control of important shipping lanes in the Mediterranean Sea. Many of these shipping lanes were controlled by Carthage, a powerful city in North Africa. Rome's attempt to control shipping throughout the Mediterranean led to a series of three wars against Carthage, from 264 BCE to 146 BCE, known as the Punic Wars.

In the first Punic War (264 BCE–241 BCE), Rome built up a powerful navy and used it to win control of the islands of Sicily, Sardinia, and Corsica, which had previously been controlled by Carthage. Carthage was defeated, but still remained powerful. They hoped to take revenge on Rome and regain the territory they had lost.

In the second Punic War (218 BCE–201 BCE), a Carthaginian leader named Hannibal led troops across Spain and over the Alps to the Po River valley in Italy, to the north of Rome. Hannibal conquered a large part of the Italian Peninsula but did not capture the city of Rome. Roman forces eventually drove the Carthaginian forces back and they retreated to North Africa. A Roman general named Scipio defeated Hannibal at the battle of Zama in North Africa, which forced Carthage to end the war. As part of the treaty that ended the war, Rome gained control of what is modern-day Spain and several of the Mediterranean islands.

By the time of the third Punic War, fought from 149 BCE to 146 BCE, Carthage had started to regain some of the power it lost in the second war. In response, Rome attacked Carthage and, after two years of fighting, defeated the Carthaginians and destroyed the city. All of its former territory in North Africa became part of the Roman Empire.

The Punic Wars began the spread of Roman influence throughout the region. Rome would continue to expand its territory and influence. As Romans moved to new regions, they brought with them their culture and their ideas.

Even as the Roman Empire grew, though, it faced internal conflict. Members of the government disagreed about whether to continue expanding Roman territory. Some thought the empire was growing too large, while others wanted to gain more land and power. These political conflicts sometimes led to violence. In addition, conflicts between the social classes became more extreme. As Rome expanded, it conquered new territories that produced more goods. It had less need for the crops that Roman farmers grew. Many farmers and other members of the working class could no longer make enough money to survive. This, too, led to violence.

**Consider the Essential Question:**

Was the Roman Republic democratic?

Go online to complete the Social Studies Explanation.

**Check for Understanding:**

What did citizenship mean to the Romans? What are the similarities and differences between the Roman concept of citizenship and the American concept of citizenship?

Discovery | SOCIAL STUDIES
EDUCATION | TECHBOOK

How did Rome's transition from republic to empire impact its citizens?

# 2.3 From Republic to Empire

# LESSON OVERVIEW

## Introduction

In this concept, you will investigate the events that caused a significant change in the Roman political system and the impact it had on the people of Rome.

## Essential Question

How did Rome's transition from republic to empire impact its citizens?

## Lesson Objectives

By the end of this lesson, you should be able to:

- Analyze the causes and effects of Rome's transition from a republic to an empire.

- Trace the expansion of the Roman Empire from the rise of Caesar to 476 CE.

## Key Vocabulary

Which terms do you already know?

| | |
|---|---|
| ☐ aqueduct | ☐ Macedonia |
| ☐ Brutus | ☐ Mark Antony |
| ☐ Caligula | ☐ Mediterranean |
| ☐ Carthage | Sea |
| ☐ Charlemagne | ☐ Middle East |
| ☐ citizen | ☐ Nero |
| ☐ Claudius | ☐ Octavian |
| ☐ Cleopatra VII | ☐ Pax Romana |
| ☐ consul | ☐ Ptolemy |
| ☐ dictator | ☐ Roman Empire |
| ☐ Egypt | ☐ Roman Republic |
| ☐ Emperor | ☐ Rome |
| Augustus | ☐ Rubicon River |
| ☐ Greece | ☐ Spain |
| ☐ Hannibal | ☐ Tiberius |
| ☐ Julius Caesar | ☐ triumvirate |

# ENGAGE

**How did Julius Caesar change the course of history?**
**Visit Engage to learn more.**

## Essential Question

How did Rome's transition from republic to empire impact its citizens?

# EXPLORE

## The Rise of Julius Caesar

*How did Julius Caesar come to power?*

From 264 to 146 BCE, the Romans fought three wars against Carthage, known as the Punic Wars. The two great powers fought for control of strategic islands throughout the Mediterranean region. Rome eventually destroyed Carthage and took control of its lands. After its success against Carthage, the Roman Republic continued to expand by conquering new lands. These new lands were organized into provinces and put under the control of local governors.

This focus on expansion led to negative effects on the city of Rome and its surrounding areas. Agriculture in the provinces was more successful than in the areas surrounding Rome. Local farmers lost business to the competition from the new provinces, which contributed to a widening gap in wealth between the commoners and the elite members of society. This led to growing unrest in the republic.

During this time, Gaius Julius Caesar (100–44 BCE) was born into a wealthy family. "Caesar" was actually a family name used by those in Gaius Julius's line. The term was eventually adopted as an imperial title, and it continued to be used even when the crown passed on to other families. Today, when people speak about Caesar, however, they are usually referring to Julius Caesar. For clarity, that is how the term will be used in this lesson.

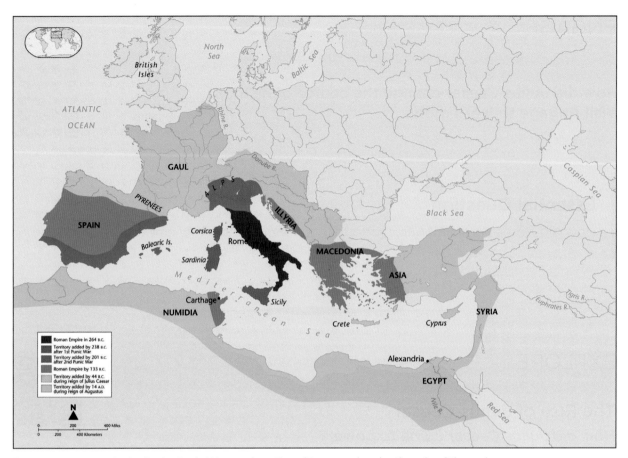

Rome won new territories in the Punic Wars and continued to expand under the rule of the early emperors.

## Political and Military Success

Caesar was very ambitious. He served in the Roman military and was a skillful soldier. He also was a clever politician and a skilled writer and speaker. In 60 BCE, he formed a political alliance with Pompey the Great and Crassus, two other political leaders. This alliance is known as the First Triumvirate. Together, these three leaders were able to influence and control much of the political life of Rome. The following year, 59 BCE, Caesar was elected consul, one of the highest political offices in Rome.

After his one-year term as consul, Caesar was appointed governor of Gaul, which is in modern France. An uprising of the northern tribes in Gaul gave Caesar an opportunity to gain political power through battle. In 57 BCE, he conquered the northern tribes and began a campaign to conquer all of Gaul and expand Roman territory. This military campaign lasted several years.

Military success in Gaul provided Caesar with increased political power, money, and popularity. Pompey, who was also very ambitious, saw Caesar's increasing power as a threat to his own quest for power and began working to undermine him. The triumvirate broke apart and Caesar and Pompey became enemies. Pompey began to try to prevent Caesar from gaining more power.

## Dictator for Life

### *How did Julius Caesar become dictator for life?*

Under the influence of Pompey, who had powerful connections in Rome, the Senate commanded Caesar to give up command of his army and return to Rome alone. Caesar agreed only on the condition that Pompey would also give up command of his army. When the Senate refused Caesar's request, he ignored their order, and in 49 BCE he led his army across the Rubicon River into Italy to fight Pompey and his army.

photo: Getty Images

*This 1747 painting depicts Julius Caesar meeting Cleopatra.*

By ignoring the Senate and crossing the Rubicon River, Caesar was seen as having committed an act of war. Because of this, many historians see Caesar's crossing of the Rubicon as the end of the Roman Republic. The expression "crossing the Rubicon" is used to this day to mean reaching a point of no return. Caesar pursued Pompey's army through Greece and Spain, where Caesar defeated them. He then crossed the Adriatic Sea to face Pompey himself at Pharsalus in 48 BCE. Ultimately, Caesar triumphed and Pompey fled to Egypt, where he was killed in September of that year.

With Pompey out of the way, Caesar continued his conquests by traveling to Egypt to claim it for Rome. At the time, Cleopatra ruled Egypt. Cleopatra was the last ruler of the Macedonian dynasty, which had been established by Ptolemy, a Greek general under Alexander the Great. Ptolemy had established himself as the ruler of Egypt after the death of Alexander. Caesar's conquest of Egypt further expanded the territory of Rome and increased Caesar's reputation.

After the successful campaign in Egypt, Caesar returned to Rome in triumph. He was very generous toward the commoners in Rome, which made him very popular. Caesar was declared dictator for life instead of the normal term of six months. Dictators were given ultimate power over the government, which is why terms were usually limited. Caesar named himself Imperator, the Roman word for "emperor." This made many senators uneasy.

## The Ides of March

### Why was Julius Caesar murdered?

The rise of Caesar made some members of the Roman Senate fear he was gaining too much power. They wanted Rome to remain a republic, and they thought that Caesar was trying to establish himself as a monarch, or king. If that happened, each leader would pass the crown to his heir instead of being elected. This would mean the crown would stay in a single family line, creating a dynasty, and the Senate would lose much of its power.

One group of senators believed that they could restore the republic if they assassinated, or killed, Caesar. This group was led by the Senator Gaius Cassius Longinus, a general in the Roman army, and Marcus Junius Brutus. Brutus had been a supporter of Pompey, but after Pompey's defeat at Pharsalus, Caesar pardoned Brutus to make him the governor of Gaul.

photo: Getty Images

*Caesar was murdered by a group of senators who feared he had become too powerful.*

According to legend, Caesar was warned about the attack by a soothsayer, or fortune teller, who told him to be careful on the Ides of March (March 15). His wife Calpurnia had dreams of disasters, such as the house collapsing. Because of these omens, as well as his poor health, Caesar thought about staying home on March 15. Unfortunately for him, he decided against this, in part because Brutus advised him not to believe in the omens.

**Explore this interactive and learn more about ideas for ruling the Roman Empire.**

As Caesar entered the senate-house, the senators took out the knives hidden under their togas and stabbed Caesar 35 times until he fell dead on the senate-house floor. Following his murder in 44 BCE, Rome fell into a period of chaos.

## Civil War

### How was stability restored to Rome after the death of Julius Caesar?

Not everyone in Rome had agreed that Caesar was a danger. His death left the country without a clear leader. As a result, a civil war began between the supporters of Caesar and the armies of Cassius and Brutus. This struggle would last for approximately 20 years and claim thousands of lives.

## Octavian and Antony

When the civil war broke out after Caesar's death, Octavian, Caesar's nephew, claimed the throne. Octavian allied himself with a former rival, Mark Antony, and the general Marcus Aemilius Lepidus, to form the Second Triumvirate. These three allies opposed the supporters of Cassius and Brutus. They fought to avenge the death of Caesar and to support Octavian's claim to the throne.

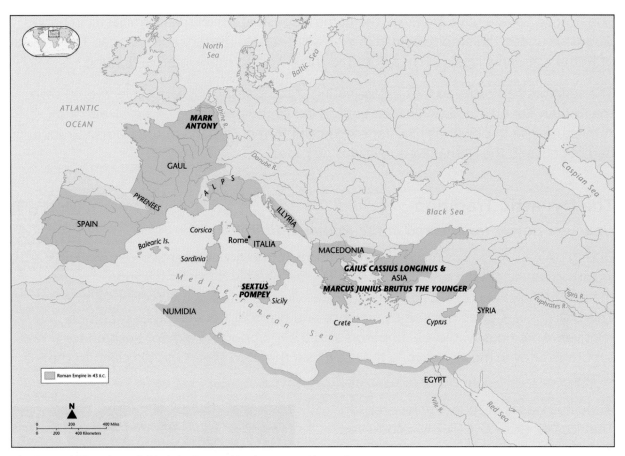

*The Second Triumvirate divided the Roman Empire among themselves.*

The armies led by Octavian and Mark Antony finally defeated the armies of Cassius and Brutus in Philippi, Macedonia. Both Cassius and Brutus killed themselves after their defeat. The members of the Second Triumvirate divided control of the land among themselves. Lepidus was given the provinces of Africa; Antony received the eastern provinces and married Octavian's sister Octavia. Octavian took control of the west, including the city of Rome itself. Eventually, Lepidus was forced out of power.

**The New Emperor**

Antony, who had divorced Octavia, went to Egypt, where he married Cleopatra, the queen of Egypt. Octavian saw this marriage as a threat to his power. He recalled Mark Antony to Rome and attacked Cleopatra's forces in Egypt. In 30 BCE, Octavian's forces won the war against Egypt and Mark Antony and Cleopatra both killed themselves. This left Octavian with no one to challenge his claim as ruler of the Roman Empire. When Octavian took the throne, he added Caesar to his name out of respect for his uncle. The Roman Senate gave Octavian the name Augustus, which means majestic in Latin. Augustus united the empire by naming himself the sole military commander. The armies of Rome were now loyal to him alone, and there was no more internal fighting.

The senators had believed that assassinating Julius Caesar 14 years earlier would save the Roman Republic. However, their actions led to the beginning of a civil war and Augustus's rise to power as the first emperor of Rome. The age of the Roman Empire had begun, and the Roman Republic was no more.

## The Dynastic Tradition
### *How was power transferred in the Roman Empire?*

During his rule, Augustus made several reforms to the government, including the establishment of a dynasty. Under the new dynastic tradition, the position of emperor was passed on to the descendants of the previous emperor. This process was often marked by violence and disorder between the emperor's relatives. Ambitious would-be emperors and their supporters did not hesitate to sabotage or even murder anyone they saw as a threat to their possible claim to the throne.

Augustus was succeeded by his stepson, Tiberius (42 BCE–37 CE). It was believed that Tiberius ordered the murder of one of the challengers to his claim as emperor. He was an efficient ruler, but he was considered cold and unlikeable.

Tiberius was followed by the notoriously cruel Caligula (12 BCE–41 CE), who is believed to have gone insane after an illness. He was killed by the Praetorian guards and succeeded by his uncle Claudius (10 BCE–54 CE).

photo: Getty Images

*Burning Rome was only one of Nero's crimes against his people.*

Claudius was believed to have been poisoned by his wife Agrippina, who wanted her son, Nero, to become emperor. Nero (37–54 CE) was one of the most notorious of the Roman emperors. He had his mother assassinated and allowed a fire to destroy the city of Rome. He was the last emperor of the dynastic line of Julius and Augustus Caesar.

Structure and organization were important parts of the Roman way of life. Even though the succession process was often messy and violent, life in the Roman Empire in general remained stable for the citizens of Rome.

## Portrait of an Empire

### What was life like in the Roman Empire?

The chaos and violence that often accompanied the succession at the highest levels of Roman government were not reflected in Roman society. Stability and order were important to the Romans, and their effects were seen throughout the empire. The beginning of the Roman Empire was also the beginning of a time of peace and prosperity within the Roman Empire known as the Pax Romana.

photo: Library of Congress

*Aqueducts, like this one in Spain, were built by the Romans to bring water to their cities throughout the empire.*

There was a strong sense of consistency between Roman cities, which were all designed and built to look similar to each other. All Roman cities had a theater, religious temples dedicated to various gods, aqueducts to carry water, and public bathhouses. Buildings in even the most distant provinces were designed to look like those in Rome. Wealthy Romans often funded civic ventures such as these.

Citizens throughout the Roman Empire were also treated the same. They spoke Latin, used the same currency, and used the same calendar (the Julian calendar, which was named after Julius Caesar, its creator). All of these elements meant that all cities and people throughout the empire were connected. This was even true of cities that Rome conquered and added to its growing empire.

## The Empire Grows

### How did the Roman Empire expand?

Although many of the internal struggles of Rome ended during the Pax Romana, Rome continued its conquest of other cities and civilizations. Rome's location near the Mediterranean Sea was an important factor in the growth of the Roman Empire. This location meant that Rome had a mild climate and a long growing season. This helped them provide supplies to their armies. It also provided the Romans with easy routes for travel, trade, and conquest.

### Expanding the Empire

Following the death of Julius Caesar, the Emperor Augustus and, a century later, Emperor Hadrian expanded the empire north and east, conquering parts of Europe. However, Rome did not attack territories without strategic planning. Conquests were chosen with care, based on how the new territory could benefit the empire. Rome also offered some members of the conquered civilizations the chance to become citizens. The Roman Empire often adopted or adapted elements of the civilizations' religion and culture.

photo: Getty Images
*Hadrian's Wall, present-day England.*

At its height, the Roman Empire reached northward to what is now the United Kingdom, controlling much of Europe. It also included parts of northern Africa and stretched as far east as the Persian Gulf. Augustus eventually became concerned about the rapid growth of the empire. He was afraid it would get so large that it would be impossible to govern. Later emperors, including Hadrian and Claudius, would continue to add territory to the Roman Empire, but their additions were much smaller than the gains made under Augustus.

## The Benefits of Expansion

### *How did expansion benefit the Roman Empire?*

The Roman Empire was largest under the emperor Trajan in 117 CE. The empire extended from Spain to the Middle East and from Britain to North Africa. Roman influence can still be seen in these regions. Europe in particular is filled with Roman roads, walls, ruins, and artwork.

The expansion of the empire brought great material wealth to Rome, both in money and natural resources. Rome's trade network expanded as far as China, from which Romans received silk that was very popular at the time. Rome's expansion also brought a great deal of intellectual and cultural diversity. The empire included Greeks, Celts, Gauls, Egyptians, and Africans. Features of all their cultures were adopted and added to the culture of Rome. Despite this diversity, the Roman Empire wanted to make the lands and people it had conquered Roman.

photo: Getty Images
*The ruins of this amphitheater in present-day Tunisia are evidence of Rome's far-reaching influence.*

The standardization of architecture in all conquered cities made the provinces look like Rome. The common language, money, religion, and calendar made the people speak and behave like Romans. The entertainment made them happy to think of themselves as Roman. This commonality helped keep people happy and loyal and made the empire prosperous.

**Consider the Essential Question:**

How did Rome's transition from republic to empire impact its citizens?

Go online to complete the Social Studies Explanation.

**Check for Understanding:**

What factors allowed the Roman Empire to expand so rapidly and effectively? What impact did the Roman Empire have on the areas it conquered?

Discovery EDUCATION | SOCIAL STUDIES TECHBOOK.

How did the spread of Roman culture influence life throughout the empire?

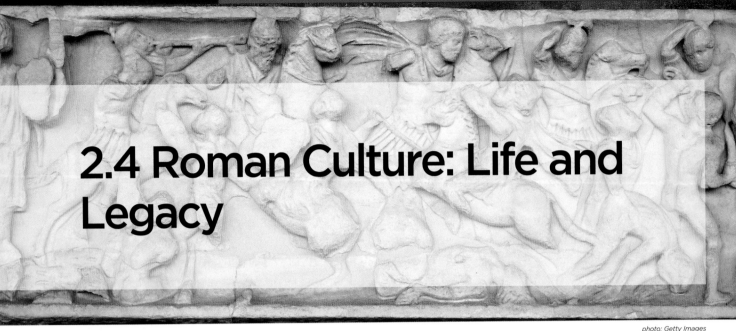

photo: Getty Images

# 2.4 Roman Culture: Life and Legacy

## LESSON OVERVIEW

### Introduction

In this concept, you will learn about the cultural roles and lives of the different classes of Roman society. You will also examine how the culture and influence of Rome spread through the ancient world and continue to influence people and nations today.

### Essential Question

How did the spread of Roman culture influence life throughout the empire?

### Lesson Objectives

By the end of this lesson, you should be able to:

- Analyze relationships of power between Roman rulers, citizens, and slaves.

- Analyze the impact of Roman government infrastructure programs on Roman life and culture and on life and culture today.

- Trace the influence of the Roman Empire on language.

### Key Vocabulary
Which terms do you already know?

- ☐ aqueduct
- ☐ architecture
- ☐ census
- ☐ Circus Maximus
- ☐ Colosseum
- ☐ Egypt
- ☐ Emperor Augustus
- ☐ Europe
- ☐ gladiator
- ☐ hierarchy
- ☐ irrigation
- ☐ Latin
- ☐ legionnaires
- ☐ North Africa
- ☐ Octavian
- ☐ Pantheon
- ☐ paterfamilias
- ☐ patrician
- ☐ Pax Romana
- ☐ Phoenicians
- ☐ plebian
- ☐ Roman Empire
- ☐ Rome
- ☐ Sicily
- ☐ taxes
- ☐ Twelve Tables

## ENGAGE

**How did Romans dwell in the lands they conquered?
Visit Engage to learn more.**

### Essential Question

How did the spread of Roman culture influence life throughout the empire?

## EXPLORE

### Roman Society

*How was Roman society structured?*

*photo: Getty Images*
*A drawing of Roman vestals.*

History is generally written from the viewpoint of those who have the power in a society. Early historians, like the people they wrote about, were primarily interested in politics and the power that went with it. This is also true about the history of ancient Rome. More is known about the interests and points of view of the members of the ancient Roman ruling class (known as the patricians), than of the ancient Roman commoners (called plebeians), enslaved persons, and—to some extent—women. However, contemporary historians have also learned much about the lower classes of Roman society by searching archaeological ruins, studying art, and analyzing works by early historians.

The center of Roman society was the family, or *familia*, in which the members were bound by blood relationships, marriage, and duty. Societal roles were determined by a pyramid-style hierarchy. The father was the head of the family, or the **paterfamilias**, and had absolute power. The other male members of the family—nephews, uncles, and cousins—were on the next level of the pyramid. The bottom of the pyramid consisted of the women, the children, and the enslaved people of the household.

Discovery EDUCATION | SOCIAL STUDIES TECHBOOK

How did the spread of Roman culture influence life throughout the empire?

Early Rome (753–509 BCE) was ruled by individual kings, and large families were encouraged to continue family lines and strengthen the paterfamilias. The paterfamilias, and then the other male members of the family, controlled all the property. The women were expected to stay at home and raise the children. Women also managed the enslaved persons in the household. Over time, as Rome's middle class increased, social roles changed. Around the beginning of the Roman Republic in 509 BCE, women were allowed more freedoms and more education. They could go to school and learn to read and write. However, women still lived with their families and were controlled by the male members of the household, unless they were widowed or enslaved.

## Patrons and Clients

### What was patronage?

Patrician families traced their family lines back to the founding of Rome and the first senators. The patricians were privileged aristocrats who

owned much of the land. Plebeians were the common people of ancient Rome, including the poor and landless. By approximately 450 BCE, many members of the plebeian class lived outside the city on small farms where they worked unless they were called into military service. Plebeians and patricians, although different in almost every aspect of their identities, depended on one another for survival. The

photo: Getty Images

*A modern drawing of Roman workers, circa 100 CE.*

dependence was seen in a social system that provided financial and political protection for plebeians and security and a source of labor for the patricians.

To make sure they were protected and had a greater say in the public sphere, plebeians known as clients sought the patronage, or support, of a member of the patrician class known as a patron. Clients provided the paterfamilias with loyalty and assistance in his public and private affairs. In the period of the later republic, the client could also be called upon to provide military support and in return was represented by the patron politically and legally. Although the relationship was more beneficial to the patricians, it worked both ways and went beyond the individuals to the family and descendants of both: a client would be loyal to the patron's son if the patron died, and the patron would continue to protect the family of the client after the client's death.

This gap in wealth and influence between the two classes began to cause problems. As the gap between the patrician and plebeian classes continued to grow during the time of the Roman Republic, the plebeian class began to fight for greater political power and economic equality. This fight eventually led to the creation of the Twelve Tables, the first set of written laws in Rome.

The concept of citizenship changed throughout Rome's history as more people gained the right to become citizens. Roman Consul Gaius Marius granted citizenship to members of the military as a reward for their service. Later, Consul Lucius extended citizenship to any Italian who wanted to become a Roman. Over time, nearly all people living in Roman territories were considered citizens of the Roman Republic.

Enslaved people were not considered Roman citizens. Both patricians and plebeians could own enslaved people. The number of enslaved people they owned was one of many indications of their wealth and power. In the first few centuries after Rome was founded, people did not tend to have many enslaved people. But as Rome expanded its territories to include most of Europe and North Africa, the enslaved population soared. Some estimates put the number in the first century CE at about 300,000, out of a total population in the city of about 900,000.

## Slavery in Ancient Rome

*What role did slavery play in the Roman Empire?*

As in many other ancient civilizations, slavery existed in ancient Rome. The majority of the enslaved people in ancient Rome were prisoners of war. Other people may have begun life free and been sold by their parents into slavery or been sentenced to slavery as punishment for a criminal offense. Some enslaved people had even been prosperous and educated as free men.

Enslaved people were an important part of Roman life and the Roman economy. They worked in a variety of roles. Slave labor was used for mining, farming, and domestic work in wealthy households. Enslaved people were often treated cruelly by their owners. Some enslaved people were even forced to fight to the death as gladiators, or professional fighters. There were no laws that protected enslaved people, they had no rights, and they were not allowed to participate in government. There was nothing to control an owner's treatment of his enslaved people other than the opinion of his peers.

### Slave Revolts

Because of the large number of enslaved people, and the poor conditions they often faced, Romans feared that the enslaved population might revolt. To help prevent revolts, the Romans used the possibility of manumission, the ability to buy one's freedom, as an incentive for good behavior. Some enslaved people saved money given to them by owners. This may have played a significant part in explaining the infrequency of slave revolts in the Roman Empire. Other factors included the fear of reprisal and the differences among the members of the enslaved population. They spoke different languages, had belonged to different social classes, believed in different religions, and had different levels of education. Creating a sense of solidarity among such a mix of people was almost impossible. And yet, uprisings did occur.

Discovery EDUCATION | SOCIAL STUDIES TECHBOOK

How did the spread of Roman culture influence life throughout the empire?

In Sicily, there was a rebellion led by Eunus, a popular and charismatic slave leader, that lasted from 136 to 132 BCE. Another rebellion happened in Sicily when 20,000 enslaved persons revolted under the leadership of a slave named Flavius, which lasted from 104 to 100 BCE. A third revolt occurred with more than 100,000 enslaved persons under Spartacus, a gladiator, which lasted from 73 to 71 BCE. These revolts were usually met with extreme cruelty to deter future rebellions. After Spartacus's rebellion, for instance, the Romans crucified 6,000 enslaved persons along the Appian Way

photo: Getty Images

*Illustration of the death of Spartacus.*

from Rome to Capua, a city more than 100 miles to the south. The revolts did not stop Romans from relying on slavery. During the last years of the republic and the first two centuries of the empire, there was an increase in the number of enslaved people.

## Slavery and the Economy of Rome

Besides the threat of revolt, slavery caused other unexpected problems for Rome. The vast numbers of enslaved people that made up the labor force meant that there was not enough work for the plebeians to do. Why pay men for what you can get for free? Many plebeians lost work and fell into poverty. They were forced to survive on food from the government. Historians refer to this group of people as the mob: the unemployed whose dependence on the state and lack of work led them to riot when tempers flared.

Many modern historians point to a decline in morals, values, and ethics as a consequence of the idleness resulting from having so many slaves. As long as there were enslaved people to do the work, there was little for the plebeians to do. In addition, there was no incentive to develop new technologies to make the production of goods any easier.

# Bread and Circuses

*How did the ruling classes attempt to keep the poorer members of society happy?*

Because the wealthy classes did not have to pay for labor, many spent their riches on luxury goods. The rich could purchase paintings or fine art at auctions. They also could buy expensive, rare items, such as gold, jewels, pearls, and silk at markets. Many of these luxuries were brought into Rome through trade routes. However, not everyone could afford these fine goods.

During the first century CE, Rome was a difficult place to live. The increasing inequality of Roman society led to tension between the upper classes and the lower class. Murder and theft were reportedly common in the city. The daily diet of grain, served as bread or porridge, and watered-down wine for the poor led to many people being malnourished. In addition, the city was very overcrowded: Approximately one million people lived within eight square miles.

This limited space in Rome made class divisions even worse. Wealthy citizens continued to build grand villas and elaborate civic buildings. This left little room for ordinary housing. Poorer members of society lived in privately owned tenement housing, which averaged three to four stories. These buildings were made of concrete, one of Rome's greatest inventions. However, landlord patricians often used low-quality concrete to cut costs. This could lead to the building collapsing. There were also no toilets, no running water, and frequent fires. These poor conditions may have been the root of the lower classes' unhappiness.

## Entertainment for the Masses

The elite members of society feared a possible uprising by the growing poor. To maintain peace, they used a method that the Roman poet Juvenal called "bread and circuses." This meant that they kept the poor happy and distracted with entertainment such as chariot races and gladiator fights.

*photo: Getty Images*
*Relief portraying an event at the Circus Maximus.*

The state tried to keep the people amused. Circuses—arenas or theaters that hosted races, fights, and other entertainment—were provided as a solution. Circuses such as the Circus Maximus in Rome had U-shaped tracks for chariot racing and could hold up to 150,000 people. The enormous building called the Colosseum served as an arena hosting gladiator fights and other elaborate entertainments. These forms of entertainment caught on throughout the empire, with circuses and theaters built in North Africa, Europe, and the Middle East.

Meaning "circle" in Latin, *circus* became the name for an entertainment performed in a circular arena, such as the more lighthearted and fun circuses we think of today.

The poor eagerly looked forward to these entertainments, not just for the excitement, but also for the possibility of meat from the animals that were sometimes used and killed in fights. Mosaics of the time frequently depicted excited crowds cheering while they watch gladiators fight to the death. Umpires regulated the fights, which followed an intricate set of rules. The heavy cost of the games was usually paid for by the emperor, although politicians sponsored them as well. It was an expensive but effective way of keeping the poor entertained.

Discovery EDUCATION | SOCIAL STUDIES TECHBOOK

How did the spread of Roman culture influence life throughout the empire?

Food was also used as a way of keeping the lower classes happy during the period of the republic when the state provided free or low-cost grain to the poor. Toward the end of the first century BCE, approximately 200,000 Romans were living off this grain. One of the army's main priorities was ensuring a constant grain supply from Egypt because shortages could lead to riots.

## Writers and Thinkers

Many great writers emerged in Rome, providing the public with both entertainment and information. Juvenal and Virgil wrote popular poetry. Pliny the Elder wrote *Natural History*, an encyclopedia that many Romans used to learn about astronomy, zoology, and other sciences. The philosopher Plutarch wrote *Lives*, which provides biographies of famous Roman soldiers and statesmen, such as Alexander the Great and Julius Caesar.

## Pax Romana

### What led to the Pax Romana?

Rome continued to expand through its conquest of other lands. Rome imposed its system of government and culture on the new lands to create consistency throughout all of the territories. After the civil wars that led to the foundation of the Roman Empire, Emperor Augustus set out to combine Rome's territories and establish boundaries to help create unity throughout the empire. Called the Pax Augustus or Pax Romana, this period of relative peace lasted 200 years.

Although there was no more civil war within Rome, small wars in other areas did occur. Rome continued its conquests and maintained a presence in all of its provinces to stop any rebellions that might occur. In peacetime, the Roman soldiers were kept busy building and repairing forts, bridges, camps, aqueducts, and roads.

## Paying for Public Projects

Another intricate part of Rome's civilization was its tax system, which paid for the city's infrastructure—its roads and aqueducts. One of the Roman kings, Servius Tullius, is believed to have introduced the idea of a census, a system of counting members of a society. The results were used to determine who to tax and how much to tax each individual or family. All the men in Rome were ordered to assemble in a pasture outside the city. Each one was counted and provided information on the size of his family,

photo: Getty Images

*Marble relief depicting the Roman census.*

how much land he owned, and the number of servants, enslaved persons, and livestock he owned. As the republic shifted to empire, a new tax system was developed.

Emperor Augustus established financial bodies to control taxation throughout the empire and levied a common tax paid with money called tribute, or *tributum*. In addition, indirect taxes were imposed on various activities related to the slave market, as well as inheritances.

## Moving People, Moving Water

*How did public projects impact culture in the Roman Empire?*

Since 351 BCE, Rome had been constructing roads. These roads eventually created a vast network that helped to hold the empire together. Soldiers, surveyors, and engineers laid out the roads, always considering the straightest and fastest routes. Roads were built in advance of the invading armies, which helped the

*photo: Getty Images*
*Modern photograph of Roman bath ruins, Trier, Germany.*

Romans to conquer new lands. Afterward, these roads made it possible for an army of 180,000 legionnaires, or soldiers, to control a population of 55 million people. Roads were constructed by creating a strong foundation and then adding several layers of construction materials, including stones and pebbles. Workers then covered the surface of the road with slabs of stone. These roads not only made military deployment swift and economical, but also allowed commerce and information to pass quickly from one end of the empire to the other. Remnants of Roman roads are still in use today in Europe, Asia, and North Africa.

Another important technological achievement of the Roman Empire was the construction of aqueducts. Aqueducts were used to carry water over great distances. They looked like large bridges supported by great columns. Some of these ancient aqueducts are still in use

**Explore this interactive to learn more about how Roman culture spread throughout the empire.**

today such as the one in Almunecar, Spain. Eleven aqueducts kept the city of Rome and its surrounding areas supplied with water for drinking and use in the irrigation of fields. Aqueducts were also built in all the colonies. Water was especially important for citizens because of the cultural activity of community bathing.

Public baths were a part of daily life in ancient Rome. No day was complete without an afternoon visit to the neighborhood bath. Here, men would discuss business, political contracts, and even the local gossip. Baths usually included an adjoining gymnasium for workouts as well as hot and cold rooms. Women had separate bathhouses, but theirs were usually smaller and less luxurious.

**Discovery** SOCIAL STUDIES
EDUCATION | **TECHBOOK**

How did the spread of Roman culture influence life throughout the empire?

Visiting the baths became a custom shared by the vastly different cultures throughout the empire. Although they were technically open to everyone, there was an entry fee, which often excluded the poorer members of society from attending.

## A Practical Art

### *What kind of influence has Roman art and architecture had on Western culture?*

In addition to the roads and aqueducts the Romans built, they made contributions to the cultural world through their art and architecture. Roman art was heavily influenced by Greece. Greek art was everywhere during the empire, and the work of Roman artists was clearly influenced by it. The Greeks had developed techniques such as bronze casting, relief, vase art, and mosaic. Roman artists adopted these practices and applied them to art forms such as landscaping, portraiture, and a style of art that creates the illusion of three-dimensionality known as *trompe l'oeil* (literally translated as "fools the eye").

Unlike the Greeks, however, the Romans did not place a high value on art. As a result, Roman artists and craftspeople made practical items such as jewelry, coins, and mosaics. Roman art adopted and adapted styles from the local cultures of conquered lands such as Egypt, Carthage, Spain, and Britain.

photo: Getty Images

*The Pantheon in Rome is one of the most widely copied examples of Roman architecture.*

Roman sculptures and murals often depict scenes from everyday life. Large, realistic paintings on plaster called frescoes have been uncovered on walls of buildings in Pompeii, Italy. Romans also valued art and luxury goods from Carthage, Iberia, Britain, and Germany.

Roman architectural influence can be seen in buildings around the world. The Pantheon, constructed of concrete and brick, was built as a temple to ancient Roman gods. The front of the building consists of Corinthian-style columns with a gabled roof. Behind this entrance, the building is circular and topped by a concrete dome that at the time was the largest ever constructed. The Pantheon has been the most widely copied of Roman architecture. Some buildings borrowed directly from the original, such as the main public library of Sarasota, Florida. Other buildings, such as the U.S. Capitol building, did so indirectly. The U.S. Capitol is a replica of Rome's Tempietto of San Pietro, built in 1459 CE, which in turn had been influenced by the dome, rotunda, and towering pillars of the Pantheon.

In many ways, Rome's art and architecture exemplify the kind of influences Roman culture has had on Europe and North America. Roman culture often imitated what it admired and improved on what it needed from other cultures. Over a 900-year period, it came up with useful inventions, such as concrete, and improved on invaluable resources such as roads and aqueducts. Both its creations and improvements—directly or indirectly—have supported the expressions of its culture.

## Latin: Dead or Alive

*How did Latin influence the world?*

The modern 26-letter alphabet that is used throughout the Americas, Europe, and Africa is the descendent of a set of letters the Romans used to read and write. The Romans inherited the alphabet from the Etruscans, an earlier Italian civilization, who had received it from the Greeks, who had borrowed it from the Phoenician traders from the eastern Mediterranean. Each time the alphabet was adopted by a different culture, it was modified to adapt to the needs of the people using it. The Romans adapted this alphabet to use with their language, which was known as Latin.

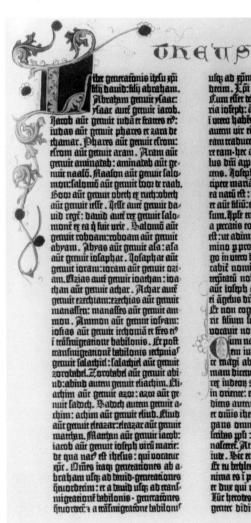

photo: Library of Congress

*The Gutenberg Bible, one of the first books ever printed, was printed in Latin.*

### Latin: Written and Spoken

Latin as a spoken language was used throughout the course of Roman history. Romans had to be able to speak Latin to be citizens. According to some historians, most citizens in the city of Rome were bilingual, or spoke two languages. They would speak Latin publicly and Greek in private. People even inserted Greek expressions into their Latin conversations.

Discovery EDUCATION | SOCIAL STUDIES TECHBOOK

How did the spread of Roman culture influence life throughout the empire?

Latin became an essential part of life. Latin helped unite the diverse cultures within the Roman Empire and would influence the creation of many languages that are common today. It developed into vulgar Latin (meaning common Latin), which was spoken by the army and the lower classes, and classic Latin, used by the upper classes. Vulgar Latin became the common language of Europe. Vulgar Latin acted as a bridge language between classic Latin and the other languages spoken in the empire. Latin mixed with the languages of Rome's conquered territories such as Gaul (modern-day France) and the Iberian Peninsula (modern-day Spain). Today, many modern languages including French, Spanish, Italian, Portuguese, and Romanian are called Romance languages because they developed from the Roman language of Latin. The influence of Latin is even evident in about two-thirds of words in the English language.

**Rome Declines, but Latin Remains**

With the decline of the Roman Empire and the rise of Christianity, Latin became the spoken and written language of the Roman Catholic Church. Even in the United States, Catholic mass was conducted only in Latin as late as the 1960s. Classic Latin was spoken by European intellectuals until the 1700s and continues to be used in science, mathematics, and legal terminology.

Like many of the cultural achievements of the Roman Empire, Latin is a combination of influences from other cultures that was made uniquely Roman and went on to influence civilizations throughout the ancient world and into modern times.

Rome's legacy has been ensured by the multiple ways the rest of the world has recognized, admired, and adopted aspects of its character. True to form, in technology, art, and language, Rome displays its uncanny ability to draw what it could from everything that came its way, while adding its own unique stamp.

**Consider the Essential Question:**

How did the spread of Roman culture influence life throughout the empire?

Go online to complete the Social Studies Explanation.

**Check for Understanding:**

Identify the social classes in the Roman Empire and describe each class. Explain two ways the social classes interacted with one another.

photo: Getty Images

# 2.5 A Weakening Empire

## LESSON OVERVIEW

### Introduction

In this concept, you will analyze the political, geographic, and cultural factors that contributed to the fall of the Roman Empire.

### Essential Question

Why did Rome decline and fall?

### Lesson Objectives

By the end of this lesson, you should be able to:

- Analyze and explain the political, geographic, and cultural factors that led to the fall of the Roman Empire.

- Explain how Constantine's establishment of the new capital in Constantinople helped lead to the Western Empire's fall.

- Describe the sack of Rome and analyze the impact of the dismantling of the empire.

## Key Vocabulary
Which terms do you already know?

- [ ] Alaric
- [ ] Attila
- [ ] Battle of Adrianople
- [ ] Byzantine Empire
- [ ] Catholicism/ Roman Catholicism
- [ ] Celtic peoples
- [ ] Christianity
- [ ] citizen
- [ ] Constantine
- [ ] Constantinople
- [ ] Diocletian
- [ ] Division of the Roman Empire
- [ ] Eastern Orthodox Christianity

- [ ] empire
- [ ] Gaul
- [ ] Germanic peoples
- [ ] Goths
- [ ] Huns
- [ ] migration
- [ ] nomadic
- [ ] province
- [ ] Roman Empire
- [ ] Roman Senate
- [ ] Rome
- [ ] Spain
- [ ] taxes
- [ ] technology
- [ ] trade

# ENGAGE

Was Rome "one fatherland of many nations"? Visit Engage to learn more.

### Essential Question

Why did Rome decline and fall?

# EXPLORE

## Who Was Emperor? Who Was Not Emperor?
*How did Rome become politically unstable?*

The Roman emperor Septimus Severus died in Britain in the year 235 CE. His dying advice to his sons was, "Make the soldiers rich and don't bother about the rest." That guiding principle weakened the empire and helped lead to its end.

The emperor of Rome, despite his enormous power, was not a king. He was the first citizen of the state. His authority came from the idea that he represented the Roman Senate and people. Of course, the emperor did not answer to the Senate or the people. Nor did he inherit authority as a descendant of a family or from the gods. The idea remained that he was given his power. Who gave it to him? The word *emperor* means "supreme military commander." The Roman Empire's foundation rested not on a constitution but on force, and force was with the army. This is evidenced by Emperor Augustus who, after winning power over Mark Antony and Cleopatra in 30 BCE, gained the allegiance of the army.

By the 200s CE, there was no single Roman army. The empire was too big and its enemies too many. It contained all or part of more than 30 countries that exist today. To the east, an ancient enemy, Parthia (Persia), was gathering strength. To the south, in Africa, Berber tribes raided Roman towns. And to the north were the Germanic peoples that Rome had not been able to conquer. Marcus Aurelius, last of the "five good emperors," died of cancer in 180 CE while fighting the tribes on the northern frontier. For the next hundred years, most emperors were the commanders of whichever frontier army could seize power.

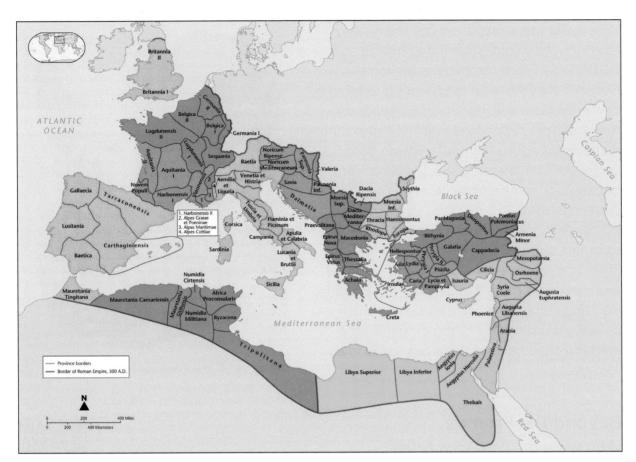

*This map shows the Roman Empire at its greatest extent.*

## Chaos in the Armies

### *How did internal conflict weaken the empire?*

Armies fought with each other to place their own man in power. The soldiers of the one who backed the next emperor would be rewarded with wealth and power. A poor general was of no use to his army. Soldiers might elevate a man with no military experience as long as he was rich, like the emperor Didius Julianus. He reigned for 66 days in 193 CE before another faction of the army killed him. Other emperors were killed because their discipline was too strict or because the soldiers grew restless for change. During the years 235–284, 30 generals were proclaimed emperor by their armies. Few reigned as long as three years; one lasted less than three weeks.

These emperors did not win victories like Roman generals in the past, except over each other. Instead of defeating the tribes on the frontier, they bribed the tribes to keep them from raiding Roman territory. The money Rome paid in bribes came to equal the army's entire payroll. In 251, the Goths, a large Germanic tribe, crossed the empire's northern border and defeated a Roman army, killing the emperor Decius. In 260, the emperor Valerian was captured in battle by the Parthians. The Persian king Sapor humiliated the emperor by using him as a footstool to mount his horse. A legend has it that when Valerian died, his skin was dyed red and stuffed, like a hunting trophy, and displayed in a Persian temple.

Where did these emperors get the money to enrich their soldiers and pay off the barbarians? From the citizens of Rome. Because they were no longer conquering new countries from which they could get money, the emperors raised taxes. At the same time, mines were not turning out enough gold and silver to make coins. So, the emperors debased, or reduced the value of, the currency. "Silver" coins came to be made of 90 percent copper. Prices of basic items, such as bread, were 200 times higher by the late 200s than in the early 200s. Trade declined, and more and more Romans fell into poverty. Roman landowners lost their lands, which became the property of the emperor. The emperor then handed them out to his loyal soldiers.

photo: Getty Images
*An illustration of the Goths crossing the Alps.*

## Beyond the Frontier
*Who were the barbarian tribes?*

### The Barbarian Tribes

What image comes to mind when you hear the word *barbarian*? In popular culture, the word suggests large, hairy savages wearing animal skins and swinging huge double-edged axes. This was not far from the way Romans thought about the Germanic tribes beyond their northern frontier. In the year 9, a Roman army was sent to subdue the tribes in the forest beyond the Rhine River. The army was massacred, almost to the last man. After that, the Romans accepted the Rhine and Danube Rivers as their border. They stationed legions at strategic points along these rivers to prevent raids, but they made no more attempts to conquer the tribes.

*Barbarian* comes from a Greek word meaning "foreign." To the Romans, it meant anyone not a part of the empire. The Germanic tribes' original home was in the Scandinavian lands of today's Norway, Sweden, and Denmark. As their population grew, their migrations carried them south into present-day Germany in search of better land. Before 100 BCE, they had drawn the notice of the Romans. Kept out of Roman territory, they expanded eastward, conquering the Celtic tribes of the region. There were many Germanic tribes, but by the 300s, five main tribes were ranged along the Roman frontier. They were the Franks, Saxons, Vandals, Visigoths (western Goths), and Ostrogoths (eastern Goths).

The tribes traded with the Romans more often than they fought with them. Roman merchants dealt in farm and household tools, wine, and jewelry. In exchange, the Germans sold them enslaved people captured in their raids to the north and east. The tribes closest to the frontier adopted Roman customs. Some came to speak a form of Latin and developed a taste for Roman civilization. By the 200s, the barbarians were also furnishing free warriors as soldiers for the Roman army. By 400, most of the Roman army was made up of barbarians. There were even barbarian generals such as Stilicho the Vandal, who led Roman troops in battle against other Germanic tribes.

**The Huns**

In the east, in what is now southern Russia, loomed a threat to the tribes that the Romans barely noticed. This threat was the Huns, a nomadic or wandering people originally from Central Asia. They may have been the same people against whom the

photo: Getty Images

*An illustration of a Goth family fleeing the Huns during the fourth or fifth century.*

Chinese had built their Great Wall several centuries earlier. The Huns "had no country but the back of a horse," as a saying went, and were fearsome warriors who could shoot arrows accurately while at a gallop.

In the 300s, the Huns were on the move. They pressed westward against the territory of the Germanic tribes. The terrified tribes were pushed against the Rhine and Danube frontier of the Roman Empire. The Romans, unable to stop the movement of the Germanic tribes across their borders, offered some of them land in Roman territory and money to pay their warriors. In exchange, the Germanic tribes would declare loyalty to the emperor and protect a portion of the Roman Empire border.

## The Empire Divided

*Why was the capital of the Roman Empire moved?*

In the anarchy of the 200s, the Roman Empire seemed about to fall apart. In 284, Diocletian was raised to the throne and quickly restored order. Although he was a citizen, he ruled as a king, surrounded by a court of officials with new titles. He introduced the idea that the emperor was given his power by the gods and demanded that all who approached him bow down to him.

But Diocletian was an expert organizer. He reorganized the government, breaking up old provinces into more than 100 smaller ones, each with its own officials. He increased the size of the army but broke it up into smaller units, each with its own command structure.

Because money was scarce, he increased the amount of taxes based on the number of people and their wealth. He sent officials all over the empire to collect census data to determine how much each province, town, and citizen should be taxed.

photo: Getty Images
*Gold coins showing the heads of Emperors Constantine and Diocletian.*

Diocletian realized that the empire was too big for one man to rule. He appointed a co-emperor, Maximian, to rule under him, both emperors taking the title of "Augustus." Diocletian would rule the Eastern Roman Empire; Maximian would rule the Western. Each then appointed a "Caesar" to rule some of the provinces in his half of the empire and to become "Augustus" when he died. Then, in the year 305, Diocletian did a remarkable thing: He voluntarily gave up his throne and retired to his estates, persuading his fellow Augustus to do the same. Diocletian's system fell apart almost at once. By 311, there were four men claiming the title of Augustus, each supported by his own soldiers. The following year, one of these generals, Constantine, defeated his rivals and became emperor.

## The Empire in the East
### *How did Constantinople become Rome's second capital?*

Constantine understood that the Western Roman Empire had been so drained by taxes that it was no longer producing wealth for the state. Even the city of Rome was no longer important, either economically or strategically. The future of the empire lay in the east, where the Germanic tribes were not pressing on the frontier. In 330, Constantine abandoned Rome. He moved the capital to the old Greek city of Byzantium, in what is now Turkey. There, he built a splendid "New Rome," which he named Constantinople, which translates to "Constantine City."

If the western part of the empire had been weak before, it now grew even weaker. As the barbarians, pressured by the Huns, in turn increased their pressure on Roman territory, future emperors withdrew legions from their western provinces to strengthen the east.

photo: Getty Images
*An illustration of the walls of Constantinople.*

Taxes to pay for defense grew so heavy that there were complaints to Constantine that his taxes had "drained our very life." The jobs of town and provincial officials, once an honor, now became a burden. Officials were required to pay their district's share of taxes even if the land and people they governed were too poor to raise the required amount.

As a result, nobody wanted to hold public office, and people had to be forced to take the job.

Constantine and his successors increasingly used their power to control the people. A son had to follow the same occupation as his father. To support the government and the army, farmers were bound to their land, city workers to their trades. The sense of community that had bound Romans together for centuries disappeared. People still spoke of "Roman citizenship," but in effect all Romans had become enslaved to the state. On large, wealthy estates in the west, a few landowners like Rutilius Claudius Namatianus dreamed of the return of Roman glory. But most people had stopped caring about Roman culture and no longer took pride in being Roman.

## Attacks from the East

### *Why did Germanic tribes attack Rome?*

In 376, the Huns were again moving westward. The Visigoths, one of the largest and most powerful of the Germanic tribes, appeared on the empire's Danube frontier and appealed to the emperor for help. They were allowed to settle in Roman territory as allies against other invaders. The Romans, however, treated them as a conquered people. They were not given enough land, their weapons were seized, and many Visigoths were sold into slavery. Roman officials sold them spoiled grain at high prices. The Visigoths were insulted and enraged. In the Battle of Adrianople, they attacked a Roman army, claiming a decisive victory for the Goths and the beginning of the end for Rome.

The Germanic tribes had no wish to destroy Rome, only to share in its riches. They had been growing stronger and more populous as Rome grew weaker. They needed more land to feed themselves, and because they were a warrior people, they sought it by conquest. The Visigoths swept through Rome's Balkan provinces, taking whatever they could. In 395, they were settled on lands in northern Greece. This land lay on the border between the Eastern and Western Roman Empire. Now and then, the Goths found themselves being attacked on both sides. Under Alaric, who became the Goths' king in 396, they began raiding Italy itself.

*photo: Getty Images*
*Alaric I, king of the Visigoths, enters Athens.*

# The Fall of Rome
### *How did Rome fall to Germanic tribes?*

In the weakened west, the general Stilicho commanded the Roman armies. To defend the city of Rome against the Visigoths, he pulled Roman legions out of Britain and Gaul. On December 31, 406, the Rhine River was frozen over. Led by the Vandals, Germanic tribes crossed the river, and Gaul effectively ceased to be a Roman province. The emperor Honorius blamed Stilicho and had him executed. The Roman legions slaughtered the families of 30,000 Germanic tribesmen who were serving in the Roman army.

Alaric now declared war against the Roman Empire. He invaded Italy and surrounded Rome. On August 24, 410, sympathizers inside the city opened the gates to his soldiers. For the first time in 800 years, Rome was at the mercy of a "barbarian" army. Alaric's soldiers left the buildings largely intact, though for three days they were allowed to steal whatever they could. As news of the sack of Rome spread throughout the empire, people greeted it with shock and disbelief. It was almost unimaginable. There could no longer be any doubt of how weak Rome had become.

photo: Getty Images

*The sack of Rome by the Visigoths in 401.*

The city of Rome survived, but the Western Roman Empire was finished. Germanic tribes chipped away at its territories in Gaul, Spain, and northwest Africa. In 451, Germanic tribes and Romans made common cause against the Huns, who had invaded Gaul under their most famous king, Attila. The following year, after being defeated in Gaul, Attila swept through northern Italy. But he died soon after, and without his leadership, the Huns ceased to be a threat. The Germanic tribes resumed their wars against Rome. In 455, Rome was sacked again, this time by the Vandals.

**Explore this interactive to learn more about events leading to Rome's decline and fall.**

The last Western Roman emperor was Romulus Augustulus. The name meant "little Augustus," and in fact he was a child. In 476, a Gothic chief named Odoacer, who had been a general in the Roman army, seized command of Italy and removed Romulus Augustulus from his throne. Seventeen years later, Odoacer was himself defeated and killed by Theodoric, the Ostrogoth. Theodoric tried to rule in the Roman manner under Roman law. He repaired Roman aqueducts and ports, but he was among the last to do so. It is likely that the people of Rome still thought of themselves as Romans. Now that they were no longer part of the Roman Empire, they were subjects of a Gothic Kingdom of Italy.

# After the Fall of Rome
*What happened after the fall of the Western Roman Empire?*

## The Western Roman Empire

The empire in the west was gone, but the idea of Rome still remained. "Barbarian" kings ruled former Roman provinces. Gaul was now part of the kingdom of the Franks, who would eventually give their name to the nation of France. Most of Spain had been conquered by the Visigoths. Italy and the territories to the north now made up the kingdom of the Ostrogoths. Rome's African provinces were taken by the Vandals, and smaller pieces of the empire were carved out by other tribes.

In all these places, Latin remained the language of government and the educated classes. Gradually, however, Roman culture was forgotten. Cities and towns were abandoned because the economy could no longer support an urban population and the infrastructure fell into decay. Roman law and customs were replaced by the folk traditions of the Germanic peoples. Further invasions and civil wars led to periodic famine, or severe food shortages. Europe had entered its early Middle Ages, sometimes known as the Dark Ages.

## The Eastern Empire

In a wide arc around the Mediterranean Sea from Greece to Egypt, the Eastern Roman Empire, which historians call the Byzantine Empire, survived. Its emperors, the heirs of Constantine, still called themselves emperors of Rome, and its people still thought of themselves as Romans. For a time, Constantinople was the most populous city in the world. The Eastern Roman Empire would not fall until 1453, when Constantinople was captured by the Turks.

*photo: Getty Images*

*A mosaic floor at the ruins of a Byzantine church in present-day Cyprus.*

Before the fall of the Western Roman Empire and long before the fall of the Eastern, the culture of the Roman Empire had been transformed by a new religion. Early in the 300s, Christianity was only one of many "mystery religions" that had won followers in the empire. As Rome had declined, the old gods, goddesses, and ceremonies no longer were meaningful to many people. Still, priests maintained the temples and continued to make the sacrifices.

Then in 324, the emperor Constantine became a Christian, and Christianity became a religion that was approved and supported by the state.

By the end of the 300s, Christianity had become the official religion of the empire. Later, as the "barbarians" swept into the empire, Romans discovered that these people also followed the new religion. For centuries, Christianity was the only unifying force in Europe. The little that was remembered of Roman culture was preserved in Christian monasteries. The Roman Empire, which had unified much of Europe, was gone. The different geographical, cultural, economic, and political issues that impacted Rome had been too great for the empire to survive.

**Consider the Essential Question:**

Why did Rome decline and fall?

Go online to complete the Social Studies Explanation.

**Check for Understanding:**

How did the geographical size of the Roman Empire contribute to its decline and fall?

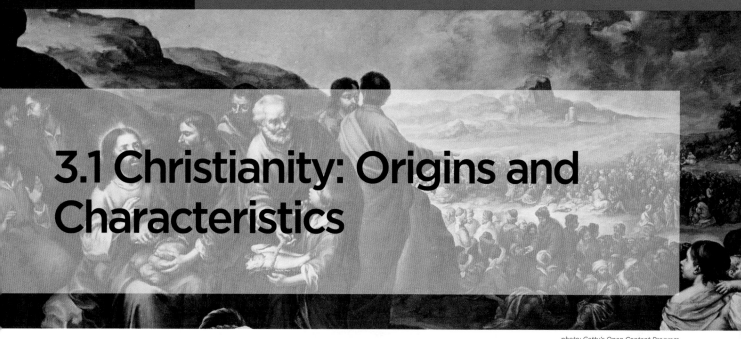

# 3.1 Christianity: Origins and Characteristics

*photo: Getty's Open Content Program*

# LESSON OVERVIEW

## Introduction

In this concept, you will explore the world in which Christianity emerged, how Christianity developed, and its basic teachings and characteristics.

## Essential Question

How did Christianity develop?

## Lesson Objectives

By the end of this lesson, you should be able to:

- Explain the origins of Christianity based on the life and teachings of Jesus.

- Describe the characteristics of Christianity.

## Key Vocabulary
Which terms do you already know?

- [ ] Abraham
- [ ] apostle
- [ ] beginning of Christianity
- [ ] Bethlehem
- [ ] bishop
- [ ] Christianity
- [ ] Constantine
- [ ] Hebrews
- [ ] Herod the Great
- [ ] Israel
- [ ] Jerusalem
- [ ] Jesus
- [ ] Judaism
- [ ] Judea
- [ ] King David
- [ ] King Solomon
- [ ] Mecca
- [ ] Messiah
- [ ] missionary
- [ ] monotheism
- [ ] Moses
- [ ] Muhammad
- [ ] Nazareth
- [ ] Nebuchadnezzar
- [ ] New Testament
- [ ] Palestine
- [ ] parable
- [ ] Phoenicians
- [ ] polytheism
- [ ] proselytizing religion/ universalizing religion
- [ ] Roman Empire
- [ ] Rome
- [ ] Ruth
- [ ] Saul
- [ ] Ten Commandments

# ENGAGE

What does the Sermon on the Mount reveal about Christianity? Visit Engage to learn more.

## Essential Question

How did Christianity develop?

---

# EXPLORE

## Judea Under Roman Rule

*What was Judea like when Christianity began to develop?*

When Christianity began to develop as a religion, the Roman Empire was the strongest power in the Western world. When the Roman Empire conquered a nation, the conquered people were allowed to continue worshipping their own gods, but they were also required to accept the Roman gods. The Romans practiced polytheism, or a belief in many gods and goddesses. The Romans also believed that their emperors were chosen to rule by the gods. Some Roman emperors were even worshipped as gods after their deaths.

photo: Getty Images
*Evidence of Roman rule can still be seen in Israel.*

In 63 BCE, Pompey the Great captured Jerusalem, bringing what is modern-day Israel under the control of the Roman Empire. At the time, most of this region was called Judea. This land was populated mostly by the Hebrew people, who practiced Judaism. Unlike most people who were conquered by Rome, however, many of the Hebrews refused to assimilate, or adopt Roman ways of life. Jewish law forbade them from worshipping the Roman gods. To try to improve the situation, the Roman Senate appointed Herod the Great as king of Judea in 39 BCE. Herod had been born in Judea and was a practicing Jew. However, the people of Judea resented him. They saw him as an outsider and felt he was a cruel leader.

The situation in Roman-ruled Judea was very tense. It was into this environment that an important figure would be born and would help shape a new religion that would transform the Western world.

## The Birth of Jesus

### What do Christians believe about the birth of Jesus?

The story of the life of Jesus is outlined in the New Testament, a portion of the Christian Bible. This story is told in the books of the Bible known as the Gospels, which means "good news." These first four books of the New Testament are traditionally believed to have been authored by two of Jesus's initial followers—Matthew and John—and by two men who helped bring Jesus's message to non-Jews outside Judea—Mark and Luke.

photo: Getty Images

*According to tradition, this star marks the location of Christ's birth in Bethlehem.*

According to the New Testament, Jesus was born around the year 1 CE in Bethlehem, a city in Judea. In the Christian calendar, one of the most commonly used calendars today, the years are counted based on the year Jesus was born. Dates ending with BC (which corresponds to BCE) occurred before Jesus's birth, and dates ending with AD (which corresponds to CE) occur after the birth of Jesus. Although Christians believe that Jesus was born in 1 CE, historians disagree about the exact date. They believe the actual date may be between 6 and 4 BCE.

The name *Jesus* is a Greek translation of the Hebrew name *Yehoshua*, or *Joshua*. The honorific "Christ" is also based on the Greek word ***christos***, meaning "savior" or "messiah."

Christians believe that Jesus was born to a mortal mother, named Mary, but was actually the son of God. Many Christians see Mary as a holy figure. Jesus's birth is celebrated during the Christian holiday of Christmas.

## Who Was Jesus?

### *What do Christians believe about Jesus's life?*

Most of what is known about Jesus's life comes from the Gospels. However, historians and religious scholars do not agree about how much of the Gospels is literally true. The Gospels were all written between 40 and 60 years after the death of Jesus. Although there is nonbiblical evidence to show that Jesus was a historical figure, there is limited evidence outside the Gospels documenting the events of his life.

Very little is written about Jesus's early life. There are only a few Bible passages that describe him before the age of 30. According to the Bible, at the age of 30, Jesus, who was Jewish, was baptized by a Jewish prophet known as John the Baptist. Jesus then went into the desert alone to fast and pray for 40 days. When he returned, he began teaching. He gathered 12 followers, known as disciples, and traveled from town to town, teaching about God and healing the sick. Within a few years, Jesus had attracted a sizable following, much of it drawn from the lower orders of society.

photo: Library of Congress

*Christians believe that after he was crucified, Jesus rose from the dead before ascending into heaven.*

According to the Bible, the local Jewish leaders became worried about Jesus. They felt that some of Jesus's teachings contradicted or challenged Jewish law. The Romans felt threatened by Jesus, fearing his teachings would turn the people against Roman rule. Eventually, the Bible says that Jesus was betrayed by one of his disciples, a man named Judas. Jesus was arrested by the Romans for calling himself King of the Jews. The Bible does not make it clear whether this was a title Jesus gave himself or whether he was only called that by some of his followers. Approximately in the year 30, Jesus was convicted and sentenced to death by crucifixion, a form of capital punishment that the Romans often used for rebellious slaves or political or religious dissidents.

After his death, his mother and a few other followers buried Jesus in a cave. The Gospels recount that three days after his death, Jesus was resurrected, or brought back to life. He returned for a brief period to speak with his followers and give them a few last lessons. Then, he is said to have ascended, or risen, to Heaven to join God, his father. This was the beginning of Christianity.

## Jesus's Teachings

*What were the teachings of Jesus?*

photo: Getty's Open Content Program

*Depiction of Christ delivering his Sermon on the Mount.*

### Jesus the Storyteller

During Jesus's life, he traveled from town to town. As he traveled, he taught those who followed him, as well as individuals and crowds who gathered to question him or hear him speak.

Many of Jesus's lessons were delivered through the telling of stories. These stories are called parables. The parables that Jesus told were simple and easy to understand. They explained difficult concepts using familiar images and characters that his audience encountered every day.

The Bible contains many parables that Jesus told. Two parables that Christians study are the parable of the good Samaritan and the parable of the prodigal son. These parables emphasize the importance of love and forgiveness for other people. Other parables tell stories about loving God. Love of God and humanity were important themes of Jesus's teachings that Christian communities still study today.

**Explore this interactive to learn how medieval stained glass windows reveal basic tenets of the Christian faith.**

## Building the Bible

*What was included in the Christian Bible?*

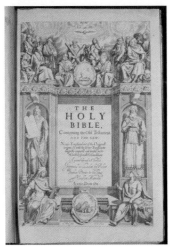

photo: Getty Images

*Image of the cover of a King James Bible.*

After the death of Jesus, his teachings were initially passed along by oral tradition. Around the year 50, Jesus's followers wrote down his teachings. These writings were eventually gathered together and would become part of the New Testament.

Many different Gospels were written by the followers of Jesus, but only four were used to construct the text of the Bible as it exists today. The books that were not used in the Bible are called the Apocrypha. Some of the Apocrypha are studied today for what they tell us about the history of early Christianity. Different branches of Christianity also accept different books as part of the Bible.

The books of the New Testament were combined with the Torah and other books of the Hebrew Bible that are used in the Jewish faith. These older books became known in Christianity as the Old Testament. Over the next century, many additional pieces of writing were created and added to the Bible. They include letters, hymns, poetry, parables, and prophecies.

## Spreading the Faith

### *How did Christianity spread?*

From the earliest days of Christianity, Christians have believed that an important part of their faith was to teach others about Jesus and Christianity. The Bible tells that in a post-resurrection appearance to his apostles, Jesus commanded: "Go and make disciples of all nations, baptize them in the name of the Father and the Son and the Holy Spirit, and teach them to obey all the commands I have laid on you." The New Testament book Acts of the Apostles recounts the travels and trials of his disciples as they attempted to carry out this commission.

### Christianity's Impact

From its beginnings, Christianity caused tension within the Roman Empire. Because of their beliefs, Christians did not conform to all Roman laws or religious ideas, including participation in the cult of the emperor. The cult of the emperor was a belief that the Roman emperor was one of the gods. This belief was one of few things that Roman citizens had in common, so this refusal to conform hurt the unity of the Roman Empire.

photo: Getty Images

*Remains of an early Christian church that began in the fifth century at the site of Roman baths.*

Also, despite the similarities of the religions, Jewish leadership had disagreements with some common Christian practices. Christians did not follow all of the traditional Hebrew laws. Christians also interpreted some laws differently than the Hebrew scholars did. For example, Christians did not strictly follow Jewish dietary laws, and some Christians ate foods that had traditionally been considered unclean. One Bible passage that supported this new attitude toward food was a scene in the Acts of the Apostles. The disciple, Peter, has a vision where a sheet full of birds, reptiles, and other animals appears in front of him. Some of these animals were considered unclean according to Jewish law. Peter then hears God tell him that all creation is now clean. In 50 CE, some apostles met at the Council of Jerusalem. They officially decided that Christians were exempt from Jewish dietary laws.

## Changing Attitudes in Rome

Initially, the Roman Empire outlawed Christianity. Christians often had to meet in secret, in private homes or in the catacombs—burial places beneath the streets of Rome. Those who practiced the new religion were sometimes punished or even put to death. Paradoxically, stories of the sufferings of these early martyrs—who remained faithful to the Christian message even as they were publicly tortured or killed—served as a powerful inspiration to their fellow Christians and sometimes won new converts to the religion.

**Consider the Essential Question:**

How did Christianity develop?

Go online to complete the Social Studies Explanation.

**Check for Understanding:**

Based on what you have read about Christianity's origins and characteristics, explain why its message spread throughout the Roman world.

photo: Getty Images

# 3.2 Christianity's Spread

## LESSON OVERVIEW

### Introduction

In this concept, you will learn how missionaries for Christianity converted people throughout the world in the years after the religion's founding. You will explore how Christians were persecuted for their beliefs. You will also learn how Emperor Constantine helped spread Christianity and how a great rift split the church in two.

### Essential Question

How did Christianity become the world's largest religion?

### Lesson Objectives

By the end of this lesson, you should be able to:

- Analyze the factors that led to the diffusion of Christianity throughout the Roman Empire and other parts of Europe.

- Explain the importance of monks, missionaries, and the Christian church itself in the spread of Christianity throughout Europe.

- Describe the impact of the fall of the Western Roman Empire on Christianity.

### Key Vocabulary

Which terms do you already know?

- ☐ bishop
- ☐ Catholic Church
- ☐ Christianity
- ☐ Constantine
- ☐ convert
- ☐ disciple
- ☐ missionary
- ☐ monastery
- ☐ monk
- ☐ Paul
- ☐ pope
- ☐ propaganda
- ☐ proselytizing religion/universalizing religion
- ☐ Saint Anthony
- ☐ Saint Patrick

## ENGAGE

How did a message from the Apostle Paul help the spread of Christianity? Visit Engage to learn more.

### Essential Question

How did Christianity become the world's largest religion?

## EXPLORE

### Disciples Spread the Story

*Who spread Christianity after Jesus died?*

After Jesus died, his 12 disciples and other followers told his story. They began to preach among the Jews of Palestine and the rest of the Roman world. They were able to convince more people to become Christians.

photo: Getty Images

*Image of a gold-plated mosaic depicting the apostle Paul in the Hagia Sofia, Istanbul, Turkey.*

Peter, one of the disciples, is credited with establishing Christianity in Rome. However, another early Christian, Paul, perhaps did more to spread Christianity than any of his contemporaries. Paul, a Jew from Asia Minor, was not one of the 12 disciples that lived and worked with Jesus, but Paul believed that Jesus appeared to him in a vision. He immediately became a Christian and began traveling around the Mediterranean region. Paul established churches, had long discussions about church doctrine, and wrote many letters to different people throughout the region. His letters explained Jesus's teachings and sacrifice.

### Paul's Travels

Paul preached the Christian beliefs that Jesus was the son of God and that whoever followed him received forgiveness for their sins and everlasting life after death. Paul believed that anyone could become Christian, whether or not they followed Jewish law. He created a formal theology, which he wrote in Greek. This appealed to the upper class.

Paul and the others who traveled and gained converts were called missionaries. Missionaries played an important role in the spread of Christianity. They were sent into areas that were not Christian. They taught the local people about Christianity, hoping to convince them to join the faith. For example, missionaries worked to convert the Germanic tribes from their polytheistic religions to Christianity. Missionaries played an important role in spreading Christianity to several other regions as well.

### Saint Patrick

Four hundred years after Paul's travels around the Mediterranean, a young Roman Briton named Patrick was kidnapped from his home, taken to Ireland, and enslaved.

Explore this interactive to learn more about events that contributed to Christianity's spread.

After escaping home to Britain, Patrick had a dream in which he felt himself called to return to Ireland so he could Christianize it. He trained as a missionary for 12 years in continental Europe and then went to Ireland. By the time of his death, nearly all of Ireland had become Christian.

## Suffering for Beliefs

*How and why were Christians persecuted for their beliefs?*

As Christianity began, many followers found themselves persecuted by the Romans. The Romans accused Christians of being disloyal to the emperor because Christians refused to worship the Roman gods and to recognize the emperor as a god.

Roman officials often saw Christianity as a religion that encouraged rebellion while reducing the power of the emperor. Some Romans persecuted Christians mercilessly in an attempt to discourage others from converting to the religion. Sometimes, they employed public execution and torture; at other times, they burned religious texts or confiscated church property.

### The Appeal of Christianity

Despite the persecution, Christianity attracted many new followers. At a time when many people in the Roman Empire and beyond were enslaved, people flocked to a message that elevated the poor and the weak, promised the love of a divine being, and guaranteed a reward in the afterlife.

photo: Getty Images

*Mid-19th century illustration of Roman persecution of Christians.*

The church also created a community of individuals who were equal and supportive of each other. Churches took care of widows, fed the hungry, and even provided rudimentary health services.

Women played a crucial role in the early survival of the Christian church. A Christian woman, Fabiola, helped create the first Christian hospital. Women were also part of missionary journeys because they could enter other women's homes to speak with them about Christianity. Even though Christian leadership was mostly male, there were many influential women converts, including wealthy Roman noblewomen. One well-known woman was Perpetua. She kept a diary in prison and was ultimately killed for being a Christian. She wrote about her prophetic visions and her fellowship with other women in prison.

### Early Christian Worship

During the earliest years of Christianity, many worshippers did not worship in actual churches. Services were held in people's homes. Women held leadership positions in many house churches in cities throughout the Roman Empire. As a church clergy hierarchy developed, some churches assigned worthy women the title of "deaconess."

Despite the early persecution, Christianity continued to spread throughout the Roman Empire. By the 300s, about 10 percent of the Roman Empire had converted to Christianity. Christianity was on its way to becoming the most popular religion in the world.

## The Emperor Constantine Adopts Christianity
### *How did Constantine influence Christianity?*

The influence of Rome and the spread of its culture also helped Christianity spread. Paul and other missionaries used the vast network of Roman roads and the Roman trade routes on the Mediterranean Sea to travel to new lands and teach more people about Christianity in an attempt to gain new converts.

In 312, Christianity gained one of its greatest converts. Emperor Constantine was not a stranger to Christianity. He had been raised by a Christian mother, Empress Helena. Before a great battle, Emperor Constantine had a vision. He dreamed that Jesus Christ appeared to him and instructed him to put the first two letters of his name in Greek on the shields of his warriors.

When he woke, he looked at the sun. There, he saw a cross and the message "in this sign you will be victor." When Constantine's army won, the ruler adopted Christianity. He also issued the Edict of Milan, which ended persecution of Christians within the Roman Empire.

The Edict of Milan and its enforcement by Constantine gave protection to Christians. He encouraged the construction of churches in the empire, which helped Christianity spread even more quickly. Although Constantine had long been a believer in Christianity, he was not baptized until shortly before his death. He died wearing his white baptismal robe in 337. The support and protection that Constantine had given to Christians during his reign helped make Christianity the official religion of Rome by 391.

photo: Getty Images

*Illustration of Constantine presiding over the Council of Nicea in 325.*

In the 300s, two major Christian councils established the Nicene Creed. These were the Council of Nicaea in 325 and the Council of Constantinople in 381. The Nicene Creed states the most fundamental beliefs of Christianity—the beliefs that God created the world, that Jesus is God's son, and that Jesus died and was resurrected. Constantine organized the Council of Nicaea to resolve a religious controversy and unify Christian belief. He issued policies that exempted the Church from legal, financial, and civic burdens. Once Christianity became the official religion of Rome, many Christian leaders gave their support to the Roman Empire.

## Monks and Monasteries Help Christianity Expand

*How did monks help Christianity grow into the world's largest religion?*

Over time, Christianity became an institution. Christians formed a community based on equality. They addressed each other as "brother" and "sister." Christians gathered each Sabbath day, Sunday, to worship and pray together, breaking bread and drinking wine to commune with Jesus Christ, whom they believed to be their savior.

photo: Getty Images

*Walls surround the Coptic Monastery of St. Anthony in Egypt, constructed in 356. How do you think Christianity spread to northern Africa?*

As Christianity grew, a hierarchy of church leaders emerged. At the local level, a priest was in charge of each Christian community. Priests answered to a bishop, a church official who supervised a large area called a diocese.

## The First Monks

In Egypt during the 300s, a group of worshippers turned to the solitude and heat of the desert to worship. The first of these Desert Fathers, as they came to be known, was Saint Anthony, who started Christian monasticism in the Egyptian desert. There, the Desert Fathers sought a peaceful, holy life centered on study of the Scriptures.

As Christianity became more popular, some people believed the religion was becoming diluted. They felt the best way to follow the word of God was to leave society and practice Christianity in solitude, away from distractions and temptation. Some of these people became monks.

Monks were men who devoted their lives to prayer and religious works. They created monasteries, communities where they lived simple lives, studying and praying in an effort to dedicate their lives to God. While some monks withdrew from society entirely, most monks continued to interact with others. Christian monks focused on prayer, faith, and service to others. They became an important force in recruiting new Christians, performing worship services, and preaching God's word. They gave a sense of safety and security to a world that often seemed to be in turmoil.

There were many early Christian monasteries located throughout Egypt and the Middle East. Pachomius founded one of the first communal monasteries 320 CE in Tabennisi, Egypt. In 386 CE, Jerome established several monasteries in Bethlehem. The Monastery of St. Samuel, established by the saint in the 600s CE, is located in Egypt's Western Desert.

## Rules for Monks

Saint Benedict of Nursia created a set of rules for the early monastic movement. While studying in Rome, Benedict developed an urge to flee from the temptations and vices of the papal city. After he fled into the wilderness, he began to draw disciples. Benedict created a community of monks at Monte Cassino, near Rome. He created rules for this community. The leader of the community, or abbot, was sovereign. The other monks were obliged to obey the abbot, live a lifestyle of moderation, and follow the daily routine of work, prayer, and study.

## Christianity Spreads After the Empire Falls

*How did the fall of the Roman Empire affect Christianity?*

Several political, geographic, and cultural factors led to the fall of the Roman Empire. However, as Rome died, Christianity survived and even became stronger.

By the time of the fall of Rome, Christianity had spread into northern Europe. Missionaries had also spread the message of the religion to Scandinavia and into eastern Europe, converting Czechs, Hungarians, and Poles. They also traveled to the Middle East, North Africa, and east Africa. By the time they reached South Asia, Christianity had become a worldwide religion.

photo: Getty Images

*Portrait of Charlemagne, circa 800.*

A growing number of monasteries also helped sustain Christianity after the fall of the Roman Empire. Some wealthy families even constructed monasteries on their own estates. By the early 500s, the Byzantine capital of Constantinople was home to more than 70 monasteries. Therefore, Christianity had a foothold beyond the political influence of Rome, especially among members of the Germanic tribes. Charlemagne was king of the Franks in the 800s. He used Christianity to unite many kingdoms, forcing the Saxons to convert. He executed anyone who did not convert because he saw himself as a defender of the faith. In the 900s, Christianity helped establish Poland as a nation.

As Rome's influence declined, Germanic kingdoms began to rise in power and influence. Many Germans had converted to Christianity before the fall of the Roman Empire. Missionaries continued to convert Saxons, Goths, and Vandals. German Christians developed strong ties to the Catholic Church. The Germanic tribes that replaced Rome continued to practice and spread Christianity. Rulers who adopted Christianity often forced their subjects to convert as well.

The survival of Christianity after the fall of Rome was aided by the rise of the Byzantine Empire in the east. Emperor Constantine rebuilt the city of Byzantium and named it Constantinople. Constantinople became the capital of the Eastern Roman Empire. The location of the city allowed it to control key trade routes and made Constantinople a wealthy city. Greek, Roman, and Christian traditions blended together within the city, further strengthening the religion.

## The Church Splits

*How did the East-West Schism lead to two separate Christian churches?*

Christians in Western Europe and the Byzantine Empire worshipped the same God. However, they disagreed over several important issues. The Byzantine emperor selected the patriarch, or highest church official, in Constantinople. Byzantine Christians did not feel they needed to obey the directives of the pope, the church leader in the West.

photo: Getty Images

*The new orthodox church in Nachodka, Russia.*

Other differences emerged. Byzantine priests could marry, but priests in the West could not. The holiest day of the year for both Byzantines and Westerners was Easter, but the two groups calculated the date of the holiday differently.

In the 700s, a Byzantine emperor outlawed the use of icons in worship, including images of Jesus; his mother, Mary; and the saints. From his seat in Rome, the pope excommunicated the emperor. Excommunication was a serious punishment. Those who had been excommunicated could not achieve heavenly salvation.

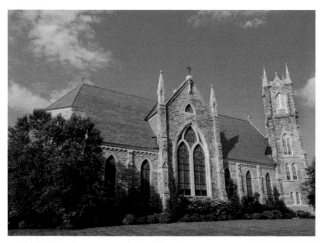

photo: Getty Images

*This Roman Catholic church in Vermont was constructed in 1892.*

By 1054, a permanent split, called the East-West Schism, existed in the Christian church. The pope in the West and the patriarch in the East excommunicated each other. The Eastern Greek Orthodox Church and Roman Catholic Church became entirely separate, even though they belonged to the same religion.

Despite this split, Christianity remained a powerful force and continued to spread. From its beginnings as a small religion in Rome, Christianity had become a global religion.

## Consider the Essential Question:

How did Christianity become the world's largest religion?

Go online to complete the Social Studies Explanation.

## Check for Understanding:

How did Constantine influence Christianity's spread? Would Christianity have spread as far and as fast as it did without Constantine's help? Why or why not?

DISCOVERY EDUCATION | SOCIAL STUDIES TECHBOOK

How did power and social class impact life in medieval Europe?

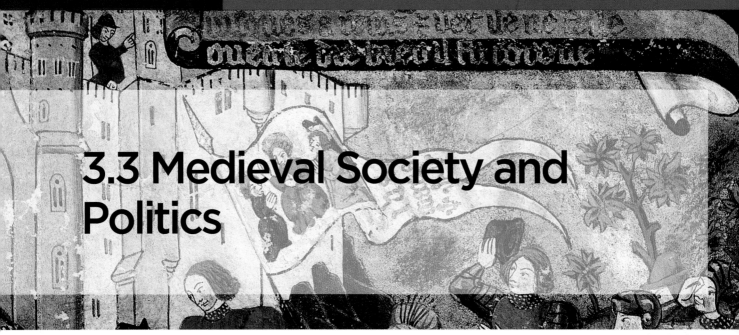

photo: Getty Images

# 3.3 Medieval Society and Politics

## LESSON OVERVIEW

### Introduction

In this concept, you will learn about people's way of life during the Middle Ages in Europe. You will also analyze the emergence of nation-states and the effect of major conflicts among Eurasian powers on medieval society.

### Essential Question

How did power and social class impact life in medieval Europe?

### Lesson Objectives

By the end of this lesson, you should be able to:

*   Describe social structures during the Middle Ages, including feudalism and manorialism.

*   Explain the emergence of nation-states (France, England, Spain, Russia) and their political structures.

*   Analyze the effects of various conflicts (for example, Crusades, Mongol conquests, fall of Constantinople) among Eurasian powers.

### Key Vocabulary
Which terms do you already know?

- [ ] Appalachian Mountains
- [ ] agriculture
- [ ] Byzantine Empire
- [ ] Charlemagne
- [ ] chivalry
- [ ] citadel
- [ ] civil war
- [ ] conscription
- [ ] Crusaders/ Crusades
- [ ] Diocletian
- [ ] England
- [ ] English Bill of Rights
- [ ] feudalism
- [ ] fief
- [ ] Genghis Khan
- [ ] goods
- [ ] guild
- [ ] Hundred Years' War
- [ ] Istanbul
- [ ] Joan of Arc
- [ ] King Ferdinand

- [ ] King John of England
- [ ] knight
- [ ] lord
- [ ] Magna Carta
- [ ] manor
- [ ] manorialism
- [ ] Mediterranean Sea
- [ ] merchant
- [ ] Middle Ages
- [ ] monarch
- [ ] monarchy
- [ ] Mongols
- [ ] nation-state
- [ ] Normandy
- [ ] Queen Isabella
- [ ] Renaissance
- [ ] Roman Empire
- [ ] Rome
- [ ] serf
- [ ] socialism
- [ ] trade
- [ ] tsar/czar
- [ ] vassal
- [ ] William of Normandy

# ENGAGE

**What can castles tell us about the society of medieval Europe? Visit Engage to learn more.**

> ## Essential Question
> How did power and social class impact life in medieval Europe?

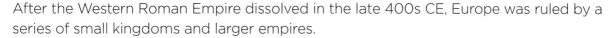

# EXPLORE

## The Feudal System

*How did the fall of Rome impact Europe?*

After the Western Roman Empire dissolved in the late 400s CE, Europe was ruled by a series of small kingdoms and larger empires.

### Ruling Europe

The European continent is part of the larger Eurasian landmass. Europe is bordered by the Ural Mountains and the Black Sea in the east, the Atlantic Ocean in the west, the Arctic Ocean in the north, and the Mediterranean Sea to the south. It includes the British Isles, the Scandinavian Peninsula, and the Iberian Peninsula. The Alps, a high mountain range, separate the southern regions from the northern. Several long, slow-moving rivers—including the Rhine, the Danube, Dnieper, and the Loire—flow from the mountains to the seas and oceans. The climate of Europe is temperate and, across most of the continent, there are reliable rains year-round. Much of Europe was once covered in woods such as the Black Forest of Germany, but humans have cut many of the forests and farmed the soil for thousands of years.

In ancient and early modern times, areas in southern Europe along the Mediterranean Sea had access by water to the great cities of Egypt, Mesopotamia, and Persia. Rome, Athens, and Constantinople were part of larger global networks. Cities were smaller, and most people lived in farming villages. North of the Alps, however, there were fewer large cities. The Roman Empire united much of this area, but it was at a remove from the center of global encounters. As Christianity spread throughout the Roman Empire, it became popular on both sides of the Alps and became an important religious and political influence on the region.

The Middle Ages in Europe lasted from about 500 to 1500. This period can be divided into three sections: the Early Middle Ages (400–1000), the High Middle Ages (1000–1300), and the Late Middle Ages (1300–1500). The term *Middle Ages* is derived from the term *medieval*, which comes from the Latin words for *middle* and *age*. The Middle Ages are the period in Europe between the fall of the Roman Empire and the beginning of the Renaissance. During this time, Europe was divided into smaller kingdoms. Secular and religious authorities struggled for control and influence within these states.

In 284, Diocletian became the emperor of the Roman Empire. Realizing that the empire had become too big for one man to govern, Diocletian divided the Roman Empire into the Eastern Roman Empire and the Western Roman Empire. The constant pressure and attacks on the Western Roman Empire by barbarian tribes weakened the empire considerably. In 410, the city of Rome was invaded by the Visigoths. This was the beginning of the end of the Western Roman Empire. The Visigoths controlled parts of the Iberian Peninsula for hundreds of years, and later a Muslim dynasty took control.

The fall of the Western Roman Empire in 476 had a great impact on Europe. The Roman Empire had provided cultural unity throughout Europe, as well as protection against outside forces. Without the empire, stability was lost. Many of the advances in technology and culture that occurred during the Roman Empire halted during this time and Europe divided into numerous small kingdoms.

### Charlemagne's Rule

During the late 700s and 800s, the ruler Charlemagne conquered much of central and eastern Europe. He reunited many small kingdoms into an empire. He developed a strong relationship with the Church as an ally of the pope, who gave religious blessing to Charlemagne's power. In 799, Pope Leo III was attacked and forced from Rome by influential Romans. Charlemagne protected the pope and escorted him back to Rome to reclaim his power. In 800, Charlemagne was crowned as the Holy Roman Emperor by Pope Leo III. This title showed the relationship between the Church and power. It made Charlemagne the successor of great Roman emperors such as Constantine. It also showed that the blessing of the pope could make a leader into an emperor.

photo: Getty Images

*The Coronation of Charlemagne. What differences does the image reveal between medieval and modern-day politics?*

Charlemagne was a well-respected and powerful king who promoted Christianity. He reformed the Christian Church to clarify Christian values, responsibilities, and morals. He opened missions in new territories and, according to some historians, he forced many of the people he conquered to convert to Christianity. He also aimed to make his people, especially the clergy, more educated.

He ordered that all clergy should learn how to read because he felt this was essential to helping them understand Christianity and the world. Charlemagne revived Roman culture as well. He promoted the visual arts and architecture, spending riches from his conquests on cathedrals and decorations. Charlemagne also established diplomatic relationships with powerful kings across Eurasia, including the Muslim leaders in the Middle East.

After Charlemagne's death in 814, the empire again fragmented, or broke apart, into smaller kingdoms. Each of these kingdoms was divided into smaller sections, called fiefs or estates. Although Charlemagne was a famous and powerful ruler, his rule was unusual in Europe during his time. In the Early Middle Ages, most kings did not have much control over their kingdoms. However, many of the people who controlled the fiefs gained a large amount of power.

## A New System

*What political system arose in Europe after the fall of the Western Roman Empire?*

Soon after the death of Charlemagne in 814, a political and military system called feudalism developed. Within this system, lords owned huge amounts of land. A lord could be any nobleman, member of a high-ranking class, or church official who owned a fief and allowed a person to use part of it, usually for agriculture, in return for services. Therefore, a lord could be a king, a prince, a knight, or a clergyman.

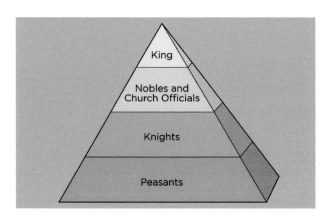

*The feudal system developed in Europe after the fall of the Roman Empire.*

Individuals who agreed to use a portion of a lord's land were known as vassals. Ownership of the land remained with the lord, but he allowed the vassal to tax the peasants on the land and keep the proceeds. Also, the vassals received a portion of the crops that these peasants produced. In return, the vassal promised to be loyal to and fight for his lord. Because of this, vassals often kept an army composed of professional soldiers called knights. To ensure a knight's loyalty, a vassal would sometimes grant part of his fief to his knights. By doing this, the vassal would become the lord of his knights, who would become his vassals. Indeed, a nobleman could be both a lord and a vassal. He could be a lord by granting land to knights, clergy, and other nobles. However, he could also be a vassal to a more powerful lord who had granted land to him.

Lords often made alliances with other lords to increase their power and their land. The more vassals a lord had, the more dominant the lord would become. However, sometimes lords and vassals often fought each other over land or other matters.

Some of these disputes were settled in the lord's court. In medieval England, some courts used a judicial system in which vassals, called peers, would judge a vassal suspected of wrongdoing. Over time, this practice became a key feature of English law, and, eventually, the laws of the United States of America.

## Feudal Society

### *What was feudal society like in the Middle Ages?*

Feudalism gave rise to a hierarchical social system that consisted of four classes: kings, nobles and church officials, knights, and peasants.

### Kings

A king was the ruler of a kingdom and, because of this, sat at the top of the social structure. However, in reality, kings did not have a lot of power, and they only ruled over their royal lands. The lords who ruled over fiefs had direct control over that land. In the Early Middle Ages, some lords who ruled large fiefs could amass as much or more power than their king. However, as the feudal system moved into the High and Late Middle Ages, the kings gradually gained more power.

photo: Getty Images

*Medieval king sitting on a throne surrounded by knights.*

### Nobles and Church Officials

Many members of the nobility (such as dukes and barons) and church officials (such as bishops) were lords who controlled fiefs. The nobility spent much of their time trying to gain new lands or defending their land against the attacks of enemies. Although the clergy devoted their lives to the Church, they still had a large amount of wealth and power in the feudal system. Not all nobles were men. Women, too, could serve as nobles under the feudal system.

### Knights

Knights were professional soldiers who were loyal to their lord. They went through years of hard training in order to prepare for battle. If a knight excelled in serving his lord, the lord sometimes granted land to the knight. In this way, a knight could become a vassal. Knights were also expected to follow a code of behavior called chivalry. According to this code, a knight should be courageous in combat, be loyal to his lord, defend the Church, and be gallant toward women. However, in reality, many knights did not always live up to this code.

**Peasants**

Peasants worked the land for their lord and had few rights. In addition, peasants performed other tasks required by their lord, such as cutting wood and repairing roads. They often lived in crude huts, slept on straw, and ate simple food.

## Manorialism

*What was manorialism?*

Within the fiefs of medieval Europe, an economic system called manorialism developed. In this system, the central focus of each fief was the lord's manor house. Some lords developed the manor house into a castle, which was often surrounded by thick stone walls for protection. Castles included living space for the lord and his family, servants, and soldiers. Many castles also included kitchens and a chapel.

The people living on these estates formed a self-sufficient community. The land surrounding the castle was used for farm buildings, peasant houses, a grain mill, orchards, and gardens. The farmland extended beyond this. The peasants did most of the work that was needed on the manor, including growing food, building shelters, and making clothes. In return for their work, the lord provided protection for the peasants by maintaining an army. If the fief was attacked, the peasants were allowed to enter the castle.

Many peasants who worked on manors were serfs. A serf was a person who was allowed to have a house and a plot of land in return for paying rent to his or her lord. This rent could be a payment in the form of crops, such as wheat, or a certain number of workdays. During workdays, serfs farmed their lord's land instead of their own. Serfs were not slaves because they could not be bought or sold. However, serfs did not have the freedom to leave the manor. So, in this way, they were bound to their lord's estate. Some serfs bought their freedom from their lord and others ran away.

*photo: Getty Images*

*Image of a knight on horseback.*

*photo: Getty Images*

*Medieval farmers plowing and sowing fields.*

Manorialism impacted the environmental development of medieval Europe. As people clustered around a lord's manor, they set up common areas, residential sectors, and farmlands. Over time, this led to the development of villages, rather than single-family homesteads. The population also increased as a result of close contact between many different families and the need to produce more children to work the land. On a manor, work was organized to support large-scale farming. Lords and overseers controlled and managed resources, such as water and access to mills for grinding grain. They could dictate what could be planted and where.

Economically, manorialism supported the aristocracy. This system kept peasants and serfs living in poor conditions. While this system did not always benefit the peasants, it did improve overall crop yield and provide food for growing populations. The eventual development of a money-based economy replaced the manorial system of living on land in exchange for performing services.

## The Rise of Kings

### How did kings gain more power?

During the High Middle Ages (1000–1300), the economy of Europe began to get stronger. Farms yielded more crops, more people became prosperous, and the population grew significantly. Soon, a merchant class began to arise.

These merchants began traveling farther in search of goods to trade. Trade routes developed along rivers, and main thoroughfares and towns sprang up along these routes. These towns were also populated by peasants who, because of the improved economic conditions, were able to save money and leave their manors. There, they often found work as craftspeople or merchants. Other peasants started their own farms near towns in order to provide food for the increasing populations.

photo: Getty Images

*This illustration shows people tending to a farm during the Middle Ages.*

This movement of peasants from manors to towns caused the system of manorialism to break apart and feudalism to weaken. The economic revival caused by improved agriculture and trade gave lords more access to money, which allowed them to pay for services rather than sacrificing control of their lands by offering fiefs. The economic recovery also made kings wealthier. Because of this, kings hired powerful armies, gained control over their lords, and established control over larger areas of their kingdoms. The royal armies often had access to the newest weapons, such as pikes and longbows, which gave them an advantage over an army of knights. Also, kings gained the support of middle-class people such as merchants and craftspeople. These people agreed to pay taxes to the king in return for protection and good government.

During the Late Middle Ages (1300–1500), many kingdoms continued to increase in size and power and eventually formed nation-states. A nation-state is an independent country united under one government and linked by a common culture and language. During the Late Middle Ages, four powerful kingdoms developed into nation-states—England, France, Spain, and Russia.

**Explore this interactive to learn more about different perspectives in the medieval world.**

## England

*How did the kingdom of England develop?*

During the Early Middle Ages, two tribes dominated the kingdom of England—the Angles and the Saxons. The Angles resided mostly in northern, central, and eastern England, and the Saxons mainly occupied southern England. In the 800s, King Alfred defeated Danish invaders and united the various regions of England into one Anglo-Saxon country. He supported Christianity and formed a code of laws.

photo: Getty Images

*This tapestry depicts the Battle of Hastings. Why was this battle an important event in world history?*

In 1066, the Anglo-Saxon king Edward the Confessor died without leaving a direct heir to the throne. The nobles appointed Harold, Earl of Wessex, as the new king. However, a French nobleman named William of Normandy, who would later be known as William the Conqueror, claimed that Edward had promised the English throne to him and that he should be king. After Harold became king, William led an invasion against England. William and his Norman knights killed Harold and defeated his forces at the Battle of Hastings in 1066.

William became king of England. He set up a strong central government and established an advisory council to assist him with governing. The Normans became the new nobility of England, and most of the Anglo-Saxons became serfs under them. Over the years, the differences between the Anglo-Saxons and Normans lessened. For example, the French language spoken by the Normans combined with the Anglo-Saxon language to form the modern English language.

William's wife, Matilda, was a powerful and well-respected woman. She became William's trusted advisor and partner. During William's invasion of England, Matilda stayed behind to rule Normandy, and she earned the praise of her people for her moral behavior. She also helped establish several monasteries and churches.

William the Conqueror became the first in a line of kings that attempted to strengthen their rule over the English lords. For example, Henry II increased his power and expanded the system of jury trials. He also applied one code of law to all of England, thereby replacing regional laws that could vary greatly from one place to another. By doing this, Henry established the English system of common law—laws that apply equally throughout England.

## The Great Charter
### What is the Magna Carta?

After the death of Henry II, Richard I, called Richard the Lion-Hearted, became king of England. He proved to be an ineffective ruler, however, because he spent most of his time away from England fighting in the Crusades, religious wars against Islamic nations. Indeed, scholars estimate that Richard only spent about six months of his reign in England.

After Richard's death, his brother John gained the throne. At this time, there were many conflicts between the different social classes. Common people were worried about being forced off their land by the higher classes. They wanted their property rights to be protected. Meanwhile, King John angered the nobles with a series of laws and decrees that the nobles believed were unfair. A group of barons and church officials, angry with the laws, rebelled against John and, in 1215, forced him to agree with a settlement. This agreement is called the Magna Carta.

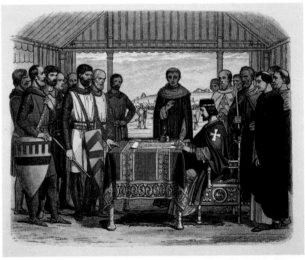

photo: Getty Images

*King John signs the Magna Carta at Runnymede, England, in 1215.*

In the Magna Carta, King John granted a list of rights to the nobles, thereby limiting royal power. The common person, though, gained few rights from this document. Even so, the Magna Carta later became a model for people who demanded democratic rights for all. For example, the Magna Carta guaranteed that people accused of crimes had the right to face a jury of their peers. This concept of due process was adopted into later English statutes, as well as the U.S. Constitution and the Bill of Rights. It assured that people would receive fair treatment in the legal system.

Even though the power of English kings was somewhat limited by the Magna Carta, many of them still managed to strengthen the power of the kingdom. For instance, in 1283, Edward I brought Wales under English control.

## France

*How did the kingdom of France develop?*

During the Early Middle Ages, a group of people called the Franks, ancestors of the French people, lived in the region that is modern-day France. In the early 800s, Charlemagne, the King of the Franks, formed an empire that reached beyond the present-day borders of France. This realm was called the Holy Roman Empire. However, after Charlemagne's death, his kingdom broke apart.

*photo: Getty Images*

*Louis IX was known for being a devout Catholic. He was canonized (made a saint) in 1297 by Pope Boniface VIII.*

In the late 900s, the French nobles chose Hugh Capet as their king, thereby starting the Capetian dynasty. At first, Capetian kings ruled only their royal land, which extended from Paris to Orleans. However, starting in the late 1000s, these kings gradually expanded and strengthened the French kingdom. Around 1180, Philip II doubled the size of the royal lands.

In 1226, Louis IX became the King of France at the age of 12. His mother ruled for Louis until he reached the age of 21. Until that time, Louis was tutored in the skills of politics and governing a kingdom. When he took control, Louis strengthened the French kingdom by reorganizing the administration. In addition, to prevent corruption, he defined the duties of royal officials and supervised their actions. Furthermore, he enforced strict penalties on counterfeiting and outlawed duels and ordeal by battle. He is remembered as a wise and just ruler.

The last Capetian King, Charles IV, died in 1328. Then, Philip VI came to the throne, beginning the Valois dynasty. Soon, France entered a period of constant warfare, marked by the start of the Hundred Years' War in 1337.

## Spain

*How did the kingdom of Spain develop?*

During the early 700s, Muslim Arabs and Berbers invaded Spain and by the early 1000s had conquered most of the region. Muslim rulers tolerated Jews, Christians, and other religions, leading to a cultural golden age in Spain. Education improved as scholars of different religions exchanged ideas and translated ancient Greek and Roman texts into Arabic. The city of Cordoba became one of the most important centers of learning in the world. It contained a massive library, a music academy, and a highly respected university that taught science, mathematics, and medicine. This golden age also honored art and beauty. Cordoba featured stone-paved streets, marble balconies, and fine gardens.

A pocket of Christian people remained independent of Muslim rule in the far northern part of Spain. This Christian stronghold began a campaign called the Reconquista to reconquer Spain and drive out the Muslims. By the late 1200s, the Christian Spanish had pushed the Muslims out of all of Spain except for the Kingdom of Granada in the south. The Reconquista brought an end to the golden age of cooperation between religions in Spain. At that time, Christian Spain consisted of two kingdoms: Aragon and Castile. However, in 1469, Prince Ferdinand of Aragon and Princess Isabella of Castile married, thereby uniting the two kingdoms.

Ferdinand and Isabella continued the conquest to regain Spanish lands from Muslim control. Soon, the troops of Ferdinand and Isabella defeated the Muslims in Granada and later in Navarre. These victories ended Muslim control in Spain. However, many Muslims and Jews still lived in Spain. Ferdinand and Isabella viewed these people as a threat to their crown and, as a result, took part in the Inquisition.

photo: Getty Images

*This image shows a ceramic statue of a Spanish inquisitor.*

## The Inquisition

The Inquisition was an attempt by the Catholic Church to fight heresy—beliefs that contradicted the teachings of the Church. To accomplish this, the Church appointed inquisitors to find people suspected of heresy. These people were put on trial without the benefit of a defense lawyer. The reason for this is that any lawyer defending a possible heretic would be suspected of heresy himself. If convicted, heretics were given the chance to recant, or reject their beliefs. If they did, they would be given a penance to perform. However, if a heretic refused to recant, he or she would be burned at the stake.

The Inquisition took place in many Christian countries, including France, Germany, and Italy. However, nowhere was it applied with more force than in Spain. Ferdinand and Isabella wanted to ensure loyalty to the Catholic Church and the Spanish crown. As a result, they became intent on rooting out people who practiced Islam or Judaism.

During the Spanish Inquisition, thousands of suspects were tortured and burnt at the stake. The exact number of victims is difficult to estimate. Later, the Spanish Inquisition extended throughout the Spanish Empire and was applied to Protestants. Although it was enforced with more strength during certain periods than others, the Spanish Inquisition lasted until 1834.

## Russia

### *How did the kingdom of Russia develop?*

During the 900s, Russia, or Kievan Rus as it was called at the time, consisted of a group of principalities that were each independently ruled by a prince. Kiev emerged as the most important principality, and the ruler of this principality was known as the grand prince to indicate his rank above the other princes. Around 988, Grand Prince Vladimir I converted to Christianity and made it the state religion. However, after Vladimir's reign, Kiev declined and other principalities gained strength.

### Mongol Conquests

Weakened by civil war, Kiev and the other principalities fell to Mongol invaders in the 1200s. The Mongols, led by Genghis Khan, destroyed Kiev in 1240 and incorporated Russia into the Mongol Empire. Mongol rule of Russia lasted for more than 200 years. They forced the Russian princes to pay heavy taxes and pledge their allegiance to the Golden Horde, the name given to the Russian part of the Mongol Empire. However, the Mongols did not interfere much in the daily lives of Russians.

In the 1300s, the principality of Moscow began to increase its power. After Prince Yuri of Moscow married the sister of the Golden Horde's ruler, the Mongols let him collect taxes from his people. With this additional money, Prince Yuri started to expand his territory and increase the size and strength of his army. In 1380, Moscow's army defeated the Mongols at the Battle of Kulikovo and drove them out of the region. The Mongols regained control of Moscow, but were not as powerful as before. Then, in the late 1400s, Ivan III of Moscow refused to pay taxes to the Mongols. The Mongols sent troops to attack Moscow, but they eventually retreated back to their capital. This ended the Mongol rule of Russia.

photo: Getty Images

*Ivan the Terrible was a strong but extremely suspicious ruler.*

### Rise of the Tsar

In 1547, the grand prince of Moscow, Ivan IV, became the first to rule all of Russia. This ruler came to be called the tsar. Ivan feared that other nobles might attempt to overthrow him. To suppress any possible rebellion, he arrested and murdered thousands of nobles. Ivan also required that each landowner supply a certain number of soldiers and horses to the Russian army. In addition, he passed laws that bound peasants to the land, making them serfs. In this way, Russia retained an aspect of feudalism for hundreds of years. Serfdom was not abolished in Russia until the 1800s.

**Discovery** SOCIAL STUDIES
EDUCATION | **TECHBOOK**

How did power and social class impact life in medieval Europe?

# Growing Power of the Church

*How did religious power and political power overlap in Medieval Europe?*

By the Middle Ages, Christianity was central to the lives of many Europeans. It was so widespread that Europe became known as "Christendom," meaning the land where Christians lived. Two cities—Rome and Constantinople—were centers of power for Christianity. Rome was the capital of the Roman Empire until 330, when it moved to Constantinople. The bishop of Rome increasingly claimed power over other bishops throughout Europe. He argued that the Roman bishop derived his authority through the apostle Peter, who was the original bishop of Rome and was crucified there. By the 500s, the Roman bishop, now also known as the pope, was recognized as the leader of the Church in Western Europe.

photo: Getty Images

*An illustration of the capture of Constantinople in 1204.*

## Two Centers of Power

When Western Europe decentralized, the Roman Empire shifted to Eastern Europe and became known as the Byzantine Empire. During this time, the bishop of Constantinople became increasingly powerful. He became second only to the Roman pope in the Church's hierarchy. Because the empire was centered in Constantinople, this city's bishop, or the patriarch, played a more important role in the lives of Christians in the Byzantine Empire.

The medieval Church in both Western and Eastern Europe encouraged missionaries to spread Christianity. It also supported the founding of monastic orders, or groups of clerics (also known as monks) who would pledge to live by a certain set of rules. These rules included lifelong poverty, communal living, and devotion to prayer, charity, preaching, and even military service on behalf of Christendom. These clerics lived differently from the average Christian. The average citizen attended church on Sundays and took part in religious rituals to mark major life events. Church teachings helped medieval Europeans better understand events in their own lives as well as their place in society.

In the West, the Church filled the power vacuum that resulted from the fall of the Western Roman Empire in 476. The pope claimed the right to crown kings in Western Europe. This was cemented in 800 when Pope Leo III crowned Charlemagne on Christmas Day. In the 900s, kings and nobles competed with one and other for the support of the Church. At the same time, political leaders and feudal lords controlled the land, wealth, and armies in Europe. Powerful political leaders could influence and even threaten the leaders of the Church. But in the 1000s, a series of popes began reforming the Church. These reforms strengthened Catholicism's power in the West. The most notable of these popes was Gregory VII, who began to rid the Church of secular, or nonreligious, influence. He declared that only popes, not kings, had the power to make a person a bishop or to write Church laws.

In the small, divided kingdoms of Western Europe, the power of the Church was often more important than the power of any individual ruler. Religious courts, run by bishops, were usually more powerful than the law-enforcement powers of a ruler. Because kings were usually crowned in elaborate religious ceremonies, powerful lords needed the support of Church officials to actually claim the throne.

**East and West**

The emperor and the patriarch of Constantinople officially shared power in Eastern Europe, but in practice, the two offices competed for authority. After the fall of the Roman Empire in the West, the Eastern wing of the Church eventually became known as the Orthodox Church. Eastern Europeans tended to see the emperor as the true head of the Church rather than the pope. They also developed distinct beliefs from Roman Catholics, such as the belief that God's essence is the source of the Holy Spirit. Missionaries spread Orthodox Christianity throughout Eastern Europe and into Russia. Meanwhile, the Catholic Church in the West continued to fall out of favor among the Byzantines. The relationship between the eastern and western wings of the Christian church gradually declined until a formal division was made in 1054.

Many Byzantines thought the division would be temporary, especially as Western and Eastern Europeans agreed to fight the spread of Islam together. Instead, the Crusades put a definitive end to the idea of a united Christian church in Europe when the Western Europeans attacked the Eastern Europeans. The split was made final in 1204 when crusaders from Venice sacked and plundered Constantinople on Good Friday.

## The Beginning of the Crusades
*What were the Crusades?*

Christians, Muslims, and Jews consider the land in present-day Israel, along the east coast of the Mediterranean Sea, a sacred place. During the Middle Ages, many Christians made pilgrimages to shrines in the Holy Land. In the 500s, the Byzantine Empire—a Christian domain—controlled the Holy Land. However, in the 600s, Muslim Arabs conquered this land. While many Muslim rulers allowed Christians to continue to make pilgrimages to their holy sites in the region, in 1071 a new group of rulers, the Seljuk Turks, began to limit Christian access to religious sites.

The Seljuk Turks also captured additional lands in the Byzantine Empire and threatened the capital city of Constantinople. The Byzantine emperor asked his rival, the pope of the Roman Church, for help fighting against the Turks. In 1095, Pope Urban II called a Church meeting in which he declared that European Christians should unite and capture the Holy Land from the Muslims. Thus began the Crusades.

The Crusades were a series of military campaigns by Christian nations in Europe. They were intended to stop the expansion of Islamic nations and reclaim Muslim-controlled lands that were considered holy by Christians. Four major campaigns took place from 1095 to 1212.

During the First Crusade, an army consisting of mostly French and Norman knights attacked Jerusalem in 1099. Eventually, they captured the city, after which most of the crusaders went home. Some stayed and divided the

photo: Getty Images

*Taken from a French manuscript from the 1300s, this picture shows Crusaders (right) fighting Muslims (left).*

conquered land into four Christian states. However, in 1144, Muslim Turks captured one of these states and threatened the remaining three. This action prompted the Second Crusade—an effort spearheaded by the kings of France and Germany. Their armies, though, were defeated by the Muslims before they reached the Holy Land.

## The End of the Crusades

*What were the major events of the Third and Fourth Crusades?*

In 1187, Saladin, the sultan of Egypt and Syria, led a Muslim force against Jerusalem and conquered the city. However, the cities of Tyre, Tripoli, and Antioch remained under Christian control. In an attempt to defend these cities and recapture Jerusalem, Richard III of England, Philip II of France, and Frederick I of Germany launched the Third Crusade. This crusade had some military victories but failed to capture Jerusalem.

The Fourth Crusade became embroiled in political issues with the Byzantine Empire and, therefore, failed to recapture Jerusalem. After this, many poor boys and girls in Europe became convinced that God would help them conquer Jerusalem.

photo: Getty Images

*A 19th-century depiction of a victorious Saladin, who conquered Jerusalem in 1187.*

Bolstered by their belief, thousands of them began to travel to the Holy Land in 1212. This event is called the Children's Crusade. Many of these children starved or froze to death on their journey. Others were drowned at sea or sold into slavery. None of them reached the Holy Land.

Although the Crusaders succeeded in controlling part of the Holy Land for periods of time, they failed in their goal of permanently controlling the region. Also, their efforts caused bitter feelings between Muslims and Christians for centuries. However, the Crusades did spur economic growth. Trade increased between cities along the Mediterranean Sea, and the Italian cities of Genoa, Pisa, and Venice made huge profits by transporting crusaders and their supplies.

## Hundred Years' War
### *What was the Hundred Years' War?*

From 1337 to 1453, the Hundred Years' War raged between the French and English over control of France. This conflict was not one long war, but rather a series of wars divided by various broken treaties. Many factors led to the outbreak of this war. French and English sailors had disputes about fishing rights in the English Channel. Also, the French assisted the Scots in their fight against the English.

photo: Getty Images

*The Battle of Agincourt in 1415.*

The conflict started in 1337 when King Philip VI of France decided to capture Guyenne, an English-controlled region in southwest France. In addition, King Edward III of England claimed the French throne because his mother was the sister of French royalty. During the war, the English won most of the battles, including the Battle of Crecy (1346) and the Battle of Agincourt (1415).

The English achieved victory in these battles with the aid of a new weapon—the longbow. The arrows shot from the longbow traveled long distances and could pierce the plate armor of the knights. For example, at Agincourt, an English army of about 6,000 soldiers faced a French army of about 25,000 soldiers, which consisted of many knights clad in heavy armor. By using the longbow, the English killed thousands of French knights as they charged.

Discovery EDUCATION | SOCIAL STUDIES TECHBOOK.

How did power and social class impact life in medieval Europe?

Because of this defeat, the French agreed to the Treaty of Troyes (1420), which made the English king, Henry V, the heir to the French throne. However, after Henry died, the French disputed this claim and war started again. Once again, the fighting turned against the French as the English forces swept through northern France. Soon, the English laid siege to the city of Orleans in 1429. However, events—including the actions of a 17-year-old girl—occurred that would begin to change the course of the war.

## The End of the Wars

*How did the Hundred Years' War end?*

### Joan of Arc

Joan of Arc was a French peasant girl who believed she had religious visions during which she heard the voices of saints instructing her. She believed that these voices told

*A portrait of Joan of Arc.*

photo: Getty Images

her that God had chosen the French king, Charles VII, to defeat the English and drive them from France. She managed to receive an audience with the king and told him about the divine message she received. The king was at first skeptical, but eventually believed that Joan truly received visions from God. Soon, he gave Joan the command of the army.

Wearing armor and holding a banner, Joan on horseback led the French army toward Orleans. The French leaders were initially hesitant about obeying her. They became convinced to follow her, though, when they realized that the orders she gave all had positive results for the French army. Inspired by Joan's leadership, the French troops broke the English siege of Orleans, and the English fled.

Later in 1429, Joan was wounded in a battle and captured by the Burgundians, who sold her to the English. The English convicted her of heresy and witchcraft and sentenced her to death. She was burned at the stake in Rouen, France, in 1431. The Catholic Church declared her a saint in 1920.

## The End of the War

After Joan's death, Philip the Good, the Duke of Burgundy, who had been a supporter of England, switched sides in 1435, aiding the French cause. Internal struggles related to which dynasty would assume control further weakened England. Taking advantage of these situations, French troops were able to drive the English out of France (except for Calais) by 1453, and win the Hundred Years' War. The French also used advanced weaponry, such as the cannon, to help them achieve this victory. This began a new age in warfare. Indeed, the war contributed to the decline of feudalism, as castles were not an effective defense against cannons.

The war strengthened the monarchs and central governments in both England and France. In England, the monarchs stopped trying to gain holdings in continental Europe and focused on developing their government, which helped unify their nation. In France, the king had developed a strong military during the war, which helped unify the country after the war. Also, Joan of Arc became a unifying figure for the French people, thereby helping form a French cultural identity.

**Consider the Essential Question:**

How did power and social class impact life in medieval Europe?

Go online to complete the Social Studies Explanation.

**Check for Understanding:**

Was Europe more stable under the political system of feudalism or under the strong monarchy that existed during the rise of nation-states?

Discovery EDUCATION | SOCIAL STUDIES TECHBOOK

How did the Black Death spark social, political, and economic change throughout Europe?

# 3.4 The Black Death

*photo: Getty Images*

## LESSON OVERVIEW

### Introduction

In this concept, you will learn about the plague known as the Black Death that struck Europe in the 1300s. You will also investigate how the plague affected the social, political, and economic systems of Europe.

### Essential Question

How did the Black Death spark social, political, and economic change throughout Europe?

### Lesson Objectives

By the end of this lesson, you should be able to:

- Describe the Black Death and its effect on Eurasia and the world.

- Identify patterns related to the spread and recovery of people suffering from the Black Death.

### Key Vocabulary

Which terms do you already know?

- ☐ Black Plague/Black Death (bubonic plague)
- ☐ epidemic
- ☐ Europe
- ☐ feudalism
- ☐ flagellants
- ☐ Mediterranean Sea
- ☐ Mongols

## ENGAGE

What were the symptoms of the Black Death? Visit Engage to learn more.

### Essential Question

How did the Black Death spark social, political, and economic change throughout Europe?

## EXPLORE

### The Plague Begins

*What was the origin of the bubonic plague?*

Plagues, infectious diseases that spread among a large population of people, were not uncommon in the Middle Ages. Plagues had broken out before in East Asia and spread to Europe and North Africa, but they usually subsided.

photo: Getty Images

*Ruins of the Italian fortress at Caffa.*

A strain of the bubonic plague, also known as the Black Death, survived in Mongolia. In the 1200s, Mongol armies conquered many cities in Asia. As they continued to spread the borders of their empire, they carried the plague with them. It was the Mongol armies that were responsible for bringing the Black Death to China and to the wealthy Italian trading city of Caffa, located on the Black Sea.

Caffa was a walled city. As part of their attack on the city, the Mongol warriors catapulted dead plague victims over the walls of the city of Caffa. The Caffans fell sick, and the Mongols took over the city with ease. However, a small group of Italian sailors escaped and sailed back to Genoa. Although they did not know it, the sailors had been infected and had brought bubonic plague with them.

Discovery Education | SOCIAL STUDIES TECHBOOK

How did the Black Death spark social, political, and economic change throughout Europe?

The plague then began to spread across Europe. The bubonic plague had two forms in which it could spread from person to person. The disease could infect the victim's blood. In this case, boils would appear on his or her skin. The person would then begin to bleed internally. Simple physical contact, such as a hug, a kiss, or even a handshake could spread the disease. In the pneumonic form of the disease, coughing, sneezing, and breathing could spread the disease. With this form, physical contact between people was not necessary for the disease to spread. People could get infected without even touching a victim.

## The Black Death Spreads Across Europe

### How did the Black Death spread through Europe?

Not only were the Italian sailors infected, but the rats on their ship also carried the plague. The Black Death was thus carried to Mediterranean ports, following the trade routes. In 1347, the Black Death appeared in Genoa and other Mediterranean cities. From Constantinople, Athens, Crete, Alexandria, and Sicily, the Black Death began an unstoppable march across Europe and Asia. By 1348, there were more than 1,000 deaths each day in the city of Alexandria alone.

After appearing at seaports in Europe and Africa, the disease moved inland. By spring 1348, most of Spain and France had experienced outbreaks. The Black Death even killed half the people in London! By 1349, it had blanketed Scandinavia and Eastern Europe. In 1350, it entered Russia.

In some cities, death rates exceeded 50 percent of the population. Handcarts passed through the city streets, their carters calling for the bodies of the dead. Bodies were piled onto the cart. Many estimates state that the Black Death was responsible for killing one-third of Europe's population in the 1300s.

photo: Getty Images

*A figure of a woman infected with the plague in the Medieval Museum, Sweden.*

Approximately every 10 years between 1400 and 1500, a new outbreak of the disease would return. Each new outbreak brought with it fear, panic, and more deaths. There were around 8 million deaths by 1347, 30 million by 1353, and perhaps as many as 200 million deaths in the 300 years afterward. In China, the Black Death reduced the population from 125 million in 1328 to 90 million only 50 years later.

## Living Conditions Assist the Spread of the Black Death

*How did hygiene practices help spread the Black Death?*

The Black Death spread quickly and easily throughout Europe and Asia. The hygienic practices of Medieval Europe helped spread the disease. Much of the poor hygiene of the period was due to a lack of knowledge.

For example, many peasants used rushes for their floor covering. Rushes are grasslike plants that grow near the water. They have long, thin, hollow stems. When they are dried, they can be made into floor coverings. But the bottom layer of the rushes was hard to replace. At the bottom, food scraps, spilled drinks, and contributions from sick babies and pets stewed, creating a rotting breeding ground for germs.

*photo: Getty Images*

*A cathedral painting of a young saint fearlessly hugging a body affected by the plague. According to legend, the young girl's prayers saved the city of Este, Italy, from the Black Death.*

People threw food scraps, garbage, and even human waste out of the windows of their homes into the streets below. Open sewers in the street were packed with garbage. Occasionally, the garbage would be pushed into the closest river.

Rats thrived and multiplied in the waste, finding shelter and food in the vast piles of refuse. As the rat population increased, this provided the infected fleas more hosts to live and feed on. Even if people were able to avoid contact with infected humans, rats were so common throughout Europe during this time that it was almost impossible to avoid them and the tiny fleas that also carried the disease.

## The Black Death Transforms Society

*What social changes resulted from the Black Death?*

Because the Black Death was so contagious, people tried to find ways to avoid contact with one another. The impulse to flee from the sick and dying overpowered any notion of family and friendship for many. Even professional members of society began to ignore their duties. Doctors would not go to see patients. Lawyers would not visit the sick to create a last will. Priests were afraid to administer last rites to the dying. Because confession of sins was an essential part of the Christian faith, the Church allowed victims to confess their sins to one another. Pope Clement VI even provided a blanket forgiveness of sins to all who died of the Black Death.

Many city residents fled to the countryside where there was more space. However, even those in the countryside fell victim to the merciless Black Death. Farmers died in their homes and in their fields. Crops were left unharvested, and farm animals were unfed or roamed freely. Many of these animals also became infected with the Black Death.

**Discovery** SOCIAL STUDIES
EDUCATION | **TECHBOOK**

How did the Black Death spark social, political, and economic change throughout Europe?

Sheep, cows, pigs, and chickens died in great numbers throughout Europe.

Some people believed that the plague was a punishment from God. To earn mercy and forgiveness, they lashed, or beat themselves and each other with whips. People who punished themselves this way were called flagellants. They vowed not to bathe, shave their beards, sleep in beds, change their clothes, or talk to the opposite sex.

photo: Getty Images

*A Procession of Flagellants, 1815–1819, by Francisco de Goya. Oil on canvas. In this 19th-century painting, a group of Roman Catholic flagellants whip their own backs in penitence.*

Many other believers were affected in the opposite way. Many found their faith undermined by the Black Death. They could not figure out why God was punishing them, or how a just God could allow so much suffering. As a result, some people began to turn away from religion and look for answers in other areas such as science.

**Explore this interactive to learn more about the impact of the Black Death throughout Europe.**

## Europe Depopulates

*How did a reduction in population affect European economics?*

Throughout Europe, almost one-third of the population died as a result of the Black Death, and in some places, such as London, the number was as high as one-half of the population. As a result of this catastrophic loss of life, the labor force was drastically depleted. This depopulation had a major effect on the economy of Europe.

photo: Getty Images

*An etching shows townspeople attempting to flee the plague while being watched over by skeletons holding hourglasses.*

The loss of so much labor meant that many projects in Europe were left abandoned. Other projects, particularly construction projects, were completed much more simply than originally planned because of the loss of qualified craftsmen. The loss of labor also meant that there were not enough workers to tend the existing farmland.

Many fields were left untended or converted to pasture, where animals could graze because it required fewer workers. This meant a loss of revenue for European landowners, many of whom were eventually ruined.

The plague also led to a decrease in trade. Like laborers, there were fewer merchants and sailors available to make the long voyages. In addition, many people correctly suspected that trade and contact with other cultures was helping to spread the plague. Fear of further infection played a role in the reduction of trade. However, this slowdown was short lived.

With fewer laborers available, greater value was placed on workers, and their wages grew. Those who survived were able to negotiate better working conditions, boosting both their income and their social status. Many people also gained wealth through inheritances from family members who had died in the plague. This increase in wealth meant that they were willing to pay higher prices for goods. Higher wages led to inflation, an increase in the cost of most items. The increase in wealth and social status would also impact the political structure of Europe.

## Political Impact of the Black Death

*How did a reduction in population affect European politics?*

Prior to the plague, Europe was a feudal society. However, as the labor force began to decline, feudalism began to fall apart. With fewer surviving farmers competing to work on the land, paid laborers could demand higher wages and tenant farmers could demand better treatment and lower service requirements. Tenants could

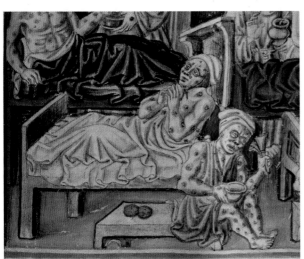

photo: Getty Images

*Patients with the plague.*

leave the lands of one landowner and seek better conditions on another farm or find work as tradespeople in a city. This decreased the power of the landowners, who depended on tenants to work fields, produce goods, and even serve as soldiers. Workers in cities also saw the wages for skilled labor increase.

This increase in wages and ability to move to new jobs in the city provided peasants with new opportunities to move up through the social classes. A serf could move to a city, learn a trade like shoemaking, and begin to earn money of his own. Under the strict hierarchy of feudal life, this had never been possible. The reduction of the workforce and this new social mobility began to weaken the existing political structure, and feudalism began to decline.

Discovery EDUCATION | SOCIAL STUDIES TECHBOOK

How did the Black Death spark social, political, and economic change throughout Europe?

The existing social order was also affected by people's shifting attitudes toward religion. The plague made some people lose faith in God as they questioned why the plague had occurred and whether God was able or willing to protect them in the face of similar disasters. As people began to turn away from religion, the Catholic Church began to lose some of its power and influence over people at this time.

The massive loss of life was only one aspect of the Black Death. The disease and the high casualties it caused impacted every aspect of life in Europe during the Middle Ages. It changed the way people thought, what they believed, and the way they structured their society and lives.

**Consider the Essential Question:**

How did the Black Death spark social, political, and economic change throughout Europe?

Go online to complete the Social Studies Explanation.

**Check for Understanding:**

How did the plague affect religion, the economy, and feudalism in Europe? Explain.

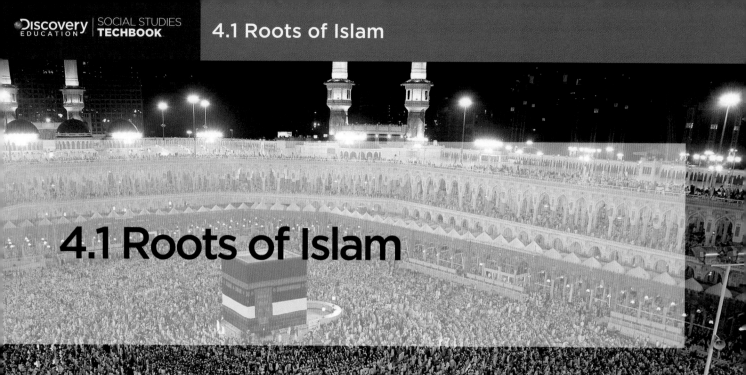

# 4.1 Roots of Islam

photo: Getty Images

# LESSON OVERVIEW

## Introduction

In this concept, you will learn about Islam's origins and teachings. You will also explore its effects on the lives of people in the Islamic world.

## Essential Question

How did Islam develop?

## Lesson Objectives

By the end of this lesson, you should be able to:

- Describe how the geography of the Arabian Peninsula shaped the way of life of the people living there.

- Identify Muhammad, his teachings, and his contributions to the growth of Islam in Asia.

- Describe the origins and characteristics of Islam.

- Explain the importance of the religion to culture and politics in the Islamic world.

## Key Vocabulary
Which terms do you already know?

- ☐ Abu Bakr
- ☐ Ali
- ☐ Arabia
- ☐ Arabian Peninsula
- ☐ Arabian Sea
- ☐ Bedouin
- ☐ beginning of Islam
- ☐ caravan
- ☐ desert
- ☐ Egyptians
- ☐ Five Pillars of Islam
- ☐ imam
- ☐ Indian Ocean
- ☐ Islam
- ☐ Kaaba
- ☐ Mecca
- ☐ Medina

- ☐ merchant
- ☐ Mesopotamia
- ☐ Middle East
- ☐ monotheism
- ☐ mosque
- ☐ Muhammad
- ☐ Muslims
- ☐ nomadic
- ☐ oasis
- ☐ peninsula
- ☐ Persian Gulf
- ☐ polytheism
- ☐ Quran
- ☐ Red Sea
- ☐ Shari'ah
- ☐ Shi'a Islam
- ☐ Southwest Asia
- ☐ Sunnah
- ☐ trade
- ☐ Yemen

# ENGAGE

How do Muslims express their faith in daily life? Visit Engage to learn more.

## Essential Question

How did Islam develop?

---

# EXPLORE

## The Birthplace of Islam

*Where did Islam begin?*

Islam began in 610 on the Arabian Peninsula. The Arabian Peninsula is located in Southwest Asia, south of the Fertile Crescent. It is bordered by the Red Sea to the west, the Indian Ocean to the south, and the Persian Gulf to the east. It is part of the Middle East, the rest of which lies to the north. The Arabian Peninsula was surrounded by important ancient civilizations, from the Mesopotamians to the north to the Egyptians across the Red Sea to the west. As such, it developed as a center of trade between ancient civilizations. The history of the Arabian Peninsula has been shaped by its geographic features. These include desert, oases, mountains, and fertile coastland.

### Desert

When most people think of the Arabian Peninsula, they think of vast stretches of sandy desert. Indeed, about three-fourths of the Arabian Peninsula is covered in desert. Parts of the desert are rolling dunes of sand, but other areas include dry plains and plateaus.

Weather in the desert is harsh, with temperatures reaching 120 degrees Fahrenheit or more during the day but sometimes plunging close to freezing during the night. Rain is scarce, with droughts sometimes lasting for years. However, the occasional torrential rain can cause flash floods. Windstorms sweep the desert, reducing visibility to near blindness and reshaping the sand into tall dunes.

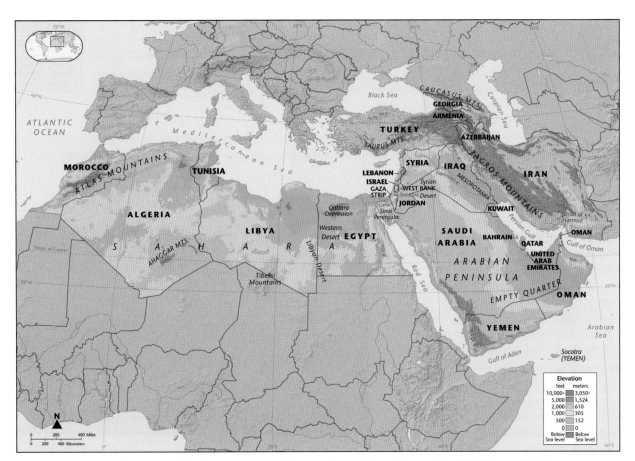

*The Arabian Peninsula is covered in desert, oases, and mountains and ringed by a strip of fertile coastland.*

## Oases

Oases appear throughout the desert, where there is freshwater available at a spring or water hole. Oases are marked by the trees and plant life that surround them. Oases can be small—only a few acres. Others are much larger. The Al-Hasa oasis in eastern Saudi Arabia is 47 square miles and contains large areas of trees and irrigated cropland.

## Mountains

Mountains cover the western part and the southeastern tip of the Arabian Peninsula. The mountains provide a barrier between the coastland and the desert. These mountains receive much more rain than the desert, up to 20 inches a year, and are cooler than the rest of the peninsula. Dry riverbeds cross the mountains, and flash floods occur as the riverbeds fill with water during rainstorms. The mountains also keep rain from falling on the desert; most rain falls on the mountains before reaching the desert areas.

## Fertile Coastland

The Arabian Peninsula is ringed by an area of fertile coastland, between 5 and 50 miles wide. Rain falls regularly in this area. This is the area of the Arabian Peninsula most suited to farming. Ancient farmers dug irrigation canals and conserved rainwater to irrigate their fields. The coast also has a few natural harbors for ships. Riverbeds cut across the plains and occasionally fill with water after a heavy rainfall.

## Deserts and Nomads

### *How did the geography of the Arabian Peninsula shape life there?*

The geography of the Arabian Peninsula shaped the lives of the people who lived there, whether they lived in the desert, at oases, in the mountains, or on the coast. The Arabian Peninsula was located near the Persian Sasanian Empire. Zoroastrianism, a monotheist religion, was the official religion of the Sasanian Empire. While early Zoroastrian empires had been tolerant of many religions, the Sasanian Empire was not as tolerant of other religions as in the past. Jews, Christians, Buddhists, and followers of other religions were persecuted.

Some residents of the Arabian Peninsula chose to adopt a nomadic lifestyle, traveling from oasis to oasis with their herds of animals. These nomads were called Bedouins. Bedouins used camels as their primary mode of transportation because camels were well suited for the dry and hot climate. Bedouins also raised sheep and goats. They used their animals for food, clothing, and shelter and traded for the things they could not produce.

photo: Getty Images

*A Bedouin encampment near the Sinai Mountains.*

Some Bedouins became traders, crossing the desert in caravans of camels from trade center to trade center and oasis to oasis. With their camels, they could travel long distances, as far as Jordan, Syria, and Iraq. Traders in and around the Arabian Peninsula moved goods from faraway kingdoms in West Africa and South Asia. Other Bedouins decided to settle down in the oases and begin to farm. They cultivated date palm trees, which thrived in the hot, dry climate. The date palm trees offered shade, food, and materials for shelter. Date palm trees are found throughout the Arabian Peninsula. Some of these oases evolved into small trading centers, where caravans would stop and rest while trading their goods. Nomads would also come into oasis towns to trade their animal products for farmers' crops.

In the mountains, farmers created terraces to farm the steep land. These people were isolated from the rest of the peninsula and developed separate ways of life. Farmers used irrigation systems to bring water to their fields and grew crops, such as melons, and trees that produced frankincense.

Along the coast, both farming and trading thrived. Trade centers grew up around the few natural harbors as people from along the Red Sea and the Persian Gulf came to trade their goods. Some people came from as far away as East Africa and India to trade goods. Both farming and trade made the coastal areas rich, and powerful kingdoms formed along the coasts.

## Muhammad—The Trader

*How did Muhammad begin to teach the religion of Islam?*

Muhammad, the founder of Islam, was born in Mecca, one of the main trading centers of the Arabian Peninsula, around 570. He was orphaned at an early age and was cared for by his grandfather and then his uncle, who was a trader. At least once, Muhammad traveled with his uncle on his trading voyages, going as far as modern-day Syria.

### Muhammad's Early Life

During the time of Muhammad, Mecca was a quickly growing trading center at the heart of the trade between the Mediterranean Sea and the Indian Ocean. However, Mecca was also a spiritual center, containing a shrine to the gods, called the Kaaba. The Arabs were polytheists, or believed in many gods, so the Kaaba, a cube-shaped building, contained idols of hundreds of local deities. Each year, people throughout the region took a pilgrimage to Mecca and the Kaaba to worship the gods. Although most Arabs were polytheists, Christian, Zoroastrian, and Jewish traders traveled to Mecca to participate in trade. Growing up, Muhammad was influenced by the traders who believed in one god instead of many.

The Mecca of Muhammad's early life was marked by tensions between the old ways and the new. Mecca was the center of traditional Arab and Bedouin religious life, but it was rapidly changing because its role as a trade center brought prosperity and the rise of a merchant class.

photo: Getty Images

*An illustration of the holy sanctuary at Mecca.*

### Changing Beliefs

Muhammad grew to become a respected member of Meccan society. He was a successful trader, but he also had a rich spiritual life, traveling into the mountains to pray and reflect on his rapidly changing world. According to Islamic teachings, in 610, during one of Muhammad's prayer retreats at the age of 40, the angel Gabriel spoke to Muhammad and told him to "recite."

Muslims believe this was the beginning of 22 years of revelations that the angel Gabriel transmitted from God to Muhammad.

## The Revelations and Teachings of Muhammad
### *What message did Muhammad spread to the people of Mecca?*

When Muhammad returned from the mountains in 610, he thought he might be going crazy. But when he talked to his wife, Khadijah, she convinced him that he was receiving messages from Allah, the Arabic word for "God." Khadijah became the first convert to Islam. Muhammad shared his revelations orally, first with family and friends and then with others. His followers later recorded his teachings in the Quran, which became Islam's holy book.

photo: Getty Images

*The Prophet Mohammed preaching to followers.*

Muhammad taught that Meccans should abandon their many gods and worship the one true God. This God, called Allah in Arabic, was the same monotheistic God that spoke to Abraham and was followed by the Jewish people and Christians. Muhammad denounced the worship of idols. These teachings were also followed by the Jewish people and Christians. He called for followers to submit their will to the will of Allah. People who followed Muhammad's teaching became known as Muslims, or "those who surrender to God." The Quran contains many stories about humanity's unwillingness to listen to the teachings and be united with God. Islam teaches that people who repent are able to achieve this unity and have their sins cleansed. The Quran also describes the Islamic view of final judgment. According to this view, people will be judged by their actions. Some people and communities will be saved and enjoy paradise. Others will be condemned to eternal suffering.

Muhammad also taught about social issues. He taught that all Muslims were equal in the eyes of God. He preached that the wealthy should share their wealth with the poor. He spoke out against the mistreatment of women and told Meccans to take care of orphans.

Muhammad gained followers among his own clan and among some of the dispossessed of Mecca. But many of Mecca's elite were very displeased with Muhammad's message.

## Reaction and Resistance

### *How did the people of Mecca react to Muhammad's message?*

The Meccan elite disliked Muhammad's message for several reasons. First, he was encouraging people to stop worshipping the many idols of gods housed in the Kaaba. Not only was this disturbing to faithful polytheists, but the Meccan merchants relied on the trade gained from the many pilgrims who came to Mecca to visit the Kaaba each year. They worried that new converts to Islam would stop coming to Mecca on pilgrimage. Second, Muhammad's message of equality in the eyes of God and his teachings that the rich should give away their money did not sit well with the wealthy Meccan elite. They did not want to share their wealth.

photo: Getty Images

*A portrait of the Prophet Mohammed, founder of Islam.*

Muhammad's opponents fought against the spread of Islam. They called Muhammad a liar, tortured some of his followers, and stopped doing business with Muslims.

Then, Muhammad was invited by some recent converts to Islam to come to Medina, a nearby town, to resolve a dispute. In 622, he and about 200 of his followers left Mecca and moved to Medina. The people of Medina were much more receptive to Muhammad's message. Gradually, Islam spread throughout Medina and to surrounding Arab communities. However, Meccans still attacked Muhammad and his followers. War raged between the Meccans and the Muslims until finally, in 630, Muhammad and his followers marched peacefully from Medina to Mecca, threw the idols out of the Kaaba, and rededicated it to Allah. Muhammad forgave his enemies. He returned to Medina and continued to unite the Arabian Peninsula under Islam. In 632, Muhammad made a pilgrimage from Medina to Mecca that became the model for Islamic pilgrimages.

The Rashidun Caliphate was the first caliphate without Muhammad's leadership. The leaders of this caliphate were known as patriarchs. They carried on many of the same tasks that Muhammad had, such as leading prayers and heading the army. Under the Rashidun caliphs, an Islamic

**Explore this interactive to learn more about how geography influenced the development of Islam.**

calendar was created and religious scholarship expanded. A controversy also arose during this period that divided Islam into two groups: the Shi'tes and the Sunnis.

# Faith, Prayer, Charity, Fasting, and Pilgrimage
## *What are Muslims required to do?*

Muslims follow five core practices, called the Five Pillars of Islam. They are faith, prayer, charity, fasting, and pilgrimage.

### Faith, or *Shahadah*

Muslims are required to proclaim their faith by saying, "There is no god but God, and Muhammad is his prophet." In this brief sentence, they proclaim their belief in one God and in Muhammad's teachings because Muhammad is the prophet of God. The *shahadah* is an integral part of Islamic life. Parents whisper it into their children's ears at birth. The shahadah also proclaims the centrality of God to each Muslim's life. A common phrase spoken by Muslims is "Insha'Allah," or "if God wills":

*Will you be home for dinner?*

*Yes, Insha'Allah.*

*When will we get to Grandma's house?*

*In three hours, Insha'Allah.*

### Prayer, or *Salat*

The second pillar is called *salat*. Muslims are required to pray five times a day. Muslims may pray by themselves, but in Muslim communities, they try to gather at the mosque. There, they wash their faces, hands, and feet to be clean before God. Muslims form lines behind the prayer leader and follow his lead as they face Mecca and stand, kneel, and prostrate themselves on the floor. The prayer leader punctuates the prayers with the phrase *"Allah u akbar!,"* or "God is great!" On Fridays, many Muslims gather together for Friday afternoon prayer and a sermon from the imam, or leader of the mosque.

### Charity, or *Zakat*

The third pillar is charity. Muhammad told his followers to take care of the orphans and the poor. According to the teachings of Islam, Muslims are required to share a portion of their wealth with their poorer neighbors. Some Muslims give this amount directly to the poor. Others donate it to a religious organization that then distributes the money. *Zakat* helps with everything, including offering shelter to the poor, caring for orphans, ensuring access to clean water, and providing schooling.

photo: Getty Images

*What role do prayers play in the daily lives of Muslims?*

## Fasting, or *Siyam*

During the ninth month of the Islamic calendar, Muslims are required to fast. This month is called Ramadan and, according to Islamic teachings, it is when Muhammad first received a revelation from God. From sunrise to sundown, most Muslims do not eat or drink, although children, the elderly, sick or injured people, travelers, and pregnant women are not expected to fast. During the month of Ramadan, Muslims rise before the sun to eat breakfast. After fasting all day, they then break their fast with a small snack, traditionally dates, and then perform the sunset prayer. After the prayer, they gather with friends and family for a large meal. Ramadan is also a time for giving charity. Fasting helps Muslims to realize what it is like to be hungry. Wealthier Muslims will often provide Ramadan feasts for others. At the end of Ramadan, Muslims celebrate Eid al-Fitr with gifts and feasts.

## Pilgrimage, or *Hajj*

All Muslims who are able are required to travel to Mecca once in their lifetimes on pilgrimage. Muslims usually travel to Mecca during the celebration of Eid al-Adhah. This holiday celebrates the prophet Abraham's willingness to obey God, even when asked to sacrifice his son, Ishmael. Just before Abraham was about to commit the act of sacrifice, God stopped him, letting him kill a ram instead.

## A Holy Book and Guides to Follow

*Where do Muslims receive guidance for how to live their lives?*

Muslims base their religion on the Quran and the Sunnah. Together, these writings offer Muslims spiritual guidance.

*photo: Getty Images*

*The Quran, the holy book of Islam, provides guidance to Muslims on how to live their lives.*

The Quran is the collection of revelations that Muhammad is believed to have received from the angel Gabriel. Because others wrote down the teachings of Muhammad, many different early accounts existed. In 651, about 20 years after the death of Muhammad, Caliph Uthman, the third ruler after Muhammad's death, compiled an official version of the Quran. He consulted with those followers who had been present at the time of Muhammad's revelations, and together they compiled a version that most followers agreed was the truest to what Muhammad had said. Then, Uthman ordered all other versions destroyed.

Many Muslims memorize the Quran in Arabic because they believe that translating the Quran into other languages dilutes its message. Muslim children often go to Quranic school and begin to memorize verses, later learning their meaning. Muslims who memorize the entire Quran are celebrated for their accomplishment.

The Quran contains stories similar to the Jewish and Christian holy books about earlier prophets, such as Abraham and Jesus. It also gives instructions on how to live as a faithful Muslim. It is the first source of guidance for all Muslims because it is believed to be the revelation of God through the angel Gabriel to Muhammad.

### Jihad

Jihad, though not a pillar of Islam, is an Islamic idea. *Jihad* means "to struggle." The Quran tells Muslims that they should fight to protect themselves or to right a horrible wrong. However, Muhammad declared this the "lesser jihad." The "greater jihad" was the struggle within oneself to submit to God's will and reject evil. Examples of the greater jihad would include the following:

- fasting during Ramadan despite going to school with nonfasting classmates

- rising early to pray even though you would rather sleep in

- listening to your parents

- working hard at your job

### Sunnah

The Sunnah is a collection of stories about the sayings and actions of Muhammad. They are not given the weight of divine revelation, such as the Quran, but are followed as the good example of a holy man. There are thousands of stories about Muhammad and the things he did and said. These stories are called *hadith* and are used to guide actions when the Quran does not offer guidance on what to do. As Islam developed, the Quran and Sunnah spread throughout the Muslim world.

From its beginnings with Muhammad, Islam spread throughout the Arabian Peninsula and beyond. The Quran and the teachings of Islam would go on to shape the culture of the region for generations to come.

### Sharia

Sharia is Islamic religious law. It was developed in the 700s and 800s by scholars and judges who drew on the Quran, hadith, and Sunnah for guidance in legal matters. Sharia describes ritual practices for worship, such as prayer practices; legal structures for Islamic societies, including some outlines for criminal and civil laws; and standards for ethical behavior. Sharia law is a guiding principle in Islamic society.

There are several schools of sharia and many ethical and legal questions open for interpretation and debate. In early Islamic societies, sharia law also left room for criminal and commercial courts that were led by local political leaders. These courts could settle simple disputes quickly.

Like most religions and legal traditions of the era, Islamic law is based on a patriarchy, in which men have rights that women do not. Still, sharia law provided some protections for women that were not common in other societies. For example, husbands were legally required to provide for their wives and a wife could obtain a divorce from her husband if she could prove mistreatment or neglect.

**Consider the Essential Question:**

How did Islam develop?

Go online to complete the Social Studies Explanation.

**Check for Understanding:**

How did the core teachings of Islam appeal to people from different countries, who practiced different religions and spoke different languages, and unite them as Muslims? Explain.

Discovery EDUCATION | SOCIAL STUDIES TECHBOOK.

What factors led to the rapid growth of Islam around Africa, Asia, and Eastern Europe?

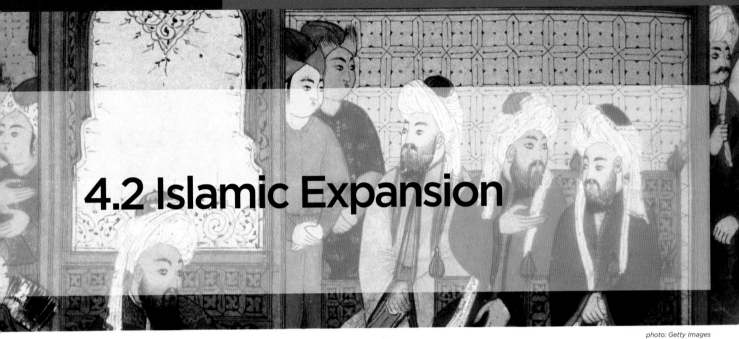

# 4.2 Islamic Expansion

photo: Getty Images

# LESSON OVERVIEW

## Introduction

In this concept, you will learn how Islam spread to Africa, Asia, and Europe, and you will examine the conflicts and challenges that stemmed from this expansion.

## Essential Question

What factors led to the rapid growth of Islam around Africa, Asia, and Eastern Europe?

## Lesson Objectives

By the end of this lesson, you should be able to:

- Identify important figures and then analyze their significance to the development, spread, and division of Islam.

- Trace Islamic expansion throughout Asia and Africa as a result of military conquests and unprepared adversaries.

- Describe the encounters between Muslims and Christians during the expansion of the Islamic world.

## Key Vocabulary
Which terms do you already know?

- ☐ Abbasid dynasty
- ☐ Abu Bakr
- ☐ annex
- ☐ astrolabe
- ☐ Byzantine Empire
- ☐ caliphate
- ☐ Crusaders/ Crusades
- ☐ Egypt
- ☐ First Fitna
- ☐ heretic
- ☐ imam
- ☐ Iraq
- ☐ Islam
- ☐ jihad
- ☐ Mecca
- ☐ Medina
- ☐ Mesopotamia
- ☐ Mombasa
- ☐ Moors

- ☐ Morocco
- ☐ Muhammad
- ☐ People of the Book
- ☐ Quran
- ☐ Rashidun caliphate
- ☐ Riddah Wars
- ☐ Sassanid Empire
- ☐ Shi'a Islam
- ☐ Southwest Asia
- ☐ Spain
- ☐ subcontinent
- ☐ Sunnah
- ☐ Sunni Islam
- ☐ Syria
- ☐ Umar
- ☐ Umayyad dynasty
- ☐ ummah
- ☐ Uthman

## ENGAGE

What happens to "he who becomes a Muslim"? Visit Engage to learn more.

### Essential Question

What factors led to the rapid growth of Islam around Africa, Asia, and Eastern Europe?

## EXPLORE

### Arab Unity or Separation?

*How important was Arab unity to Islamic expansion?*

By the time Muhammad died in 632, his message had spread and his power had grown. Still, it was not clear who would continue to lead the Muslim faith and the political state that he had founded. At Muhammad's death, Muslim Arabs numbered about 100,000. After he died, many of the tribes he had converted fell away, and the tradition of intertribal raids and feuds revived. These activities were, after all, an important source of income. Some tribes refused to pay *zakat*, the charitable tithe required of all Muslims. Some tribes found new prophets to inspire them.

**Caliph Abu Bakr**

Abu Bakr was one of Muhammad's original followers. After Muhammad's death, a council of many of Muhammad's closest advisors agreed that Abu Bakr should become the caliph, or leader of both the religious movement and the political power that Muhammad had established. Abu's first task was to reunite the community, which was beginning to fall apart. Under the rule of Muhammad, based on the teaching of the Quran, there was a prohibition against infighting.

Caliph Abu Bakr immediately set about forcing the tribes to return to Islam. Historians refer to Abu's military campaigns in 633 against ex-Muslims as the Riddah Wars. Abu not only revived Islam among the tribes, but he also redirected infighting among smaller Arab groups toward wars against other empires.

By all accounts, Abu Bakr was a practical as well as a religious man. According to many accounts, he began the process of preparing a formal record of Muhammad's revelations that would eventually be codified in the Quran so all Muslims would share a common holy book. Although he died in 634, only two years after Muhammad, his leadership helped keep Islam together.

### Caliphs Umar and Uthman

The next caliphs, Caliph Umar (634–644) and Caliph Uthman (644–656), were also aware that Arab unity was essential. They worked to lay the foundations of an Islamic state to administer the new lands conquered by Arab armies. According to many scholars, they also carried on where Abu left off and commissioned a committee to complete the standardization of the Quran based on accounts from people who were present when Muhammad preached in Medina and Mecca. This project was completed in 652. Uthman then ordered all other versions to be destroyed. This ensured that all Arabs were reciting the same words from the same book, which strengthened the foundation of Islam.

## The First Wave of Islamic Expansion
### *How did the Islamic expansions begin?*

The term *Islamic expansion* refers to the military campaigns made by Muslim armies after the death of Muhammad in 632. The first wave of the expansion took place during the first 100 or so years after Muhammad's death. It followed the rapid expansion of territory under Arab rule.

After the death of Muhammad, his successors united the Arab tribes, who led their armies in conquests against surrounding territories. Islam was used as a unifying force, although for some tribal leaders the promise of expansion may have been a greater factor. Their efforts were aided by the situation in nearby empires.

### Conquering Empires

The Byzantine and Sassanid Empires had been in conflict for years. By Muhammad's death, they were exhausted and weakened by inner religious and political turmoil. It was the perfect time for an invading army to attack. In 634, Caliph Abu Bakr declared *jihad*, or holy war, on the Byzantine Empire, which was peopled mostly by Greek-speaking Christians. Abu died shortly after, so his successor Caliph Umar took control. Under his rule, Arabs conquered Jerusalem. They also conquered Iraq, Syria, Palestine, and Egypt and annexed Mesopotamia.

The Sassanid Empire, or Persian Empire, was the second empire the Arabs attacked. The state religion of the Sassanid Empire was Zoroastrianism, which followed the words of their prophet Zarathustra and is considered one of the first major monotheistic religions. By 750, the Arabs and their conquered territories stretched from the Atlantic Ocean to India. Umar allowed Jews and Christians to continue to worship as long as they paid a tribute to the leaders. This precedent was followed in subsequent Muslim empires.

**New Dynasties**

Arab expansion continued for the next 100 years. A new set of rulers called the Umayyad dynasty (661–750) doubled the size of the empire by adding North Africa, Spain, and parts of central Asia. The larger the empire, the more difficult it was to govern. In 750, rebels overthrew the Umayyad dynasty, and a new dynasty emerged called the Abbasid dynasty (750–1258).

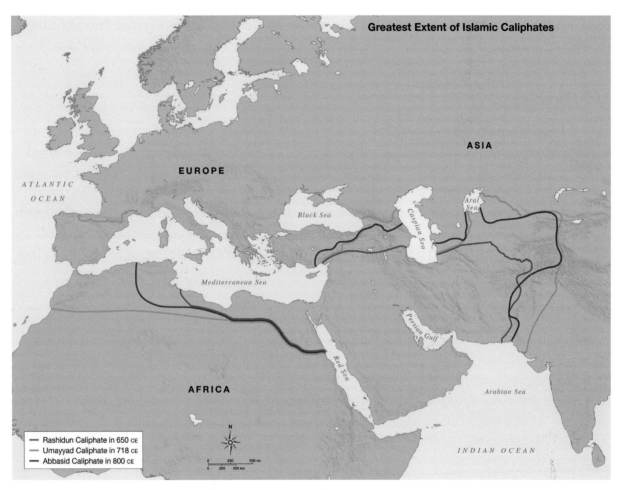

*A map uses three colors to show the greatest extent of three Islamic caliphates.*

## A Split Develops

*How did the split between Shi'a and Sunni Muslims originate?*

As the 62-year-old prophet Muhammad lay dying, many believed he said something regarding those who would succeed him. No one today is sure what he said. In one version, he is said to have uttered, "Oh God, have pity on those who succeed me." If this is true, perhaps Muhammad realized that his failure to name a successor would create discord in his *ummah*, or community of believers. There are, however, Muslims who do not agree with this story. Some of them are among those who insist that Muhammad had already chosen his heir: his cousin and son-in-law, Ali.

**Discovery EDUCATION | SOCIAL STUDIES TECHBOOK**

What factors led to the rapid growth of Islam around Africa, Asia, and Eastern Europe?

### Shi'a Muslims

A man of strong spiritual beliefs, Ali had grown up in the same household as Muhammad. He had declared his belief in his cousin as the messenger of God when he was 10 years old. His later marriage to Muhammad's daughter, Fatimah, solidified the family connection. Many Muslims believe that Ali should have been named Muhammad's successor because Ali was the closest male relative to the Prophet Muhammad. Today, those who believe that Ali should have been named the successor are called Shi'a Muslims. *Shi'a* is a contraction of *Shiat Ali*, meaning "faction of Ali." Today, the Shi'a make up about 15 percent of Muslims. They are mostly found in Iran, Iraq, Lebanon, Pakistan, and Afghanistan.

### Sunni Muslims

Sunni Muslims make up the majority of the Islamic world today. *Sunni* comes from the word *sunnah*, which is the sum of all the words, customs, and practices of Muhammad. While Shi'as believed that political leadership of the Islamic community rightly belonged to Ali and his descendants, Sunnis accepted the rule of other leaders as long as they had the support of the community and followed Muhammad's teachings. Disagreement between Shi'a and Sunni regarding how leadership in Islam should have been passed on after Muhammad's death in 632 sowed the seeds of a conflict that troubles Islam to this day.

### Ali's Leadership

In 656, Ali became the head of the Muslim state. He assumed the position following the assassination of his predecessor, Uthman. For the Shi'a, Ali became the first *imam* (teacher) and the rightful successor of Muhammad. For the Sunni, Ali became the fourth caliph and last ruler in what is called the Rashidun Caliphate, or "rightly guided" caliphate. These early rulers were believed to be rightly guided because they were all personally close to Muhammad and connected all decisions directly to religious teachings and practices.

Ali remains a controversial figure in the eyes of many Muslims. By the time he came to rule, he had been passed over three times. His rule was troubled from the start. Although some historians believe he had nothing to do with Uthman's assassination, Ali's rise to caliph set off the First Fitnah, or civil war, in which Muslim factions fought amongst themselves to gain political leadership. The war created long-lasting tension within the Islamic community, and in 661, Ali was assassinated.

*photo: Getty Images*

*The Dome of the Rock in Jerusalem is the oldest existing Muslim monument. It was completed in 691.*

## A Special Relationship

### *What was the relationship between Muslims and Christians in the Islamic world?*

Historical evidence indicates that Muslims treated their Christian and other non-Muslim subjects well. An example of the Muslim treatment of Christians is Islamic Spain (711–1492).

photo: Getty Images

*The Castle of Gormaz in Spain, built after 756.*

During Muslim rule in Spain, the continued survival of the Christian and Jewish populations suggests that they were tolerated and treated fairly. Muslim tolerance of non-Muslims may come from the example set by Muhammad. According to Islamic beliefs, when Muhammad first began receiving the Quranic revelations in about 610, he looked to the local Christian and Jewish authorities for recognition of spiritual kinship. Even when their leaders rejected him as a false prophet, Muhammad still believed that Jews and Christians were, like Muslims, "People of the Book," who also followed the written teachings of God's prophets and so were alike in some ways.

When Muhammad put together a document called the Constitution of Medina in about 622 to establish the first Islamic state, he assigned Jews and Christians certain rights and responsibilities. He gave them freedom of religion in return for the payment of a special tax. This tax was later exacted from Christians as well as Jews residing in all conquered territories. It marked them as *dhimmis*, or protected people in the Muslim state. The tax became an important part of the caliphate budget. This, some historians believe, explains why there was little effort during the early years of Islamic expansion to convert people to Islam: the Muslim state needed the taxes paid by members of other faiths.

During this period of history, it was the practice of invading armies to kill or enslave the conquered people. As in the case of the armies of the Roman Empire, however, the Muslim armies did not always do so. Arab policy was to maintain a military presence in camps outside the conquered city to prepare for the next stage of conquest and to keep an eye out for any challenge to their authority. Once Arab rule was acknowledged, those who had surrendered were left alone, and the administration of the conquered city was left intact. In this way, the Muslim state could keep the money flowing but ensure that it was directed into their hands.

Discovery | SOCIAL STUDIES
EDUCATION | TECHBOOK

What factors led to the rapid growth of Islam around Africa, Asia, and Eastern Europe?

# Time Is Mightier Than the Sword

### How did Islam spread?

Older histories of the Islamic expansion often describe Islam as having been "spread by the sword," meaning that the Muslim armies forced Islam on the peoples they conquered. Modern historians, however, have reversed this idea. While armies and empires led by Muslim rulers conquered vast territories, they rarely forced non-Muslims to convert to Islam.

## Conversion to Islam

One reason was that the Quran explicitly forbids forcible conversion because it is unlikely to be a true conversion. What use is a false believer to people of the faith? Only against Arab tribes was force used wholesale to ensure that all were of one faith.

Although non-Muslims were rarely forced to convert, sometimes alternatives were less attractive. Some converted to Islam while others adapted to the new rulers. It was not unusual for the conquered people to submit and to become Muslim if they did not want to pay a tax to practice their own faith.

Most countries conquered by the Muslim armies eventually chose conversion rather than being forced. In Iran, for example, under the Umayyad dynasty from 651 to 750, only about 10 percent of non-Muslims converted to Islam. By about 850, under the more tolerant Abbasid dynasty, Iran's Muslim population had grown to about 40 percent. By the end of the 1000s, the Iranian population was nearly 100 percent Muslim.

## Reasons for Conversion

This progression in the rate of conversion, as suggested earlier, reflects an attitude of tolerance. But there were other reasons as well. The success of the Muslim armies, for instance, validated Islam not only in the eyes of any wavering Muslim converts but also in the eyes of the freshly conquered. For the Muslims, success meant extraordinary wealth unlike any that had been won in intertribal raids. For the non-Muslims, Islamic military success sometimes signaled an improvement in how they were treated. The Islamic custom of the seclusion of women, especially by the wearing of concealing clothing, originated in the Persian culture and was adopted throughout the Islamic empires.

photo: Getty Images

*A silver dirham (coin) of the Abbasid dynasty.*

Aside from any religious feelings that might inspire non-Muslims to convert to Islam, there were other reasons to convert as well. As Muslims, they would no longer have to pay the tax required of those of other faiths. They were no longer restricted in what they could wear, and they were no longer excluded from the political process. Once converted, however, there was no going back. *Shariah*, the religious law of Islam, spells out the price paid for leaving the faith once converted: death.

**Explore this interactive to learn more about how Islam spread to Africa, Asia, and Europe.**

## A World Religion

*How did Islam expand after the year 750?*

Military conquests by Arab armies created the Muslim world in the Middle East during the first 100 years following the death of Muhammad. By the fall of the Umayyad dynasty, the word *Muslim* had come to define more than just Arabs, and the armies included soldiers from all over the empire. In 711, for instance, converted Berbers made up the Muslim armies that invaded southern Spain and established Islamic control over most of the Iberian Peninsula that lasted for centuries.

photo: Getty Images

*The Spiral Minaret of the Mosque at Samarra, present-day Iraq.*

Armies were not the only vehicle by which Islam spread, however. Islam was carried peacefully by missionaries and traders to Southeast Asia—Indonesia, the southern Philippines, and the Malaysian Peninsula. Later, they were followed by migrants from Persia and southern Arabia. Sufi missionaries also played an important role in the expansion of Islamic ideas through education, literature, and poetry. Sufism is the mystical part of Islam that focuses on rituals and spiritual truths. Traders and conquests in Africa also helped spread Islam. Parts of East and West Africa became Muslim. By the 1300s, vibrant commercial centers reportedly thrived in East African Islamic cities, such as Mogadishu, Mombasa, and Kilwa. Typically, chiefs and kings would become Muslim first; only gradually did the people convert, usually incorporating Muslim beliefs to their local religions.

The only obstacle in Islam's path was the repeated fracturing of the centers of power. Muslim kingdoms fought for power while the Abbasid dynasty (750 CE–1258 CE) tried to stay in control. In the 900s CE and 1000s CE, the Seljuks, ancestors of modern-day Turks, seized parts of the Abbasid territories and pieces of the Byzantine Empire in Asia Minor. The Seljuks also captured Jerusalem, Syria, and Palestine.

# The Crusades

## *What were the Crusades?*

In 638, Islamic armies had captured Jerusalem in order to protect one of their holy sites. Now, Christians invaded Jerusalem for the same reason—to protect their holy city and people on pilgrimage. The actual reasons may have been more political. Kingdoms in Europe were growing in strength and competing with Islamic kingdoms for trade routes and revenue. European rulers saw the Crusades as an opportunity to demonstrate, as well as increase, their power, influence, and wealth.

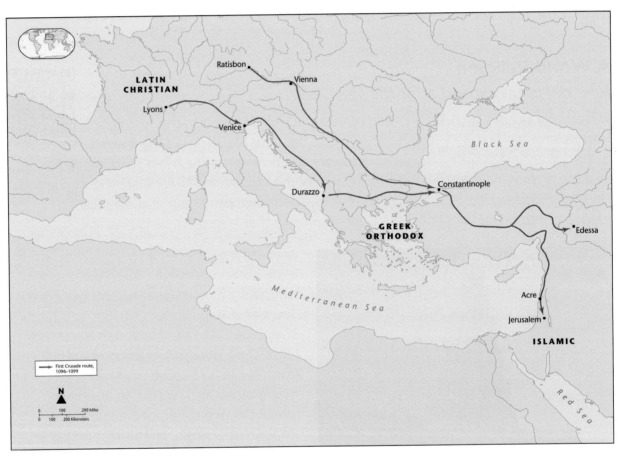

*Route of the First Crusade, 1096–1099.*

## Struggle for the "Holy Land"

The Crusades (1095–1291) were a violent series of campaigns by Christian armies against the Muslim world. There were nine crusades made to modern-day Israel, where so many holy places associated with Christianity and Islam existed.

The Crusades were extensive, as Christians tried to retake lands that had been captured by the Islamic Empire. Major fighting centered on Jerusalem, the holy city, but also took place in the regions of Palestine, Syria, Egypt, and Anatolia. However, the Crusades also reached Islamic cities in Spain. As the armies advanced and tried to establish control over the conquered lands, they established Crusader states, such as Edessa, Galilee, Antioch, and Tripoli.

During the Fourth Crusade in the early 1200s, the Crusaders never reached the Holy Land and, instead, attacked Constantinople, the capital of the Orthodox Christian Byzantine Empire. Jews and Eastern Orthodox Christians were killed because they were believed to be heretics by members of the western Church. Even more successful Crusades did little to expand Christian power in the Middle East because the Crusaders were isolated in a few walled cities. In later Crusades, Muslims regained control of Jerusalem. In 1291, the Crusaders met with defeat, and Muslim armies were once again in control of the entire region.

From the 600s to the 1400s, Islam served as a unifying force among people living in various parts of Asia, Europe, and Africa, contributing to their indigenous cultural landscapes. Although Islam's arrival in a region was often accompanied by violence, in time it became the one element that the diverse populations under Muslim rule had in common.

**Consider the Essential Question:**

What factors led to the rapid growth of Islam around Africa, Asia, and Eastern Europe?

Go online to complete the Social Studies Explanation.

**Check for Understanding:**

What was the main cause of Islam's split into the Shi'a and Sunni sects? Be sure to provide details and examples to support your response.

*photo: Getty Images*

# 4.3 Life in the Islamic Empires

## LESSON OVERVIEW

### Introduction

In this concept, you will learn about the achievements of Islamic societies and how the Islamic religion affected life in these societies.

### Essential Question

How did trade, religion, and innovation shape society in Islamic cultures?

### Lesson Objectives

By the end of this lesson, you should be able to:

- Explain how the development of trade routes led to the growth of cities and the economy in Islamic society.

- Analyze how the Islamic religion affected life for men and women in the region.

- Connect important innovations under Islamic empires to the expansion of global trade and cultural diffusion.

## Key Vocabulary
Which terms do you already know?

- [ ] Abbas the Great
- [ ] Africa
- [ ] Arabia
- [ ] Arabian Peninsula
- [ ] Arabian Sea
- [ ] Asia
- [ ] Byzantine Empire
- [ ] camel
- [ ] caravan
- [ ] Delhi Sultanate
- [ ] domestication
- [ ] Europe
- [ ] Five Pillars of Islam
- [ ] hijab
- [ ] Ibn Battuta
- [ ] India
- [ ] Indian subcontinent
- [ ] Janissaries
- [ ] Mecca
- [ ] Medina
- [ ] Middle East
- [ ] millets
- [ ] oasis
- [ ] patriarchal
- [ ] pilgrimage
- [ ] polytheism
- [ ] Ptolemy
- [ ] Quran
- [ ] Red Sea
- [ ] reform/social reform
- [ ] shah
- [ ] Shari'ah
- [ ] Spain
- [ ] sultan
- [ ] Umar
- [ ] Uthman

## ENGAGE

What was it like to be a boy in ancient Yemen? Visit Engage to learn more.

> ### Essential Question
> How did trade, religion, and innovation shape society in Islamic cultures?

## EXPLORE

### Geography and Trade

*How did the geography of the Arabian Peninsula affect how people in the region traded?*

Located on the southwestern edge of Asia, the Arabian Peninsula, also known as Arabia, which makes up a part of the modern-day Middle East, offered several geographic advantages to the traders who lived there. Its location, weather patterns, and climate all combined to impact trade throughout the region.

The location of Arabia made it a center of trade in the region. Arabia is the meeting place for three continents: Africa to the west, Asia to the east, and Europe to the north. Arabia is also surrounded by important bodies of water: the Red Sea, the Gulf of Aden, the Arabian Sea, the Gulf of Oman, and the Persian Gulf. These bodies of water provided important trade routes throughout the region. It also made it possible to move heavier and larger amounts of goods that were difficult to move over land. Travel by sea was also aided by the weather patterns in the region.

Seasonal weather patterns also affected trade in the region. In the winter and summer, monsoon winds blow from the Indian Ocean to the southeast of the Arabian Peninsula. They are strong winds that blow from the southwest during the winter and then shift during the summer and blow from the northeast during the summer. These winds helped ships travel from Arabia to Africa in the summer and return in the winter. Muslim traders gave thanks to God for these winds. The relative ease of travel through the water was important because the climate in the region made travel over land more difficult.

**Discovery** SOCIAL STUDIES
EDUCATION | **TECHBOOK**

How did trade, religion, and innovation shape society in Islamic cultures?

Despite the bodies of water that surround the peninsula, the interior of the peninsula is dominated by harsh, dry deserts. This climate made it difficult for travelers and traders to move across the land. However, the domestication, or breeding and raising, of camels allowed people to travel more easily through the deserts. They were also able to use pack saddles to carry large amounts of supplies and goods, which allowed them to travel much farther that they could on foot. This helped the Arabian Peninsula become a center of trade for people from Africa, the Middle East, and the Indian subcontinent.

photo: Getty Images

*Camels allowed people to travel farther into the desert than they would have been capable of on their own.*

## The Spread of Islam

### *How did traders help spread Islam?*

Because of the arid climate that dominated most of the Arabian Peninsula, a reliable source of water was important to the development of cities in Arabia. For this reason, cities on the Arabian Peninsula developed as people gathered in areas where an oasis (a fertile area within a desert), a well, or other water source, could be found.

Two cities that were particularly important to the development of Islamic society were Mecca and Medina. Mecca is located on the west side of the Arabian Peninsula on an old trade route. Mecca had wells that provided drinking water but did not have enough water for agriculture. Because of this, trade was a necessary part of life in the city. Mecca had been a religious center for polytheistic religions and later became an Islamic holy city because Muhammad was born in Mecca and began Islam there.

When Muhammad was forced out of Mecca because of his religious beliefs, he settled in Yathrib, later known as Medina, located in the western part of modern-day Saudi Arabia.

photo: Getty Images

*In early Islamic society, trade routes were important to the spread of Islam.*

Medina was another city that was important for trade in the region. While in Medina, Muhammad and his followers shared Islam with other people and cultures. Muhammad later died in Medina, and it became a holy city to Muslims.

**Explore this investigation and take a position on how other cultures impacted the development of Islamic empires.**

The cities of Mecca and Medina helped spread Islam because they were both holy cities and important centers for trade. Muslim traders from these cities traveled in caravans, large groups of traders who traveled together, to other lands along the trade routes. Silk, spices, and incense were among the many goods traded along these routes, which extended across the Arabian Peninsula to eastern Africa. Traders brought their religious practices with them and taught the local people about their religious beliefs and customs. Some of these people converted to Islam and, in turn, shared the religion with others as they traveled farther along the trade routes. As the economy of the world grew, Islam grew as well. As Islam spread, the rules and laws of Islam shaped new societies.

## The Ottomans

*How did Islam become the primary religion for powerful empires?*

By 750, Islamic rulers had expanded the boundaries of their empires across North Africa, Southwest Asia, and into Central and South Asia. By the 1200s, Muslim emperors controlled land on three continents and Muslim merchants controlled trade throughout the Eastern Hemisphere. Rulers of these empires became incredibly wealthy and powerful.

### A Growing Empire

In the 1200s, groups of Islamic nomads from central Asia began to move into the Anatolian Peninsula (modern Turkey) and gain power. These groups began to unify under a leader named Osman and became known as the Ottomans. The Ottomans slowly gained territory in the Eastern Roman Empire, then called the Byzantine Empire. The Ottomans attacked the city of Constantinople several times. In 1453, the Ottomans conquered Constantinople and made it the center of an empire that would last, in some form, for nearly 500 years.

The military strength of the Ottoman Empire came from its skilled corps of soldiers, led by an elite group called the janissaries. These soldiers were young war captives, usually from Christian families, who were taken away to receive special training. They converted to Islam, learned to read and write, and became skilled warriors. The janissaries were considered property of the Ottoman emperor, or sultan, and served him directly. Janissaries who excelled were promoted to the highest levels of government.

## The Golden Age

Led by the janissaries, the Ottoman army conquered much of the Islamic world. After the fall of Constantinople, the armies spread through Greece and the Balkans into Europe, across North Africa, and into the Arabian Peninsula. By 1519, the Ottoman sultan controlled the Muslim holy cities of Mecca and Medina, earning him the title of "Protector of the Sacred Places." The Ottoman Empire also ruled over much of the Mediterranean coast and the links between the Chinese Silk Road and Europe, giving it power to control trade across three continents.

In 1520, a young sultan named Suleyman (SOO lay mahn) took over the empire. Suleyman boldly pushed the limits of his empire to the west and the east, attacking the city of Vienna in modern-day Austria and capturing the cities of Baghdad and Basra in modern-day Iraq. He became well known in Europe as Suleyman "the Magnificent" because of his wealth and power. In his own kingdom, he was called Suleyman "the Lawgiver" because he improved the justice system. Under Suleyman, arts and architecture flourished. The Christian-born janissary and architect Sanin converted to Islam and built hundreds of mosques, palaces, schools, and other public buildings that are still considered some of the finest examples of Islamic architecture.

photo: Getty Images

*A portrait of Sultan Sulyman the Magnificent.*

## Decline

Many historians see the death of Suleyman in 1566 as the beginning of the long, slow decline of the Ottoman Empire. Over the next several hundred years, Europeans found new trade routes. This meant they did not have to deal with the Ottoman traders, which weakened the Ottoman economy. Rebellions inside the janissary corps and power struggles in the elite families weakened the government. The empire shrank as lands were conquered by rivals. Still, the empire persisted until 1923, when the sultans finally gave up power and the republic of Turkey was established.

## Persia and South Asia

*How did other Islamic empires expand their influence?*

While the Ottomans gained power along the Mediterranean, two other powerful empires flourished in the east.

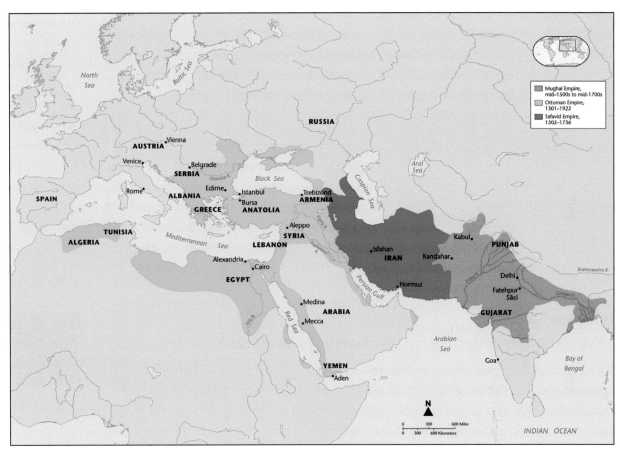

*This map shows the boundaries of the Mughal, Ottoman, and Safavid Empires.*

### The Safavid Empire

Persia, the land near modern-day Iran, has been a center for culture and political power since ancient times. Persians have fought and conquered powerful neighbors, including Greeks, Arabs, and Turks. By the 1400s, almost all Persians had converted to Islam. Like most Muslims in the region and in the neighboring Ottoman Empire, they were largely Sunni. However, by the late 1400s, a small group of Shi'a Persians called the Safavids (sah FAH weeds) began to gain power.

Between 1500 and 1722, the Safavid Empire grew to control all of modern-day Iran and portions of modern-day Iraq. Its armies engaged in constant battles with the Sunni Ottoman Empire on its borders. Under the Safavids, Persian culture thrived and its influence grew. The shah, or ruler, Abbas the Great (1571–1629) encouraged artisans and craftsmen. According to legends, Abbas would disguise himself as a commoner and walk through the cities of his empire. He also was a skilled diplomat and entered into alliances with Christian rulers in Europe against the Ottoman Empire.

### The Delhi Sultanate and the Mughals

By 711, Arab armies had conquered portions of the Indus valley, bringing Islam to South Asia. In the 1100s and 1200s, Islamic rulers began to expand their territory by conquering Hindu regions. While the Islamic armies triumphed on the battlefield, the Islamic religion also gained power. In some regions, lower-caste Hindus, who could not expect to gain social status inside the caste system, were drawn to Islam's message of equality. From 1206 to 1526, Muslim leaders ruled a portion of northern India called the Delhi Sultanate. Under the Delhi Sultanate, cultures and traditions from Hindu South Asians and Islamic central Asians blended, though there were often tensions.

In 1526, Turkish and Mongol armies invaded the Delhi Sultanate, led by a general named Babur (BAH bur) and established a new empire called the Mughal Empire. Babur and his successors expanded the Mughal Empire throughout most of South Asia. They continued traditions of blending Hindu and Muslim cultures, creating unique literature, art, and architecture. In 1631, the Mughal emperor Shah Jahan's beloved wife Mumtaz Mahal died in childbirth. The shah commissioned one of the most recognizable buildings in the world, the Taj Mahal, to serve as her tomb. During the 1700s, Mughals gradually lost power to European traders, but their influence on South Asia is still apparent today.

## Islamic Society

### How did Islam affect society in the Muslim empires?

Before the spread of Islam, there was no strong central government in the Arabian Peninsula. People in this region were members of tribes, or local groups. Most tribes practiced polytheism, meaning they worshipped more than one god. Because people believed in different gods and practiced different religions, there was not one common set of rules about how people should live their lives. The spread of Islam changed this by providing this common set of guidelines. The Quran, the holy book of the Muslim religion, detailed the laws of the Islamic faith, called Sharia, the rules for how Muslim people should live their lives.

### Social Reforms

The teachings of the Quran led to social reform. Islam taught that Muslims should help those who may be suffering or in need. This included the poor, orphans, women, and enslaved people. Muslims in many Islamic societies were required to pay a tax each year based on the amount of property they owned. This money was then distributed to those in need.

### Life for Women in Islamic Society

Before the spread of Islam, many of the tribal societies on the Arabian Peninsula were patriarchal, meaning men were in charge of society and the family. Women at that time did not have many rights. They were not allowed to buy, sell, or own property. If a woman received an inheritance from her parents when they died, it automatically went to her husband.

photo: Getty Images

*The Quran requires Muslim women to be very modest, so many women cover their faces in public. Some Muslim women wear hijab today.*

The Quran taught that women and men were equal in the eyes of Allah, or God. Because of this, Islam helped improve the lives of women and gave them more rights. In Islamic society, women were allowed to buy, sell, and own property, including an inheritance from their parents. Although Muslims believed that family was one of the most important parts of society, the Quran gave women the right to ask for a divorce in many situations. Women were also given more rights to education because a certain time was allowed each day for both men and women to learn about Islam. This led to increased literacy throughout society, especially for women.

Because Islam taught that women were to be honored, Muslim women were expected to live more reserved lives than they had before. Some women chose to wear a *hijab*, or a traditional scarf that covers women's hair, neck, and sometimes face. Some later Islamic societies required women to wear a hijab, but in many societies women were given the choice.

**Explore this interactive to learn more about four different perspectives on life in the Islamic empires.**

## The Role of Other Religions

*How were members of other religions treated in the Islamic empires?*

As Islam spread along trade routes, Muslims lived along with people of many other religions. Many Muslim empires such as Islamic Spain, the Ottomans, and the Mughals allowed members of other religions to worship freely inside their empires. However, the members of other religions were not allowed to hold positions of power, and they also were required to pay tribute to the Muslim leadership.

In the Ottoman Empire, non-Muslims were allowed to practice their own religions in communities called millets. Each millet was allowed to govern itself, develop its own schools, and even follow many of its own laws. They collected taxes and reported to the sultan.

In some areas, even these restrictions did not apply. For example, the ruler Akbar the Great, Emperor of the Mughal Empire, is noted for his tolerance. He could not read or write, and he chose religious leaders and scholars from all faiths as his top advisors. He abolished the tax that non-Muslims needed to pay in order to worship and avoid military service. Most notable, however, was his relationship with the large numbers of Hindus in the empire. Hindus were able to hold high government positions within Akbar's government, including governor and general.

This attitude of tolerance in Islamic empires helped Islamic society to become a place where ideas and traditions from across the world came together. Muslim artists encountered the work of Chinese artisans and incorporated features of their artwork, such as the use of jade, in their designs. Hindu and Muslim cultures intermingled. Many languages and traditions blended under the Islamic empires, including Persian, Arabic, Swahili, and Urdu. This led to several cultural and technological innovations.

photo: Getty Images

*Akbar supported religious tolerance in the Mughal Empire.*

## Muslim Scholars

### *How did Muslim scholars use the past work of ancient civilizations?*

As Islam spread and united people from Spain to northern India, the Arabic language spread as well. Having a common language helped unite people from such various backgrounds. The shared Arabic language also helped scholars bring together important writings from other societies.

Early Muslim scholars were exposed to the ideas, philosophies, and technological advances of other societies. They translated texts from Greek, Roman, Indian, and Persian thinkers into Arabic. Many of these historic texts were almost forgotten before the time of Islam. Without the Arabic translations, many of these texts would have been lost and would not have been available to modern society.

photo: Getty Images

*A 13th-century manuscript depicting Arab travelers on camels.*

Muslim scholars did not only translate the historic texts. They studied the ideas presented in the texts carefully and expanded on them. Scholars such as Al-Farabi, an Arab philosopher who lived from 878 to 950, adapted the philosophies of Plato and Aristotle to Islam. Much of Al-Farabi's writings focused on how to best order and organize the state. He believed that as God ruled the universe, wise philosophers were the best suited to run governments. This was similar to Plato's idea of the philosopher-king. Al-Farabi also wrote about music, science, and philosophy.

## Advances in the Sciences and Mathematics

*What advances were made by Muslim scholars?*

Muslim rituals encouraged learning and travel. These beliefs and the activities of Muslim traders led to important innovations in science and medicine.

One of the five pillars of Islam, the *hajj*, requires Muslims to make a pilgrimage, or religious journey, to the city of Mecca once in their lifetime, if possible. To make the pilgrimage, it was important for Muslims to know where Mecca was and the best way to travel there. Muslim scholars used the works of Greek astrologers, such as Ptolemy, and simple mathematics to develop a system of determining longitude and latitude. They also adapted and improved upon a tool, known as the astrolabe, used by Greek navigators. This tool aided navigation by allowing sailors to calculate the position of the sun and other important navigational stars. These advances in navigation also helped Muslim traders find their way to new places and would influence the work of later astrologers and navigators.

photo: Getty Images

*A 19th-century illustration of Ibn Battuta in Egypt.*

One famous Muslim traveler named Ibn Battuta went on his pilgrimage to Mecca from his home in Morocco in 1325 when he was 20 years old. After visiting Mecca, Ibn Battuta kept traveling for the next 30 years. He visited Asia, Africa, and parts of Europe. Ibn Battuta returned home in 1354 and wrote about his travels. He described all of the places he visited. Ibn Battuta's books helped other people learn about the geography of the Islamic empires.

Another one of the five pillars of Islam is *salat*. Salat requires that Muslims pray five times each day while facing the city of Mecca. The correct times to pray are not standard but are based on the times of sunrise and sunset. It was difficult to determine what the right time for each prayer was, but the Muslims used advanced math skills to determine the correct times and help them perform their daily prayers correctly.

Discovery EDUCATION | SOCIAL STUDIES TECHBOOK

How did trade, religion, and innovation shape society in Islamic cultures?

In studying the works of other civilizations, the Islamic mathematicians spread existing ideas. When Muslims reached India, they learned Indian mathematics, including the concept of zero and their decimal place-value system. Muslim scholars studied these ideas and spread them to new people and civilizations. Muslim scholars also used the work of Greek and Indian mathematicians to develop new concepts. For example, the Arab mathematician Muhammed Al-Khwarizmi developed new concepts and ideas that would lead to the development of algebra around 830. Khwarizmi is still known as the "Father of Algebra." Muslim scholars shared these new ideas with other civilizations throughout the world.

## Medical Knowledge

### What advances did Islamic society make in medicine?

As was the case in other scientific fields, Muslim doctors studied the works of Greek, Roman, and Indian doctors. They used this knowledge as a basis and then improved upon it to make significant advances in medicine.

Muslim doctors identified bacteria as the source of infection. This knowledge helped them prevent and treat diseases. This effort was aided by advances in chemistry. Many chemists during that time practiced alchemy—they tried to find a way to turn common metals into gold using chemicals. However, during these experiments, they recorded the characteristics of the chemicals they used. Some of these chemicals were found to have medicinal properties and so were used in the treatment of disease. Arab chemists also discovered medicinal herbs. Some drugs still in use today can be traced back to these chemists.

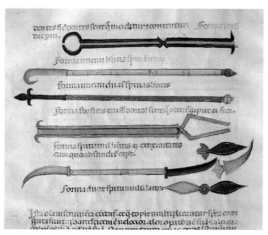

photo: Getty Images

*An illustration of Arab surgical instruments in Abu al-Qasim's* Treatise on Surgery.

Although surgeries had been performed by other ancient cultures, including the Greek and Roman cultures, Muslim doctors improved upon the existing methods. The famous surgeon Abu al-Qasim wrote a book on general surgery that included illustrations of instruments. This text would influence surgical procedures throughout the Islamic empires and would also influence European surgeons through the Renaissance.

## Islamic Art

### How did the spread of Islam shape art and architecture?

There was little recorded art in the Arabian Peninsula before Islam. Some Arabs wrote poetry, but they did not widely practice visual arts, such as painting and sculpture. Under Islamic society, however, many forms of art blossomed.

According to the teachings of Islam, drawings or sculptures of living things, including human beings, are not permitted. Therefore, most Islamic art consists of geometric patterns and calligraphy. The calligraphy is often of verses from the Quran. These styles are evident in textiles, such as clothing, rugs, and fabrics, which were often created by women and used in daily prayers and religious services. They can also be seen in Islamic buildings. Architecture, especially the building and decorating of mosques, was an important form of early Islamic art.

photo: Paul Fuqua

*This mosaic, made from small, colorful tiles, represents the decorative patterns that are typical in Islamic art.*

Other forms of art that flourished in the Islamic empires were music and literature. One famous piece of literature from Islamic society is *The Arabian Nights*, which is a book of Arab folktales from many different authors. Have you ever heard the story of Aladdin? Aladdin, Sinbad the Sailor, and Ali Baba were all characters in *The Arabian Nights*. Music in Islamic society was based on the chanting of the Quran. Like many elements of society, it was heavily influenced by religion.

The Islamic faith was a major influence on Islamic society. Innovation in science and technology, architecture, artwork, and cultural traditions were all influenced by Islam.

**Consider the Essential Question:**

How did trade, religion, and innovation shape society in Islamic cultures?

Go online to complete the Social Studies Explanation.

**Check for Understanding:**

How did the growth of Muslim empires encourage scientific, literary, and technological innovations? Be sure to provide details and examples in your response.

Discovery EDUCATION | SOCIAL STUDIES TECHBOOK

What changes and accomplishments defined South Asia's Golden Age?

# 5.1 South Asia

photo: Getty Images

## LESSON OVERVIEW

### Introduction

In this concept, you will learn about the rise of various empires and cultures in South Asian countries between 300 and 1200 CE. You will also explore the influence of these cultures on the development of the medieval West.

### Key Vocabulary
Which terms do you already know?

- ☐ bhakti movement
- ☐ Buddhism
- ☐ Gupta Empire
- ☐ Jainism
- ☐ pilgrimage
- ☐ Sanskrit
- ☐ Silk Road

### Essential Question

What changes and accomplishments defined South Asia's Golden Age?

### Lesson Objectives

By the end of this lesson, you should be able to:

- Describe the cultural, religious, and economic impact of the reunification of South Asia under the Gupta Empire.

- Analyze the changes and growth of South Asian religions between 300 and 1200 CE.

- Describe the impact of Islam and the founding of the Delhi Sultanate on South Asia.

# ENGAGE

Why is it important to learn about medieval events outside Europe? Visit Engage to learn more.

## Essential Question

What changes and accomplishments defined South Asia's Golden Age?

# EXPLORE

## Rise of the Gupta Empire

*In what ways did the Gupta Empire consolidate power and culture in South Asia?*

After the fall of the Mauryan Empire in 185 BCE, India was ruled by many small kingdoms, each controlling a small piece of the subcontinent. Chandra Gupta I was a member of a family living in northern India. By the early 300s CE, the previously unknown Gupta family had grown so wealthy and influential that they controlled the kingdom of Magadha, which had been the center of the earlier Mauryan Empire.

The year 320 is considered the beginning of the Gupta Empire. Some historians believe this was the year that Chandra Gupta became the *maharajadhiraja*, or ruler of the Magadha kingdom. Others believe it was the year Magadha became fully independent. Chandra reigned for 10 years. He added land to his kingdom by marrying a princess from the nearby Licchavi kingdom. A set of gold coins was made to commemorate the marriage.

### Samudra's Empire

In 330, Chandra passed on the throne to his son, Samudra, who reigned until 380. Like his father, Samudra's deeds were depicted on gold coins. Other coins made at the same time suggest that he might have had a rival for the throne. Historians know a great deal about Samudra's reign and accomplishments from a long poem carved on a pillar in the city of Allahabad.

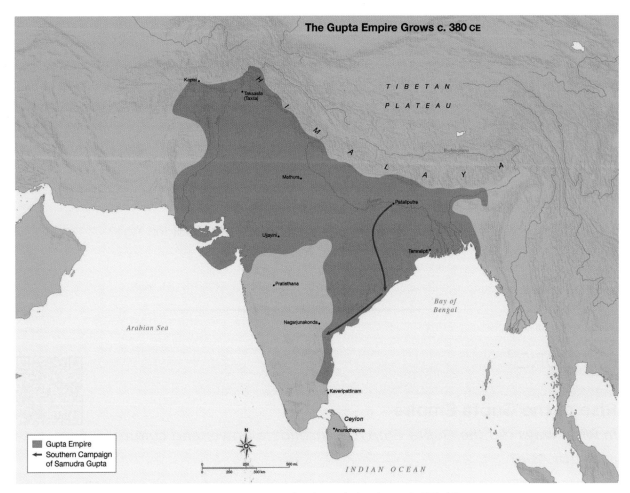

**The Gupta Empire Grows c. 380 CE**

Samudra expanded the territory of his father's empire after he took the throne in 330 CE.

Samudra was ambitious and passionate about conquest. Under his reign, the Gupta Empire expanded in all directions. By 380, it stretched north to the Himalaya Mountains, including modern-day Nepal; west to the Indus valley region, which includes parts of modern-day India and Pakistan; and east, including modern-day Myanmar. When Samudra conquered some of the remote areas in the east, he made them tributaries. This means he allowed the conquered rulers to keep governing their own lands as long as they paid tribute to him and acknowledged him as their ruler. These tributary rulers were called *samanta*, meaning "neighbors." Samudra's son, Chandra II, also increased the size of the empire, both through conquest and marriage.

**Creating a Common Culture**

For the Gupta dynasty, and especially for Chandra II, building an empire meant more than just power and wealth. It also meant creating a common culture across much of the empire. Under Chandra II, the empire grew peaceful and prosperous, supporting the arts and scholarship. Roads were built, connecting the various regions and cities and making travel and trade easier. Chandra also built many schools, hospitals, and temples celebrating the Buddhist, Hindu, and Jain faiths.

These developments also increased contact with other people in the South Asia region. The art and architecture developed under the Guptas influenced South Asian culture for centuries to come. In 402, a Buddhist monk from China named Faxian, or Fa-hsien, made a pilgrimage to India. Faxian came to India because it was the birthplace of the Buddha. He wanted to learn more about Buddhism by visiting shrines and studying Buddhist texts. Faxian wrote about his pilgrimage in great detail. He described India under the Guptas as "very productive, with the people happy and prosperous beyond compare."

# India's Golden Age

*What were the most important scientific and cultural contributions of the Gupta Empire?*

Some historians call Chandra II's reign a "Golden Age" for India. Unlike Samudra, Chandra II was not interested in conquering more lands or growing wealthier. Instead, he focused on supporting artists and encouraging scientific and technological discoveries. This led to many advances in the fields of science, mathematics, and art. Artists were even paid for their work, which was unusual at the time. As a result, many forms of art flourished, including music, dance, and literature.

## Science and Math

In the Gupta era, many discoveries were made that helped shape the worlds of math and science. Aryabhata (476–550) is often called the father of algebra. His books

*photo: Getty Images*

*A gold coin with the image of Gupta king Samudra.*

described the Indian number system. Some historians even believe he helped popularize the ideas of zero and base-10 math, or using a number system based on 10 numerals. This simple system made it easier to count and make calculations.

Aryabhata also studied astronomy. He calculated that Earth and other planets were round and that they rotate on an axis. He also correctly described eclipses as shadows cast by different celestial bodies, and he could accurately calculate the length of a lunar eclipse. Many of the astronomical discoveries made by Aryabhata and other Gupta-era scientists would not be made in the West for around 1,500 years.

Discovery SOCIAL STUDIES
EDUCATION TECHBOOK

What changes and accomplishments defined South Asia's Golden Age?

## Sweet Discoveries

The innovations of the Gupta era were not limited to math and astronomy. Around 350, people learned how to crystallize the sugar from sugarcane juice. This made sugar easier to transport and trade. Sailors also used crystallized sugar as food for long trips.

Another popular invention of the Gupta period was the game of chess. Many historians believe it developed around the 500s. Chess may have evolved out of an earlier strategy board game called Chaturanga. The earliest mentions of chess terms are written in Sanskrit, a historically Indian language. As India traded with other countries, chess spread into Persia, Arabia, and China along a trade path known as the Silk Road. The game eventually reached Europe by around the 1100s. Chess is still played around the world today.

Music and dance flourished in the Gupta period as well. Music had always been a part of Indian culture, especially in religion. Chanting hymns was part of the Vedic rituals, and many Hindu stories were set to music. Medieval Indians also played a variety of instruments, including flutes, drums, cymbals, and the veena, a stringed instrument similar to a lute. Samudra was a musician as well as a conqueror. Several gold coins from his reign show him playing the veena. Like music, dance began as a religious ritual. Dancers were invited to perform these religious dances at court. The dances involved elaborate gestures, body movements, and facial expressions. Many of these dances are still performed today.

## Language and Literature

Sanskrit was the language used in many religious texts. Gupta rulers encouraged poets and writers to produce a wide range of Sanskrit literature. This royal patronage helped the language flourish and spread, particularly among educated groups. Sanskrit literature included both religious texts and stories that focused on humans. Fables and fantasy stories often had animals playing human roles. Romantic stories were also popular. The most famous writer of this period, Kalidasa, wrote poems and dramas that drew on rituals and ideas from the sacred Vedas, but added human emotions and rich descriptions of the natural world.

Many nonfiction works were written as well, including books on medicine, astronomy, and math, like the ones Aryabhata wrote. Sanskrit was the language used in religious writing by both Hindus and Buddhists. Many of these texts survive to this day. They help reveal how people lived in medieval South Asia.

# India After the Guptas

## *How did South Asia change after the Gupta era?*

The reign of Chandra II was the high point of the Gupta era. After that, the empire began to shrink. Around 450, warriors from the Hunas kingdoms of central Asia began to attack the Gupta Empire's borders. The Hunas were nomads, also known as the Hepthalites, or Huns. The same groups also attacked kingdoms and empires in Europe during this era. After decades of peace, the Guptas' military was unprepared for these attacks. The empire had also grown weak from reduced trade, internal conflicts, and the need to keep conquered territories from rebelling. Skanda Gupta, who ruled from 455 to 457, managed to hold off the Huns' attacks until his death. After that, the Huns kept pressing their attacks. By around 550, the Gupta Empire had shrunk to a small kingdom.

## South India Rises

The fall of the Gupta Empire did not mean the end of South Asia's golden medieval age. Various kingdoms arose in northern India over the next few centuries, although none of them was as powerful or influential as the Guptas had been. However, a new power

photo: Getty Images
*A Hindu temple built during the Chola era, South India.*

emerged from southern India, which would have a strong influence on the civilizations and culture of South Asia. This new power was the Chola civilization that arose in modern-day Tamil Nadu.

The Cholas began their rise to power around the 100s. At the time, they were one of several ruling families in South India. By the 800s, they had become the strongest family in the region, and by the 1000s, they ruled most of South India and part of Sri Lanka. They would hold power until 1279. The Cholas often used symbolic actions to gain power as well as military strength. For example, Rajendra, who ruled from 1012 to 1044, claimed control over the River Ganges and the lands surrounding it by collecting water from the river and pouring it into a tank in one of his temples.

## Art and Religion Under the Cholas

Much like the Guptas, the Chola rulers were strong supporters of the arts. In particular, the Cholas built many brick and stone temples to various Hindu Gods. These temples had elaborately carved sculptures decorating their pillars, walls, and roofs. Bronze sculptures and paintings of religious scenes filled the temples. It was during the Chola age that the famous image of the God Shiva appeared in the form of Nataraja, performing the cosmic dance.

Discovery EDUCATION | SOCIAL STUDIES TECHBOOK

What changes and accomplishments defined South Asia's Golden Age?

Most people in the Chola civilization were Hindus, and most of those Hindus were Saivists, or worshipers of Shiva. Other religions such as Buddhism did survive during Chola rule, but Buddhists experienced persecution under some Chola kings. Some Chola rulers were hostile toward Vaishnavites, or worshippers of the Hindu God Vishnu, and to Jains. Although Buddhism was tolerated by the Cholas, it began to decline as Hinduism became more popular.

**The Delhi Sultanate**

In the early 1200s, a new power entered India. Muslim armies from central Asia invaded North India, and around 1206, they seized control of the region. While there were Islamic communities in South India dating back to the 700s, this was a new religion for northern South Asia. Sultan Iltutmish established a new capital city at Delhi, becoming the first ruler of the Delhi Sultanate. Muslims ruled the Delhi Sultanate until 1526, when the Mughal Empire—another Muslim empire—drove them out.

**Complete this activity to make an ad for an innovation from the Gupta or Chola era.**

Under the Delhi Sultanate, Indian and Muslim culture blended to create a unique new culture. This could be seen in the art, architecture, literature, and music of the time. Many mosques, or Muslim places of worship, were built inside the territories of the sultanate. Non-Muslims were not forced to convert, but they were forced to pay a tax if they did not. Many North Indians converted to Islam, though most remained Hindu. Eventually, Islam would become the predominant religion in some of the northernmost regions, which are now part of Pakistan. South India, which was still ruled by Hindus for most of this period, also remained mostly Hindu.

## Religious Awakenings

*What impact did the bhakti movement have on the culture of medieval South Asia?*

The bhakti movement arose in South India around 600. It focused on intense personal devotion to one of the Hindu Gods. Most followers of bhakti were devoted to one of the three major aspects of God: Brahma, Vishnu, or Shiva. Others followed one of the Hindu Goddesses, such as Shiva's wife, Parvati, or Lakshmi, the Goddess of prosperity and the wife of Vishnu. Some people believe bhakti was partly inspired by the Muslim idea of surrendering to one's God, though many ideas behind the bhakti movement date back to early Hindu texts. It also shares some characteristics of Sufism, the Muslim mystical tradition.

Bhakti first appeared as a popular social movement in the form of poems from the southern Tamil region. These poems took elements from love poetry and applied them to God instead of a human lover. Other poems compared the relationship to God with other human relationships, such as a child to a parent or a servant to a master. These poems were usually written in a common language and sung as part of rituals and celebrations. Other bhakti practices included making offerings to one's God in shrines that were built in homes and temples. Bhakti followers also wore emblems of their God and went on pilgrimages to holy sites.

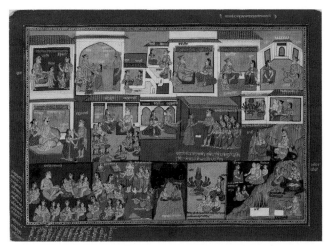

photo: Getty Images

*Page from a series on the* Bhagavata-Purana*, circa 1780.*

### The *Bhagavata-Purana*

One of the most important texts to come out of the medieval bhakti movement was the *Bhagavata-Purana*. This epic poem about the life of Krishna was written in its current form around 900. It was written in Sanskrit, unlike many bhakti poems, but it has the same theme of devotion to God. The detailed descriptions of Krishna's life and the reverent tone of the writing have made the *Bhagavata-Purana* a key text for many followers of Krishna. It has inspired many other texts, as well as countless paintings, sculptures, and other works of art.

### A Movement for the People

Perhaps because it emphasized personal devotion, the bhakti movement took religious power out of the hands of the elite clergy caste and put it into the hands of the common people. Bhakti was also very inclusive. Women could participate as well as men, as could people of every caste. In fact, women and *shudras*, or members of the lowest caste, were seen as examples of real humility. The only requirement for following the bhakti movement was passionate devotion to God. Female bhakti poets did have a harder time being accepted during their lifetimes.

## Love Poems to God

### *Who were Ramananda and Mirabai?*

Ramananda and Mirabai were religious figures from the 1400s and 1500s who wrote in the bhakti tradition. Both poets defied the customs of their time. Ramananda made his religious teachings available to anyone who wanted them. Mirabai refused to let her love and devotion for Krishna be held back by the rules of proper behavior for a woman. Although they lived and wrote toward the end of the medieval period in India, they are important examples of its artistic and innovative qualities.

## Ramananda

Ramananda was a Brahman priest living in the 1400s. He studied under Ramanujacharya, one of the most important thinkers of the movement. Ramananda became an ascetic devoted to the God Rama. Ascetics are people who devote their lives to religion, such as Christian monks. Ramananda finished his studies and became a teacher. When he was criticized for sharing meals with his students regardless of their caste, Ramananda became angry. He left and established his own ascetic sect.

Ramandanda's new sect, the Ramanandis, was more open and accepting than most Hindu religious groups at that time. He taught in Hindi, which was the common language, instead of Sanskrit. By this time, Sanskrit was only used by the upper classes and religious orders. Many Hindu scholars believe that his first 12 disciples included members of all castes and included women, a cobbler (which was considered a very low-status occupation), and a Muslim. Ramananda's actions and writings express the idea that one person could not be better than another because of his or her position in life. He taught that faith was perfect love directed toward God.

## Mirabai

Mirabai, also known as Meera Bai, was a bhakti poet who lived in the early 1500s. Mirabai was devoted to the God Krishna. Many Hindus believe she was an incarnation of Krishna's human lover, Radha. Mirabai had been devoted to Krishna since she was a child. She sang and danced before images of the God and even slept with a statue of Krishna in her bed.

When she grew up, Mirabai was married to a nobleman, but she did not give up her devotion to Krishna. She continued to sing and dance in public, proclaiming her love for Krishna in songs and poems. This angered her new family, who did not think her behavior was acceptable for a woman. They plotted against her many times, and once they even tried to poison her. Eventually, Mirabai left her home to make a pilgrimage and walked barefoot across the desert to visit temples to Krishna. She died in 1557, in a temple in the city of Ranchod.

Mirabai's poems, like her life, are devoted to the celebration of Krishna. She wrote about the joy of being connected to one's God and the pain of losing that connection. Her poems are filled with descriptions of longing for the divine and the joy that comes with it.

photo: Getty Images

*A poster of Mirabai, present-day India.*

# The Growth of Faiths

## *How did Hinduism and Buddhism spread and change?*

Hinduism and Buddhism both originally appeared in India. During the Middle Ages, India became a greater international power. As a result, these religions spread from India to other countries in South and East Asia. As they spread, each religion changed.

## Monastic Traditions

During this time, both Hinduism and Buddhism developed ascetic, or monastic, traditions. In Hinduism, an ascetic is someone who has retreated from the world instead of living as a householder. Hindu ascetics separate themselves from everyday life and focus on spirituality. Many Hindu ascetics practice separating themselves from worldly needs. Some early Hindu ascetics subjected themselves to pain such as staring at the sun until they went blind or fasting for very long periods of time. This was intended to lead to greater spiritual awareness by reducing attachment to the spiritual body.

Buddhism has always had a monastic tradition as well. This is because the goal of Buddhism is to end suffering by getting rid of attachment. Buddhist tradition tells that Buddha himself was an ascetic. He gave up a privileged life of wealth to pursue spiritual enlightenment. In the early days of Buddhism, ascetics wandered among different communities. Eventually, they created permanent settlements, or monasteries, where they developed monastic rules to govern life in these institutions.

## Buddhism Goes Underground

From 300 to 1200 CE, Hinduism and Buddhism were the major religions in India. Both the Guptas and the Cholas were Hindu and Hinduism grew during their reigns. Though rulers in both dynasties supported the construction of Buddhist temples and monuments, Buddhism began to decline during the Gupta and Chola ages. This decline continued under the Delhi Sultanate. During this time, many Buddhists moved their religious practice to beautifully decorated caves, where they could pray and meditate in peace. One of these Buddhist retreats is the Ajanta Caves. These caves, located near Mumbai, are filled with paintings and sculptures.

## Out of India

India became more of a global power over time. As merchants traveled to other countries to trade, they brought their religious ideas with them. Merchants and pilgrims from other countries also traveled to India. Some, such as Faxian from China, were already Buddhist. Others were exposed to Buddhism and Hinduism and brought the new religions back to their homes.

Hinduism spread through South Asia into Borneo, the Khmer Empire, Indonesia, and what are now Cambodia and Vietnam. These new countries made minor changes to Hindu practice. For example, in Khmer, Hindu practice often focused on the story of churning of the sea of milk, which was a minor story in Indian Hinduism. The main structure of Hinduism changed very little, however.

## The Changing Face of Buddhism

While Hinduism mainly spread south, Buddhism spread north into Burma, Nepal, Tibet, Korea, China, and eventually Japan. In the 300s BCE, India's emperor Asoka adopted Buddhist principles and sent missionaries into central Asia. Pilgrims such as Faxian traveled to India during this time. They translated Buddhist texts into Chinese and brought them back. This helped Buddhism expand throughout China.

Unlike Hinduism, Buddhism changed significantly as it expanded through Asia. Mahayana Buddhism, or "Great Vehicle" Buddhism, arose in India, but it became very popular in other countries, including Tibet, Korea, China, and Japan. Mahayana Buddhism focuses on the idea of the bodhisattva. A bodhisattva is a person who wants to become enlightened by helping others reach enlightenment as well. In India, most Buddhists practiced the more traditional form of Buddhism. By the 800s, many Buddhist ideas were absorbed by Hinduism, so some historians believe that many Buddhists

photo: Getty Images

*Carving of Buddha in the Ajanta Caves.*

converted to Hinduism. Gandharan Buddhism emerged in modern-day Afghanistan. It treated Buddha as a God to worship, focusing on his miracles and ignoring his past lives.

## Buddhism in Japan

Xuanzang was a Buddhist monk who lived in China in the 600s. In 629, he began a 16-year pilgrimage to India along the Silk Road, which was a network of trade routes between China and the western world. Like Faxian, he wanted to learn more about Indian Buddhism. Xuanzang translated Buddhist texts into Chinese and brought them home, where he was offered a court position by the emperor. In 653, a Japanese monk named Dosho came to study in the school that Xuanzang founded. Dosho brought Xuanzang's knowledge back to Japan and opened his own schools there. These schools became the most influential schools of Buddhism in Japan.

Buddhism in Japan was influenced by Shinto, the local religion of Japan. In Shinto, everything is alive and has its own spirit, including animals, plants, and stones. In the 1200s, a new form of Buddhism called Chan came from China to Japan, where it was renamed Zen. Zen Buddhism focuses on gaining enlightenment through meditation. In Zen, enlightenment often comes as a sudden flash of inspiration. By the 1500s, Zen had become the most popular form of Buddhism in Japan.

## East Meets West

### How did South Asia influence medieval Europe?

The innovations and discoveries made in medieval India had a strong influence on medieval Europe as well. The Gupta and Chola civilizations traded with countries in Southwest Asia, including Persia (modern-day Iran), Turkey, and Arabia, and in North Africa. These countries also traded with European merchants, mostly from Italy. They brought spices and cotton from India as well as silk and other goods from China. The trade route from China to Europe was called the Silk Road.

The Silk Road was not the only trade route that involved South Asia. Trade routes across the Indian Ocean allowed Indian merchants to sell goods to the Middle East and Africa. Calicut was one major Indian trade city famous for the fabric calico. Using the monsoon currents, Indian merchants used the Indian Ocean routes to trade with countries as far as Mozambique and China.

### South Asian Ideas in Europe

European merchants who traded with India and other South Asian countries often brought back more than silk and spices. The game of chess spread from India to Persia, and then to Italy by around 900 and the rest of Europe soon afterward. By around 1100, the discoveries in math and astronomy made by Indians began to spread to Europe as well. The Moors of North Africa brought algebra to Spain and Portugal around this time. Trade also exposed Europe to India's religious ideas, although medieval Europe stayed primarily Christian.

The spread of these ideas from the East would help bring Europe out of its so-called Dark Ages and into a rebirth of knowledge known as the Renaissance. The new ideas that reached Europe through trade with South Asia helped inspire many thinkers and scientists. Indian discoveries such as the decimal system gave Europeans a foundation on which to build modern math and science. The rediscovery of Greek and Roman knowledge, preserved in Islamic texts, also helped bring this about.

**Discovery** SOCIAL STUDIES
EDUCATION | **TECHBOOK**

What changes and accomplishments defined South Asia's Golden Age?

## The Age of Exploration

Western merchants wanted to buy spices and other goods directly from India, instead of paying extra money to Arabian merchants. Around 1400, many Western explorers began searching for a new sea route to India and the rest of Asia. This became known as the Age of Exploration. This sea route would allow them to trade directly with India and the rest of Asia. Although they did not find a simple sea route, the Age of Exploration led Europeans to find many new markets, as well as new lands to colonize. These new lands included the continents of North and South America.

photo: Getty Images

*Part of the collection at the Calico Museum of Textiles, Gujarat, India.*

### Consider the Essential Question:

What changes and accomplishments defined South Asia's Golden Age?

Go online to complete the Social Studies Explanation.

### Check for Understanding:

Describe the qualities of the Gupta Empire that would make it a golden age for North India. How did the actions of Gupta rulers contribute to the emergence of a golden age?

# 5.2 China's Reunification and Development

photo: Getty Images

## LESSON OVERVIEW

### Introduction

In this concept, you will explore Chinese history from the fall of the Han dynasty to the restoration of order in the Tang and Song dynasties. You will also learn about the artistic and philosophical contributions made during these dynasties.

### Key Vocabulary
Which terms do you already know?

- [ ] Buddhism
- [ ] census
- [ ] Chang'an
- [ ] China
- [ ] civil war
- [ ] Confucianism
- [ ] Daoism/ Taoism
- [ ] Europe
- [ ] Grand School
- [ ] Great Wall of China
- [ ] Han dynasty
- [ ] junk
- [ ] Li Yuan
- [ ] Mandate of Heaven
- [ ] Marco Polo
- [ ] Mediterranean Sea
- [ ] Middle East
- [ ] Neo- Confucianism
- [ ] Silk Road
- [ ] Song dynasty
- [ ] Tang Empire
- [ ] unification
- [ ] Yellow Turban Rebellion

### Essential Question

What were the greatest achievements of the Tang and Song dynasties?

### Lesson Objectives

By the end of this lesson, you should be able to:

- Explain the reasons for the fracturing of China.

- Identify important Chinese dynasties (Tang dynasty, Song dynasty) and the developments of Chinese culture during this era before the Mongol invasion.

- Analyze the evolution of Confucianism during this period and its impact on governmental systems.

## ENGAGE

**How has the meaning of "made in China" changed over time? Visit Engage to learn more.**

### Essential Question

What were the greatest achievements of the Tang and Song dynasties?

---

## EXPLORE

### The Fall of the Han Dynasty

*What led to the collapse of the Han dynasty?*

The Han dynasty ruled China from approximately 206 BCE to 220 CE. Many historians view this era as an important and prosperous period in Chinese culture and history. Even today, the Chinese people refer to themselves as "the people of Han."

The last ruler of the Han dynasty was Emperor Xiandi, who reigned until 220 CE, when he was forced to abdicate, or give up, the throne. Xiandi was not a strong emperor. Under his reign, court officials became corrupt and worked for their own gain instead of the good of China. Three main groups struggled for power within the government: court officials, the emperor's servants and bodyguards, and clansmen of the empress. But while these three powerful groups were fighting within, other powerful forces who were unsatisfied with the corrupt government were also battling for power and control.

#### A Shift in Beliefs

In China, the wealthy elite, or upper class, owned most of the land. This land was typically worked by peasants. The work the peasants did helped make the members of the elite class richer while the peasants remained poor. Hungry and powerless, the peasants turned away from the state religion of Confucianism, which taught that people should follow the rules of society, and turned to the philosophy of Daoism (also known as Taoism).

photo: Getty Images

*Lao Tzu is the chief figure associated with early Daosim (Taoism).*

Daoism, unlike Confucianism, taught that people should live simply and in harmony with the world around them. This harmony, called the Dao, or "The Way," was more important than any laws or social structure. In more practical, real-world terms, Daoism called for a return to a simple agricultural life. Daoism spread rapidly throughout China's peasants. Followers of Daoism believed that human intervention, even intervention by rulers, would disrupt the natural order. They did not believe that loyalty to the government was as important as followers of Confucianism did.

The peasants became increasingly frustrated with their positions and the growing corruption in government. They believed the emperor's servants had too much power over the emperor. In 184, these peasants attacked the North China Plains in the Yellow Turban Rebellion. This rebellion was led by Zhang Jue, a Daoist faith healer. The government spent great amounts of money from their trade and tax revenue to raise armies to counter the revolution. However, inefficiencies and corruption in the government prevented these efforts from being successful. The rebellion would continue for 20 years and would give rise to a time of uprisings and political turmoil. Eventually, warlords would begin to fight each other, dividing the power of the empire and leading to the end of the Han dynasty.

**Explore this interactive to learn more about key events that shaped China's reunification.**

## The Three Kingdoms

*What happened after the fall of the Han dynasty?*

With the central government weakened, ambitious generals and warlords took advantage of the power vacuum to try to seize control of China. The result was constant, brutal war that cost many thousands of lives. As a result of this fighting, the most powerful warlords eventually took control and divided China into three separate kingdoms: Wei, Wu, and Shu-Han. Without a strong emperor or central government, China descended into chaos and civil war. This fighting would last for approximately 60 years from 220 to 280. Although one of China's greatest poets, Dao Yuanming, came from this era, overall there was very little cultural development during this time. It was a time that was similar to the Dark Ages in Europe. However, unlike the Dark Ages, the Chinese people did not lose their knowledge or skills during the Three Kingdoms era.

The leader of each kingdom claimed to be the next emperor of all of China. The strongest of the three leaders was General Cao Cao, who had once been a protector of Emperor Xiandi. Cao Cao founded the Wei kingdom in northern China. Xiandi remained the leader of the new kingdom in title, but Cao Cao held the true power. When Cao Cao died in 220, Xiandi turned over the imperial throne to Cao Cao's son, Cao Pi. This was the beginning of the Wei dynasty. The Wei conquered the Shu-Han Kingdom in approximately 263, leaving only two powers in China.

photo: Getty Images

*A statue of a knight in armor, Wei dynasty.*

Despite its success against the Shu-Han, the Wei dynasty did not last long. In 265, less than 50 years after its founding, a Wei general named Wudi (also referred to as Sima Yan) turned against Cao Pi and seized the throne from him. In 280, Wudi conquered the Wu kingdom, declared himself emperor, and founded the Jin dynasty.

Wudi died only 10 years after taking the throne. He had briefly reunited China, but the country was too weakened by decades of fighting to stay together after his death. China's fragile unity was quickly destroyed by internal revolts and invading nomads from the north. The Jin dynasty ruled until 420, but was under constant attacks from outside forces and internal unrest. The dynasty ended over 200 years before China was truly unified.

## The Sui Dynasty

### How was China finally reunited?

Emperor Wendi, the man who would finally reunite China, was not entirely Chinese. He was also partly Mongolian, the country to the north of China. In the 400 years after the fall of the Han dynasty, constant warfare and rapid changes of leadership fragmented China. Wendi was an official in the Bei Zhou court of northern China. When the system collapsed in 581, Wendi took advantage of the chaos and established the Sui dynasty. During the 580s, Wendi conquered the western and southern regions of China. He united the entire country under a single emperor for the first time in 400 years.

photo: Getty Images

*Lead Bactrian camel produced in the late Sui or early Tang dynasty.*

### Life During the Sui Dynasty

Wendi did more than just bring back the unity of the Han dynasty. He also restored many of the policies that had made the Han dynasty strong. Confucian rituals were once again used in government. Laws, land distribution systems, and taxes were simplified and made fairer. A careful census, or counting of the population, was taken to learn how many people were living in China. Wendi also developed a network of administrators who would make local laws consistent and fair.

The Sui dynasty was also the beginning of a golden age of art and culture. Wendi supported scholars and received their support in return. Wendi became a patron, or supporter, of the arts. Painters came to his court from all over the country. The religion of Buddhism was encouraged to flourish alongside Confucianism. Many large and beautiful stone Buddha statues throughout China were constructed during the Sui era. Buddhism grew in popularity over the course of the Sui era, and experienced a golden age in China during the next era of the Tang dynasty.

### The Fall of the Sui Dynasty

After Wendi's death in 604, his heir, Yangdi, continued his policies. Yangdi strengthened his position in South China, and developed a set of Confucian tests for government officials that would be used in the Tang and Song dynasties. Unfortunately, he was also greedy and cruel.

Yangdi loved luxury and wanted to increase his wealth and power. Under his reign, relations with the Turks, the people to the west, broke down. This led to the threat of invasion and rebellion. Yangdi also started a war with Korea and forced many peasants into military service. As a result, there were few farmers left to grow food. This led to famine and rebellion. The war in Korea failed, and Yangdi was killed by a member of his court in 618.

Gongdi was the third and last Sui emperor. He reigned for less than a year before he was overthrown by Li Yuan, who would go on to establish the Tang dynasty.

## The Tang Dynasty

*How did the Tang dynasty succeed where the Sui dynasty failed?*

Li Yuan (566–635) was a general during the Sui era. When the Sui dynasty collapsed in 618, Li Yuan headed one of several groups fighting to take control during the period of rebellion and chaos. By 621, he had taken control of eastern China. By 624, he held most of the country, with only a few groups of rebels remaining in the north.

The influence of the Tang dynasty reached much farther than China. The neighboring regions of Japan, Korea, and Vietnam recognized China as the dominant regional power. Chinese culture heavily influenced their cultures. Military success spread this powerful Chinese influence throughout central Asia. The expansion of trade through the Silk Road led to cultural exchanges that stretched through much of Eurasia.

Discovery SOCIAL STUDIES
EDUCATION | TECHBOOK

What were the greatest achievements of the Tang and Song dynasties?

One of the major reasons Li Yuan succeeded was that he built on the good ideas of the Sui dynasty, while avoiding its mistakes. In fact, because the Sui dynasty was so short, and so many of its achievements were continued by the Tang dynasty, the two are sometimes considered part of the same era.

The Tang dynasty was an age of prosperity. Many civic improvements were made throughout the empire. One of the most important developments was the Grand Canal. The canal, which was begun under Sui emperor Yangdi, connected a network of canals that already existed across northern and southern China. The canal improved trade and travel throughout the empire and brought wealth to more of the country than ever before.

The restoration of Han policies that began during the Sui dynasty expanded during the Tang dynasty. The Han dynasty had staffed a bureaucracy with civil servants recommended by local officials. The Sui dynasty systematized this process and made it official. The Tang dynasty set up schools where civil service candidates could study. The candidates were tested on their knowledge of Confucianism, which was also restored by the Sui and supported by the Tang dynasty.

The golden age of Chinese culture that had begun in the Sui dynasty was brought to new heights during the Tang dynasty. Music from Persia and central Asia was played alongside traditional Chinese court music and common music. The famous poet Li Bo (701–762, also known as Li Bai), a Daoist wanderer, wrote during the Tang era.

photo: Getty Images

*The Grand Canal made transportation through China much easier.*

Poems often accompanied paintings. It was believed that the elaborate brushstroke calligraphy used in Chinese writing added beauty to the paintings. Portraits of important figures, along with paintings of court scenes, were popular during this age. Sculpture and metalwork also flourished during this time. Sculptures often focused on religious subjects, especially the Buddha. Metalworkers created jewelry and ritual objects. Gold and silver were commonly used during this time.

In the second half of the 700s, rebellions broke out in the northeast. Emperor Xuanzong fled west to the Sichuan region. The rebellions were eventually stopped, but the country's sense of unity was splintered. By the second half of the 800s, more rebellions broke out and the government grew weaker. In 907, the Tang dynasty collapsed and China split into five separate kingdoms.

# A Golden Age

## How did the Song dynasty rise to power?

The era following the end of the Tang dynasty in 907 was known as the Five Dynasties period in the north. It was called the Five Dynasties period because there were five short-lived dynasties that gained control of China before the Song dynasty established long-term control. In the south, it was known as the Ten Kingdoms period because that region split into ten small, independent nations.

photo: Getty Images

*The Zhonghua Gate, Nanjing, China, was built during the Ten Kingdoms.*

In the north, the military inspector-general Taizu (927–976) seized the throne. Taizu founded the Song dynasty, which would last until 1279. After 1127, the northern Song kingdom was destroyed by the Jin, so only the southern kingdom remained.

Many historians consider the era of the Song dynasty to be a golden age. Many policies from the Sui and Tang dynasties were carried on. These included the systems of land distribution and taxation. The Song dynasty leaders also built on the Han dynasty ideas of meritocracy, promoting the most skilled to positions of wealth and power. The leaders strengthened the education system and created a civil service exam, a test taken by the candidates for government jobs. These tests stressed the teachings of Confucius. An individual's performance on the tests determined whether or not he received the job. These tests laid the basis for future meritocracies, social systems that give opportunities to people based on their merit or ability. Civil service exams are still used to screen candidates for government jobs in many countries throughout the world today.

The exams were open only to men. Although technically open to all social classes, the tests were usually taken by wealthier, more educated members of society who could afford to study for the tests. Once in a governmental position, individuals could be promoted based on performance. The civil service system helped create a government with qualified professionals in many important positions. However, the civil service exams did not eliminate corruption. Occasionally, individuals cheated on the tests, and powerful families were still able to use their influence to place their children in high positions, with or without qualifications.

**Explore this resource to analyze Chinese landscape painting, and then design your own creation.**

The population exploded during this time, and more people began living in cities. This led to the growth of restaurants and food markets, theaters, and seasonal festivals. With more people living in the cities, the culture of China also went through a golden age.

# Art and War

## What achievements occurred during the Song dynasty?

The Song dynasty was a time of incredible innovation. The Chinese had had the ability to print since the Han dynasty, but during the Song dynasty, they began to create paper money. The money helped standardize currency across the empire. Movable type was also invented during the Song era, based on the technique of making prints from carved blocks of wood. However, the large number of Chinese characters made movable type printing less practical than it would be in the West, so it was not used often.

There were also great scientific innovations during this period. One of the most impressive was the invention of the first mechanical clock, which was driven by water. The clock was used mostly as a show piece, but the technology developed to create it would serve as the foundation for future mechanical clocks.

Farming technology improved greatly during the Song dynasty. Farmers began to use complex tools such as the three-shared plow and the harrow, both of which made farming more efficient. The introduction of Champa rice, a drought-resistant strain of rice from the area that is now Vietnam, also advanced agricultural development.

The Chinese also made significant advances in military technology. Gunpowder was accidentally discovered by alchemists, or mystical scientists, during this time. It was first used in fireworks, and then later was used in battle to propel arrows. The crossbow was another significant invention of the time. While a bow and arrow depended on the strength of the bowman, the crossbow could be fired by using a trigger. This made the weapon more efficient, reliable, and accurate.

photo: Getty Images

*A sample of Song-era printing.*

The arts during this time became less stiff and formal, and more natural, as you can see in the poems of Dao Qian, also known as Dao Yuanming. Natural scenes, especially mountains, rivers, and flowers, were very popular paintings during this time. Huge statues of the Buddha were carved in China, Japan, and Korea. Architectural styles, such as the famous curved pavilion roof, also date from this period.

Porcelain, commonly called "china" in the West, and other ceramics were used for everything from cookware and plates to decorative vases and detailed figurines. Then, of course, there was silk. Luxurious silk fabric was one of China's most valuable products—and one of its most closely guarded secrets.

The Chinese traded these goods, and transportation was a crucial aspect of the Song economy. Water transport was the cheapest method, with rivers proving very useful in the South. In the North, water transport was also employed, but it was often directed through the Grand Canal, which led to the Yangtze River.

## Silk and the Silk Road

### How did silk impact trade in China?

Silk was China's most important export during the Song dynasty, and it remains so to this day. It is strong, soft, lightweight, and lustrous. Silk has been considered a luxury for centuries, and was often reserved for royalty. Silk fabric was used to make clothing, banners, painting surfaces, fans, and many other things.

For hundreds of years, China was the only country that produced silk because the process of making silk was a carefully guarded secret. Exporting silkworm eggs was a crime. There are many stories of people smuggling silk and silkworm caterpillars out of China during this time. Many of them are romantic fables, but eventually the secret did get out. Around 550, two monks hid silkworm eggs in hollow bamboo staffs and brought them to the court of the Byzantine emperor Justinian. Eventually, silk production spread throughout Europe and the Middle East. But while China was no longer the only country producing silk, the high quality and exotic beauty of Chinese silk still made it very popular.

The network of roads taken by merchants traveling west was known as the Silk Road. It was originally established during the Han dynasty. However, trade increased during the Sui and Tang dynasties, along with interest in Western art, music, and ideas. The Silk Road's traffic reached its peak during the Song dynasty, which was tied to the era's improving prosperity and culture. The increased trade led to a prosperous and growing middle class in China.

The Silk Road ran from Chang'an in north-central China through central Asia to the east coast of the Mediterranean Sea. Merchants loaded up camels with goods to sell from China: furs, spices, silk, ceramics, jade, bronze, and iron, and animals and plants. They brought back money and goods from Turkey, Persia, Greece, and other countries from the Mediterranean region, including gold, jewels, ivory, and glass.

Discovery EDUCATION | SOCIAL STUDIES TECHBOOK

What were the greatest achievements of the Tang and Song dynasties?

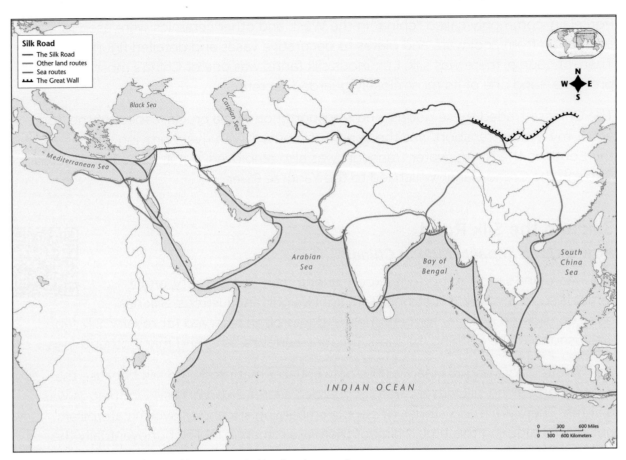

*The Silk Road consisted of several interconnected land and sea routes.*

Travelers along the Silk Road were protected by the Great Wall of China. Originally built to keep out invaders from the north, the wall was expanded as trade with the Western world increased. Open trade with the West brought great wealth and new ideas to both regions. In the 1200s, Italian explorer Marco Polo visited China and brought Chinese culture back to Europe. Chinese influences spread to the West, and ideas from central Asia and the Middle East were brought back to China. This increased the wealth and diversity of Chinese culture.

## The Rise of Neo-Confucianism

*How did Confucianism rise in popularity during the Song dynasty?*

During the Han dynasty, Emperor Wudi made Confucianism the state philosophy of China. However, after the fall of the Han dynasty, and the period of unrest that followed, Daoism and Buddhism became extremely popular among the Chinese people. Confucianism became a less popular and influential way of life.

photo: Getty Images
*Figure of Bodhisattva Guanyin from the Song dynasty.*

This would change with the rise of Neo-Confucianism (or "new" Confucianism) during the Song dynasty. Emperor Wendi of the Sui dynasty saw that Confucianism could help strengthen his rule. Confucianism supported an emperor's right to rule with the Mandate of Heaven, which stated that emperors were chosen to rule by the gods. Confucianism also called for following the rule of law, loyalty to a just and fair monarch, and respect for one's rulers and ancestors.

During the Tang dynasty, the rulers were generally Daoist. However, they encouraged Buddhism, which greatly expanded in popularity during this period. In 845, the Tang emperor Wuzong reversed this position by persecuting Buddhists and destroying many Buddhist temples. Even so, the religion remained popular.

By the time of the Song dynasty, Buddhism and Daoism had become very popular among the population. Buddhism, unlike Daoism and Confucianism, did not begin in China. Buddhism was brought to China by travelers and traders from India. Buddhists believe that to end suffering, which is caused by desire, one must end his or her attachment to things of this world. This is accomplished through meditation, good deeds, and compassion to all living things.

Neo-Confucianism used elements of Buddhism and Daoism to create a system that was more compassionate and accessible than the original Confucian faith had been. These changes increased the popularity of Neo-Confucianism. Its popularity was also increased by the actions of the government, which used Neo-Confucianism to strengthen its authority.

## Neo-Confucianism in the Song Dynasty

*Why was Neo-Confucianism important to the Song dynasty?*

Neo-Confucianism helped strengthen the power of the rulers of the Song dynasty. The Mandate of Heaven placed an importance on loyalty and the order of law. It was also an important tool for selecting government officials. During the Three Kingdoms period, government positions were given to those with power, wealth, or connections. But in the Sui dynasty, similar to the Han dynasty, positions were once again awarded on a system of merit.

Discovery EDUCATION | SOCIAL STUDIES TECHBOOK

What were the greatest achievements of the Tang and Song dynasties?

In this meritocracy, government positions were given to those who proved they were most qualified by passing a civil service examination. The Tang and Song emperors not only carried on this process, but also strengthened it. This system of merit created a prestigious scholar-official class. This class consisted of government officials who possessed superior academic skills and demonstrated political clout.

During the Song period, candidates could no longer be recommended by other government officials. To become a government official in the Song dynasty, candidates had to pass a test based on Confucian ideas and beliefs. Written tests had been used in some degree since the Sui dynasty, but now they were the standard path for success and were much more difficult.

photo: Getty Images

*Confucian temple, built during the Song dynasty, Nanjing, China.*

The tests were designed to draw men with literary and artistic educations to the government to counteract the presence of the military-minded leaders already present. Candidates were required to know the Confucian texts such as the *Four Books* and the *Five Classics*. They also had to write poetry and answer questions on policy, although the tests focused more on general knowledge than on political and governmental issues.

The tests were usually taken by male members of the wealthy land-holding classes who could afford to study, but they were open to anyone. The tests were difficult and passing them carried a certain degree of prestige. Candidates typically had to take the tests several times before passing. This rigorous standard for obtaining government offices led to a class of leaders known as the scholar-officials.

The order that was restored to the government mirrored the order that was restored to the country by China's reunification. The Tang and Song dynasties brought order back to the Chinese empire and government and created an environment where innovation and cultural achievement were possible.

**Consider the Essential Question:**

What were the greatest achievements of the Tang and Song dynasties?

Go online to complete the Social Studies Explanation.

**Check for Understanding:**

How did the silk trade shape the development of China during the Song dynasty? Be sure to provide examples and details in your answer.

photo: Getty Images

# 5.3 The Mongols

## LESSON OVERVIEW

### Introduction

In this concept, you will learn about the rise of the Mongol Empire and how the Mongols' rule affected China and neighboring civilizations.

### Essential Question

How did Mongol conquest change relations between regional societies?

### Lesson Objectives

By the end of this lesson, you should be able to:

- Explain the expansion of the Mongolian Empire.
- Analyze the impact of Mongol rule on Chinese civilization and other cultures.

### Key Vocabulary

Which terms do you already know?

- [ ] Africa
- [ ] Baghdad
- [ ] Beijing
- [ ] Black Sea
- [ ] Catholic Church
- [ ] China
- [ ] Christopher Columbus
- [ ] commonwealth
- [ ] Crusaders/ Crusades
- [ ] England
- [ ] Eurasia
- [ ] Genghis Khan
- [ ] Gobi Desert
- [ ] Great Schism
- [ ] Great Wall of China
- [ ] Himalayas
- [ ] Huns
- [ ] Iraq
- [ ] John Calvin
- [ ] King Henry VIII
- [ ] Korea
- [ ] Marco Polo
- [ ] Martin Luther
- [ ] Mediterranean Sea
- [ ] Mongolia
- [ ] Mongols
- [ ] Muslims
- [ ] New Testament
- [ ] nomadic
- [ ] Pax Mongolica
- [ ] Pax Romana
- [ ] Persian Gulf
- [ ] pope
- [ ] Protestant Church
- [ ] Protestant Reformation
- [ ] Protestantism
- [ ] reform/social reform
- [ ] Silk Road
- [ ] Song dynasty
- [ ] steppe
- [ ] trade
- [ ] William Tyndale

## ENGAGE

**Why was Marco Polo's adventure an important historical event? Visit Engage to learn more.**

### Essential Question

How did Mongol conquest change relations between regional societies?

## EXPLORE

### The Beginnings of the Mongol Empire

*How did Genghis Khan establish the Mongol Empire?*

North of the Great Wall of China and southeast of Lake Baikal in Russia lies the nation of Mongolia, a mixture of climates, desert, and steppe. A steppe is a large area of flat grassland. In the 1100s, this region was occupied by many related nomadic tribes. The tribes were made up of sheep and horse herders, who were dependent on those animals for food. The tribes often formed shifting alliances that were usually at war with one another. The Mongols were one of these tribes, and not necessarily the most dangerous one. Around 1155, a son was born to Hoelun, the wife of the Mongol *khan*, a term which means "leader." His name was Temujin (te MOO jin).

Legends are told about Temujin's childhood and his rise to power. As with all legends, it can be hard to determine how much of the information is based on facts. It is said that Temujin declared himself the leader of the Mongols when he was 12, after his father was poisoned at a feast by members of a rival tribe. To cement his power, the young leader killed his half-brother. However, at the age of 20, he was captured and enslaved by another enemy tribe. He escaped and joined other members of his tribe and several related clans to form a strong force of 20,000 men.

*photo: Getty Images*
*A small, present-day Mongol village on the steppe.*

Temujin defeated enemy tribes through a combination of military force, shrewd diplomacy, and merciless brutality. He made use of spies and a signaling system that combined smoke, fire, drums, and flags. His mounted warriors could live for days on horseback. Their saddlebags carried food, spare clothes, tools, and weapons. The saddlebags were waterproof and could be used as life preservers when crossing rivers. By commanding horses with the pressure of their legs alone, Mongol warriors could even shoot arrows at a full gallop. When closing on the enemy, they used hooked lances that could pull men off their horses. By 1206, through alliances and conquests, Temujin had united all the tribes of Mongolia and built a force of 80,000 men. Tribal leaders granted him the title of Supreme Ruler—Genghis Khan.

Genghis Khan set out to build a new state by taking already established laws and customs of the tribes and formulating his own. The old tribal names no longer mattered, he declared, because the people were now all part of the Great Mongol Nation. He abolished the old noble titles among the tribes and clans. All such titles now belonged to the state, not to individuals or families. He divided his army into well-disciplined units of 1,000 and 10,000. Warriors who showed they had leadership abilities became generals, even if they came from lowly families. He even set some as commanders over members of his own family.

## Laws of the Mongol Empire

*How did Genghis Khan rule his empire?*

Genghis's first new law outlawed the kidnapping of women from rival tribes. Genghis's wife, Borte, had once been kidnapped, and it was uncertain

*photo: Getty Images*

*A portrait of Ghengis Khan.*

whether her first son had been fathered by Khan or by her kidnapper. The chieftain declared all Mongol children legitimate, whether born to a man's legal wife or not. Other laws he declared included forbidding one Mongol to enslave another. Horse thievery was to be punished by death. Anyone who found stolen goods and failed to turn them in to the proper authorities would be punished. He forbade hunting during the spring and summer breeding seasons. The rest of the year, hunters had to limit their kill to what they needed for food.

Genghis proclaimed these laws in the traditional Mongol way, which was in a great meeting of the tribes on the open steppe. To each new announcement, the assembled men and women voiced their approval with the traditional Mongol cry, "Hurray! Hurray! Hurray!" Six years of peace followed Temujin's elevation to Genghis Khan. He forged alliances with neighboring nations by declaring them relatives of the Mongols when he married his daughters to their leaders.

They cemented their alliances to Genghis by bringing rich gifts all the way from China, across the Gobi Desert. Some of the gifts came from the Muslim lands of western Asia. Genghis was aware that he ruled a powerful nation, but one that was poor in trade goods. Soon, the chance would come for him to change that situation.

## The Mongol Conquest of China
### *How did the Mongols gain control of China?*

China was not a united empire when Genghis Khan turned his sights south. The Song dynasty ruled the southern part of China, while the north was ruled by a group of small states that were formerly nomadic tribes. The largest of these states was the Jurched kingdom. It controlled much of northern China from its capital at Zhongdu (modern-day Beijing) and claimed lordship over the tribes of the steppe. In 1211, the Jurched king demanded that Genghis Khan acknowledge that the Jurched rulers were his overlords. Genghis's response was to cross the Gobi Desert, invade the Jurched kingdom, and make it his first conquest.

The Mongols had several advantages over other armies. Their force consisted only of horsemen, with no foot soldiers to slow them down. They also traveled without supply wagons. Each soldier carried food for 10 days, "cooking" his meat only by placing it under his saddle until it was soft enough to chew. They could camp without fires, which might

photo: Pixabay

*Ghengis Khan, founder of the Mongol Empire.*

warn enemies of their approach. Instead of marching in tight columns, they spread out over wide areas. They sent scouts to spy out the territory they would cover each day. Because they had no written language, orders were transmitted orally after being memorized. And unlike other warrior cultures, the Mongols saw no glory in a brave death during battle. Their goal was to win with as little loss of Mongol life as possible.

The Mongols were practiced in steppe warfare but had no experience in attacking fortified cities. They learned quickly. They learned to defeat their enemies before a battle even began by breaking their spirit. Mongols would appear outside cities, destroy the food supply, and then ride away for a day or two. They would only return when the enemy thought they were safe. The Mongol soldiers made secret alliances with the tribes their enemies ruled, turning the subordinates against their rulers when the fighting began. They drove crowds of refugees before them as they would livestock, and they used enemy captives as human shields. They also spread rumors to create hope, fear, or confusion. Once a city was subjected to the Mongols' tactics and had been demoralized, the sudden attack would follow from all directions. By 1215, Genghis Khan was lord of northern China.

## Mongol Conquests

*How did the Mongols expand their empire in Asia?*

The riches of the Silk Road were now flowing northward out of China toward the steppe. The Mongols now had more silk than they knew what to do with. Genghis already knew that trade along the great east-west road was controlled by Persian merchants in the central Asian cities of Bukhara and Samarkand (now in Uzbekistan). Because no one power controlled all of the Silk Road, it was not possible to travel from one end to the other safely. Traders from China, the Muslim Caliphates, and Europeans sold their goods to Persian middlemen who made huge profits selling them to other traders going in the opposite direction.

The central power in these central Asian lands was a Turkish dynasty called Khwarazim. In 1217, Genghis sent a diplomatic mission to establish trade relations with the Turks. A provincial governor captured and killed the envoys, possibly believing they were spies. Genghis sent a diplomat to the Khwarazim ruler, Shah Muhammad. He demanded that the offending governor be sent to him as a prisoner. Shah Muhammad had the diplomat killed and sent his head back instead. This gave Genghis Khan the excuse he needed to invade the Khwarazim Empire. In 1219, he led a force of 200,000 men against the Khwarazim cities.

*photo: Getty Images*

*An illustration of battle between the Khwarazim army and the Mongols.*

By then, the Mongols had perfected the tactics that they had used against the Chinese cities. They swept through central Asia, sparing cities that surrendered without a fight but destroying those that resisted. People who survived the sieges were driven in front of the Mongol armies as human shields. Pyramids of skulls were all that remained where once there were thriving cities. Irrigation systems were destroyed so that the land was only good for grazing and not farming. By 1221, the Mongols were masters of central Asia.

## From China to Hungary

*What happened to the Mongol Empire after Genghis Khan died?*

Genghis Khan died in 1227, dividing his empire among his sons. Legends surround his death, as they did his life. Some say he fell off a horse while hunting; others say he died of a lung disease. He was buried in a secret place near his tribal homeland, and supposedly anyone who learned where his grave was located was killed. Genghis's favorite son, Ogedei, was given China and the rest of eastern Asia. Chagatai took over central Asia, while Genghis's grandson Batu controlled the western part of the empire.

Other empires based on the conquests of one ruler, such as Alexander the Great, did not long survive their founders. This did not happen with the Mongol Empire. Though Genghis's sons and grandsons sometimes fought each other for control, the empire continued to expand. In 1235, Mongol forces invaded the Chinese territory of the Song dynasty. By 1240, the Mongols controlled Kiev, Russia's greatest trading center. A force of German knights could not keep them from taking over the rich grazing lands of Hungary in 1241. The Arab cultural capital of Baghdad was sacked by the Mongols in 1258. The following year, Kublai Khan, Genghis's grandson, completed the conquest of China.

photo: Getty Images

*An illustration of Kublai Khan, Great Khan of the Mongol Empire.*

**Explore this interactive to learn more about how the Mongols were able to conquer so much territory.**

By 1290, the Mongols reigned from the Pacific Ocean to the Black and Mediterranean Seas, from the Himalayan Mountains to the Persian Gulf. The laws that Genghis Khan had decreed for the tribes of the steppe were in force from Vietnam to Hungary, from Korea to Iraq. Blood feuds, theft, and lying for one's own advantage were outlawed. Even the environment was protected under Mongol laws. Bathing in rivers and streams that were used for drinking water was forbidden. If a Mongol soldier dropped any item while on the march, the soldier behind him was under orders to pick it up.

## Life Under the Mongols

*What was life like in the Mongol Empire?*

Women held more rights under the Mongol Empire than in most other cultures at that time. Because Mongol men were all mobilized for war, women took on many economic roles. Some even served in the army. They had the right to divorce and to own property. These Mongol customs became laws throughout the empire. Genghis Khan's daughter-in-law, Sorkhokhtani (Su oh loo he ti en ee) was one of the most remarkable leaders of her time. She respected Chinese culture, protected Chinese peasants, and guided her son Kublai Khan to follow her example.

The Mongols imposed their laws on the peoples they conquered but did not interfere with their culture. The ancient Romans had forced conquered peoples to learn Latin and grow foods that Romans ate. The Romans also built cities, following the Roman plan, across the empire, regardless of local custom. The Mongols did not force any such changes on their subjects. They respected local customs and languages. They granted freedom of religion to all, including lands that had been dominated by Muslims, Buddhists, Christians, and other traditional religions. The laws even kept religious leaders and certain other professionals exempt from paying taxes.

photo: Getty Images

*Kublai Khan established himself as the emperor of China.*

Kublai Khan established himself in China as the Great Khan over his brother and cousins, who ruled other parts of the empire, thus establishing the Yuan dynasty in China. He reorganized the Chinese government and made a point of mixing foreigners with Chinese officials so they could learn from one another. He had a staff of scribes and translators fluent in all the major languages of his empire. He even tried to invent an alphabet that could be used for all languages. Most important, he followed his mother's lead in honoring ancient Chinese traditions. He built schools that taught the texts long studied by Chinese scholars and organized Chinese peasants in a form of local self-government, building more than 20,000 public schools for their children.

## The Pax Mongolica

### *How did trade flourish under the Mongols?*

In just 50 years, the Mongols had conquered the largest empire the world had ever known. Now, across their vast realm, warfare all but ceased. A Pax Mongolica—Latin for "Mongolian peace"—was in force. Historians use this term to compare it with the Pax Romana. With most of Eurasia under one law, nations, tribes, and religious communities that had been enemies for centuries were forced to respect one another. With peace came a stability that allowed trade to grow. For the grandsons of Genghis Khan, war gave way to a passion for business.

### Transporting Goods

The Mongols were not an urban people. They did not concentrate business and wealth in a single capital. They recognized that parts of their empire produced goods that were scarce and greatly desired in other parts. Moving them efficiently from one place to another would benefit all; taxing the buying and selling of these goods would increase their own wealth. Along the major trade routes, the Mongols established shelters stocked with provisions a day's travel apart. They issued tablets of gold, silver, or wood for traders to wear around their necks. These passes allowed their bearers to travel freely throughout the empire. They guaranteed the traders transport, guides, protection, places to stay, credit, and freedom from local taxes.

As with goods, so it was with people. The Mongol rulers identified craftspeople, engineers, translators, scientists, and others with special skills, including artists and entertainers. They moved them from one part of the empire to another along the trade routes, wherever their talents might be best used.

In this way, Persian doctors learned techniques of Chinese medicine, while Arabs, who were more skilled in surgery, taught the Chinese. Kublai Khan brought together scholars who were experts in Chinese, Arab, and Greek geography. The result was the creation of the most accurate maps and globes of the time period. Mongol traders used this knowledge to move goods by sea more efficiently.

photo: Getty Images

*An illustrated map depicting Marco Polo's journey on the Silk Road.*

Crops, along with the tools and techniques used in farming and cooking them, also found new uses in new places. The Mongols introduced Chinese goods such as tea and rice to other parts of their empire and lemon trees from the Middle East to China. Civilians experimented with fruits and vegetables to find which varieties would grow best in certain climate zones. They developed new varieties and hybrids.

## Mongol Peace

The entire Silk Road now lay under the protection of the Mongol Peace. For more than 150 years, Christians and Muslims had been fighting the wars known as the Crusades. Europeans had been blocked from trade with East Asia by the Muslim states that lay between them. Now, the Mongols had split the Muslim world. Peace reigned along the entire length of the great trade route. For the first time, European traders were beginning to venture eastward toward the almost legendary land they knew as Cathay. The first to arrive at Kublai Khan's court were Europeans in 1266 named the Polos. Their relationship with the Mongols was to reveal the wealth and culture of China to Europeans. The resulting desire for trade with East Asia aroused European imagination and changed the course of world history.

# West Meets East

## *Who was Marco Polo?*

While the Mongols were expanding trade through their empire, the Italian city-state of Venice was the richest trading power in Europe, rivaled only by Genoa. Both of these powerful city-states traded by sea, using advances in nautical technology to increase the number of voyages they could make and the amount of goods they could trade. The Genoese established several hundred ports across the Mediterranean and Atlantic coast of Europe. The Venetians sent six fleets out every year to places as far as England, Russia, and Northwest Africa. Both city-states controlled trade with Asia, sending metal products and silver from Europe to China in exchange for silk and other goods from the East. By the middle of the 1200s, Venetian traders were probing by land eastward along the Silk Road.

The brothers Niccolo and Maffeo Polo, stranded for three years by a local war in central Asia, were rescued by a Mongol ambassador. He told them that the Great Khan had never met a Western European before and would be pleased to host them at his court. They were escorted over land to Beijing, where they were received lavishly by Kublai Khan in 1266.

### The Polo Family

The Polo brothers spoke a Turkic traders' dialect that Kublai could understand. He was curious about their homeland. They told him about the pope and the Catholic Church, and he hinted that he might be interested in becoming a Christian. The Polos returned to Italy as the Khan's official ambassadors to the pope. The head of the Catholic Church was not much interested in China. Instead of the 100 priests the khan had requested for the brothers to bring back to China, he sent two friars. The friars turned back early in the journey.

*photo: Getty Images*

*Marco Polo in the presence of Kublai Khan.*

Also on the Polos' second journey to China was Niccolo's teenage son, Marco. Young Marco Polo impressed the khan with his intelligence and his skill at learning languages. He was made an official of the khan's government and served as a diplomat on missions all over China, Southeast Asia, and the Mongol homeland. His father and uncle also served Kublai Khan as advisers. They were anxious to get home, however, as the khan was getting old. They did not know how they and the great fortune they had amassed would fare if the khan were to die. In 1292, they were asked to escort a Mongol princess to her wedding in Iran. Traveling by sea, they completed their mission and continued home. Marco Polo had spent 17 years in China and returned home a wealthy man.

## Marco Polo's Book

*How did Marco Polo's travels influence Europe?*

Six years later, Marco Polo was serving as captain of a ship in Venice's navy. He was captured in battle and spent a year in prison. During that year, he dictated the story of his travels to another prisoner, who happened to be a writer. Upon his release, Polo published *Description of the World* or *The Travels of Marco Polo*. For many Europeans, it was their first exposure to China and the Mongol Empire, which they had known about only through tales of Mongol ferocity in battle. They learned of China's wealth and technology; its food, plants, and animals; and its canal-based transportation system. Polo's book described paper money and the khan's swift postal system. It also described China's industries, economy, its great cities, and the wonders of the khan's court.

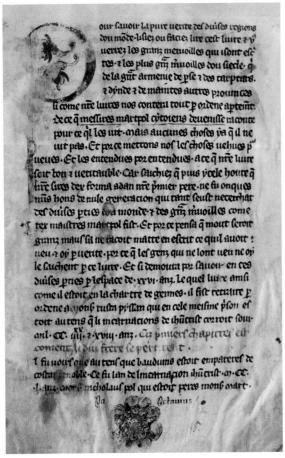

*Marco Polo arriving at Hormuz in the Persian Gulf.*

*Marco Polo kept records of all that he saw in his travels. Later, these records became a book known as* The Travels of Marco Polo.

Polo's book was translated into nearly every European language. Many people could not believe that what he described was true. They ridiculed him as "Marco of a million lies." Yet, the book described the journey to China in such accurate detail that merchants and travelers used it as a guide well into the 1800s. European traders now could aspire to profits from trade with China. Its products included not only silk, but also the fine ceramics still known today as "china," as well as spices from the islands of the Southwest Pacific.

The Mongol Empire broke apart in the 1400s. It lost control of China and the Middle East. The plague epidemic known as the Black Death disrupted trade. A new power, the Ottoman Turks, now controlled the western part of the Silk Road, once again blocking European merchants from its trade. But Marco Polo's accounts of China still excited the imagination of European merchants and rulers. By the 1400s, Europeans were thinking of trying to reach Asia by sea. When Christopher Columbus sailed from Spain in the hope of reaching Asia by traveling west, he carried a copy of *The Travels of Marco Polo* in his cabin.

## Consider the Essential Question:

How did Mongol conquest change relations between regional societies?

Go online to complete the Social Studies Explanation.

## Check for Understanding:

Discuss the impact that Marco Polo's writings had on Europe and the Europeans' relations with the people of the East.

# 5.4 The Ming Dynasty

*photo: Pixabay*

## LESSON OVERVIEW

### Introduction

In this concept, you will learn about the spread of Chinese culture and the growth of the empire. You will discover how overseas trade impacted and expanded Chinese society and how China later cut off these overseas expeditions. Finally, you will analyze the impact of these events on China's economy and culture.

### Key Vocabulary
Which terms do you already know?

| | |
|---|---|
| ☐ Africa | ☐ Indian Ocean |
| ☐ Asia | ☐ junk |
| ☐ Beijing | ☐ Ming dynasty |
| ☐ Europe | ☐ Mongols |
| ☐ Genghis Khan | ☐ porcelain |
| ☐ Great Wall of China | ☐ Silk Road |
| | ☐ Song dynasty |
| ☐ gunpowder | ☐ Zheng He |
| ☐ India | ☐ Zhu Yuanzhang |

### Essential Question

How did trade shape Chinese society during the Ming dynasty?

### Lesson Objectives

By the end of this lesson, you should be able to:

- Explain how trade under the Ming dynasty spread Chinese ideas and goods across the world.

- Discuss how the expansion of trade in China led to the growth of the empire and its people.

- Evaluate the decision by Ming emperors to cut off overseas expeditions and outlaw foreign trade.

How did trade shape Chinese society during the Ming dynasty?

# ENGAGE

**How did trade fuel the Ming dynasty? Visit Engage to learn more.**

## Essential Question

How did trade shape Chinese society during the Ming dynasty?

# EXPLORE

## Birth of a Dynasty

*How did the Ming dynasty begin?*

In the early 1200s, the Mongol chieftain Genghis Khan's goal was to create a Mongol empire that stretched from the East China Sea to Eastern Europe. He united the Mongol tribes and took over China and other countries. For much of the 1200s and 1300s, peace and order reigned across Asia. Political stability, cultural exchange, and economic growth were realized under the leadership of the Mongols.

Despite these benefits, most Chinese were not happy with the government under the Yuan, or Mongol, dynasty. Unlike previous dynasties, the Mongol leaders did not strive for Chinese unity. Most of the government officials were Mongols, or even Europeans. The native Chinese were angered by this and wanted to depose, or remove, the foreign rulers.

Zhu Yuanzhang, the founder and first emperor of the Ming dynasty, became the leader of a rebel army and led them against the Mongols. He first succeeded in capturing the southern portion of the country. In 1363, Zhu's army won a decisive naval battle at Lake Poyang, and gained an advantage in the northern provinces.

photo: Getty Images

*Portrait of Zhu Yuanzhang, founder of the Ming dynasty.*

By August 1368, Zhu had captured the Yuan capital at Dadu, modern-day Beijing. Soon after, the Mongols were driven back beyond the Great Wall of China. After successfully taking control from the Mongols, Zhu founded a new dynasty in 1368 that he called *Ming*, meaning "brilliant."

## Culture and Trade

*How did a renewed interest in culture increase trade during the Ming dynasty?*

The arts flourished, trade expanded, and the economy prospered during the Ming dynasty. With the revival of art and literature, painters employed unique styles of landscape painting. Chinese writers produced novels and poetry, and music and dance thrived.

photo: Pixabay

*The blue and white decoration of porcelain Ming vases was copied throughout the world.*

As a result of the renewed interest in the arts, trade expanded. Chinese industries increased the production of silk and tools. They also invented a special type of clay pottery called porcelain, from which dishes were made. The popularity of porcelain in the West today is why some people refer to their dishes as "china." Ming porcelain was commonly decorated in blue and white. Blue was one of the few paint colors that did not burn away in the extreme temperatures needed to create the porcelain pieces. This color would come to symbolize Ming pottery and would be copied throughout the world, especially in Japan and Korea. Ming vases became valuable and popular, even in the West.

The economy continued to grow with the expansion of trade. Farmers used improvements in planting techniques to gather bigger yields from their rich farmland. When specimens of corn and sweet potatoes reached China through trade from other civilizations, the Chinese eagerly adopted these crops. The Ming dynasty lived up to its name—brilliant.

## Masters of the Oceans

*How did the Ming rule the seas?*

During the Ming dynasty, rulers sent fleets of Chinese ships across the oceans of the world. The Chinese made several advances in sailing and navigation that made this type of exploration possible.

Chinese sailors had long been using navigation equipment such as the magnetic compass, which was invented during the Song dynasty. However, improvements in the ships themselves also helped advance exploration. Chinese shipbuilders had become masters of their craft before the time of the Ming dynasty. As well-built ships were critical to a successful sea trade, elaborate systems were in place to keep the ships in good working order. Supporting industries around the shipyards created sails, ropes, and nails and helped provide jobs to the Chinese people.

photo: The New York Public Library

*This image shows the first Chinese junk, a type of ship, to sail to Europe. Europeans soon copied Chinese ship design.*

Although many of these innovations had occurred before the Ming period, the Ming continued to improve on existing designs. One of the most popular boats in the Chinese fleet was called a junk. Its hull design was unique. A typical junk had a high stern (back end) and a bow (front end) that projected out over the water. In addition, junks were divided into as many as 12 compartments by walls, known as bulkheads, which ran the length and width of the ships. These walls made the ships stronger than other ships of this time and helped protect them from damage that could occur in rough seas.

The sails and rudders used on junks also were important. The boats contained as many as five masts that held the sails. The sails were flattened by strips of bamboo, called battens, which allowed them to be opened and closed quickly. The sails could also be angled in different directions, allowing junks to sail into the wind. The rudders could be raised or lowered into the water. Sailors could adjust the rudder according to the depth of the water through which they sailed, allowing the sailors to steer the junk through shallower waters. This allowed for greater exploration options. Europeans began to use many design modifications like the mounted rudders and multiple sails of the Chinese junks to improve their own ships.

## The Explorations of Admiral Zheng He
### *How did advances in navigation and shipbuilding impact exploration?*

The advances in shipbuilding and navigation made prior to and during the Ming dynasty made exploration easier for the Chinese. One of the best-known Chinese explorers was Admiral Zheng He.

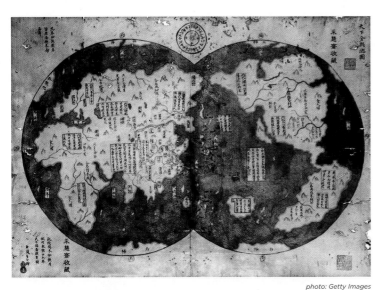

*A 1763 copy of a world map drawn by Zheng He.*

photo: Getty Images

In 1405, Zheng was selected to be the leader of expeditions to explore the "Western Oceans." On his first voyage, Zheng He was in command of a fleet consisting of approximately 30,000 sailors and 62 large ships. He and his crew traveled across the Indian Ocean to the Calicut, on the western coast of India. He returned to China in 1407.

From 1408 to 1433, Zheng He would make six more voyages. During these voyages, Zheng He sailed to the Hormuz in the Persian Gulf, and southward down the eastern coast of the African continent. These voyages, made possible by earlier Chinese innovations in shipping, helped spread Chinese goods and trade and also increased China's influence and control of the waters around Asia.

## Reading and Writing

*How did culture grow during the Ming dynasty?*

During the Ming dynasty, China made many contributions to enhance its culture. China improved literacy among its people by refining the papermaking process. Early Chinese paper, which dated back to the Han dynasty, was made from bamboo. In the Ming dynasty, the refined method had papermakers gathering tree bark, bamboo, and other plant fibers. These materials were beaten into a pulp and put into a mold. Later, starch was added to paper to help

*Chinese landscape painted on gold-speckled paper, Ming dynasty.*

photo: Getty Images

adjust its size. The Chinese also added a yellow dye to the paper that repelled insects. This new paper was thinner and easier to use than the old bamboo writing tablets. This development paved the way for the papermaking process used today.

Writers in the Ming dynasty had to pass a competitive literary examination to earn respect. They had to be able to compose a *baguwen*, or eight-legged essay, that became the classic way to determine a writer's ability. The advances in papermaking and the expanded use of moveable-type printing presses, which had been invented during the Song dynasty, helped poetry and literature thrive during the Ming dynasty.

## Transcontinental Trade

### How did demand for Chinese products abroad impact trade?

China's luxury goods were in high demand outside of China. Chinese merchants carried these goods to other countries using the Silk Road, a network of interconnected trade routes. The trade routes linked Asia with Europe and Africa. The Chinese also worked to improve the canal system, which had been built under previous dynasties, to improve and increase travel and trade.

Large quantities of silk in many colors and textures made their way across the Silk Road. Silk was worth almost as much as its weight in gold. While silk was China's major trade item, many other goods traversed the Silk Road, such as gold, ivory, exotic plants, and animals. Precious stones, glass, and items made of bronze or iron were also popular trade items. Traders also exchanged ideas, technology, and culture as they traveled the Silk Road.

photo: Getty Images

*The manufacturing of raw silk is known as sericulture.*

### Global Demand

To wealthy European leaders and nobles, silk, porcelain, and other goods from China were symbols of success and power. Explorers and traders from Europe were eager to expand this trade. Many Europeans hoped to find a route to Chinese cities that did not require traveling across the Islamic empires that controlled the Silk Road routes.

Because of the increased trade by land and sea during the first years of the Ming dynasty, the merchant class grew in wealth, power, and status. At first, merchants were strictly regulated and had low social status. They were told where they could live, how they could run their businesses, and where they could travel. However, as Chinese trade with outsiders increased, some of these restrictions eased and the merchant class rose.

## The Empire Turns Inward

### Why did Ming emperors cut off outside trade and ban overseas expeditions?

Early in the Ming dynasty, exploration and trade expanded. China's sailors such as Admiral Zheng He went on vast expeditions to explore new lands and open new trade routes. In the process, they also spread Chinese culture.

After Zheng He's death in 1433, however, the expeditions were halted. The government determined that transoceanic voyages were too expensive. Soon after, the emperor reduced the Chinese fleet to one-third of its original size and prevented the building of large ships.

photo: Getty Images

*Just as China closed itself off to the outside world under the Ming dynasty, the Forbidden City was closed off to Chinese not working within the government.*

With the ending of trade, the government began to turn inward. As China reduced its contact with the outside world, traders from across the world, still eager for Chinese products, had no other choice but to come to China to trade for the goods they desired. These trade items included jade, porcelain, and Chinese silk. China's closure of its overseas trade expeditions decreased the availability of Chinese goods, which in turn increased the demand for them as well as their value. It also motivated Western countries to search for new and quicker trade routes to the east. This would open a new era of exploration by mariners, including one of the most well-known explorers of the time, Christopher Columbus.

Trade had a significant impact on Chinese society and culture. A strong and prosperous middle class developed. The exchange of ideas with other cultures led to advances in science and technology, and improvements in navigation and naval technology led to exploration. All of these achievements were driven in some part by trade. The Ming dynasty's decision to reduce its trade and contact with other nations would affect not only Chinese society, but also other cultures.

**Explore this interactive to learn more about life in the Ming dynasty for a variety of groups.**

**Consider the Essential Question:**

How did trade shape Chinese society during the Ming dynasty?

Go online to complete the Social Studies Explanation.

**Check for Understanding:**

How did trade increase the wealth and power of the early Ming dynasty? How did the discontinuation of trade voyages later in the Ming dynasty impact the Chinese economy?

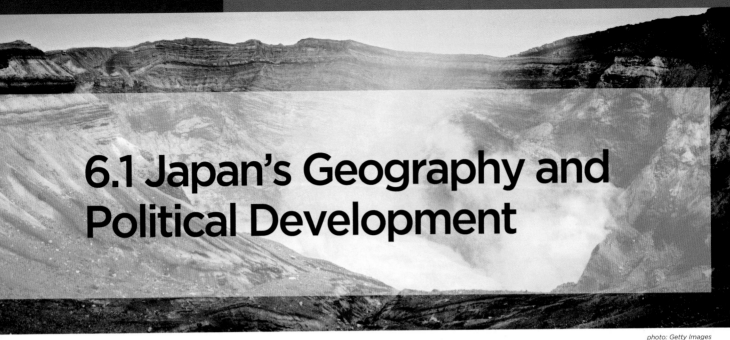

# 6.1 Japan's Geography and Political Development

photo: Getty Images

## LESSON OVERVIEW

### Introduction

In this concept, you will explore how the geography of Japan shaped the lives of its people. You will also learn about the different political, economic, and religious systems that have affected Japan's history.

### Essential Question

How did physical geography influence Japan's cultural development?

### Lesson Objectives

By the end of this lesson, you should be able to:

- Locate Japan's boundaries, important cities, and bodies of water on a map.

- Describe how the geography of the region shaped the way of life of the people living there.

- Trace the major political, economic, and religious developments in Japanese history.

### Key Vocabulary
Which terms do you already know?

- [ ] Ainu
- [ ] archipelago
- [ ] Asia
- [ ] Buddhism
- [ ] China
- [ ] Confucius
- [ ] daimyo
- [ ] Edo
- [ ] empire
- [ ] Heian period
- [ ] Japan
- [ ] Kyoto
- [ ] Lady Murasaki
- [ ] Minamoto Yoritomo
- [ ] Mount Fuji
- [ ] Prince Shotoku
- [ ] province
- [ ] shogun
- [ ] *The Tale of Genji*
- [ ] *The Tale of the Heike*
- [ ] Tokugawa Ieyasu
- [ ] Tokugawa shogunate
- [ ] Tokyo
- [ ] Toyotomi Hideyoshi

# ENGAGE

**How did the threat of earthquakes influence daily life in Japan? Visit Engage to learn more.**

## Essential Question

How did physical geography influence Japan's cultural development?

# EXPLORE

## An Island Nation

*What are the important geographical features of Japan?*

Japan is an archipelago, a group of islands, lying in the northwest Pacific Ocean. It is too far off the coast of Asia to be seen from the mainland. Japan is made up of four main islands and almost 1,000 smaller ones. Honshu, the main island, contains most of the major cities. The cities on Honshu include Tokyo, Japan's capital since 1603 and one of the biggest cities in the world, and Kyoto, which was the ancient capital.

Southwest of Honshu is the island of Kyushu, where Japanese civilization began. East of Kyushu is mostly rural Shikoku, smallest of the main islands. And to the north, near the coast of Russia, is the island of Hokkaido. Separating Honshu from Shikoku is the narrow inland Sea of Japan, and north and west of the islands, the Sea of Japan forms both a sea route and a barrier between Japan and China.

Four-fifths of Japan is covered by forested or snow-covered mountains. In some parts of the islands, the mountain slopes come all the way down to the edge of the sea. But between the mountain ranges are several large plains, wide river valleys, and smaller areas that are suitable for farming. Rice is

**Explore this interactive to learn more about how geography affected Japan's development.**

the main food crop grown in Japan. Until recent times, rice farming was the occupation of the majority of the population.

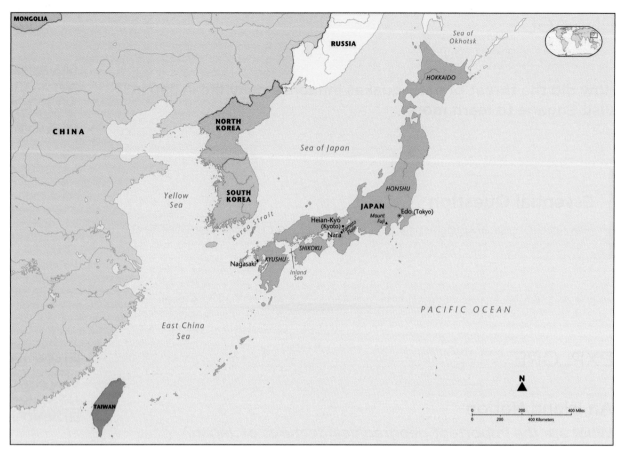

*A map of modern Japan shows the country surrounded by water, isolated from its mainland neighbors, China and Korea.*

## Potential Threats

### *What problems are caused by Japan's location?*

About 200 of Japan's mountains are volcanic. They include the country's most famous peak, Mount Fuji, which is 12,388 feet high (3,776 meters). Fuji is the most-climbed mountain in the world, with about 100,000 people ascending to its crater every year. Its name comes from *Fuchi*, an ancient Japanese fire goddess. Both of Japan's main religions, Shinto and Buddhism, consider Fuji to be sacred.

Mount Fuji last erupted in 1708, but other Japanese volcanoes have been active more recently. Japan is part of the Ring of Fire, the most seismically active region on the planet. Earthquakes are frequent and

*photo: Getty Images*
*Devastation caused by the 2011 earthquake in Japan.*

sometimes quite severe. A quake that struck Tokyo in 1923 caused fires that destroyed half the city. It killed about 142,000 people and left nearly two million homeless.

The earthquake and resulting tsunami (a long, high sea wave) that struck northeastern Honshu on March 11, 2011, left more than 28,000 dead or missing and flooded entire cities. Far more frequent are the Pacific hurricanes, or typhoons, that can drench the islands with rain, uproot trees, and flood narrow river valleys.

When the earth and weather are peaceful, however, Japan is a beautiful land of breathtaking natural views. Abundant rainfall nourishes the country's fertile farms. The same seismic system, an area where tectonic plates meet, that causes Japan's volcanoes also creates hundreds of hot springs, which are used often for bathing by the Japanese people.

## An Island People

*How have mountains and sea affected the Japanese people?*

### Japan's People

It is uncertain when people first came to Japan. However, scientists believe that people first crossed over land bridges in the north and south that connected Japan with the Asian mainland between 30,000 to 35,000 years ago. One of the earliest recorded cultures on Japan was the Jōmon culture, which dates from approximately 10,500 to 300 BCE. The Ainu, the indigenous people of Japan, claim to be descendants of the Jōmon culture. Although many of the Ainu have died, or assimilated into Japanese

culture, a few thousand Ainu people still live in northern Japan practicing their traditional culture. Historically, they have been treated poorly by many Japanese, much as Native Americans were by European settlers.

Through genetic research, historians have connected the ancestors of the Japanese people to early Koreans. Their language, however, has not been positively connected with other known languages. They arrived in Kyushu from the mainland of Asia

*photo: Getty Images*
*Traditional Ainu thatched houses, Shikotsu National Park, Japan.*

between 300 and 100 BCE and gradually spread across the island and in the process overwhelmed the culture of the Jōmon civilization.

### Geography's Impact

The culture of the people who arrived in Kyushu was based on rice farming and the sea. Travel by land was difficult. Except in the cities, wheeled vehicles were not generally used until modern times, as they would have been useless for crossing Japan's rugged mountains and rushing rivers. Ocean transport was usually the easiest way to get from one part of an island to another, even when a land route was a shorter distance.

The Japanese people mainly grew rice and vegetables, but a major part of their diet came from the sea. Fishing is still a major occupation. The Japanese enjoy eating an enormous variety of sea creatures, many of which are not often found on dinner tables in other countries, including the pufferfish, which is poisonous if not prepared with great care. The diet also includes several types of seaweed, which the Japanese do not consider to be weeds. As rice-growing land was considered too valuable to use on livestock, meat other than fish was not an important part of the diet.

For many centuries, the ocean isolated the Japanese from the influence of other cultures. When at last the influence of their enormous neighbor, China, reached the islands, the Japanese adopted much of what they liked about Chinese culture. Between 200 and 500 CE, many Chinese and Korean people migrated to Japan, bringing metallurgy techniques, systems of writing and papermaking, silk, textiles, and knowledge of weaving.

The sea also protected the Japanese from invasion. In the 1200s, when the Mongols under Kublai Khan attempted to add Japan to their empire, their horsemen were fighting in an unfamiliar element. The Japanese harried, or pillaged, the Mongol invasion fleet using small boats before a typhoon wrecked and scattered it. The forces of nature had tormented the people of Japan at times, but those forces also prevented the nation from being invaded from the Asian mainland.

## A Divine Emperor

### Who ruled early Japan?

A Chinese traveler visited Japan in 238, calling it Wa. He described it as divided into many small states, one of which was ruled by a powerful witch-queen named Pimiko. She was said to live in a palace with 1,000 female attendants and one man, who helped her communicate with her subjects. But the story of Pimiko is only a legend—the Japanese have no actual record of her. However, this legend demonstrates two important aspects of Japanese culture. One is that women often held power and influence in early Japan. Another is that much of what we know about these centuries in Japan is legend or myth. Written records from this time are scarce, and much of what is known comes from histories or stories written by Chinese historians and travelers.

Japan was ruled by an emperor, who was believed to have been descended from the gods and inspired by them, but not a god himself. The emperor had no official or permanent capital, but by about 400, his court was centered in the Yamato plain on Honshu. Although the emperor was technically the head of the government, his actual power was limited. Many of his duties were merely ceremonial. For example, as part of the native Japanese religion, called Shintō or Shintōism, the emperor carried out certain rituals that made sure that the gods looked after Japan, ensuring its prosperity. Real power was in the hands of an official who represented different noble families who were able to win control over the others. The emperor's government in Yamato had little control over the powerful families that ruled other regions.

*photo: Getty Images*

*The Japanese believed the emperor was descended from Shintō gods. Part of the emperor's duties involved carrying out certain Shintō ceremonies and rituals.*

In 552, when cultural ties with China were opened, messengers from the mainland brought to the emperor's court a bronze statue of the Buddha and some Buddhist writings. The officials who controlled the emperor's court saw Buddhism and Chinese ideas about government as a way of strengthening control over the country. The introduction of these new cultural influences began to change the power structure in Japan.

## A Practical Prince

### *Who was Prince Shotoku?*

Japanese officials who believed that they could use Buddhism and Chinese political philosophy to strengthen the government brought in Chinese books and scholars and encouraged the establishment of Buddhist monasteries in Japan. In time, Buddhism would join Shintō as one of Japan's national religions, with many people observing the rituals of both. Shintō is a polytheistic religion that worships the powers of nature, which are represented by many gods, goddesses, and spirits. Buddhism emphasizes study, discipline, and meditation as a way of understanding humans' places in the universe. Because most Japanese did not see any conflict between the two religions, there have been very few periods of religious conflict.

*photo: Getty Images*

*Prince Shotoku introduced Buddhism and other aspects of Chinese culture to Japan.*

During Shotoku's reign, Japan was an agricultural society, in which the rich owned enslaved people and lived in houses with wooden floors, while the poor lived in huts with dirt floors. Women were comparatively powerful for the time, acting as the center of family life and raising children while fathers often lived elsewhere.

By 593, the most influential official in the emperor's court was Prince Shotoku, the nephew of the reigning Empress Suiko. Shotoku enthusiastically embraced Chinese culture. Because Japan had no written language, Shotoku encouraged scholars to learn and adapt the Chinese writing system. He wrote books about Buddhism and helped spread the religion in Japan. He is also credited with the document that became Japan's first constitution, although some modern scholars dispute his authorship.

It established a government based on the principles of Confucius, emphasizing how ruling officials should behave. For example, Shotoku created 12 court ranks, named after Confucian ideals, for members of the government. Each rank had rules for proper behavior they were expected to follow. Appointment to these positions was supposed to be based on ability and merit. By Shotoku's death in 622, Chinese culture and Buddhism were well established in Japan.

One of the Chinese principles of government was a permanent location for the capital. Japan's first capital was the city of Nara. The influence of Buddhist priests became so strong in this city that they eventually dominated the government. In 784, Emperor Kammu and the Soga family that directed his government feared that the influence of religious leaders was undermining the authority of the government and decided that the ancient Shintō gods wanted a capital that was not under Buddhist influence. They established a new capital called Heian-kyo, which would become the modern city of Kyoto. It was during the Heian period (794–1185) that Japan's unique culture developed as its own, not just as an extension of China.

## Politics in the Heian Court

*What was political life like at the Heian court?*

Like other landmark cultures in history, the culture that developed in Heian-kyo was of the greatest benefit to court officials and their families, perhaps 3,000 people in all. Although much of the Japanese government was based on the Chinese model, there were some differences. For example, while officials in China were chosen by exam, the important posts in Japan were handed out based on family. Those who could trace their lineage to the wealthiest or most powerful ancestors received the top jobs. The great families that ruled the rice lands grew richer and more powerful until one family, the Fujiwara, eventually came to dominate the government. They cemented their power by marrying their daughters to emperors and their sons to imperial family members, one generation after another. This practice was meant to assure that power would always remain with members of the same family. The Fujiwara supported the emperors' extravagant lifestyle, but they held the actual power and were the real rulers of Japan.

The Heian rulers and government officials admired the Chinese and sought to be like them in every way. Buddhism, Chinese writing, and the Chinese system of government were only the first ideas and practice they adopted from the Chinese.

photo: Getty Images

*During the Heian period, the Japanese adapted Chinese Buddhism to their own culture and fused it with their traditional Shintō religion.*

Japanese traders and scholars traveled regularly to China and brought back Chinese ideas of painting, sculpture, architecture, and music. But after 838, China was troubled by invasions and civil wars between competing dynasties. Japanese contact with China was broken off for centuries. The great families that dominated the court had the chance to develop their own, unique Japanese culture.

## At the Emperor's Court

### What was cultural life like at the Heian court?

Heian court culture became one of rich tastes and formal behavior. At the center of the court was the emperor, even though he had little real power. He performed the Shintō rituals that were believed to ensure prosperity, and he was always present at celebrations and festivals. There were parties, flower-viewing ceremonies, and elaborate dress codes. For example, if just one color of one sleeve of one of the many silk robes worn by a fashionable court lady was considered to be in bad taste, she would be the subject of gossip. A person's social rise or fall could also depend on his skill at poetry or calligraphy.

A male courtier, or member of the royal court, was expected to have mastered the complicated Chinese system of writing. But the literature of Heian Japan was written almost entirely by women. Many of their letters, diaries, poems, and stories have been preserved. In fact, much of what historians know about this era of Japanese history comes from these women, especially from one author.

photo: Los Angeles County Museum of Art

*An early manuscript edition of* The Tale of Genji. *Few books in world history have drawn as much attention and praise.*

Murasaki Shikibu, usually known as Lady Murasaki, was born about 978, the daughter of a government official. As a lady-in-waiting to the empress, she began to keep a secret diary about court life. She wrote freely about the people of her class, describing their parties, arts, and ceremonies. Much of her diary consisted of gossip about the courtiers, their personalities, and their love affairs. Around the year 1003, the empress asked Lady Murasaki to write stories for the court's entertainment. She adapted her diary into *The Tale of Genji*, which she published as a series over the next several years. *The Tale of Genji* is generally considered to be the first novel.

The Japanese today consider *The Tale of Genji* one of their classic works of literature. The centerpiece of Japan's historic culture, it set the standard for Japanese language, behavior, and aesthetics. Later, Japanese empires looked to *The Tale of Genji* for guidance about what pure Japanese culture should be. The story is still popular in Japan today. It has been adapted into movies, manga (comics), and anime (animated series). But even as *The Tale of Genji* was being written, the world it described was starting to change drastically.

## The Rise of the Samurai

### *What events brought about the end of the Heian culture?*

The economy and government of Heian Japan rested on a weak base. The emperor had little more than a symbolic presence, and the government was not strong enough to control the entire country. Large landowners far from the capital refused to pay taxes to the government. These were not the members of the emperor's court. They were a tough warrior class who maintained private armies to protect their lands and increase their power. Emperors also did not require favorite courtiers and Buddhist monasteries and temples to pay taxes. In some provinces, the peasants not only had to pay high taxes, but were also mistreated by the emperor's tax collectors, who seized them for forced labor or army service. These peasants asked the nobles and members of the Buddhist monasteries and temples for protection. The nobles taxed the peasants, too, but not as much as the government did. With the nobles receiving the taxes that had previously gone to the emperor, the economic power of the government was further reduced.

As the government grew poorer, the owners of the large estates became more powerful. With no strong central government to control them, they began fighting each other to expand their territory. In the capital, the loss of tax money meant a loss of power for the Fujiwara. The emperors themselves became poor. Bands of robbers plagued the roads and even controlled sections of the capital. Even sea travel was dangerous due to the existence of pirates.

Gradually, the fighters in the provinces came to ally themselves with the two most powerful families, the Minamoto and the Taira. Warriors became the dominant class and would offer their services to powerful lords called daimyo. The armed warriors were bound to their lords by ties of personal loyalty and became known as *samurai*, or "those who serve."

*photo: Getty Images*
*Illustration of Samurai on horseback holding bow.*

By the middle of the 1100s, the samurai were loyal to lords who in turn were loyal to either the Minamoto or the Taira. The wars between them consumed Japan for a generation. Samurai on both sides slaughtered the elegant nobles of Kyoto and burned their palaces. In a climactic battle fought on the Inland Sea in 1185, the Minamoto decisively defeated the Taira. Control of the country was now theirs.

The clan's leader was the daimyo Minamoto Yoritomo. He saw his chance to reorganize the government and strengthen his control. He moved his headquarters far from the emperor to Kamakura, near modern-day Tokyo. In 1192, he appointed himself commander in chief, or shogun. He appointed officials in the provinces who maintained order through loyal daimyo and their samurai. The emperor still kept his court in Kyoto, but for centuries after the shoguns would be the most powerful figures in Japan.

## Under the Shoguns

*How did the samurai influence Japanese culture?*

With the beginning of the shogunate and the samurai era came a new growth of Buddhism. The Japanese had long ago adopted basic Buddhist beliefs, such as karma and reincarnation. Now, however, new Buddhist sects were taking root in Japan. In the 1200s, a form of Buddhism called Zen became popular among the samurai. It emphasized mental and moral discipline through meditation.

Zen temples were at first very plain. But as Zen spread among the ruling class, some establishments grew wealthy and became part of the samurai culture. They sponsored contests in fencing, wrestling, and archery for their patrons. They also encouraged poetry, painting, calligraphy, and flower arranging. The elegant arts of the Heian culture had not died. Instead, they had been adopted into the newer warrior-based culture.

The shoguns lost power when they abandoned their warrior roots. By the 1400s, they were maintaining a luxurious court in Kyoto and were more focused on their wealth than on maintaining control of their lands. The local daimyo began to regain control over their territories, supported by their samurai. By the 1500s, Japan was again engulfed in constant conflict between the daimyo and the shoguns. Men claimed the title of shogun, but they lacked the power to rule. The 1500s became known in Japanese history as the "Age of the Country at War."

In 1542, the first Europeans reached Japan. They were Portuguese traders carrying a cargo of silk from China. Because the shogun could not control the Japanese pirates off their shores, the Chinese had refused to trade with Japan because of the danger to their merchants and ships. Because of this, the Europeans and their trade were welcome. With Portuguese expeditions came Catholic missionary priests. They won many converts and also the favor of a daimyo named Oda Nobunaga, who saw them as a way of limiting or controlling the power of the Buddhist monasteries. The Portuguese also introduced firearms to Japan. Within two years, the Japanese were producing them. Guns changed Japanese warfare almost overnight. They provided certain ambitious daimyo with the power to unify the country.

**Explore this investigation and take a position on how the shoguns gained power.**

No ruler, whether emperor or shogun, had ever been able to bring all of Japan under his control. Nobunaga, though a minor daimyo, set out to do just that. In 1560, he won a decisive battle against a far more powerful daimyo. This victory brought several other daimyo over to his side.

## The Three Unifiers

### How was Japan unified?

While many daimyo and their samurai despised guns and thought them cowardly, Nobunaga saw that they were superior to the traditional samurai style of fighting with swords and bows and arrows. He built up his power slowly, winning daimyo to his side by diplomacy and battle, until he had brought central Honshu under his control. He sought information and advice from Catholic priests about their religion and about European politics, and he won their favor by destroying the power of the Buddhist monasteries. In 1575, he fought a decisive battle against a much larger force of samurai. He won it by using his small force of gun-armed men as an organized unit. They easily defeated the mounted samurai.

Nobunaga is considered the first of Japan's three unifiers, leaders who brought all of Japan together under one rule. His successor was Toyotomi Hideyoshi, a peasant soldier who had become a samurai and then a great general. Hideyoshi was the second of the three unifiers. With the help of Tokugawa Ieyasu, he succeeded in bringing all Japan under his rule by 1590. He distrusted Europeans, especially after their priests began to meddle, or interfere, in Japanese politics. At one point, he ordered the priests to leave Japan. Possibly because he feared the loss of European trade, he never carried out the order. At one point, to inspire authority, he had a number of priests and Japanese Christians put to death. But by 1598, when he died, the persecutions of Christians ended.

photo: Getty Images

*Oda Nobunga, the first of Japan's three unifiers, made war on Buddhism and the power of its priests.*

photo: Getty Images

*The White Heron castle was built by a daimyo in the 1300s and expanded and strengthened by Toyotomi Hideyoshi in 1581.*

Tokugawa Ieyasu was the third of the three unifiers. In 1600, he defeated his rival daimyo, and three years later he invited the reigning emperor to declare him shogun. He chose the previously unimportant city of Edo as his capital, which would become today's Tokyo. So began the Tokugawa Shogunate. Ieyasu and his descendants would rule Japan for the next 264 years.

## Turning Inward

*Why did Japan close itself off to the outside world?*

At first, Ieyasu was friendly to Christians and supported trade with the Portuguese. However, political and religious conflicts in Europe led Ieyasu to reconsider this position. In 1614, Ieyasu made the decision to ban Christianity in Japan, and all foreign priests and missionaries were ordered to leave.

photo: Getty Images

*Tokugawa Ieyasu united Japan. In 1614, he banned foreign priests and missionaries from Japan.*

After Ieyasu's death in 1616, his son was harsher in his attitude toward Christians and Europeans, and many were killed. The Tokugawa shoguns came to see the world outside Japan as a corrupting influence. In 1637, all foreigners were ordered to stay away from Japan under penalty of death. The only exceptions were a few Dutch trade ships that were permitted each year. A small group of Dutch merchants was allowed to live under guard on a small island in Nagasaki Harbor. Other than these, Japan would remain closed to the outside world for more than two centuries.

Japan's geography had influenced the development of its culture and political institutions. Its contact with its nearest neighbors also influenced its cultural and political development. Now, however, Japan's geography made it possible for it to remain closed to the outside word and further develop its own unique culture.

**Consider the Essential Question:**

How did physical geography influence Japan's cultural development?

Go online to complete the Social Studies Explanation.

**Check for Understanding:**

Japan consists of four major islands, and four-fifths of its land area is covered by mountains. How did these facts influence Japan's political development?

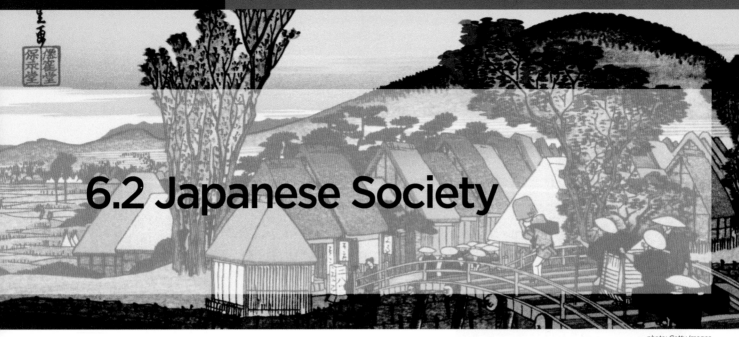

Discovery SOCIAL STUDIES EDUCATION | TECHBOOK.

What effects did power and social class have on Japanese feudal society?

# 6.2 Japanese Society

photo: Getty Images

## LESSON OVERVIEW

### Introduction

In this concept, you will analyze the social structure of ancient Japan and the importance of social classes. You will also learn about the important achievements of the Japanese culture during this time.

### Essential Question

What effects did power and social class have on Japanese feudal society?

### Lesson Objectives

By the end of this lesson, you should be able to:

- Analyze the relationship between feudal power, military rank, and social status in shogunate Japan.

- Understand the connection between Zen Buddhism and Bushido.

- Identify important achievements and contributions of the Japanese people.

### Key Vocabulary
Which terms do you already know?

- ☐ artisan
- ☐ Basho
- ☐ Buddhism
- ☐ Bushido
- ☐ civil war
- ☐ daimyo
- ☐ Edo
- ☐ emperor
- ☐ feudalism
- ☐ haiku
- ☐ Hokusai
- ☐ Japan
- ☐ merchant

- ☐ Minamoto Yoritomo
- ☐ peasant
- ☐ Prince Shotoku
- ☐ shogun
- ☐ Tokugawa Ieyasu
- ☐ Tokugawa shogunate
- ☐ Toyotomi Hideyoshi
- ☐ Zen Buddhism

# ENGAGE

How did young samurais view the world around them? Visit Engage to learn more.

## Essential Question

What effects did power and social class have on Japanese feudal society?

# EXPLORE

## Emperor, Shogun, and Daimyo

### *Who held power in feudal Japan?*

"The Son of Heaven" was one of the titles traditionally held by the emperor of Japan. There was a myth that the first emperor of Japan was the grandson of the sun goddess, Amaterasu. He was sent down from heaven around 660 BCE to establish order. He was given three tokens as symbols of his rule on Earth: the Jewel, representing kindness; the Sword, representing courage; and the Mirror, representing wisdom. Based on this tale, one of the titles traditionally held by the emperor of Japan was "The Son of Heaven." According to the archaeological evidence, however, the year 100 CE is closer to the date that one noble family in the Japanese islands won power over the others. Amazingly, his descendants have reigned as the emperors of Japan ever since, and the sword, jewel, and mirror are still important symbols in the imperial household and in Japanese culture.

Although the Japanese people believed their emperor was descended from the gods, after about 400, the emperor was little more than a religious symbol—he held no real power in the government. The real power was in the hands of the noble families, who often fought to gain control. The leading noble family chose which prince of the imperial family would be the next emperor, often by murdering his rivals. The nobles also married their daughters to members of the imperial line so that they would be related to the new emperor. In 1185, when Yoritomo of the Minamoto clan won a war for power against his rivals, the Taira, he claimed the title of shogun: supreme military dictator or commander in chief. The shogun now had the actual power in Japan.

## The Feudal Era

The power of the Minamoto, Taira, and other noble families rested on armed warriors known as samurai, or "those who serve." The samurai were fiercely loyal. The shogun used the samurai to rule the country by force. By the 1300s, however, the shogun had become almost as powerless as the emperor. There was no central power in Japan. It was a feudal system of government, very much like that which was in force in Europe at that time. Regional lords called daimyo controlled local territories and had their own group of loyal samurai. All daimyo shared an equal title, but some were more powerful than others. Some might rule many rich rice-growing provinces, while others ruled only one town or the area around their castle.

photo: Getty Images

*This engraving depicts a daimyo in court dress.*

# The End of Feudalism

### *Why did feudalism in Japan come to an end?*

By 1500, all of Japan was caught up in civil war. Samurai armies fought one another to increase their daimyo's power and wealth. In some areas, Buddhist warrior monks or armies of peasants were able to resist the local daimyo and his tax collectors. One peasant, Toyotomi Hideyoshi, rose to become a samurai and the most powerful war leader in the land by 1582. Within a few years, he had defeated his rivals and united all of Japan under his rule.

One of Hideyoshi's laws was to make the levels of Japanese society permanent. A person could move up or down within their class, but by law they and their descendants were bound to that class forever. Samurai were at the top. Samurai controlled the wealth of the country, but they considered handling money a disagreeable task, unfit for a real man. The peasant class, essential for the production of food, was just below the samurai. Below the peasant class were artisans, and at the bottom of the class structure were merchants. Merchants were held in contempt because they produced nothing but only bought and sold what others grew or made. Other members of society such as actors, bandits, and anyone whose job involved handling dead humans or animals were beneath consideration in this class system.

Hideyoshi held supreme power, but because he was of peasant birth, he could never become shogun. That honor went to Tokugawa Ieyasu, who won control after Hideyoshi's death. In 1603, after defeating his rival daimyo in battle, Ieyasu had the power to "invite" the emperor to name him shogun. So began the Tokugawa shogunate. From the capital at Edo (modern-day Tokyo), Ieyasu and his family ruled Japan for the next 264 years.

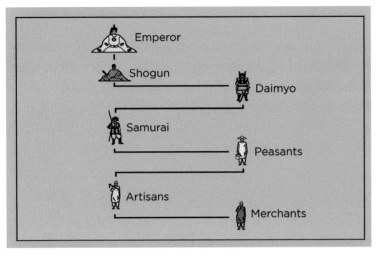

*Japanese society was based on a structured class system. Power was centralized in the wealthy classes at the top of the social pyramid.*

During the Tokugawa shogunate, the leadership and culture of Japan became centered in Edo. Wealthy landowners and powerful samurai were required to live in Edo, close to the shogun, every other year. This helped ensure that the landowners would not gain power in their own homes and become rivals of the Tokugawa family. With this influx of wealth, power, and culture, Edo became a bustling city with a vibrant culture.

## The Way of the Warrior

*What was life like for the samurai class in Tokugawa Japan?*

The samurai lived a life of privilege, but they were also expected to live their life under a strict code. The code of Bushido, the way of the warrior, was a way of life that the daimyo and their samurai were obligated to follow. Members of the lower social ranks were considered incapable of understanding it, but the samurai

*photo: Getty Images*

*An illustration of a samurai holding a sword and lance.*

were still expected to serve as examples to them. Bravery and prowess in battle, particularly skill with the sword, was at the core of Bushido. However, after Tokugawa Ieyasu took power, the samurai did not have anyone to fight. As a result, their roles shifted. They were expected to provide moral guidance for the Japanese people.

The idea of Bushido combined the courage of the warrior with loyalty, honesty, self-sacrifice, modest behavior, refined manners, and other virtues. A samurai did not work, but he was expected to obey his lord without question, and to endure any hardship in the service of his lord. He was even to commit ritual suicide (*seppuku*) if so ordered. The samurai owed loyalty to the emperor, to his parents, to his master, to his teachers, and to his friends. By demonstrating such obedience and loyalty, the samurai set an example for the lower orders.

### Social Rank

The rules of social rank were complicated but very clear. The daimyo were at the top, with different levels down to what would be called privates in a modern army. Each was paid at a specified rate depending on his rank. The Japanese language had elaborate differences in forms of address, depending on whether the person spoken to was of a higher or lower rank than the speaker. If someone below the samurai in rank failed to show due respect, the samurai were permitted under law to kill that individual.

Women could also be members of the samurai class but had their own strict rules to follow that defined their place. A woman was obligated to obey her parents as a child, her husband as a wife, and her sons when they were grown. Girls were separated from boys at the age of seven and no longer ate with their brothers. Families arranged marriages, and women had few rights in the marriage. A man could divorce his wife and leave her on her own with no resources for a variety of reasons, such as failing to have children, unseemly displays of emotion, or even for getting sick.

## Life in the Court of the Daimyo
### *What was life like for the samurai?*

The samurai made up approximately 7 percent of the population of Tokugawa Japan. The majority of the population, especially the peasant class, worked to support their luxurious lifestyle. Because the samurai did not work, they were free to develop culture, which was also part of Bushido. Along with swordsmanship, archery, and other martial arts, samurai were expected to cultivate skills in painting, flower arranging, calligraphy (handwriting), and a board game called go. Poetry contests were held in every daimyo's court, and in the shogun's, too. In fact, poetry contests were a pastime of the working classes as well as the samurai.

### Rice in Japan's Economy

For all classes, the economy of Japan was based on a rice standard. Taxes were owed to daimyo, who paid salaries to their samurai in *koku*. One koku was the amount of rice needed to sustain an average family for one year, or approximately five bushels. To keep a position as a daimyo, a samurai lord had to have a net worth of at least 10,000 koku. All items for sale in the towns and cities were priced in terms of koku. But as Japanese society under the shoguns became more urban, a money economy began to develop. This would lead to serious changes in the relationship between the samurai and the other classes.

photo: Getty Images

*The tale of the 47 loyal ronin (masterless samurai) has been told and retold in Japanese books, plays, and movies.*

## In Field and Town

*What was life like for peasants, artisans, and merchants in feudal Japan?*

### Peasants

The peasants in feudal Japan were essential to the foundation of the state because they produced the food. The shogun and daimyo needed to keep the peasants happy, but not allow them to gain too much power. Taxes on peasants ranged from 40 percent to 60 percent of what they produced. Peasants were thought by their samurai masters to be people without great intelligence. They could not be counted on to be thrifty. At harvest time, they must feed their families whatever other foods they had available besides rice. The rice they grew was the property of the daimyo and his samurai.

Peasants made up the great majority of the population. In law, they ranked just below the samurai, but they had very little power in society. They were not free to leave their daimyo's land and seek other work in the towns. Samurai organized the peasants under their control into groups of five households. Each household was the responsibility of the others in the group. If one failed in its duty, all five could be punished by the village headman. If he failed in his duty, he faced punishment by the daimyo's officials, up to and including death. Peasant responsibilities fell upon women as well as men, as specified in the shogun's law.

### Artisans

Artisans and their families lived under their own rules and restrictions. Those with skills that were valuable to the daimyo received direct payment from the taxes their lords collected. These included castle carpenters, makers of the silk kimono worn by both men and women, coin makers, artists, and especially sword smiths and other craft workers skilled at making weapons and armor. Craft workers had a system of ranks, from master to apprentice. Those with skill could earn a good living in the cities and towns.

### Merchants

At the bottom of the social ladder were merchants and shopkeepers. Under the Tokugawa shogunate, they were at first restricted to doing business within their daimyo's territory. As the city of Edo expanded in population and Japan became more urban, these restrictions were usually

**Explore this interactive to learn more about how Japanese feudalism affected life for four different groups.**

ignored. Large amounts of food and manufactured goods were flowing into the cities. The daimyo needed markets where they could exchange the rice they collected in taxes for its value in gold. Eventually, the daimyo issued their own gold and silver coins, and by 1700, Japan had a money economy.

Discovery EDUCATION | SOCIAL STUDIES TECHBOOK.

What effects did power and social class have on Japanese feudal society?

photo: Getty Images

*An artist captured this glimpse of middle-class life under the Tokugawa shogunate. What can you see in this print?*

The merchant class had a better understanding of money, credit, and banking than the samurai and the daimyo did. Merchants grew rich by shrewdly buying and selling rice. Daimyo and their samurai increasingly needed cash to pay for goods and services and to support their luxurious households. Many samurai found themselves in debt to the merchants and shopkeepers they despised. One Japanese observer around 1700 estimated that the daimyo owed 100 times as much money as there was in the whole country. Though they were legally of low status, the merchant class gained wealth and power through their control of trade.

## In the Shogun's Court

### *How did culture develop in Edo under the Tokugawa shogunate?*

Tokugawa Ieyasu understood the history of his country. A shogun could be all-powerful, but only until he was overthrown by another. Ieyasu's plan to keep his own family in power was a simple one. He required all daimyo and their families to live at his court in Edo every other year. That would keep them from mustering their samurai in rebellion. What Ieyasu could not have foreseen was how much that rule would change Edo. In less than a century, the shoguns' capital had grown from a small town to a city of almost one million. Daimyo competed with one another to build elaborate palaces in the capital and to furnish them with luxuries. With this leisure time, art and literature flourished under the samurai. Even the study of the martial arts took on aspects of religion.

## Zen Buddhism

The preferred religion of the samurai was Zen Buddhism. This was a branch of Buddhism that had its roots in Indian and Chinese forms of the religion. In one sense, Zen is not a religion at all. It does not have any gods or sets of beliefs. Like other forms of Buddhism, its goal is personal enlightenment and knowledge of the true nature of things. Zen Buddhists seek this knowledge through meditation and an emptying of one's mind.

Zen teachers guide their students in meditation through the use of stories, dialogues, and metaphors called *koan*. These often link things that are unrelated or that state apparent contradictions. One famous example is the question, "What is the sound of one hand clapping?" Other koan include the challenge to watch rocks grow or to drink tea from an empty cup.

During the Tokugawa period, Zen Buddhism was used to develop a type of morality that was used in all levels of society. This morality, and a focus on the traditional arts, provided the samurai with a balance to the violent aspects of their warrior lifestyle. Zen Buddhism also emphasized loyalty and duty, which is why the samurai were viewed as moral leaders and were expected to set an example for the lower classes.

The culture of the samurai was distinct from the culture of the rest of the court in its discipline. The samurai followed a code called Bushido that emphasized honor and loyalty and held these traits to be more important than even life. A samurai was expected to commit ritual suicide rather than dishonor himself. The samurai culture led to many aspects of Japanese society that persist today, including the tea ceremony and flower arranging.

photo: Pixabay

*This garden of interestingly shaped and carefully placed stones is an object of contemplation by Zen Buddishts.*

## A Model Samurai

Miyamoto Musashi was considered the greatest of all samurai and the model of a life based on Bushido. Born in 1584, Musashi fought in six battles and claimed to have fought in more than 60 duels by the time he was 30. After defeating his greatest rival in a duel, he retired from sword fighting and devoted himself to teaching others and to the arts. Musashi was a skilled painter, sculptor, calligrapher, and architect. But he remained a teacher of fighting strategy until 1645, the last year of his life. That was when he wrote his famous manual of swordsmanship, the *Book of Five Rings*. It is as much a book on Zen discipline as it is on swordsmanship. The book was later used by Japanese businesspeople to develop management strategies. In the 1970s, the book was translated into English and studied by business leaders in the West.

## The Floating World

### What sort of culture did the merchant class develop?

The men and women of the merchant class in Edo and other cities had little use for Zen and other aspects of samurai culture. The social structure of feudal Japan kept the classes separated, and they developed separate cultures. The thriving merchants had money to spend, and they developed a culture of their own called "the floating world."

### Ukiyo-e

The art form *ukiyo-e*, floating-world pictures, provides us with views of this culture and daily life in Edo. It was a world of restaurants, theaters, and popular singers and dancers. Instead of the martial arts of the samurai, which were barred to them, the merchant class enjoyed watching and betting on sumo, in which wrestlers tried to push each other out of a ring. Instead of the formal Noh plays that samurai performed for each other's entertainment, they developed a popular form of theater called Kabuki, performed by professional actors. This culture of pleasure and entertainment provided the actors, athletes, and celebrities who were the earliest subjects of ukiyo-e artists.

One of the first uses of ukiyo-e was in theater posters, like those we see today in front of movie theaters. The pictures were popular because they were inexpensive prints made from blocks of wood by a master artist and a team of assistants. The artist first made a drawing in ink, and an assistant made a tracing of it on paper. Then, an assistant glued the tracing upside down to a wood block. The areas not inked were carved away. This left a reverse image on the wood, like a rubber stamp. When they inked the block and pressed it onto paper, it made a copy of the artist's original drawing. After the artist approved this test copy, assistants made several prints, each inked in a different color. Finally, they pressed the blocks one at a time onto a sheet of paper to create a colorful design.

photo: Getty Images

*Print of porters carrying loaded baskets, by Katsushika Hokusai, 1835.*

### Hokusai

Ukiyo-e came from "the floating world," but by the 1760s, its artists were choosing other subjects for their prints. As the merchant class became more prominent, scenes from ordinary middle-class life became popular. Artisans at their tasks, mothers and their babies, and other domestic scenes were among the subjects of ukiyo-e. So were depictions of particular Japanese pleasures such as flower viewing and catching fireflies at night. Landscapes and scenes of nature also became popular during this time.

The most famous ukiyo-e artist was Katsushika Hokusai (1760–1849). He produced a series of prints of the Tokaido, the main road between Edo and the older capital of Kyoto. They featured human figures and showed the way of life of ordinary people at various places along the road.

## A World in 17 Syllables

*How did Japanese poets invent haiku?*

A haiku is a poem in 17 syllables, divided into three lines of five, seven, and five syllables. Haiku usually expresses feelings about a season or another aspect of nature. Chances are you have seen a haiku before and may have been reading them since a young age. You may have even written a few. What is often an elementary school exercise in some countries is an ancient and very serious art form in Japan.

Haiku may have developed from the poetry contests that were popular among samurai. These poems were usually in a form called *tanka*. They were made up of 31 syllables in five lines, grouped as 5-7-5-7-7. The judge of the contest would give the first three lines, and the court poets would each add their own version of the last two. Those first three lines may represent the origin of haiku. In Japan, the familiar 17-syllable form is sometimes called *hokku*, which means "starting verse."

### A Master Poet

By the 1200s, poems resembling haiku were being published in Japan. But the form really took shape during the Tokugawa shogunate. The first great haiku artist, and possibly the greatest of all, was Matsuo Basho. He was born into a samurai family in 1644 and served as a page to his daimyo's son. Basho wrote his first known poem when he was nine. He became famous as a poet and as a teacher of poetry. He developed the idea that a haiku should consist of two statements. The first one creates an image or a mood. The second may have nothing to do with the first, but it makes you think of the two of them together in some way. In 1681, while living in Edo, Basho began to study Zen seriously. In the 10 years of his life that remained, he wrote nearly all of his finest haiku.

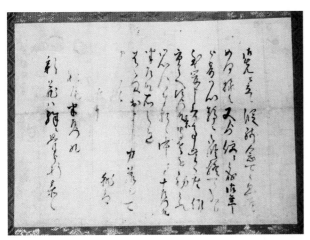

*photo: Getty Images*

*Handwritten manuscript of a poem by Matsuo Basho, written two days before his death in 1694.*

The years of the Tokugawa shogunate were the "golden age" of haiku, but the Japanese still write them today. In fact, hundreds of magazines now publish haiku in Japan and in many other countries. Like much in Japanese feudal society, these poems and their creation were influenced by the strict class structure of society.

The social structure of feudal Japan greatly influenced the lives of its inhabitants. People's rank in society determined the types of work they did, the power and wealth they had, and even the types of cultural activities they participated in and enjoyed.

**Consider the Essential Question:**

What effects did power and social class have on Japanese feudal society?

Go online to complete the Social Studies Explanation.

**Check for Understanding:**

What effects did power and social class have on Japanese feudal society? Create a mind map to address this question.

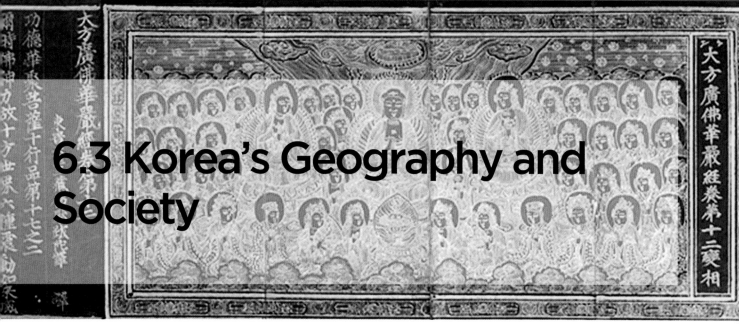

photo: Ancient History Encyclopedia

# 6.3 Korea's Geography and Society

## LESSON OVERVIEW

### Introduction

In this concept, you will learn about the location and geography of Korea. You will also investigate how Korea's location influenced its culture and the exchange of ideas between China, Korea, and Japan.

### Essential Question

How did physical location impact life in ancient Korea?

### Lesson Objectives

By the end of this lesson, you should be able to:

- Locate the boundaries, important cities, and bodies of water of Korea on a map.

- Analyze how the geography of the region shaped the way of life of the people living there.

- Explain the importance of Mongol rule on Korean society.

- Explain how Korea has served as a link between China and Japan.

### Key Vocabulary
Which terms do you already know?

- [ ] absolute monarchy
- [ ] Buddhism
- [ ] celadon
- [ ] China
- [ ] Chosŏn
- [ ] Chosŏn dynasty
- [ ] Confucianism
- [ ] Europe
- [ ] Han dynasty
- [ ] Japan
- [ ] Johannes Gutenberg
- [ ] Koguryŏ
- [ ] Korea
- [ ] Koryŏ
- [ ] Mongols
- [ ] Neo-Confucianism
- [ ] Paekche
- [ ] Silk Road
- [ ] Silla
- [ ] Taoism
- [ ] Wang Kon
- [ ] yangban

# ENGAGE

> **How did Korea's location create an exchange of culture and ideas? Visit Engage to learn more.**

## Essential Question

How did physical location impact life in ancient Korea?

# EXPLORE

## Korea's Geography

### *Where is Korea located?*

Korea is located on a peninsula in East Asia. Though Korea is not an island, it is bordered on all sides by water. To the northwest, separating Korea from China, its northern neighbor, is the Amnok River, which flows down from Mount Paektu. This river travels 500 miles southwest to the Korea Bay. When the river reaches the bay, it empties into the Yellow Sea, on Korea's western border. To the northeast, Korea is separated from China and Russia by the Tumen River. This river flows northeastward to the Sea of Japan, which borders Korea to the east.

Korea's surface is almost completely covered by mountains and hills. The country's farmland and most of its people are found along the southern and western coasts. Even these areas are not completely flat. They are covered with rolling plains and low hills.

A system of rivers flows to the west and south in the southern part of Korea. These rivers include the Han, Kum, Naktong, and Somjin Rivers. Because of the hilly terrain of Korea, these rivers are important to commerce because they make inland travel easier.

> **Explore this interactive to learn more about how geography affected Korea's development.**

Korea's proximity to Japan has been both troublesome and beneficial to Korea. However, Korea's nearest neighbor, China, has most severely and repeatedly affected Korea's history.

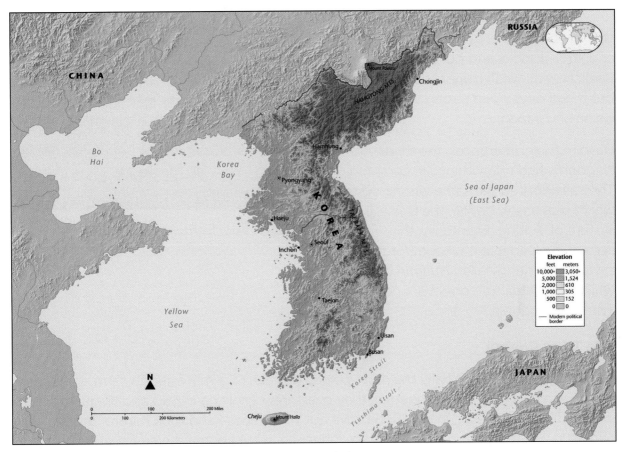

*Korea is located on the southern border of China near the island of Japan.*

## Old Chosŏn

### *How were Korea's earliest days influenced by China?*

The earliest known Korean state was Chosŏn (CHO-sən). It was established in the Taedong River basin, in the northern part of the Korean Peninsula. The legend is that Chosŏn was founded by Tan'gun, who was believed to be the child of the son of heaven and a bear in the form of a woman.

### Chinese Influence

In 108 BCE, Chosŏn was overthrown by China's Han dynasty. The Chinese then established colonies, which are settlements that are established in a distant land that are governed by and considered part of a separate country. The establishment of these colonies essentially made Korea a part of the Chinese Empire. This would be the first of many times that Korea's closest neighbor invaded.

Over time, these Chinese colonies evolved into separate tribal states. Some of these tribal states joined together into federations under one rule. Eventually, these federations of states evolved into three kingdoms: Koguryŏ (GO-gur-yo) (which existed in Korea before the Chinese invasion), Paekche (BEK-chyeh), and Silla (SHIH-lah), which took hold in the southern part of Korea where Chinese influence was not as strong.

Koguryŏ had a strong military. Silla had a strong educational system, several schools, and strong social and political institutions. Paekche was weak militarily and politically, but it had developed strong ties with China and Japan.

Despite their differences, the three kingdoms had many things in common. They all adopted the same writing system, which was based on *idu*, the Chinese system of writing. Eventually, this writing system evolved into a unique Korean system of writing called *Hunmin chongum*, which translates to "correct sounds for instructing people."

photo: Getty Images
*The image shows traditional Korean characters.*

## Silla Takes Control

Though Koguryŏ was initially the most powerful state, Silla managed to form an alliance with China's Tang dynasty. Together, they overthrew Paekche in 660 and Koguryŏ in 668. Eight years later, in 676, Silla drove out the Chinese and took control of the peninsula. Silla's culture, and its Chinese influence, would dominate and shape life in Korea for hundreds of years.

## United Under Silla

*What role did Buddhism play in Silla's Korea?*

With the three kingdoms unified under one rule, Korea was under the control of an absolute monarchy. An absolute monarchy is a government in which the monarch, usually a king or queen, has complete control. Aristocrats held government offices and controlled some land, but once they left office, they lost control of the land. In this way, the real control remained with the monarch.

Buddhism had come to Korea from China and became popular on the peninsula between the 300s and 500s. Buddhism would also become an essential part of life in Korea under Silla rule. Buddhism is a religion and philosophy that teaches that life is suffering and that freedom from suffering can only be reached by turning away from worldly desires.

photo: Getty Images
*Three stone Buddhas from the Silla period, present-day South Korea.*

Buddhism influenced almost all aspects of Korean life, including the arts, intellectual life, and politics. To this day, beautiful works of art and temples from this period can be seen throughout Korea.

Buddhism became very important to the Korean people. Over time, religious leaders became more powerful and influential than political leaders. Because of the influence of religious leaders, and the growing struggles between aristocrats, by the 800s, Silla's grip on Korea was weakening.

## Koguryŏ's Korea

### How did Korea's next dynasty come into power?

By 935, the three kingdoms were again becoming separate nations with their own identities. This time, however, it was Koguryŏ, which was now known as Koryŏ, that was the most powerful of the three. Koryŏ is where the Western name, Korea, developed from.

Koryŏ was founded by a statesman and warrior named Wang Kon. Wang Kon once again united the three kingdoms under one rule and established the Koryŏ dynasty. The Koryŏ dynasty prospered over the next hundred years, thanks in part to its system of government, which was influenced by China. The old tribal system of government was replaced with a centralized system that included civil service exams for government officials.

*photo: Getty Images*
*The Koryŏ potters were great craftsman and created many kinds of pottery.*

One product of the Koryŏ dynasty that is still greatly appreciated today is its artwork and pottery such as celadon, which is green stoneware. This pottery was inspired by Buddhism, which also flourished in this period. Buddhist monks developed the pottery because they needed beautiful vessels for their rituals and ceremonies. Later, Korean artists perfected Chinese techniques of copper glazing to add intricate designs to the celadon. This pottery became famous throughout Asia and was used to decorate palaces.

## Koryŏ Society

### What was the social structure during the Koryŏ dynasty?

Early Koryŏ society was based on a hierarchical structure. Much of the power rested in the hands of the upper classes. For example, wealthy landowners made up the majority of the ruling class. For this reason, family heritage (the status, wealth, and tradition passed on from family members) was an important part of life.

Members of the highest-ranking families were awarded government positions without needing to pass the civil service exams that were given to members of the lower classes.

The peasant, or common, class in Koryŏ worked the land for the landowning class. They paid taxes to the owners of the land they worked in return for protection. This system led to an increase in the power and wealth of the ruling class. As more and more peasants paid taxes to landowners, the government received less money. Because of this, Koryŏ leadership over the peninsula began to weaken.

photo: Getty Images

Stone statues stand guard at Kaesong, the ancient capital of the Koryŏ dynasty.

Meanwhile, the military class was feeling discriminated against. Military members were not allowed to rise beyond the second of nine government levels, which left them with little say over the government of the country. They also were given smaller allotments of land than civilians, who were awarded the same government positions. In 1170, the military revolted and overthrew the ruling class. The military became the real power behind the kings.

The internal conflict caused by this military takeover left Koryŏ open to another invasion. However, this time, the invasion did not come from China.

## Enter the Mongols

### How did Korea thrive in spite of invasion?

The Mongols, a nomadic people from the north of China, had already conquered much of Europe and Asia when they invaded Koryŏ in 1231. For nearly 30 years, the military, and even the civilians of Korea, fought back. However, the Mongols successfully took control of Koryŏ in 1259. Under the treaty signed with the Mongols, the Korean kings were able to remain in control.

The years of Mongol occupation were prosperous ones for Koryŏ. The Mongols controlled the Silk Road, a vast network of land- and sea-based trading routes that connected Asia and Europe. Korean exports and ideas spread throughout Asia and Europe along the Silk Road. In turn, Koreans imported goods and were exposed to new ideas from around the world.

*Bronze casts of Korean type, 1406.*

photo: Getty Images

## New Developments

Perhaps the greatest invention that Korea shared with its neighbors was metal movable type, similar to the wooden block version that had developed in China. This process for printing books was created in Korea 200 years before Johannes Gutenberg invented his printing press in Europe. Monarchs hired metalworkers to print books that would spread artistic and philosophical knowledge.

A feudal system developed during this time. In a feudal system, land was owned by aristocrats and worked by tenants. These tenants paid taxes to the landowners, who lived in the cities. Many tenants chose to become servants to the landowners to avoid the mandatory military service and state duties expected of tenants. By the mid-1300s, this had resulted in a depleted military.

## Political Tension

Meanwhile, strains were growing among the aristocracy. The government was no longer able to grant land to newly appointed officials. A class of scholar-officials took over the government and began to grant land to officials according to rank.

The Mongol invaders had found it difficult to take and maintain control of Korea. After several years of resistance, the new government was able to arrive at a peace treaty with the Mongol Empire. Although this treaty effectively ended Mongol control of Koryŏ, the changes to its structure were irreversible. In 1392, the Koryŏ dynasty came to an end.

## New Chosŏn

### *How did Korea change after Mongol rule?*

During the 1300s, Korea had begun to turn away from Buddhism. The people became excited about a new form of Confucianism. Confucianism, which developed in China, teaches that through virtue and ethics, in personal and community life, human beings can be taught, improved, and perfected. As Koryŏ's officials were losing direction and control, Confucianism inspired the ruling middle class to found the Chosŏn dynasty in 1392. Chosŏn was run by the yangban, an aristocratic class.

photo: Getty Images

*Portrait of Sejong the Great, fourth king of the Chosŏn dynasty, on South Korean currency.*

Members of the yangban studied Neo-Confucianism, a branch of Confucianism that combined elements of Buddhism and Taoism, and held many public offices. They established a social and political structure that would become the longest lasting dynasty in world history, not ending until 1910.

## A Distinct Culture

Chosŏn society distinguished itself from China in many ways. The Korean method of metal movable type, which was no longer being used, was brought back. In 1446, Korea developed its own alphabet, called Hangul.

For its first 200 years, Korea knew peace and prosperity. But Korea's location again threatened its peace. In 1592, Japan invaded Korea, wanting to use it as a launching point for an invasion of China. Chosŏn joined forces with China's Ming dynasty and drove Japan back in 1598.

## Japanese Invasion

One by-product of Japan's invasion was that in 1593 one of Japan's armies brought the process of metal movable type back from Korea. They adapted it, using wood instead of metal in some cases, and the process spread. Books and pamphlets could then be created more quickly and cheaply than before, which allowed information to spread more easily. Many metalworkers from Korea also traveled to Japan and shared their knowledge of the craft with their Japanese counterparts. They also carried with them elements of Chinese and Korean culture that would in turn influence the culture of Japan.

Korea's geography left it vulnerable to several attacks from the strong powers that lived nearby. However, these invading forces also brought their ideas, technology, religion, and culture, and they helped shape Korea.

**Consider the Essential Question:**

How did physical location impact life in ancient Korea?

Go online to complete the Social Studies Explanation.

**Check for Understanding:**

What aspects of Korea's location made it vulnerable to foreign invasion? How did these invasions shape Korea's history and society?

# 7.1 Early North American Cultures and the Maya

*photo: Getty Images*

## LESSON OVERVIEW

### Introduction

In this concept, you will learn about the Maya and other peoples who lived in North and South America before the arrival of European explorers. You will also analyze how the land in which each civilization developed shaped its culture.

### Essential Question

How did physical geography shape the early societies of the Americas?

### Lesson Objectives

By the end of this lesson, you should be able to:

- Locate the physical features and early American civilizations on a map of the Americas.

- Describe how the geography of the region shaped the way of life of the people living there.

- Describe Mayan culture and scientific innovations.

### Key Vocabulary
Which terms do you already know?

- [ ] Amazon River
- [ ] Andes
- [ ] Atlantic Ocean
- [ ] Aztec
- [ ] Central Plateau
- [ ] Chichén Itzá
- [ ] Christopher Columbus
- [ ] Classic Period
- [ ] climate
- [ ] codex
- [ ] colonization
- [ ] conquistador
- [ ] Copan
- [ ] Egypt
- [ ] Inca
- [ ] indentured servant
- [ ] infrastructure
- [ ] La Venta
- [ ] maize
- [ ] Maya
- [ ] mestizo
- [ ] Mexico
- [ ] Middle America
- [ ] Nile River
- [ ] Northwest Passage
- [ ] Olmec
- [ ] Peru
- [ ] polytheism
- [ ] South America
- [ ] stela
- [ ] steppe
- [ ] terrace farming
- [ ] Toltec
- [ ] treaty
- [ ] Yucatán Peninsula
- [ ] ziggurat

Discovery SOCIAL STUDIES
EDUCATION TECHBOOK

How did physical geography shape the early societies
of the Americas?

# ENGAGE

**How did geography shape home design in the ancient Americas?
Visit Engage to learn more.**

| **Essential Question**

How did physical geography shape the early societies of the Americas?

# EXPLORE

## Geography of Mesoamerica

*What are the important geographical features of the Americas?*

North America and South America are large continents, joined by a thin strip of land called Central America. The continents are bordered to the east by the Atlantic Ocean and the Gulf of Mexico and to the west by the Pacific Ocean. North America reaches up to the Arctic Circle, while the equator runs through South America.

Both of the American continents have diverse geography and climates, with coastal mountain ranges, temperate and tropical forests, and deserts. South America also includes regions covered by rain forests. In general, North America is cooler, with a larger temperate zone. However, it has deserts in the Southwest. Central and South America are hotter. They have desert and jungle regions as well as mountains and plains. The Rockies in North America and the Andes in South America are part of a single mountain spine that runs along the entire west coast of the Americas.

The Amazon River is located in the northern part of South America. It is nearly 4,000 miles long, making it the second-longest river in the world. Only the Nile River in Egypt is longer. The Amazon River flows down from the Andes Mountains in Peru, where it is fed by melting snow and ice. It flows east through the Amazon rain forest, and is joined by a huge network of rivers and tributaries before emptying into the Atlantic Ocean.

The continents of North and South America were home to a rich and diverse range of cultures that developed hundreds of years before Europeans found them. Each civilization was shaped by the land where it grew.

*This map shows the physical features of South America. How are they similar to North America?*

Human presence in Mesoamerica can be traced back as early as 21,000 BCE. Hunting-and-gathering groups existed for centuries before agricultural practices began to appear around 7000 BCE. By approximately 1500 BCE, early civilizations began to emerge in the Andes.

The Olmec are one of the oldest known Mesoamerican civilizations, dating from about 1200 to 400 BCE in southern Mexico. After 300 BCE, many other Mesoamerican cultures flourished, including the Maya, Inca, and Aztec.

## Nations of the Pre-Columbian Americas
*How did the Toltec and Olmec influence Mesoamerican culture?*

The three largest and most powerful civilizations in pre-Columbian Americas were the Maya in Central America, the Aztec in central Mexico, and the Inca in the Andes of South America. These civilizations thrived and left behind impressive artifacts that have taught modern historians much about their cultures.

Discovery EDUCATION | SOCIAL STUDIES TECHBOOK

How did physical geography shape the early societies of the Americas?

Both the Maya and the Aztec were influenced by the Olmec civilization, the earliest known civilization in Mesoamerica. Mesoamerica is the region that is now Mexico and Central America. In pre-Columbian times, it was the most densely populated region of the Americas. The Olmec lived along the Gulf Coast of modern-day Mexico in tropical rain forests and lowlands from around 1200 BCE to 400 BCE. Sculptures and temples indicate that kings or priests led the Olmec society. This focus on religious leadership influenced later civilizations in the region. At former religious centers characterized by pyramid-shaped temples, giant stone heads weighing 10 tons stood up to 11 feet tall. The Olmec also developed a form of writing, as well as a calendar. Through their trade networks, the Olmec were able to spread many characteristics of their culture, religion, architecture, and social structure north to the Valley of Mexico and around Central America.

photo: Getty Images

*This giant head sculpture, carved by the Olmec, is similar to giant sculptures the Maya would later create.*

In some ways, the Olmec were similar to the four early river valley civilizations that developed along the Nile, Tigris-Euphrates, Indus, and Yellow Rivers. Although the Olmec did not need to develop irrigation systems because they received plenty of rain, they did need to create drainage systems to control the water from this rain. Like the Fertile Crescent in Mesopotamia, the soil was rich enough to support farming. As mentioned earlier, Olmec society was based around its religion, and they created pyramid-like structures similar to those found near the Nile and Tigris-Euphrates Rivers. Also, like the first major civilizations in the Fertile Crescent, Nile valley, Indus valley, and Huang He valley, the Olmec showed the first evidence of many economic, social, and cultural patterns that would shape future civilizations throughout the region.

The Toltec were a warrior society that lived in what is now central Mexico. From the 900s through 1100s CE, they created an empire through conquest and military strength. The Toltec military power provided a model for future civilizations, such as the Aztec. Many scholars believe that Toltec culture and religion also had a strong influence on future civilizations.

The Aztec and the Maya each branched away from their common origin and developed their own unique features. The Inca built a large empire in the Andes Mountains of South America. The cultures and characteristics of these empires were affected by the climate and geography of the regions where they developed. This was also true of smaller Mesoamerican groups.

## Ancient Builders

*How did geography shape the development of early North American people?*

### Mound Builders

The early people who lived in North America constructed mounds out of earth. Some mounds date to before 5000 BCE. Some of the best-known earthen mounds in the United States were constructed from about 700 BCE to 1000 BCE by people living in the areas that today make up the midwest and southeast United States. These mound builders are known as Mississippians. Many of these mounds can be found today in the Ohio and Mississippi River valleys. Floodplains and river valleys were good for farming, so villages and towns developed in these areas. Some of these communities still existed when Europeans arrived in North America beginning in the mid-1500s.

photo: Getty Images

*Archeologists thought this huge earthen structure might have been the lost City of the Sun.*

These societies used the mounds in several ways. Round or conical mounds were individual homes or burial sites. Some mounds were built in the shape of animals, such as Serpent Mound in Ohio. Temples and other public buildings stood on top of large platform mounds. They were often built around an open central plaza.

Some mounds, called midden mounds, were used to store garbage. These mounds are the ancestors of modern landfills. Midden mounds are some of the oldest mounds archeologists have discovered, which shows that the problem of what to do with garbage is not a new one. Archeologists have learned a lot about these civilizations by examining what was thrown away.

photo: Getty Images

*Example of a cliff dwelling in Mesa Verde National Park, Colorado.*

### Cliff Dwellers

The Ancestral Pueblo, sometimes called the Anasazi, were the ancestors of the modern Pueblo tribes. These include groups such as the Hopi, Zuni, Acoma, and Laguna, who continue to live in the modern-day southwestern United States. As the Ancestral Pueblo shifted from hunting and gathering to farming, they built settlements and irrigation systems so they could farm in the desert.

At first, the Ancestral Pueblo lived in houses built partially underground, or on top of rocky plateaus known as mesas. Around 1150, they began building cliff dwellings out of sandstone, wooden beams, and adobe mortar, made from mud.

Some of these cliff dwellings were essentially villages, having anywhere from 20 to 1,000 rooms. To get from one floor to the next, people climbed up ladders. The Ancestral Pueblo may have built these villages in the cliffs for protection against invaders. They abandoned the cliff dwellings by the 1300s, perhaps because of a severe drought. The influence of the Ancestral Pueblo and their descendants can still be seen in modern architecture styles in the American Southwest.

## The Maya

### What were the characteristics of the Mayan civilization?

The Maya started settling in villages around 1500 BCE. The Mayan civilization started to become more complex around 250 CE. Cities grew and trade increased. The Mayan civilization thrived until around 900 CE. It had declined by the time European explorers arrived. Before the arrival of the Spanish conquistadors, the Maya were one of the most advanced civilizations of Mesoamerica.

The Maya lived in modern-day southern Mexico and Central America, including the areas that are today Belize, El Salvador, Guatemala, and Honduras. They were an agriculture-based society.

At its height, the Mayan civilization reached from the lowlands of the Yucatan Peninsula to the highlands of northern Central America. Today, many of the descendants of those early Maya live in Belize, Guatemala, Honduras, and Mexico.

Modern-day Maya still engage in some of the same practices as those of the ancient Maya. They grow the same crops, such as corn, beans, and squash, and practice many of the same crafts, such as weaving and pottery. Modern-day Maya even speak languages that developed from the original Maya languages.

photo: Paul Fuqua

*Mayan temples included giant limestone pyramids like this one from Chichén Itzá.*

Their central location made it very easy for the Maya to trade and interact with other cultures from North and South America. This enriched the Mayan culture, as they absorbed many ideas from the peoples with whom they traded. The Maya built a large and complex system of roads to stay connected with other cities and peoples.

Many remains of Mayan cities can be found in the jungles of Central America. The city of Chichén Itzá, in the Yucatan, is home to a large number of ancient Mayan ruins, including sculptures of giant serpents, a huge ziggurat, or pyramid, and an observatory used by astronomers. Mayan buildings were often covered with plaster and painted red. Traces of plaster and paint can be found on the ruins today.

## Mayan Agriculture

*What role did agriculture play in the Mayan civilization?*

The climate through most of Mesoamerica was warm, and the majority of the land was very fertile. Mayan farmers who lived in the hilly highlands

photo: Getty Images

*A stone bust of the Mayan Maize God, circa 600–800 CE.*

practiced slash and burn agriculture to clear out the rain forests, and also utilized irrigation systems and terrace farming. They carved steps, or terraces, into their land so they could farm more efficiently. The Maya also raised turkeys for their meat and feathers.

Corn, called maize, was a primary crop for all Mesoamerican cultures, including the Maya. Other crops included squash, beans, and hot peppers. The Maya grew cacao beans, which are used today to make chocolate. Mayan chocolate was not sweet like we think of it today, but a hot, bitter drink. The Maya also used cacao beans as a form of money.

Another unusual Mayan crop was rubber. The Maya cut slits in the bark of the rubber tree and collected its sap. They used the dried sap to make water-resistant shoes and clothing. Rubber was also used to make balls. The Maya played games in enclosed, I-shaped courts with the rubber balls. These ball games took on a ritual significance and were an important part of Mayan culture.

**Explore this interactive to learn more about the importance of calendars to Mayan daily life.**

## Mayan Religion

### What was the religious culture of the Maya?

The Mayan religion was polytheistic, meaning that the Maya believed in many gods. These gods represented the natural world, such as the sun, moon, and corn. At the top of pyramid-shaped temples, powerful priests conducted ceremonies believed to ensure good harvests and success in war.

The Maya believed that the gods were responsible for many aspects of life and could provide good weather and good health, or cause illness and misfortune. Priests, who were believed to have magical powers, conducted ritual ceremonies and sacrifices to encourage the gods to help them, as well as to celebrate victories. They made sacrifices of plants, animals, and humans. Many of the sacrificed humans were prisoners of war and enslaved people. Other ceremonies involved praying,

photo: Paul Fuqua

*This stone carving shows a Maya warrior and a skull. Why might artists carve this in their city?*

music, and ball games. All of the rituals were based on a 260-day calendar, which the priests interpreted. In addition to determining which rituals to perform, the priests also informed people of which days were best for activities such as building houses, weddings, and paying debts.

The Maya built large, stepped pyramids that served as temples in the center of many of their cities. While the priests conducted sacrifices and other rituals on a platform at the top of the pyramid, audiences watched from a large plaza below. Some rulers were buried in the temples.

## A Decentralized Nation

### How did the Maya organize their society?

The Maya were among the first agricultural societies in Mesoamerica. In fact, agriculture was the basis of their culture. The warm climate and fertile valleys made it easy to grow crops. Over time, some of the Mayan population that lived in small villages united under larger cities. Unlike the Inca and the Aztec, the Maya did not have a single ruler, such as an emperor, or a central government. Instead, each city had its own individual leader. This ruler organized military leaders and officials, who could then organize workers to build irrigation systems, grow food, and construct buildings. A typical Mayan city had a marketplace where food, ceramics, and a variety of other goods could be traded. Many Mayan cities had special courts to play a ball game that was a combination of modern soccer and basketball. These sorts of courts have been found in ancient cities across Mesoamerica and the southwestern United States.

photo: Paul Fuqua

*In Mayan ball courts such as this, battles between cities were reenacted. The losing team was often sacrificed.*

Until the mid-1900s, historians thought that the ancient Maya had a peaceful society. However, as they deciphered Mayan hieroglyphics, historians learned that the Maya were more warlike than previously believed. Because they were not united under a central ruler, Mayan cities often fought each other in bloody wars to gain additional territory, wealth, or power. The victors then often sacrificed the leaders and nobility of the conquered city. In some cases, after a battle, the victorious army would play a ball game against their prisoners to re-create the battle. The victorious army would always win, and the prisoners were often sacrificed afterward.

Around 750 CE, the Mayan civilization entered a period of increased warfare, leading to decreased trade and the construction of fewer monumental buildings. Deforestation and drought may have also been factors in the decline of trade. River and land trade routes became disrupted, and the human population in cities dwindled.

Although the Mayan civilization collapsed around 900, possibly due to a combination of warfare, overpopulation, and failed crops, Maya continued to survive as farmers in small villages in the south. In the north, the Toltec and other groups may have ruled over still-thriving Mayan societies until the

**Explore this resource and write a script for a documentary about Mayan ball games.**

Spanish conquistadors arrived. When the Spanish conquistadors arrived in the 1500s, they found that fighting the Maya was much harder than conquering other groups, such as the Aztec and the Inca, because the Maya did not have a single ruler who could be toppled. Instead, the Spanish had to fight each Mayan city separately. While they were fighting one city, others would band together and drive the Spanish back. The Maya fought fiercely for several years. However, by 1524, only one Mayan group, the Itza, remained unconquered.

## A Society of Thinkers

*What scientific innovations did the Maya develop?*

The Maya made a number of significant advances in learning. They developed a hieroglyphic writing system as well as a number system that was one of the first to include the concept of zero. They also advanced innovations that originated with earlier societies. For example, although some historians believe the Maya may have started with an early Olmec calendar, they improved upon it and developed it into a very precise calendar.

**Discovery** | SOCIAL STUDIES
EDUCATION | **TECHBOOK**

How did physical geography shape the early societies
of the Americas?

The Maya were skilled builders, mathematicians, and astronomers. They left numerous written records of their achievements. Some records were carved or painted into a stone column called a stela. Others were written on deer hide or on paper made from wild fig trees, which was folded into a type of book called a codex.

photo: Paul Fuqua

*This Mayan observatory is called a caracol, or snail, because of its round tower.*

The Maya had several different calendars. One of them was a solar calendar, based on the movements of the sun. It had 360 days, along with a month of five unlucky days. On these "bad" days, the Maya made sacrifices to their gods. This came to a total of 365 days—very close to the calendars we use today. The second calendar was a ritual calendar, used by priests to determine which days were good days and which were bad. This one had only 260 days. These two calendars were combined into a "Calendar Round" system, where it took 52 years for a date to repeat. One of the main purposes of the Mayan calendar was to ensure that rulers and priests knew when to hold religious ceremonies.

## Language and Math

*What cultural innovations did the Mayan civilization develop?*

Not only did the Maya develop a complex calendar, they also developed a unique number system that included the concept of zero. It used only three different symbols. It was likely based on an earlier system used by the Zapotec Indians who lived nearby in Mexico. Mayan math may look primitive, but it was incredibly flexible and could be used to solve complex calculations.

The Maya also developed a sophisticated hieroglyphic writing system that contains more than 800 characters. Some of the signs are pictures that represent words. Others represent syllables. This variety of characters made it difficult to decipher. It was not until the late 1900s that scholars were able to make significant progress in interpreting Mayan writings.

In the 1500s, Spanish priests trying to convert the Maya to Christianity burned many Mayan codices. The few that survived have allowed historians to learn more about Mayan religious practices. Although Mayan written texts were destroyed, their spoken language survived the arrival of the Spanish settlers. About 30 variations of the original Mayan languages are still spoken today by many people in Central America and Mexico.

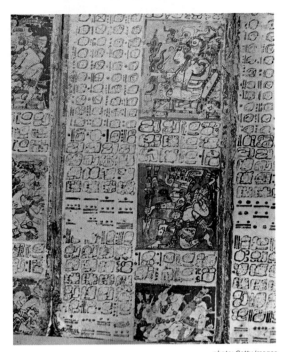
*photo: Getty Images*
*The Maya wrote using a combination of images.*

A large number of modern Mayan people speak a language called Yucatec. Other Maya speak related languages that include the following: Huastec, Chanabal, Chol, Chontal, Chorti, Chuj, Jacaltec, Motozintlec, Tzental, Tzotzil, Kekchi, Pokomam, Pokonchi, Cakchiquel, Quiche, Tzutuhil, Uspantec, Aguacatec, Ixil, and Mam.

The movement of the Maya into several geographic regions helped their culture and language survive. The Maya built many of their cities near rivers, which allowed people from other Mayan cities, as well as other civilizations, to easily reach them. This encouraged an exchange of goods and ideas. Mayan culture survived the fall of their civilization, and today, many Mayan communities continue to preserve their traditional culture.

Geography influenced other Mesoamerican groups as well. As other Mesoamerican people adapted to the climate and geography of the regions in which they settled, they, like the Maya, developed distinct societies and cultures.

**Consider the Essential Question:**

How did physical geography shape the early societies of the Americas?

Go online to complete the Social Studies Explanation.

**Check for Understanding:**

What are the main geographical differences between the locations of the Mayan and Anasazi civilizations? How might these differences have affected the people who lived there?

**Discovery** | SOCIAL STUDIES
EDUCATION | **TECHBOOK**

How did the Aztec Empire become so powerful with such speed?

# 7.2 The Aztec Empire

## LESSON OVERVIEW

### Introduction

In this concept, you will learn about the rise and growth of the Aztec Empire. You will also examine the political and social structure of Aztec civilization.

### Essential Question

How did the Aztec Empire become so powerful with such speed?

### Lesson Objectives

By the end of this lesson, you should be able to:

- Explain the rise and growth of the Aztec Empire.

- Analyze the political and social structure of Aztec civilization.

### Key Vocabulary
Which terms do you already know?

- ☐ Aztec
- ☐ Aztec Empire
- ☐ conquistador
- ☐ Hernán Cortés
- ☐ Itzcóatl
- ☐ Lake Texcoco
- ☐ Mayans
- ☐ Mexica
- ☐ Mexico
- ☐ Montezuma
- ☐ polytheism
- ☐ social class
- ☐ tribute

## ENGAGE

When the Spanish first encountered the Aztec, what did they find? Visit Engage to learn more.

### Essential Question

How did the Aztec Empire become so powerful with such speed?

## EXPLORE

### The Earliest Days of Mexico

*Who were the Aztec people?*

The beginnings of the Aztec civilization occurred in the desert of modern-day Mexico. As you will read later, the Aztec civilization grew to become a great empire after King Itzcóatl took power in 1428 CE.

*photo: Getty Images*

*Aztec carving depicting an eagle, with the date of the founding of Tenochtitlán. What is the significance of the eagle in Aztec lore?*

The origins of the Aztec people are uncertain. None of the earliest people of Latin America called themselves the Aztec; this name appeared only later, after the Spanish conquest. According to Aztec legend, the Toltec Empire started around 800 CE and spanned most of what is now Mexico and Central America. One group of people ruled by the Toltecs was the Mexica. When the Toltec Empire collapsed, around 1150 CE, the Mexica were forced out of their homeland, which they called Aztlán. The name Aztec developed in part from Aztlán, the name of their homeland. Though part of Aztec legend, historians believe that these events are historically accurate.

The Mexica or Aztec had a reputation for savage warfare and were therefore unwelcome wherever they went. As a result, they lived as nomads, looking for a permanent place to settle.

Explore this interactive to learn more about how the Spanish used drawings to depict elements of Aztec society.

Another Aztec legend was the story of Copil and his uncle, the god Huitzilopochtli. Copil resented and tormented the Aztec because they were Huitzilopochtli's chosen people. Copil was also angry at Huitzilopochtli because he believed the god had treated his mother unfairly. Copil planned to ambush Huitzilopochtli, but before he could do so, Huitzilopochtli killed Copil. Huitzilopochtli cut out Copil's heart and threw it into a lake. Later, Huitzilopochtli told the Aztec to settle where Copil's heart could be found. They would know the place when they saw an eagle perched on a cactus, eating a snake.

While the Aztec were roaming around the marshes surrounding Lake Texcoco, they saw the cactus and eagle and stopped on the spot to build their empire. In 1325, they settled on an island in the southwestern portion of Lake Texcoco. They named this place Tenochtitlán.

Today, the ruins of Tenochtitlán lie in Mexico City, the capital of modern-day Mexico. During the time of the Aztec Empire, Tenochtitlán was a large city that had layers of defenses protecting it from any invading tribes. In the end, the Spanish conquistadors, or conquerors, would overcome these defenses.

## The Aztec Build an Empire

### How did the Aztec people become united?

Itzcóatl was the fourth leader of the Mexica, or Aztec, people. The Mexica called their leaders *tlatoani*, which means "emperor." Itzcóatl came to power in 1428 and created a powerful empire by joining with two neighboring peoples to form the Triple Alliance. The three allies were the leaders of the cities of Tenochtitlán, Texcoco, and Tlacopan. Rather than fight each other for supreme power over other local towns and peoples, they agreed to share power. The three rulers worked together to defeat the powerful Tepanec Empire from Atzcapotzalco in central Mexico, which had previously controlled the Aztec. During their empire, the Tepanec had a large city located on the northern side of Lake Texcoco. Since Itzcóatl's city of Tenochtitlán was on the southern side, defeating the Tepanec meant that the two sides of the lake were united politically under one ruler.

photo: Getty Images

*The Teotihuacan civilization influenced the Aztec.*

The Aztec, or Mexica, gained large areas of land with the defeat of the Tepanec. This gave Itzcóatl much power in the region, and the empire became centralized under his rule. Conquered peoples could choose to leave the land in search of a new home, or they could pay tribute, a special tax paid to the Aztec emperor. This tribute increased the wealth and resources available to Itzcóatl. These resources helped him to continue the conquests of new lands, which in turn brought further wealth and resources.

## Further Expansion

*How did the Aztec Empire continue to expand under the rule of Itzcóatl?*

The tributes collected from the conquered lands made Itzcóatl a powerful and wealthy man. As part of the tribute, every six months, 800 large white mantas, or woven blankets, had to be delivered to Itzcóatl. Additionally, every year, a tribute of two warrior costumes and shields, six bins of maize (corn), two bins of beans, and four bins of herbs were also given to the emperor. Conquered regions also sent gold and enslaved people, the latter to be used as labor or as human sacrifices, to the Aztec leader as tribute. While the Triple Alliance divided material goods and resources taken during the conquests of new lands, only the Aztec were given the tributes.

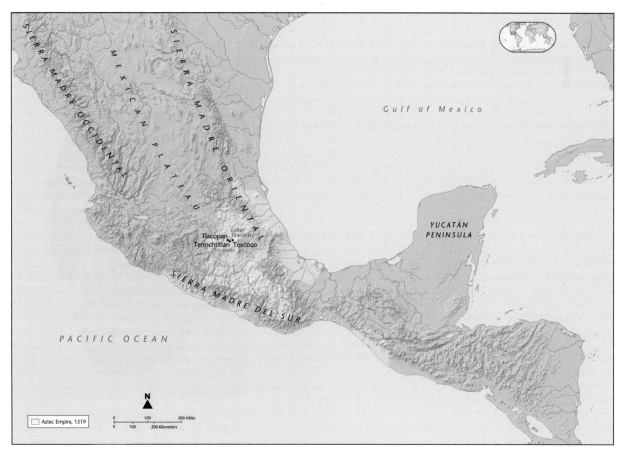

*This physical map of Mexico shows the borders of the location of the cities of the Triple Alliance and the extent of the Aztec Empire in 1519.*

As the empire continued to expand and Itzcóatl's power increased, he ordered that the existing history of the Aztec be destroyed because he believed it was inaccurate and contained lies. As a result, the empire was given a shared history that was more closely related to the legends of the Aztec. This new history presented the Aztec as a culture that had always been powerful and emphasized Itzcóatl's importance.

Itzcóatl spent his reign expanding his empire beyond the Valley of Mexico and into the surrounding areas by adopting the conquered tribes into his territory. Under his leadership, the empire spread quickly. The leaders following Itzcóatl took over additional territory, making the Aztec Empire the central block of Mexico and a powerful entity.

## Religion of the Aztec

### What role did religion play in Aztec society?

Religion played a large role in the daily life of the Aztec people. The Aztec religion was a combination of many beliefs and practices from other Mesoamerican cultures. The Aztec believed that the current world was one in a series of four worlds, called suns, which had existed before it. They believed that each of these worlds had been completely destroyed before the new world began.

Aztec religion was polytheistic, meaning the Aztec believed in many gods. Chief among these gods were Huitzilopochtli, the Aztec god of war; Quetzalcóatl, the feathered serpent; and Tonatiuh, the sun god. Considerable time and resources in the form of religious ceremonies were devoted to worshipping these gods. These religious ceremonies were dictated by the Aztec calendar, which was the one used in much of Mesoamerica, and was made up of separate calendars containing 365 days and 260 days.

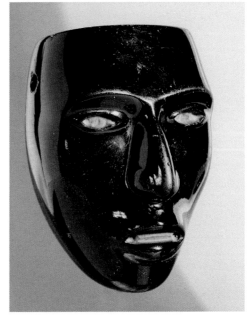

Many of the religious ceremonies performed by Aztec priests were intended to please the gods in an attempt to protect their civilization. For example, the Aztec believed that the sun god needed sacrifices of human hearts to ensure that the sun rose each day. Some of the sacrificial victims were enslaved people, but most were war captives. Many of those chosen for sacrifice were believers in the religion and thought they would go to the gods. The important role that priests played in these ceremonies meant that they held a high position within the rigid social structure of Aztec society.

photo: Getty Images

*Aztec masks like the one shown were used in religious rituals.*

## Daily Life in the Empire

### *What was life like in the Aztec Empire?*

As the Aztec expanded their empire and centralized control, a class system developed. As new lands were conquered, control of that land was removed from the conquered people. Itzcóatl gave large areas of land to his allies and friends. This class system greatly affected the daily lives of people in the empire. Classes were strictly divided—and the upper and lower classes of society never mixed. As the empire grew with each new conquest, the divide between the classes grew larger as the emperor gave more lands to the nobles and wealthy members of society. When the Spanish explorers arrived in the 1500s, they found that the lower classes of the Aztec society were not even allowed to enter the palace.

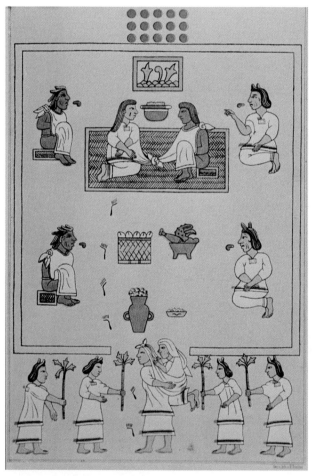

photo: Getty Images

*Depiction of an Aztec marriage on the Codex Mendoza. The Codex Mendoza features a Spanish artist's drawings of Aztec daily life.*

All Aztec children, male and female, attended school in some form. However, school and the type of education the children received differed for each social class and gender.

The education of males in Aztec society depended on their class. All boys received training as warriors. They learned fighting techniques and strategy, history, and religion and important rituals, as well as the correct social behaviors for their class. Children whose parents were skilled warriors or wealthy merchants were allowed to join the upper-class school. Members of the upper classes were trained to become temple priests or government officials and were responsible for leading the next generation of Aztec people. As a result of this, they learned the laws of the culture. Upper-class boys also learned writing, medicine, engineering, and religion, including important songs and dances.

School for young women of all classes in Aztec society was different from that for young men. Young women were educated for their roles in the home. They learned how to weave, sew, and cook. They also learned about their religion and how to sing and dance.

Despite the increasing size and wealth of the empire, there was unrest within the Aztec civilization. The poor classes did not like the restrictions placed on them by the emperor, such as the need to pay taxes and tribute to members of the upper classes. There were also many tribes who were unhappy about being a part of the empire, and as a result, there were often rebellions against the Aztec emperor. The tribes did not like having to pay tribute because it meant they had fewer resources for their own people. This restlessness in the empire paved the way for the Spanish conquest of the region.

## Montezuma and Cortés

*How were the Spanish explorers initially received by the new emperor?*

In the early 1500s, the Aztec Empire stretched from the Pacific Ocean to the coast of the Gulf of Mexico. All of central Mexico was ruled from the capital city of Tenochtitlán.

Moctezuma Xocoyotl or Montezuma II, the king we know today as Montezuma, came to power in 1502. He ruled over a vast empire. Over 15 million people in 38 provinces paid tribute to the new ruler in Tenochtitlán. Montezuma would be the last emperor of the Aztec Empire. He followed his uncle to the throne after being schooled in religion, science, and art. Like the leaders before him, Montezuma worked on expanding the Aztec Empire. He also led improvements in Tenochtitlán, enlarging the palace and creating a zoo.

In 1519, Spanish soldiers led by the explorer and conqueror Hernán Cortés landed on the shores of Montezuma's empire. Montezuma sent messengers to Cortés with gifts. Some historians believe Montezuma was convinced by the Spanish sailing ships and pale skin that the newcomers were gods. However, he also had his messengers warn the Spanish to stay away from Tenochtitlán and asked the temple priests to use charms to send them away. Montezuma was concerned that the men would endanger his throne.

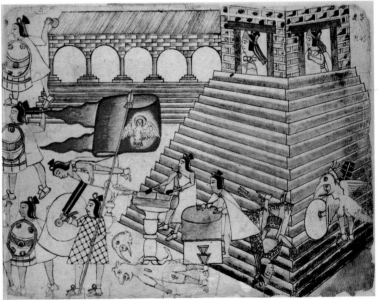

photo: Getty Images

*An illustration of Aztec warriors defending Tenochtitlán against Spanish conquistadors.*

As Cortés arrived in Tenochtitlán, Montezuma remained undecided on whether to treat the Spanish as enemies or potential allies. In the end, Montezuma decided to welcome the Spanish and invited them into his palace. This invitation set in motion events that would end in the conquest of the Aztec Empire by Spanish conquistadors. Despite its eventual fall, the Aztec Empire had been a powerful force in the region. The Aztec conquered and controlled large areas of the regions, established a lasting culture, and built advanced cities. Their impact can still be felt in the region today.

**Consider the Essential Question:**

How did the Aztec Empire become so powerful with such speed?

Go online to complete the Social Studies Explanation.

**Check for Understanding:**

In what ways did Aztec religious beliefs and practices play an important role in Aztec society? Be sure to provide details and examples to support your answer.

Discovery EDUCATION | SOCIAL STUDIES TECHBOOK

How did the Inca Empire maintain power across such a challenging geographic location?

# 7.3 The Inca Empire

photo: Paul Fuqua

## LESSON OVERVIEW

### Introduction

In this concept, you will learn how the physical geography of the Inca Empire shaped its people. You will discover how Inca political and social structures helped keep together an empire that spanned a large part of a continent.

### Key Vocabulary
Which terms do you already know?

- [ ] Andes
- [ ] Cuzco
- [ ] emperor
- [ ] Francisco Pizarro
- [ ] guano
- [ ] Inca
- [ ] irrigation
- [ ] llama
- [ ] Machu Picchu
- [ ] Pachacuti
- [ ] Peru
- [ ] South America
- [ ] terrace farming

### Essential Question

How did the Inca Empire maintain power across such a challenging geographic location?

### Lesson Objectives

By the end of this lesson, you should be able to:

- Analyze the impact of physical geography on Incan culture.

- Describe the Incan political and social structures.

## ENGAGE

> **Why were messengers so important in the Inca Empire? Visit Engage to learn more.**

## Essential Question

How did the Inca Empire maintain power across such a challenging geographic location?

## EXPLORE

### Geography of the Inca Empire

*Where was the Inca Empire located?*

The Inca were a large South American empire that rose to power in the 1400s. The empire began in the 1100s with a small group of people living in a city called Cuzco, in the southern highlands of what is now Peru. Eventually, the Inca Empire would stretch over much of the South American continent, covering parts of modern-day Argentina, Bolivia, Chile, Ecuador, and Peru.

The Inca lived in the Andes Mountains. The Andes stretch the length of the western coast of South America, which is bordered by the Pacific Ocean. The Andes are the highest mountains in the Americas, and they are separated by plateaus that are also at very high altitudes.

The climate of the Andes region varies greatly depending on a number of factors such as altitude and latitude. Although the region's average temperature does not change much over the course of a year, temperatures in a single day may vary by as much as 40 degrees Fahrenheit between the high and low. Rainfall in the region is seasonal, with the highest amount of precipitation occurring between December and March.

The geography of the Andes had a large effect on the Inca Empire. The climate of the region and the mountainous terrain presented many challenges. The Inca were forced to adapt their lifestyles to meet many of these challenges.

**Discovery** | SOCIAL STUDIES
EDUCATION | **TECHBOOK**

How did the Inca Empire maintain power across such a challenging geographic location?

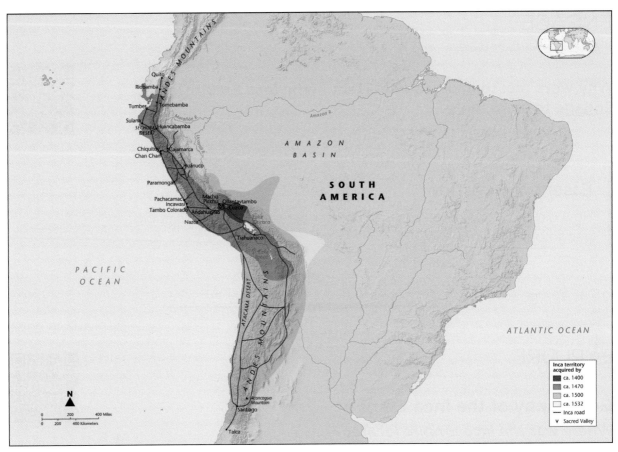

*The Inca Empire extended over much of the length of South America.*

## Farming in the Andes

*How did the physical geography of their empire impact Incan agriculture?*

Life in the Andes was challenging in many ways. Agriculture in particular was extremely difficult. The steep slopes of the mountains limited the amount of fertile land that could be used for farming. It was also difficult to find water for the crops.

To solve this problem, the Inca used a system known as terrace farming. They built walls on hillsides and filled them with soil to make terraces. Terraces are wide steps on the side of mountains. Without the terraces, the mountainous landscape would have been too steep for farmers to water, plow, and harvest. The terrace system increased the amount of land that the Inca could use for agriculture. It also kept the topsoil from washing away down the hillside in heavy rains.

photo: Getty Images

*The rugged terrain of the Inca Empire forced farmers to use terracing to boost the amount of available farmland.*

Although rain falls regularly in the Andes from December to March, the rest of the year sometimes brings extended periods with no rainfall. To ensure that they had the water they needed for their farms, the Inca built large canal systems to irrigate, or bring water to, their fields. The canals also brought water to the cities. Many streets had supplies of freshwater running through a canal. This made daily chores, such as washing clothes, much easier. To fertilize the land and improve crop production, Incan farmers in the coastal areas used bird droppings, or guano; in the highland areas, they used the remains of dead local animals, such as llamas.

Maize, squash, beans, and potatoes were the staple crops of the empire. Farmers also grew coca for its leaves, which they chewed to reduce fatigue and hunger. The farmers were taxed on all the crops they grew and gave most of their crops to the government. The government controlled how farmers used the crops that they harvested and kept a large store of food in reserve in case of prolonged drought. This system, called the mita, was a way of redistributing wealth to promote the power of the emperor. Controlling the food supply also helped the emperor keep the empire united.

## Highways and Byways

*How did geography impact travel throughout the Inca Empire?*

In addition to the challenges it created for Incan agriculture, the extreme mountain terrain of the Andes also presented many obstacles to travel and trade. The Inca created a network of roads throughout the empire.

photo: Getty Images

*Roads in the Inca Empire were tricky, but the llama was capable of navigating treacherous terrain while carrying heavy loads.*

To create this network, a labor tax was enforced. The labor tax forced peasants to provide free labor for public works projects, such as roads, forts, and bridges. Peasants were also forced to work mining precious metals.

### Mountain Highways

The transportation network consisted of two main roads linking the north and the south, and a complex web of crossroads that reached nearly every village in the empire. This system of roads was essential for maintaining communication among the geographically widespread empire. Runners were needed because many of the roads were too steep for carts. Relay runners used a 10,000-mile-long network of roads to carry messages between government officials. These runners worked in teams to cover up to 250 miles each day. The roads were also used by the military, which could travel quickly to any region to protect the empire from invasion or to stop rebellions.

Discovery EDUCATION | SOCIAL STUDIES TECHBOOK.

How did the Inca Empire maintain power across such a challenging geographic location?

The mountainous roads caused problems for traders in the region. Llamas were common in the Andes; the Inca used them as pack animals because llamas are capable of carrying heavy loads over the mountainous roadways. The llamas also provided a source of wool that was used to make cloth. Yarn was spun and boiled in dye. The dyed yarn was turned into fabric. Incan women paid their labor tax by spinning and dying wool. Llamas were also a food source for the Inca.

### Bridges

The deep river valleys, called gorges, in the Andes provided another unique challenge for the Inca. Roads were often interrupted by these gorges, which meant that some Incan cities were separated from each other. The Incas used ropes made from twined plant fibers to create suspension bridges that could reach across these gorges. Some of the bridges were over 300 feet long. One bridge, constructed in 1350 CE, lasted over 500 years. These rope-suspension bridges were similar to today's modern suspension bridges.

The roads and bridges of the Inca helped unify the empire by enabling travel and trade. The road system made communication between the four regions of the empire easier. It also allowed the army to move quickly to wherever they might be needed. This all helped the emperor keep the sprawling Inca Empire united, even as it continued to expand.

photo: Getty Images

*A portion of the Inca road Yunga Cruz, in present-day Bolivia.*

## Building the Empire

### How did the Inca Empire expand its holdings?

The Inca Empire was centered in the territory that is modern-day Peru. However, through expansion it grew over time to include parts of present-day Ecuador, Bolivia, Chile, and Argentina.

Pachacuti, who ruled from 1438 to 1471 CE, greatly expanded the Inca Empire. Under his leadership, the Inca pushed northward, conquering new territories and spreading the boundaries of the emperor.

*A statue of Pachacuti, present-day Cuzco, Peru.*

photo: Getty Images

Topa Inca, Pachacuti's son, expanded the empire into Chile, Bolivia, Argentina, and Ecuador. Under Huayna Capac, thought by many historians to be the final Incan emperor, the empire added lands in northern Peru, coastal Ecuador, and Guayaquil.

The Inca conquered some regions through the use of their strong army. Incan soldiers remained in the conquered lands to help collect tribute and to keep order among the citizens. Local governments offered tributes of gold and silver to the central Inca government.

Force was not always required, however. Sometimes, regions were invited to join the empire before conquest. The emperor sent spies to the regions he wanted to conquer to learn about their strengths and weaknesses. Then, the emperor sent messages to the leaders of these lands convincing them of the wisdom of joining the Inca Empire. Promises of safety and riches were often enough to persuade local rulers to join the empire. The local ruler's children would be brought to Cuzco to train to be Inca administrators. There, they would learn about the structure of the Incan government.

**Explore this interactive to learn more about how the Inca adapted to their geographic surroundings.**

## The Political Structure of the Inca

*What was the structure of the Incan government?*

The society of the Inca Empire was built on order. At the head of the society and the government was the emperor, who was also known as Inca and was believed to have a divine origin from the sun god Inti. As a god-king, the emperor had absolute authority and ruled over the land, its people, and all that they owned. The Incan emperor lived in luxury, eating off gold plates and dressing in the finest clothes.

The royal family of the emperor was just below the emperor in the social structure of the empire. The royal family was followed in importance by the upper aristocracy, which was composed of all the relatives and descendants of the royal family.

Those who had two Incan parents and were not previous members of one of the conquered regions could hold the highest government, religious, and military positions.

**Discovery** | SOCIAL STUDIES
EDUCATION | **TECHBOOK**

How did the Inca Empire maintain power across such a challenging geographic location?

The emperor's sons took the most important administrative posts, but the emperor also gave important jobs to the nobles of the lands the Inca had conquered. This helped promote unity within the empire.

photo: Library of Congress

*Cuzco was the center of the Incan world for three centuries.*

The next level of power was the imperial administrators. The Inca Empire was divided into four regions, with the capital city of Cuzco at its center. There was an administrator, or governor, for each quarter. The quarters were divided into smaller governmental units known as districts. District governors supervised about 10,000 peasants each. Village leaders were in charge of smaller groups of perhaps 1,000 people. Below them, 10 foremen were responsible for overseeing 100 peasants each.

It was the duty of the noble class to supervise the government officials who ran the kingdom. This expansive system of administration and organization of the government helped the Inca Empire maintain power across a vast and challenging expanse of land.

## An Organized Empire

*How did the Inca organize their growing empire?*

As the empire expanded, the structure of the government and the organization of the empire became more important to maintain control. The Inca had a central capital in Cuzco and regional capitals in four other cities.

The empire as a whole was known as Tahuantinsuyu, a Quechua word that means "Land of the Four Quarters." Quechua is the native language of the Inca. Each of the four quarters was called a suyu. The Antisuyu quarter was made of deep, heavily forested valleys east of Cuzco. The Cuntisuyu was west of Cuzco. South of Cuzco was Collasuyu, the largest of quarters, which touched present-day Bolivia, Chile, and Argentina. The Chincasuyu was composed of the land north of Cuzco. Each quarter was further divided into smaller provinces. Placing the capital at the center of the four regions helped the emperor keep control of the vast Inca Empire.

The empire was at its largest during the reign of Huayna Capac. At that time, the empire spread over 2,500 miles from north to south, and about 500 miles from east to west. Somewhere between 3.5 million and 16 million people from several different tribal backgrounds lived in a region about as big as the present-day Atlantic Coast states in the United States.

photo: Getty Images

*An example of a quipu, a tool the Inca used to keep records.*

The physical distance made communication across the empire difficult. Communication was also hampered by the fact that there was not a shared language throughout the empire. Although no written Incan language has been discovered, historians believe that the Inca used a system of knotted ropes of different colors, known as *quipu*, to record information. Many historians believe that this was a numerical system that was only used for accounting and record keeping. Others believe it was a binary code (similar to that of modern computers) that also could be used as a form of written language. However, few examples of quipu exist, and they have never been successfully translated.

The geography of the large Inca Empire made governing the empire a challenge. However, the Inca succeeded and created a great society. As great as the Inca Empire was, however, it was not powerful enough to last forever. In 1532 CE, Spanish explorers, including Francisco Pizarro, arrived in Peru and made contact with the Inca. This contact with European explorers would ultimately lead to the end of a great civilization.

## The Mystery of Machu Picchu

*What does the Inca city Machu Picchu reveal about Incan architecture and engineering?*

One Incan city still mystifies historians and archaeologists. Known as the "City in the Clouds" and the "Lost City of the Inca," it is perhaps the best-known archaeological ruin in the Americas. This city is proof of the power and architectural ability of the ancient Inca.

### City in the Clouds

Machu Picchu lies in the middle of a dense mountain forest, rising 8,000 feet above sea level. Machu Picchu is surrounded by mountains that are holy to the Quechua Indians, the descendants of the Inca, who still occupy the land today. City walls were made out of white granite. The land was terraced to aid in farming, and ramps were used to make walking up and down the steep mountain terrain easier. These elements helped make Machu Picchu the premier city of the Inca Empire.

photo: Paul Fuqua

*The central plaza of the great Incan city of Machu Picchu.*

Historians still debate why the Inca would perch a great city like this on a mountain ridge in the Peruvian Andes. Some historians think that Machu Picchu was a royal estate for Pachacuti, a famous Incan ruler and warrior who conquered much of the land that made up the Inca Empire in the 1400s.

## Engineering Machu Picchu

The Inca built the great city in less than 100 years. A nearby mountain spring provided freshwater. The Inca built an elaborate system of canals and fountains to process drinking water and prevent flooding. To help the city get rid of water from rainfall, Incan engineers used chunks of white granite left over from construction of the city walls to build an underground drainage system. There are approximately 700 terraces at Machu Picchu. Water can flow easily through the soil in the terraces, so it seeps through the ground and is safely carried away from the city. Engineers also included over 100 drainage holes to help drain rainwater from the city.

## The Decline of Machu Picchu

Machu Picchu declined as smallpox and civil war weakened the Inca Empire. Just 60 years after the death of Pachacuti, the Inca Empire collapsed. As much as historians and archaeologists have learned about Machu Picchu, it still remains a source of intrigue and wonder for many. Even today, many aspects of Incan culture are still common in societies throughout the Andes Mountains. Quechua, spoken by the ancient Inca, is still the dominant language of many rural residents in Peru and Bolivia. Religion, family life, and farming techniques used today still mirror those used by the ancient Inca.

Much of the wonder of Machu Picchu was created as a response to the challenges imposed by the environment of the Inca Empire. The geography of the Inca Empire affected all aspects of life. The links between the past and present that can be seen in Machu Picchu demonstrate how important the geography of the region continues to be.

### Consider the Essential Question:

How did the Inca Empire maintain power across such a challenging geographic location?

Go online to complete the Social Studies Explanation.

### Check for Understanding:

Identify the geographical challenges the Inca faced. What methods did the Inca use to overcome these challenges? How did they use natural resources to their advantage?

Discovery SOCIAL STUDIES EDUCATION TECHBOOK

How did the geography of Africa affect its settlement patterns and commerce?

# 8.1 Geography of Africa

photo: Getty Images

## LESSON OVERVIEW

### Introduction

In this concept, you will learn where the major cities and important geographic features of Africa are located and how they affected the development of African civilizations.

### Essential Question

How did the geography of Africa affect its settlement patterns and commerce?

### Lesson Objectives

By the end of this lesson, you should be able to:

- Locate the boundaries, important cities, and bodies of water of Africa on a map.

- Describe how the geography of the region shaped the way of life of the people living there.

## Key Vocabulary
Which terms do you already know?

- ☐ Aksum
- ☐ Atlantic Ocean
- ☐ Bantu
- ☐ Bantu Migrations
- ☐ Bartolomeu Dias
- ☐ Congo River
- ☐ Congo River basin
- ☐ desert
- ☐ East Africa
- ☐ Ethiopia
- ☐ Ghana
- ☐ Giza
- ☐ Great Rift Valley
- ☐ Great Zimbabwe
- ☐ Indian Ocean
- ☐ Kalahari Desert
- ☐ Kingdom of Benin
- ☐ Kush
- ☐ Mali
- ☐ Mogadishu
- ☐ Mombasa
- ☐ Morocco
- ☐ Mount Kilamanjaro
- ☐ Niger River
- ☐ Nile River
- ☐ nomadic
- ☐ Sahara Desert
- ☐ Sahel
- ☐ savanna
- ☐ Sofala
- ☐ Sub-Saharan Africa
- ☐ Timbuktu
- ☐ trade
- ☐ Zambezi River
- ☐ Zanzibar

# ENGAGE

What can we learn about Africa's geography from examining images? Visit Engage to learn more.

## Essential Question

How did the geography of Africa affect its settlement patterns and commerce?

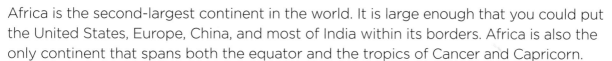

# EXPLORE

## Large Rivers and Harsh Deserts

*What geographic features shape the continent of Africa?*

Africa is the second-largest continent in the world. It is large enough that you could put the United States, Europe, China, and most of India within its borders. Africa is also the only continent that spans both the equator and the tropics of Cancer and Capricorn.

The continent of Africa is bordered by several major bodies of water. The Mediterranean Sea borders it to the north, the Red Sea and the Gulf of Aden to the northeast, the Indian Ocean to the east, and the Atlantic Ocean to the west.

One of the most significant geographic features of Africa is the Sahara Desert, which is almost as big as the United States. The Sahara divides Africa in two. Because it was so difficult to cross, the Sahara effectively isolated these two regions of Africa from each other for much of their history. North Africa consists of modern-day Morocco, Algeria, Egypt, Tunisia, and Libya. It is mostly populated by Arabic-speaking people who practice Islam. The portion of the continent south of the desert is known as Sub-Saharan Africa; the prefix *sub-* means "below," or "under." Sub-Saharan Africa is populated by people of numerous cultures. They speak many local languages and practice a variety of religions, including Islam, Christianity, and local religions.

photo: Getty Images

*Mopti Harbor on the Niger River, present-day Mali.*

Discovery EDUCATION | SOCIAL STUDIES TECHBOOK

How did the geography of Africa affect its settlement patterns and commerce?

photo: Getty Images
*Victoria Falls, present-day Zambia.*

photo: Getty Images
*Tinerhir, an oasis at the foothills of the Atlas Mountains, present-day Morocco.*

Africa is crossed by four large rivers. The Nile River begins in central Africa and winds its way north before spilling into the Mediterranean Sea. The Niger River begins in West Africa, in the country of Guinea. It loops north through Guinea and Mali before turning south again through Niger and Nigeria and spilling into the Atlantic Ocean. The Congo River begins in central Africa in Zambia. From there, it winds its way north, west, and southwest through several countries before emptying into the Atlantic Ocean in the Democratic Republic of Congo. The Zambezi River also begins in Zambia. It winds south and east through Zambia, Angola, Zimbabwe, and Mozambique to the Indian Ocean.

Except for the Niger, it is impossible to navigate these rivers from start to finish because each contains a series of cataracts, or waterfalls, as it nears the ocean. This means that, although the rivers have been used for trade upstream, there has been little trade from the ocean coming inland using these rivers. The four major rivers of Africa played an important part in agriculture.

## Climate Zones

### What types of vegetation are there in Sub-Saharan Africa?

Sub-Saharan Africa has four major climate zones. These zones affect the types of vegetation and animal life that can live in a particular area.

### Tropical Forests

A line of dense tropical forests covers the area around the equator. It rains frequently in this region, and it is always hot and humid. Although the land is covered by a wide variety of vegetation, the soils of this zone are poor. Because of the frequent heavy rains, many natural minerals and nutrients are washed away.

photo: Paul Fuqua
*The savanna is an area of grassland with sparse trees. It is where most of the large animals in Africa are found.*

## Savanna

North, east, and south of the tropical forests is a band of grasslands known as the savanna. Savannas typically have some trees, but they are mostly covered in grass. This is the area where many of Africa's familiar large animals, such as elephants, lions, and zebras, live.

The savanna has a dry and a wet season. During the dry season, it may not rain for months at a time, and smaller rivers and water holes may dry up completely. During the wet season, however, it may rain every day. These rains replenish the water sources in the area.

## Semiarid Strip

Between the savanna and the desert, there is a strip of semiarid land. *Arid* means "dry." In this zone, rain is scarce and the dry season is very long. The plants that live here are drought-resistant. The few animals that thrive in this zone have adapted to living with little water.

The northern section of semiarid land is known as the Sahel. Here, winds from the Sahara bring huge dust storms that cover everything in sand during the winter months.

## Southern Desert

Finally, after this section of semiarid lands, another desert makes up the final zone. The Kalahari Desert, in southwestern Africa, is a low area covering approximately 360,000 square miles. The Kalahari has some of the highest sand dunes in the world, and the temperature sometimes reaches over 120°F. However, some areas of this desert get seasonal rains that form large, shallow temporary lakes, called pans. These pans attract much wildlife, including migratory birds.

## Making a Living

*How did the environment affect the economy of Sub-Saharan Africa?*

The various climate zones of Africa influenced the economic activities and daily customs of each zone's residents. In the forest areas, agriculture was difficult because of the poor soils. However, farmers grew tree crops such as kola and palm trees. Kola nuts, which grow on trees similar to cocoa trees, contain caffeine and were prized for their stimulating power. Kola is still used today in some soft drinks, although most American soft-drink companies have abandoned kola in favor of artificial substitutes. Kola nuts also held a key place in the rituals of some religious groups. Various palm trees produced different products, from coconuts to palm oil. Farmers also grew various types of yams.

Discovery | SOCIAL STUDIES
EDUCATION | TECHBOOK

How did the geography of Africa affect its settlement patterns and commerce?

In the savanna, farmers grew grain crops. Depending on the amount of water available, farmers planted rice, millet, or sorghum. Farmers used irrigation to provide water and staged controlled burnings of the grasslands to provide fertile soil for their crops. Because the savanna was also home to large game animals, farmers and animals frequently came into conflict, as large wild animals trampled crops or threatened domesticated animals.

photo: Getty Images

*A village in the Sahel region.*

**Explore this interactive to learn more about how geography affected the settlement and economy of early Africa.**

In the Sahel and other semiarid areas, herding was the primary economic activity. These areas did not receive enough water for farming, but nomadic herders could move their herds of goats, sheep, or cattle from place to place in search of water and food. In the desert, herders tended to use camels, which were uniquely suited to the harsh climate.

## On the Move

### *Who were the Bantus?*

The climate and vegetation of most parts of Africa place strict demands on the people who live there. One of the most successful populations has been the Bantu people. Originally, the Bantus lived in West Africa near the mouth of the Niger River. They were traditionally farmers, fishers, and herders. They lived in small villages based on kinship, or family, networks that traced their heritage through their mothers rather than their fathers.

Around 1000 BCE, groups of Bantu people began migrating eastward and southward. After a period of about 2,000 years, the Bantu people covered much of Sub-Saharan Africa. As the Bantus spread across the continent, different ethnic groups gradually developed. Today, each of these groups has its own language and culture. Yet, all the Bantu languages are considered members of the Niger-Congo language family, and the Bantu peoples share other cultural elements as well.

Historians are not sure why the Bantu migration began. Some believe the Bantu people acquired the ability to work with iron earlier than other groups, and this allowed them to overcome the other ethnic groups and spread throughout Africa.

Other historians believe the Bantu people experienced a population explosion that prompted them to migrate out of their homelands. Some believe the Bantu migration is connected to the introduction of certain forest crops, such as yams and taro, into Africa, and that the Bantu cultivation of such crops allowed them to enter and thrive in new forest regions. Some believe Bantu migration is connected to the arrival of certain forest crops, such as yams and taro, into Africa from Southeast Asia.

One of the reasons so little evidence of ancient and medieval Sub-Saharan culture has been discovered is that the African climate quickly destroys most evidence of civilization. Wood rots, clay disintegrates, and iron rusts. Historians try to piece together a history using modern technologies, archeological discoveries, and oral history, or stories passed down through the generations. While we may not know much about the earliest Bantu peoples, their continued survival proves that the Bantu developed and mastered important tools and techniques for dealing with the African environment.

photo: Getty Images

*A wood sculpture made by the Shona, a Bantu ethnolinguistic group, present-day Zimbabwe.*

## Trade

### Why did trade routes run north and south in Sub-Saharan Africa?

Farmers in each climate zone used their environment shrewdly. However, in each area, farmers could not produce all they needed, so Africans relied on trade. Farmers in the forest areas, for example, lacked the rich soil to grow grain crops and did not have enough grazing land to support large herds of animals. Farmers in the savannas needed yams and palm products from the south and animals from the north. Herders from the Sahel needed food crops to supplement their own animal products and especially cherished the kola nuts from the tropical forests.

Because the different climate zones changed from north to south across the continent, trade routes developed along common pathways. This was especially true in West Africa. Here, farmers in the tropical forests along the coast of the Atlantic Ocean established trade routes with farmers in the savannas and herders in the Sahel. As more resources were discovered, such as gold in the forests and salt in the Sahara, trading routes grew and trading centers between these two mining areas flourished.

**Discovery** | SOCIAL STUDIES  
EDUCATION | **TECHBOOK**  

How did the geography of Africa affect its settlement patterns and commerce?

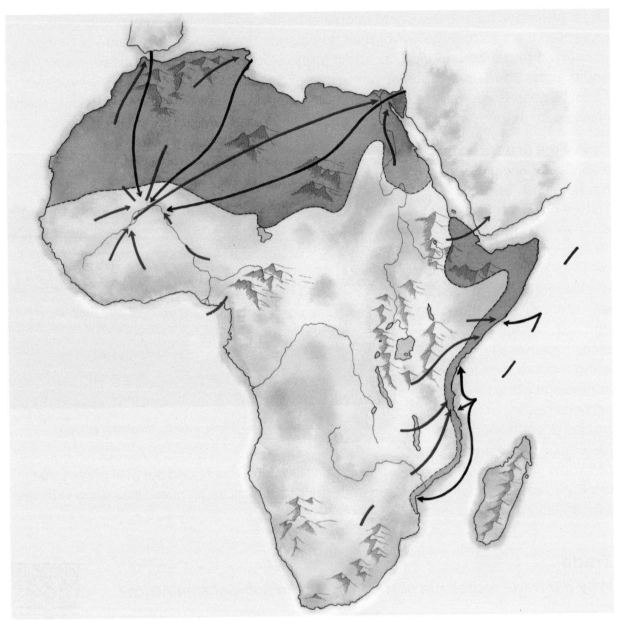

*Map depicting African trade routes in the 1400s CE.*

## Major Cities

*What were the major cities of medieval Africa?*

During the time that medieval Europe was in the grips of the Dark Ages after the fall of the Roman Empire, cities flourished throughout Africa.

Along the east coast of Africa, trading cities developed. Developing cities on the coast of Africa allowed traders to more easily take advantage of trade routes that connected to Southwest Asia, especially the Arabian Peninsula. The city of Aksum, located in the modern country of Eritrea, sat directly across the Red Sea from Arabia. Aksum grew rich on trade with cities across the Red Sea. Farther down the coast, in the modern countries of Kenya, Tanzania, and Mozambique, Kilwa and other cities were founded as Arab traders came to do business with local merchants.

*The conical tower and enclosure of Great Zimbabwe.*

photo: Getty Images

Cities also developed along trade routes in West Africa. The cities of Djenne and Timbuktu became centers of trade. They traded natural resources such as salt from the mines of the Sahara and gold from mines of the forests to the south. Djenne and Timbuktu both were along the Niger River, which helped both cities to facilitate their trade. Djenne and Timbuktu still exist in the modern state of Mali. The city of Ile-Ife in the West African forests of the modern country of Nigeria was also a center of trade.

Not all cities developed along trade routes. Other cities developed around natural resources. In southern Africa, the city of Great Zimbabwe, in the modern country of Zimbabwe, grew rich on the gold mines under its control. It traded gold with cities as far away as Kilwa, a city located on the east coast of Africa.

**Consider the Essential Question:**

How did the geography of Africa affect its settlement patterns and commerce?

Go online to complete the Social Studies Explanation.

**Check for Understanding:**

How did Bantu-speaking migrants overcome environmental challenges to survive? What resources and geographic features encouraged the growth and prosperity of the Bantu civilization?

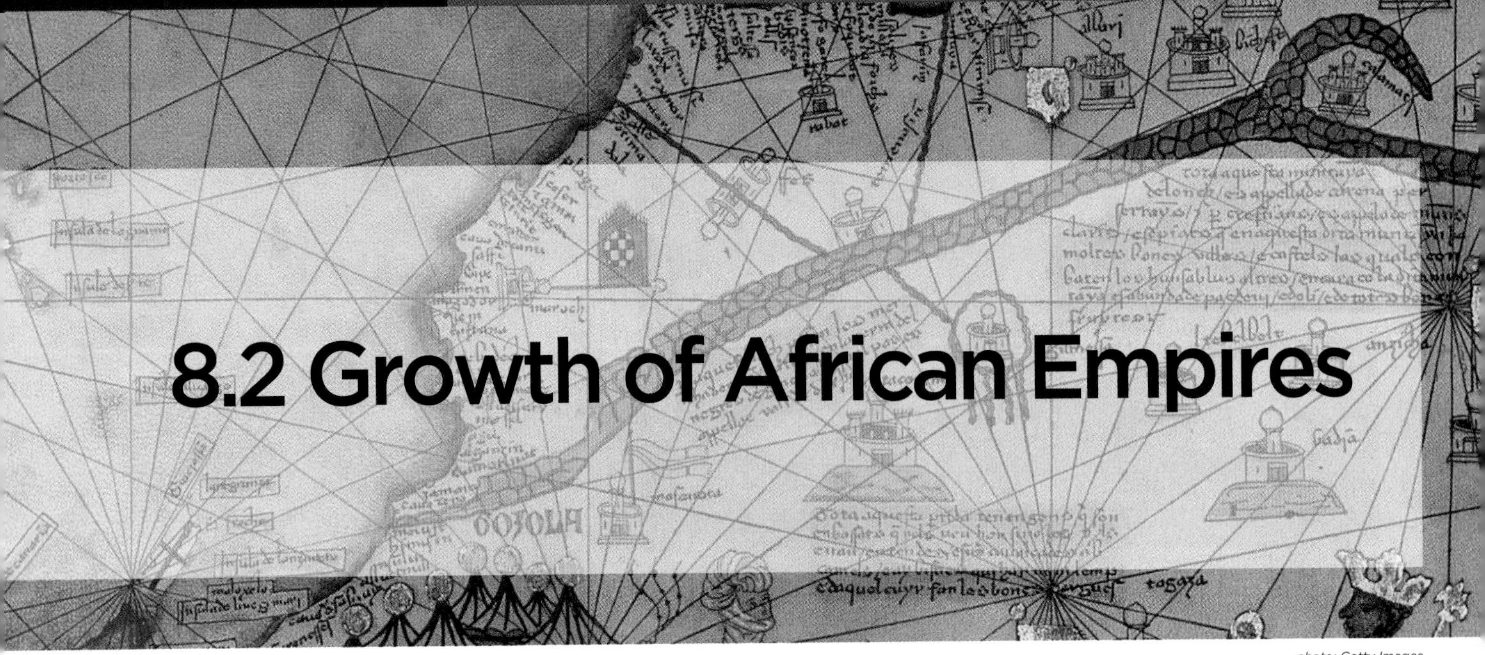

SOCIAL STUDIES
Discovery EDUCATION | TECHBOOK

# 8.2 Growth of African Empires

photo: Getty Images

## LESSON OVERVIEW

### Introduction

In this concept, you will learn about the development of several empires in Africa. You will examine the social, economic, and political characteristics that these empires shared and the characteristics that made each empire unique.

### Essential Question

How did trade influence the politics and culture of African empires?

### Lesson Objectives

By the end of this lesson, you should be able to:

- Trace the growth of the empires of Ghana, Mali, and Songhai.
- Describe the cultural, social, economic, and political characteristics of African empires.

### Key Vocabulary
Which terms do you already know?

- ☐ Aksum
- ☐ Arabian Peninsula
- ☐ Atlantic Ocean
- ☐ caravan
- ☐ China
- ☐ city-state
- ☐ desert
- ☐ Egypt
- ☐ embargo
- ☐ Ethiopia
- ☐ Europe
- ☐ Ghana
- ☐ Ghana Empire
- ☐ goods
- ☐ Great Zimbabwe
- ☐ Ibn Battuta
- ☐ Indian Ocean
- ☐ Indian subcontinent
- ☐ Kingdom of Benin

- ☐ Mali
- ☐ Mali Empire
- ☐ Mansa Musa
- ☐ markets
- ☐ Mecca
- ☐ merchant
- ☐ Mogadishu
- ☐ Morocco
- ☐ Muslims
- ☐ Niger River
- ☐ North Africa
- ☐ Nubia
- ☐ pilgrimage
- ☐ province
- ☐ Red Sea
- ☐ Sahara Desert
- ☐ Sahel
- ☐ Songhai
- ☐ Songhai Empire
- ☐ Timbuktu
- ☐ trade
- ☐ West Africa

## ENGAGE

What was life like for traveling merchants in North Africa during the days of the Mali Empire? Visit Engage to learn more.

> ## Essential Question
>
> How did trade influence the politics and culture of African empires?

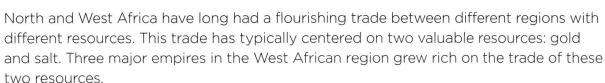

## EXPLORE

### Salt and Gold

*How did trade affect the rise of empires in West Africa?*

North and West Africa have long had a flourishing trade between different regions with different resources. This trade has typically centered on two valuable resources: gold and salt. Three major empires in the West African region grew rich on the trade of these two resources.

### Gold

The West African forests contained several different areas where gold could be mined. Historians are not sure exactly where the gold mines were because the people who mined the gold in medieval times did not record their locations to keep them a secret. However, historians believe that the mines were likely located in an area called Wangara, which was near the sources of the Niger River and Senegal River in the southern part of the modern state of Mali and the eastern portion of the modern state of Guinea.

Gold was valued throughout Europe and the Islamic world because it could be used to make coins. These coins, in turn, could be used in trade with other areas, including China. However, many of the markets for gold were separated from the rich mines of Africa by the enormous Sahara Desert. Trade from West Africa across the Sahara Desert to North Africa had gone on for thousands of years, but the introduction of the camel into the Sahara in the 200s CE allowed trade across the Sahara to increase. The camel was suited for desert travel because it was adapted to survive in the hot and dry conditions. Camels could travel for many days without water and were able to carry heavy loads. This enabled traders to move farther and faster across the desert than they would have been able to go on their own.

## Salt

While the people north of the Sahara valued gold, the people of the West African forests needed salt to replenish the natural salts lost through perspiration, or sweat, caused by the hot, humid climate of the region. They also used salt to preserve their food, or keep it from spoiling. For the West Africans, salt was more valuable than gold. However, they did not have an adequate source of salt and needed to trade with others to gain this precious commodity.

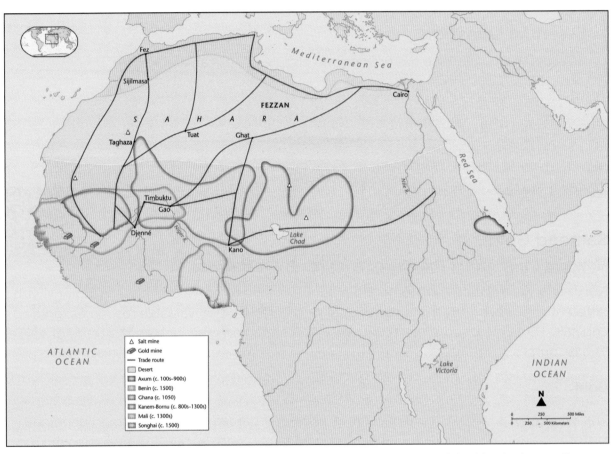

*West African empires grew by controlling the mining and trading of gold and salt. How did gold and salt get to Europe and the Middle East?*

Traders got salt from the Sahara Desert. Most of the salt they received came from the salt mines at Taghaza, a settlement located in the far northern part of modern-day Mali. Taghaza existed solely to mine salt. It was hard work that was done mostly by people enslaved by Arab merchants. The miners dug salt out of the ground, and the merchants sold it to caravans headed south to the West African Sahel, a semiarid region, and to the forests. Because Taghaza was in a desert climate and there were few natural resources other than salt, the settlement depended on the trade caravans to provide all of their food and supplies.

**Explore this interactive to learn more about how the salt and gold trade affected African empires over time.**

Trade caravans went south to Wangara bringing salt and north to Taghaza bringing gold. On this journey, the caravans needed to pass through the Sahel to get to their destinations. The people of the Sahel eventually began to take advantage of these rich trade routes as well.

## Empires Rise

### *How did the West African empires gain power?*

Between the gold fields of the west and the salt mines of the north lay the Ghana Empire. Ghana first arose around 300 CE. Although historians do not know how the kingdom of Ghana began, they do know that it grew rich and powerful due to the gold–salt trade.

As trade caravans carrying gold and salt traveled north and south, they had to cross through Ghana. Ghana charged the merchants taxes on their goods both as they entered the kingdom and as they left the kingdom. The money from these taxes went to the king. In return, the king promised safe passage through his kingdom and protected the traders from attack and theft by bandits.

The king used some of the tax money to raise and supply his army. This army grew into one of the largest and strongest in the region. It included hundreds of thousands of soldiers, including many skilled archers. The army allowed the king to conquer other territories. Members of the king's elite bodyguard often served as his ambassadors to smaller kingdoms. By the time Arab scholars became aware of the existence of the Ghana Empire in the 800s, it was already a large and powerful empire. Its capital, Kumbi, was the main market for the gold and salt trade. The city also provided a place for local traders to sell a variety of other goods.

Kumbi was home to the king and the royal court of Ghana and also to many intellectuals and religious leaders. The members of the royal court enjoyed showing off their wealth. They wore fancy necklaces and bracelets, adorning themselves in gold. Kumbi was also a city with a large Muslim population and had 12 mosques. Islamic scholars brought new ideas and Arabic language to the city. Although the king was not Muslim, many of his top advisors were.

*photo: Getty Images*

*An adobe mosque, built during the Ghana Empire, on Morfil Island in present-day Senegal.*

**DISCOVERY** EDUCATION | SOCIAL STUDIES **TECHBOOK**

How did trade influence the politics and culture of African empires?

Although the main trade was salt and gold, other goods passed through Ghana on their way north or south. Copper, woven cloth, and cowrie shells traveled south from North Africa, while West Africans traded kola nuts, ivory, and enslaved persons. Enslaved persons from West Africa were usually captives from wars or criminals who were taken across the Sahara and sold to North Africans or Europeans.

The Ghana Empire controlled the trade routes between North Africa and West Africa for over 300 years. Then, in the late 1000s, Muslim warriors from North Africa invaded Ghana. Although they only controlled Ghana for about 10 years, the Ghana Empire was weakened and it fell to an invasion from an outside kingdom in 1203. Forty years later, the neighboring kingdom of Mali conquered Ghana's capital of Kumbi, and the rule of a new great empire had begun.

## The Mali Empire
*Who was Mansa Musa?*

### Mali

While the Ghana Empire was in decline, the kingdom of Mali was expanding its borders. The kingdom of Mali began south of the kingdom of Ghana, around the source of the Niger River in what is today the southern part of Mali. Around 1230, Sundiata Keita, the king of Mali, led a rebellion against Ghana and conquered the empire. Sundiata established his capital at the city of Niani. The Mali Empire had begun. As a result of its defeat of Ghana, Mali gained control of the gold and salt trade. Mali would keep control over these valuable trade routes for about 300 years, from approximately 1200 to around 1500.

Sundiata's successors expanded the Mali empire until it stretched from the forests in the south to the Atlantic Ocean in the west, east into modern-day Niger, and north to the trading city of Timbuktu. Timbuktu, a crossroads for cultures on both sides of the Sahara, became a center for learning that attracted scientists, philosophers, and religious scholars from Egypt and Mecca. By 1450, Timbuktu was reported to have 25,000 scholars living and studying in the city. Books were very popular and

photo: Getty Images

*The grand mosque in Djenne, Mali.*

were traded often. Islamic scholars wrote books in Arabic, which helped spread the language throughout the city and the West African region. Many of their writings are now collected in libraries and museums in Timbuktu.

**Mansa Musa**

Mansa Musa ruled from 1307 to 1332. Under his rule, the Mali Empire expanded to its largest boundaries. The empire gained control of the gold-producing areas of the south as well as the salt mines of the north. Mansa Musa expanded trade throughout the empire and across the Sahara. He sent ambassadors to Islamic states in Morocco and Egypt.

Mansa Musa became well known outside West Africa when he traveled to Mecca on a pilgrimage, or religious journey, in 1324. Mansa Musa traveled by caravan across the Sahara to Morocco and then across North Africa, arriving in Cairo after eight months of travel. According to witnesses, his caravan contained over 60,000 men and 80 camels, each carrying 300 pounds of gold. In Cairo, he spent gold lavishly, so much so that by the time he left, the price of gold had dropped so significantly that it did not recover for 12 years. Europeans and North Africans were very impressed by stories of Mansa Musa's wealth, and tales of the rich kingdom spread.

However, it is Ibn Battuta, a Muslim scholar and traveler from Morocco, who gives us the clearest picture of the kingdom of Mali. In 1353, he traveled to the kingdom of Mali. He stayed in the capital, Niani, for about 50 days and wrote down his observations about the kingdom. He praised the safety of the kingdom and the swift execution of justice.

**The Decline of Mali**

After Mansa Musa's death, the Mali Empire slowly declined. The city of Gao, on the northern section of the Niger River, rebelled against Malian rule. Tuareg people from the north captured the city of Timbuktu. People in the west of the empire also rebelled. Gradually, Mali lost control of its empire and the gold–salt trade. Around 1550, Mali ceased to be an important political power and the Songhai Empire rose in its place.

## The Songhai Empire

### *How did the Songhai Empire gain power?*

Unlike the Mali Empire and the Ghana Empire before it, the Songhai Empire revolved around the city of Gao on the northern bend of the Niger River. The people of the city of Gao, after rebelling against the Mali Empire, continued to expand their territory. Ali the Great, who ruled Songhai from 1464 to 1492, formed a fierce army of cavalry (horse-riders) and infantry (foot soldiers) and captured the cities of Timbuktu and Djenne along the Niger River. He incorporated the people he conquered into his army, which helped increase its numbers and strength.

Another strong Songhai ruler was Askia Muhammed Touré, who ruled from 1493 to 1528. He overthrew the Songhai king and proclaimed himself king. He expanded the boundaries of Songhai's empire to its greatest extent.

He also created a system for governing his vast empire, dividing the empire into five provinces and appointing a governor to each province.

Like the Mali Empire before it, as it expanded, the Songhai Empire took control of the profitable north–south trade routes that connected it to North Africa. At its peak, the Songhai Empire stretched from the

photo: Getty Images

*Tomb of Askia Mohammed, ruler of the Songhai Empire, at Gao in present-day Mali.*

gold fields in the south to the salt mines in the north and from the Atlantic Ocean in the west to the modern-day countries of Niger and Nigeria in the east.

**Explore this resource and write a journal entry from the perspective of a trader visiting Timbuktu for the first time.**

Although the Songhai Empire was the largest of the three empires, it was also the shortest lived. In the 1580s, Moroccan forces from across the Sahara invaded first the salt mines of Taghaza and then the heart of the Songhai Empire. The Songhai Empire fell around 1590.

## Kanem-Bornu

### *How did Kanem-Bornu gain power?*

Kanem-Bornu was powerful from the 800s to the 1800s in the area around Lake Chad. Lake Chad was a unique water resource in the Sub-Sahara region. Kanem's importance as a trading power was also due to its location. It became a stopping point for trade between Egypt, Kush, Aksum, and Ethiopia in the east; Tripoli to the north; Ghana, Mali, Asante, and Songhai to the west; and Benin to the south.

Kanem-Bornu was ruled by the militaristic Sef (or Sayf) dynasty. The Sef began as a confederation of many nomadic peoples in the area. Like other Sub-Saharan trade empires, they gained wealth by demanding tribute from caravans. Before 1100, the Sef king Umme (Humai) converted to Islam. The Sef continued in power for more than 750 years, one of the longest dynastic rules in human history.

photo: Getty Images

*Lake Chad*

## The Kingdom of Benin

*How was the Kingdom of Benin affected by its trade with the Portuguese?*

Around the time that Mansa Musa ruled the kingdom of Mali, a small kingdom near the mouth of the Niger River was gaining power. The Kingdom of Benin began during the 1200s and was ruled by a series of obas, or kings. In the mid-1400s, the Oba Ewuare the Great expanded the Kingdom of Benin. By the mid-1500s, the Kingdom of Benin reached from the location of the modern-day city of Lagos to the mouth of the Niger River. Ewuare also consolidated power so that the oba was considered the political leader and the spiritual leader of his people.

*photo: Getty Images*

*A bronze statue from Benin, sculpted around 1750.*

Like the other African empires, the Kingdom of Benin grew rich on trade. In the 1400s, it began to trade with Portuguese merchants who had begun their voyages along the African coast. From the 1400s through the 1700s, they maintained an active trade with the Portuguese and then the Dutch. They traded a variety of goods such as leopard skins, ivory, palm oil, and pepper. The Kingdom of Benin also participated in the slave trade, capturing peoples from the interior of West Africa and bringing them to the coast to sell to the European slave traders.

One of the more significant products the Portuguese brought to Benin was brass. Benin metalworkers already knew how to make brass out of copper and zinc, but they did not possess enough of these materials to supply their immense desire for brass sculptures and plaques. So, the people of Benin bought brass from the Portuguese and then turned it into works of art. Benin's artists were skilled in brass casting as well as carving ivory and creating terra-cotta sculptures. Among other art, Benin's artists created bronze castings of their obas' heads. Rather than represent the actual features of the obas, the castings showed the ideal image of a ruler. These commemorative castings were placed on shrine altars within the royal palace in Benin City after the death of the ruler.

The king of Benin also bought guns from the European traders, which were used to fight wars against people of the interior whose weapons were inferior. Eventually, the people of Benin learned to make their own guns. Warfare allowed the king to increase his territory and thus his control over trade in the region.

## The Aksum Kingdom

*What helped trading centers to develop along the coast of the Indian Ocean in Africa?*

Just as the trans-Saharan trade helped link West Africa to North Africa, the Red Sea and Indian Ocean sea trade connected East Africa to the Arabian Peninsula, the Indian subcontinent, and North Africa.

The first large trade center of the East African coast was in the kingdom of Aksum. Located along the coast of the Red Sea, in the modern countries of Eritrea and Ethiopia, Aksum's merchants traded with merchants in Egypt and the Arabian Peninsula along the coast of the Red Sea. Through the 200s and 300s CE, the Aksum Kingdom expanded to cover most of what is now Ethiopia in Africa, and even conquered areas of the Arabian Peninsula, in what is today Yemen. The political power of the

photo: Getty Images
*Ruins of Dungur Palace, Aksum, present-day Ethiopia.*

kingdom diminished with the spread of Islam from the Arabian Peninsula in the 700s. Yet Aksum remained a strong trading center under the control of Arab merchants.

Aksum converted to Christianity around 300, around the same time it began using the name "Ethiopia." Modern Ethiopia has remained predominantly Christian.

## Swahili Traders

*How did Swahili traders contribute to a blending of cultures?*

Traders also traveled further south to the coasts of what is now Kenya and Tanzania. The Swahili people who lived along the Indian Ocean made a living through a combination of farming, fishing, and trade. It appears that traders traveled to the East African coast up to 2,000 years ago, based on the Greek and Roman coins that have been found along the coast. Around 900, Muslim traders began to visit the East African coast in search of gold, enslaved persons, ivory, and other valuable goods. In return, the merchants traded goods from Persia, India, and China, including porcelain, glass, and textiles, or fabric.

In some places, trading villages and settlements grew into city-states, with their trade controlled by a local king. Muslim, Arab, Indian, and Swahili culture and peoples mixed and blended in these city-states. Swahili culture eventually became defined by both its African and its foreign influences. For example, the Swahili language contains many Arabic words. The word *swahili* is an Arabic word meaning "people of the coast."

*photo: Getty Images*

*The dhow was a type of sailboat used in the Indian Ocean and Red Sea trade. It is still used today along the eastern coast of Africa.*

Sea traders used traditional Arab ships called *dhows*. A dhow is a sailboat with triangular sails. Smaller dhows were used for fishing and local trips while larger dhows made trips from India all the way to the coast of Africa. Dhows took advantage of the monsoon winds of the Indian Ocean, traveling to East Africa during the winter monsoons and returning to the Arabian Peninsula and India on the summer monsoons when the winds blew from the opposite direction.

The city-states of the coast grew rich trading the products of interior Africa to the merchants who arrived by sea. Kingdoms in the interior of Africa also grew rich, selling their resources to the traders of the city-states.

## Great Zimbabwe

*What made Great Zimbabwe rich?*

*Zimbabwe* means "stone houses." Great Zimbabwe refers to the complex stone city that became a center of trade.

*photo: Getty Images*

*The ruins of Great Zimbabwe.*

We do not know a great deal about the Great Zimbabwe civilization because many of the artifacts were destroyed or taken during the British colonial period. Historians do know that in the 1000s, the people of the city of Great Zimbabwe began to construct the city of the same name in what is now the southeastern part of the modern country of Zimbabwe.

The city was made of stone. To build the city, the kings of Great Zimbabwe organized their subjects to extract stones from the quarry, transport the stones to the site of Great Zimbabwe, and use the stones to construct large structures. The city of Great Zimbabwe was surrounded by a Great Wall that was up to 36 feet high. Inside the walls are the ruins of mud brick buildings.

The kings of Great Zimbabwe controlled the trade from the interior of Africa to the coastal city-states. They facilitated the transport of gold, ivory, enslaved persons, and products for the local markets across their territory. As in West Africa, controlling the trade routes across the regions brought great wealth and power to the kingdom of Great Zimbabwe.

Throughout medieval Africa, empires formed and grew by controlling trade routes and resources. These empires developed sophisticated cultures that rivaled those of Europe and Asia. Historians continue to learn new information about these empires and their influence on each other and future civilizations.

**Consider the Essential Question:**

How did trade influence the politics and culture of African empires?

Go online to complete the Social Studies Explanation.

**Check for Understanding:**

How did the effects of trade on Ghana compare with its effects on the Swahili states? Be sure to provide details and examples.

# 8.3 Religion and Culture in Africa

photo: Getty Images

## LESSON OVERVIEW

### Introduction

In this concept, you will learn about the traditional religions in Africa and how the arrival of Christianity and Islam caused important cultural changes.

### Essential Question

How did contact with other religions change life in Africa?

### Lesson Objectives

By the end of this lesson, you should be able to:

- Describe the indigenous religions practiced in Africa before the introduction of Christianity and Islam.

- Trace the influences of Islam and Christianity on African cultures.

## Key Vocabulary

Which terms do you already know?

- ☐ Aksum
- ☐ Coptic Christianity
- ☐ indigenous
- ☐ King Ezana
- ☐ Mali Empire
- ☐ Mansa Musa
- ☐ Mecca
- ☐ monotheism
- ☐ Muhammad
- ☐ polytheism
- ☐ Timbuktu

# ENGAGE

**How can religious conflict and cooperation in present-day Africa be traced to the past? Visit Engage to learn more.**

## Essential Question

How did contact with other religions change life in Africa?

# EXPLORE

## Traditional Religion in Africa

*What was traditional religion in Africa like?*

Africa has a wide variety of traditional religions that are indigenous, meaning that the religions originated in Africa. Although these religions share some overarching similarities, they are distinct from one another and have been uniquely shaped by the different civilizations and tribes in Africa that practice them. These religions have lasted for hundreds of years and have impacted the life and culture of the people in Africa.

The traditional religions of Africa practice polytheism, or the worship of many gods. Although these religions all recognize a supreme god, they also believe that people should seek guidance and help from a variety of lesser gods, as well as from the spirits of their ancestors. In some cases, they believe that the supreme god created the world and then withdrew from the concerns of daily life, which in turn is controlled or influenced by the other lesser gods.

A unique characteristic of many of the indigenous African religions is that their followers do not offer prayers or sacrifices to their supreme beings. Instead, they practice customs and rituals focused on the lesser gods, ancestral spirits, or spiritual forces of nature.

## Talking to the Gods

*What practices and customs do traditional African religions use to communicate with the gods?*

Members of many African traditional religions offer prayers for fertile land and good health. In many traditional African religions, ancestors serve as mediators to the spiritual world. Ancestors who lived healthy and morally respectable lives gained spiritual power after death and can reward or punish the living. Prayers and offerings to ancestors and spirits are common features of many traditional African religions.

photo: Getty Images

*This image shows an example of a fetish used by the Ashanti people.*

In some traditions, dancing, chanting, or drumming are used to communicate with gods or spirits. This is especially common in groups that practice vodun, a belief system with many believers in West Africa, especially in Benin, where it was officially decreed to be a religion. Worshippers believe that a person who practices these rhythmic arts can become possessed: gods or spirits are believed to take over this possessed person's body and use it to communicate with the group.

Also, for many traditional religions, statuettes called fetishes can serve as mediators between the human and spiritual worlds. These objects are thought to make spiritual beings more tangible. For instance, the Lobi people create fetishes called *bateba* that can be used to call on spirits for assistance. The bateba are believed to be extensions of the spirits and can do the spirits' bidding.

## The Importance of Ceremonies and Ancestors

*What are some of the rituals of traditional African religions?*

Traditional religions hold ceremonies that mark important occasions in an individual's life such as the passage from childhood to adulthood. In addition to their religious aspects, these initiation ceremonies teach values and skills expected of adults. In the Dinka culture of the South Sudan, for example, boys of a similar age are put through a ritual in which their skin is cut in a design to yield scars before they are considered men. After completing the ritual, they give up a chore they undertook as boys: milking cows. Masks are often an important part of this type of ceremony. Pende men, for example, wear masks that symbolize their new roles as adults after they complete their initiation rituals. Masks are also used to represent gods, goddesses, cultural heroes, and ancestors.

Although African traditional religions are still practiced in many countries, they typically have not spread far from where the groups who practice each religion live. Because of this, there were hundreds of traditional religions practiced in regions across Africa around 500 CE. However, two religions very different from the indigenous beliefs of the African people, Islam and Christianity, arrived in Africa between 100 CE and 800 CE. Islam and Christianity would change the cultural landscape of this continent. The traditional religions were polytheistic, but Islam and Christianity were monotheistic, meaning that they believed in only one god.

*photo: Getty Images*

*Dancers in Sanga village perform a ceremony depicting the Dogon culture's creation story. Masks are an important part of this and many other traditional rituals.*

## Christianity Enters Africa

### *What type of Christianity formed in Africa?*

Christianity first came to Africa around 100 CE through Egypt. At that time, the people of Egypt referred to themselves as Copts. After Islam's spread, the form of Christianity that developed in Egypt became known as Coptic Christianity. Egypt became an important center in early Christianity, especially the city of Alexandria.

During the 300s and 400s, a conflict developed between the Christian Copts and the Christian Romans living in Egypt. The conflict centered on different beliefs about the true nature of Jesus. Many Copts believed that Jesus had one nature that combined the human and the divine. Many Romans, though, claimed that Jesus had two separate natures—one divine and the other human.

In 451, at the Council of Chalcedon, Christian theologians confirmed the belief that Jesus had two natures. The Roman Catholic Church and the Eastern Orthodox Church agreed with the decision of the council. The Coptic Christian Church, however, rejected the council's decision and continued to practice their belief in Jesus's one nature. Soon, the Catholic and Orthodox churches proclaimed that the Coptic Church was heretical.

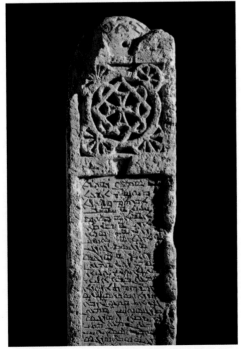

*photo: Getty Images*

*A stela with text opposing the Council of Chalcedon, sixth century.*

As a result, Coptic Christians set up their own independent church. The split between Coptic Christianity and mainstream Christianity still exists today, although these varieties of Christianity are beginning to resolve some of their differences.

## Christianity Spreads to Aksum

*How did Christianity spread to the kingdom of Aksum and other parts of Africa?*

Around 50 CE, people living in the region of present-day Ethiopia began to form a powerful kingdom called Aksum (or Axum), named for the city at its center. The leaders of the kingdom of Aksum conquered lands along the Red Sea and the Blue Nile River. As they conquered new lands, they constructed large fortresses and palaces. Soon, Aksum established a trading network that dominated the Red Sea region. The main port city of Aksum was Adulis. Adulis was a bustling city where merchants from as far away as Greece lived and worked.

photo: Getty Images
*Ruins of a 13th-century Coptic church in present-day Ethiopia.*

During the early 300s, Christianity and Christians entered Aksum through port cities such as Adulis. Before long, Christian monks began evangelizing to people throughout the kingdom. Evangelization is the process of trying to convert people to your religion or belief system. Around 321, Ezana, the king of Aksum, and his court converted to Christianity.

Aksum reached the peak of its power during the 500s. However, a century later, Islam spread swiftly through northern Africa and Muslim forces attempted to take control of Aksum. The conflict between Muslims and Aksumites lasted for approximately 300 years. By the 800s, Aksum had lost much of its territory and power. The people of Aksum held on to their Christian faith, despite being surrounded by Muslim-controlled territory. Eventually, the region of Aksum developed into the modern country of Ethiopia. Christianity, in the form of the Ethiopian Orthodox Church, served as the country's official religion until 1974, and over half of the Ethiopian people still practice some form of Christianity.

In the 1400s, Portuguese slave traders brought Christianity to West Africa. By the 1700s, other European powers, including the British, Dutch, French, and Spanish, had formed outposts along the coast of Africa. These outposts established pockets of Christian influence.

# Islam Spreads to Africa
*How did Islam impact North Africa?*

## Islam in North Africa

During the 600s, Muslim Arabs conquered Egypt and brought Islam to Africa. The Arabs then swept across northern Africa and by the mid-700s had taken control of most of the region. As a result, North Africa became part of the Muslim caliphate. The caliphate was the Muslim political and religious state. The ruler of the caliphate was the caliph, who was viewed as the successor of the Prophet Muhammad, the founder of Islam. *Caliph* means "successor" in Arabic. Throughout the history of Islam, various groups fought and struggled for control of the caliphate. The Umayyad caliphate ruled during much of the invasion of North Africa.

The Muslims encouraged the people they conquered to convert to Islam but usually did not force them to convert. Muslim Arabs, though, formed the ruling class of the area they conquered. However, Muslim non-Arabs, such as the nomadic Almoravids, were also allowed to rule states within the caliphate. Non-Arabs who practiced other religions formed the social class below the Muslim non-Arabs. The lowest class in Muslim society consisted of enslaved people.

photo: Getty Images
*The Kutubiyya Mosque, built in 1158, present-day Morocco.*

The Muslim Arabs brought their own culture and learning to North Africa. This included many great achievements in math, science, art, and literature. With the construction of mosques, Muslims brought to North Africa their distinctive form of architecture, characterized by domes and minarets, as well as geometric gardens. As Arab traders and pilgrims traveled across North Africa, they would see familiar shapes and designs in the landscape of each city, with the dome of its mosque rising above. In contrast, in Sub-Saharan Africa, Muslim architecture was not simply reproduced. Instead, mosques were built by local architect-builders using local materials, particularly clay, and traditional shapes and decorations or motifs.

## Islam Spreads to West and East Africa

During the 800s, Muslim merchants began to trade on a regular basis with parts of West Africa. This trade network was based on trading salt from North Africa for gold from West Africa. Through this trade, the merchants of West Africa were introduced to Islam. Most of the first converts to Islam in West Africa were merchants.

Many West African political leaders also converted to Islam. The spread of Islam introduced the Arabic language to West Africa. This language was popular with African scholars, who saw it as a way to connect with other cultures and to expand their education. West African leaders usually continued to allow the practice of traditional religions in their regions. Members of other religions were protected, although they commonly had to pay a tax to continue to practice their religion.

In addition, Arab merchants sailed to East Africa on ships and traded with groups in this area. Some of these merchants settled along the coast of East Africa and introduced Islam to that region. As in West Africa, Islam was brought to East Africa by merchants rather than by conquest. Rulers who converted to Islam were tolerant of those who did not convert. They incorporated Islamic rules of behavior into the laws, but they did not require non-Muslims to attend mosques or to give up their traditional religious practices and beliefs. For centuries, Islam has existed side by side with local traditional religions.

## Mansa Musa

*How did Mansa Musa impact Africa and other regions?*

### The Pilgrimage of Mansa Musa

In the 1200s, the Mali Empire in West Africa gained considerable wealth and influence through the gold-salt trade. The cities of Mali became centers for the caravan trade, which extended beyond the Sahara Desert. Most scholars believe that the empire's founder, Sundiata, had close relationships with Muslim merchants and mixed Islamic practices with traditional religions. His grandson—or perhaps grand-nephew—Mansa Musa became emperor in 1307. Mansa Musa was a devout Muslim.

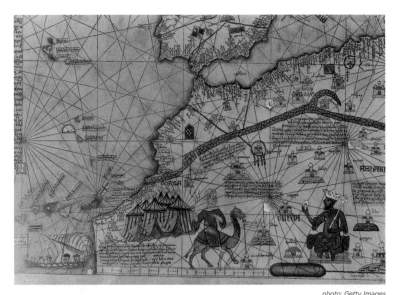

photo: Getty Images

*When the Muslim king of Mali, Mansa Musa, performed the pilgrimage to Mecca in the 14th century, he took so much gold with him that it disrupted the currency markets of Egypt.*

Islam requires that all Muslims make a pilgrimage, or hajj, to Mecca, the holy city of Islam, at least once in his or her lifetime. Mansa Musa made this pilgrimage with 60,000 of his followers. Everyone on the pilgrimage was dressed in fine clothes. The caravan traveled with camels that carried the food and supplies the travelers would need, as well as 300 pounds of gold. When Mansa Musa arrived at the city of Cairo, he initially focused on his religious observances and did not meet with the sultan of Cairo. Eventually, the sultan's officials convinced Mansa Musa to pay tribute to the sultan.

Mansa Musa not only gave tribute to the sultan, but he and his followers spent lavishly and, in so doing, flooded the Cairo market with gold. Because there was so much gold in the city, the value of gold dropped sharply. Twelve years later, the gold value in Cairo had still not fully recovered. The pilgrimage of Mansa Musa spread news of the great wealth in Mali throughout all the Muslim lands and even into Europe. Because of this, many countries sought to find the source of this amazing wealth.

**The Achievements of Mansa Musa**

Mansa Musa also made the city of Timbuktu in Mali an important trade center. From Timbuktu, Mansa Musa set up extensive caravan connections with trade cities throughout North Africa. He developed the city into a cultural center by supporting the arts and learning. For example, he made the mosque of Sankore a school for the teaching of history, law, and theology. Later, this school became the University of Sankore. In addition to his contributions to education, Mansa Musa brought an architect back with him from Egypt who designed mosques in Gao and Timbuktu. Mansa Musa died around 1332.

**Explore this interactive to analyze a source that reveals information about how trade changed life in Africa.**

Thus, Mansa Musa used Islam to increase trade with the rest of the world and to bring more prosperity to his people. However, even though King Mansa Musa was a devoted Muslim, he kept his kingdom separate from the caliphate. In this respect, Mali and the rest of West Africa were quite different from North Africa. The kingdoms of North Africa were conquered by Muslim invaders and in some cases forced to convert to Islam. In contrast, Islam was brought to Mali and other West African kingdoms peacefully and gradually. For the most part, it spread through personal influence and by word of mouth. This meant that traditional religion and Islam coexisted. Most Malians, even those who adopted Islam, retained at least some of their traditional beliefs and customs. Thus, West African culture, and even West African Islam, became a blend of local and imported practices.

**Consider the Essential Question:**

How did contact with other religions change life in Africa?

Go online to complete the Social Studies Explanation.

**Check for Understanding:**

What important similarities do the traditional religions of Africa share? Explain.

# 9.1 The Renaissance: Origins and Characteristics

*photo: Getty Images*

## LESSON OVERVIEW

### Introduction

In this concept, you will learn how the Renaissance began and how its ideas spread throughout Europe. You will also analyze the characteristics of Renaissance society.

### Essential Question

How did global contact create social and cultural change during the Renaissance?

### Lesson Objectives

By the end of this lesson, you should be able to:

- Define Renaissance and discuss its impact on society.

- Trace the origins and growth of the Renaissance from Italy throughout Europe.

## Key Vocabulary

Which terms do you already know?

- ☐ China
- ☐ Christianity
- ☐ city-state
- ☐ England
- ☐ Europe
- ☐ Florence
- ☐ France
- ☐ goods
- ☐ Greece
- ☐ Holy Roman Empire
- ☐ humanism
- ☐ Johannes Gutenberg
- ☐ Mediterranean Sea
- ☐ merchant
- ☐ Michelangelo
- ☐ Middle Ages
- ☐ Muslims
- ☐ Petrarch
- ☐ Renaissance
- ☐ republic
- ☐ republicanism
- ☐ Rome
- ☐ Sir Thomas More
- ☐ Spain
- ☐ trade

# ENGAGE

What qualities formed the ideals of the Renaissance? Visit Engage to learn more.

## Essential Question

How did global contact create social and cultural change during the Renaissance?

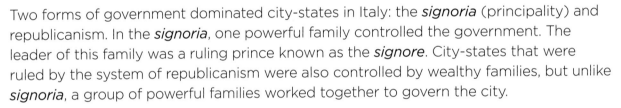

# EXPLORE

## The Governments of Italian City-States

*What types of governments did the Italian city-states have?*

Two forms of government dominated city-states in Italy: the *signoria* (principality) and republicanism. In the *signoria*, one powerful family controlled the government. The leader of this family was a ruling prince known as the *signore*. City-states that were ruled by the system of republicanism were also controlled by wealthy families, but unlike *signoria*, a group of powerful families worked together to govern the city.

### The Signoria

Many Italian city-states in the late 1200s suffered from internal conflicts. Various groups often fought each other in an attempt to gain power. A strong family sometimes defeated their opposition and established a *signoria*.

Although the establishment of a *signoria* usually ended the conflict within a city-state, average citizens had very little say in the government. The *signore* had the power to control most aspects of the government, including passing laws and choosing a successor. The *signoria* was often established in cities, such as Milan, Verona, and Padua, which had many artisans and farmers but not many other powerful families. This made it possible for one family to gain control.

### Republicanism

The larger city-states, such as Venice and Florence, had numerous strong, wealthy families. These conditions made it difficult for one family to gain control over the city-state. In city-states like these, the ruling families formed republics. In a republic, a group of wealthy families ruled together.

photo: Getty Images

*Created during the 1500s, this illustration shows the doge (center) and the Council of Ten.*

For example, in Venice, wealthy families formed a Great Council that consisted of about 1,000 members from the upper class. These members elected representatives to the Senate and the Council of Ten. The Council of Ten was very powerful and controlled the police and the judicial system. The Senate dealt with foreign policy and commerce. All of the candidates for the Senate and Council of Ten had to be members of the Great Council. In this way, the republic of Venice was a closed system. No person outside of the Great Council could play a role in government.

In Florence, the wealthy families set up a group called the *popolo*, which consisted of members of the elite class, such as wealthy merchants. The popolo elected six members of their group to serve as supreme magistrates of Florence. These magistrates supposedly ruled the city. However, in reality, the *popolo grasso* (literally "fat people") held most of the power. The popolo grasso included extremely wealthy bankers and merchants, such as the Medici family.

## A Shift in Thinking

*How did a change in thinking lead to the development of the Renaissance?*

During the Middle Ages, the religion of Christianity dominated Europe. Theology, or the study of God, was considered the most important type of learning. Because of the central role religion played in society and culture, most people focused on the goal of reaching heaven after they died. Because of this, many believed that life was merely a series of sufferings and temptations that must be endured and resisted to achieve the heavenly reward of eternal life.

In the mid-1300s, a few scholars began to change this way of thinking. They developed a philosophy that is now known as humanism. Today, the term *humanism* implies focusing on human concerns and disregarding religious matters. However, the early humanists did not reject Christianity. Instead of focusing on the afterlife, humanists used religious ideals and thoughts to look for solutions to the problems and concerns of the living. Indeed, they viewed any learning that helped people solve their problems and improve their lives to be worth pursuing.

During this time, many classical Greek and Roman texts were rediscovered, translated, and made available to a wide audience. The humanists realized that the teachings and philosophies of ancient Greece and Rome offered many ideas that could be applied to the concerns of everyday life. They identified with the logical approach the Greeks and Romans used in their philosophies and saw it as a model for using reason to find solutions to everyday problems. Like the Greeks and Romans, the humanists thought subjects such as politics, ethics, and science should be studied rationally and separated from existing preconceptions that were tied to religious doctrine.

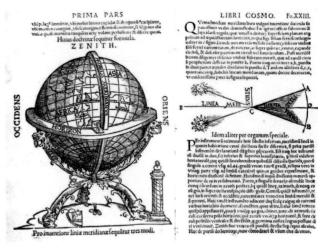

*16th-century astronomy drawings by Petrus Apianus, a German humanist.*

The humanist goal of improving life led to advances in science, literature, architecture, and the arts. In addition, humanists emphasized the importance of free inquiry and criticism in the development of new ideas. This shift in thinking brought forth a flourishing of learning that came to be called the Renaissance.

## The Development of Humanism

### *How did humanism develop?*

Two Italian scholars, Petrarch and Giovanni Boccaccio, are considered the first Renaissance humanists. These two friends realized that the works of the ancient Greeks and Romans were important and could be useful in their pursuit to improve people's lives. However, these works were not widely available in Europe in the 1300s. In an attempt to find more classical Greek and Roman manuscripts, Petrarch and Boccaccio began to search the libraries of monasteries throughout Europe. There, they found old copies of the classical works. Petrarch, Boccaccio, and other humanists studied these works, translated them, and even prepared new editions.

Petrarch, as well as other later Renaissance thinkers, believed that the ideas of Plato validated, or supported, the beliefs of Christianity. For example, both Christianity and Plato shared the belief in the immortality of the human soul and an all-powerful God who created the world.

*Portrait of Giovanni Boccaccio.*

Humanists thought that many aspects of ancient Greek and Roman civilization, such as the arts, sciences, and government, could serve as models for improving their societies. The achievements of ancient Greece and Rome began to influence scholars and artists throughout Italy and later throughout Europe. Art began to focus on humans rather than lofty religious themes. Artists painted what they observed. Science was advanced by the humanist ideals of examining the natural world and challenging existing ideals.

At the same time, cities were developing and growing throughout Europe. Medieval thinkers often viewed cities as wicked places that could lead people astray. The humanists, however, believed cities were places where people could develop and use civic virtues, such as justice, courage, and compassion. Because of this, cities would become an integral part in the development of the Renaissance.

## The Birthplace of the Renaissance
### Why did the Renaissance begin in Italy?

The Renaissance began in Italy during the mid-1300s. During the Middle Ages, most of Europe was divided into fiefs, which were ruled by lords or vassals. These fiefs often consisted of a manor house and surrounding farmland. Large cities did not exist in most of these regions. However, Italy had developed independent city-states rather than fiefs.

View of Venice, 1493.

photo: Getty Images

Italy was divided into more than 200 city-states. A city-state consists of a city and the surrounding area, and is ruled independently. Although many of these city-states were small, Italy also contained some of the largest and most powerful cities in Europe, including Florence, Milan, and Venice. In the 1300s, each of these cities had a population of at least 100,000 people. Although Italy was technically part of the Holy Roman Empire, the Italian city-states governed themselves.

Because of their access to waterways, many of the Italian city-states had become wealthy through trade. For example, Venice had established a trading empire that dominated the eastern Mediterranean. Luxury goods from Asia, such as silk and spices, flooded into the city. Because of the importance of trade to Europeans, many merchant families in Italy became wealthy and influential. Trade also gave merchant families access to people and cultures from around the world. While much of Europe was isolated from the rest of the world during the Middle Ages, Italian traders had extensive contact with the Byzantine Empire and the Muslim empires of North Africa and Southwest Asia. Cultures mixed across these empires, and leaders and scholars in these empires often drew lessons from ancient Egypt, Greece, and Rome, as well as Jewish and Muslim traditions.

Discovery EDUCATION | SOCIAL STUDIES TECHBOOK.

How did global contact create social and cultural change during the Renaissance?

Many of these families supported artists and humanist thinkers. They also encouraged the study of Greek and Roman writers because they wanted the society of their cities to be similar to those of ancient Greece and Rome. These families were considered patrons of the arts and learning. A patron is a person, family, or group that gives money or other support to artists and intellectuals. The Medici family of Florence was one of the most famous patrons in Italy. They controlled the largest bank in Europe and supported such well-known Renaissance artists as Michelangelo and Raphael.

The Renaissance was fueled by competition between the Italian city-states. As they became rich through trade, they wanted to show off their wealth, beauty, and culture. They constructed and decorated churches, libraries, and other public buildings in a race to be the best. Government rulers funded arts and education. Florence, in particular, became a center of Renaissance influence.

Before long, because of the support of wealthy patrons, Renaissance arts and learning began to flourish in Italy. These works showed a strong Greek and Roman influence; however, those civilizations were not the only influences on the Renaissance.

## Muslims and Other Peoples Influence the Renaissance

*How did ideas from regions outside of Europe influence the Renaissance?*

The Italian city-states depended on trade. Their trade networks expanded to regions all around the Mediterranean Sea, many of which were controlled by Muslims. Contact with these areas not only brought wealth, but also contributed to an exchange of ideas between Europe and the Muslim world.

Muslim-ruled areas of Spain, such as Seville and Granada, had become centers of study. Muslim thinkers during this time were strongly influenced by Greek philosophy, especially the ideas of Aristotle.

During the Middle Ages in Europe, Muslims made many scientific and cultural advances. Muslims made breakthroughs in medicine and the use of drugs to cure disease. Muslim mathematicians used their knowledge of the Indian system of numbers and decimal system to make new discoveries in mathematics, including geometry and algebra. Muslim thinkers also made important advances in the fields of astronomy, geography, and architecture.

*photo: Getty Images*
*Contemporary photo of the Court of Lions, Alhambra Palace, Granada, Spain, constructed in the 1300s.*

Much of this knowledge spread to Italy from Muslim traders. The Italians, in turn, used this knowledge to make advances in the arts and learning, thereby enriching the Renaissance. In addition, Venetian trade routes into Asia brought Italy into indirect contact with lands as far away as China. Because of this, Europeans became aware of the Chinese invention of block printing on wood and the process for papermaking that the Chinese had developed.

## The Renaissance Spreads Beyond Italy

*How did the Renaissance spread throughout Europe?*

During the late 1400s, Renaissance ideas began to spread beyond Italy and into other areas of Europe, including France, Germany, England, the

photo: Getty Images

*This picture shows the French king Francis I receiving a painting of the Holy Family by the Italian Renaissance painter Raphael.*

Netherlands, and Spain. Merchants, diplomats, and scholars from these countries sometimes visited Italy. There, they learned about the philosophy of humanism and saw great works of Renaissance art. When they returned home, they brought with them this newfound knowledge and awareness, which influenced the cultures of these other nations.

Also during the late 1400s and early 1500s, armies from France, Germany, and Spain invaded Italy. The invading soldiers were impressed by the beautiful Renaissance art and architecture. When they returned home, they spread the news of the marvels they saw in Italy.

The leaders of France, England, and Spain heard about the great advances being made by the Italians in art and learning. These monarchs wanted to incorporate these elements into their own cultures. For example, King Francis I of France brought

**Explore this interactive to take a tour of Europe during the Renaissance.**

Leonardo da Vinci and other great Italian artists and scholars to France. King Henry VII of England invited many Italian humanists to his country. These monarchs also became patrons of Renaissance artists from their own nations.

**Discovery** SOCIAL STUDIES
EDUCATION TECHBOOK

How did global contact create social and cultural change
during the Renaissance?

## A Growing Idea

*How did the ideas of the Renaissance continue to spread and grow?*

As the Renaissance spread throughout Europe, the ideas continued to advance and grow. Advances in technology also exposed more people throughout Europe to Renaissance ideas. In the 1440s, Johannes Gutenberg invented a printing press that greatly increased the speed of printing books. This invention significantly increased the number of books available to the public, thereby enhancing the spread of humanist ideas.

In northern Europe, scholars developed their own type of humanism, called Christian humanism. This movement sought to correct any errors that had been introduced to Christian writing over the years, including the Bible. Christian humanists also used education to reform the Church. For example, in his book *The Praise of Folly* (1511), the Dutchman Desiderius Erasmus criticized the lax morals of church leaders. His friend Sir Thomas More of England attempted to eliminate the abuses and inequalities that were accepted as normal in his society. In 1516, he wrote *Utopia*, which portrays an ideal society. This society has equality and justice for all citizens.

photo: Getty Images

*Johannes Gutenberg. Why was the invention of the printing press so momentous?*

By the 1500s, the influence of Renaissance ideas and art could be seen in many aspects of life throughout Europe. The increased contact between nations and the ability to record and pass on information more quickly helped the ideas of the Renaissance spread. This contact brought about great cultural changes throughout Europe.

### Consider the Essential Question:

How did global contact create social and cultural change during the Renaissance?

Go online to complete the Social Studies Explanation.

### Check for Understanding:

What six factors most contributed to the beginning of the Renaissance? Use story frames to illustrate your ideas.

# 9.2 Renaissance Cultural Contributions

*photo: Getty Images*

## LESSON OVERVIEW

### Introduction

In this concept, you will explore the many contributions that Renaissance thinkers and inventors made to Europe and to the world at large. You will get to know more about these people. You will also begin to understand how their contributions continue to influence the world in which we live.

### Essential Question

How did innovations of the Renaissance influence the development of Western society?

### Lesson Objectives

By the end of this lesson, you should be able to:

- Identify important Renaissance figures (Machiavelli, Leonardo da Vinci, Shakespeare, and Gutenberg) and developments.

- Analyze the impact of these developments on European society.

### Key Vocabulary
Which terms do you already know?

- [ ] Age of Exploration
- [ ] Andreas Vesalius
- [ ] circumnavigate
- [ ] city-state
- [ ] England
- [ ] Europe
- [ ] Florence
- [ ] France
- [ ] humanism
- [ ] Italy
- [ ] Ivan the Terrible
- [ ] Jan van Eyck
- [ ] Johannes Gutenberg
- [ ] Johannes Kepler
- [ ] King John of England
- [ ] Leonardo da Vinci
- [ ] Machiavelli
- [ ] Nicolaus Copernicus
- [ ] Raphael
- [ ] Renaissance
- [ ] Spain
- [ ] William Shakespeare

# ENGAGE

**Is it better to be loved or feared? Visit Engage to learn more.**

## Essential Question

How did innovations of the Renaissance influence the development of Western society?

---

# EXPLORE

## The Art of Politics

*What is the importance of Niccoló Machiavelli's book* The Prince?

The Renaissance was a time of cultural rebirth in Europe. Beginning in Italy in the early 1300s, new Renaissance ideas and beliefs spread through northwestern Europe until the beginning of the 1600s. It was a time of great artistic and scientific innovation. It marked the emergence of humanism. Renaissance thinkers' belief in the potential of humans led to several ideas, innovations, and artistic creations that are still relevant today.

Niccoló Machiavelli was an important Renaissance thinker. Little is known of Machiavelli's early life, except that he was born in the Florentine Republic, a city-state centered around Florence, Italy, on May 3, 1469. During Machiavelli's life, the Florentine Republic went through many changes as rival families fought for control of the region. Machiavelli held public office in the Florentine government in the late 1400s and early 1500s. This experience gave him firsthand knowledge of the use of political power and the ways that leaders asserted control.

In 1512, the Medici family took power in Florence. Machiavelli had been a member of the government from which the Medicis took power. Because of this, he was imprisoned. He was then exiled to his family's country estate. Country living was a horrible punishment for a man who loved politics! Frustrated, he turned to writing. He wrote essays and poetry and produced his most famous work, *The Prince*. It was a book about politics and how to gain and keep power. *The Prince* set the standard for the modern concept of the state and how to go about enforcing it.

photo: Getty Images
*Late 17th-century portrait of Niccoló Macchiavelli.*

In the book, Machiavelli wrote about the main qualities a prince, or leader, should possess. He also discussed the principles a leader should follow to retain power. One of the key ideas in his book was "the end justifies the means." According to Machiavelli, a leader should try to do only good, but should be able to do evil if necessary. Likewise, a ruler must be flexible and be willing to do anything to retain power. Machiavelli believed that if the results were good, then a ruler was justified in using immoral methods to achieve those results.

Through the centuries, scholars and experts have argued over Machiavelli's perspective and about whether he describes a good leader or a tyrant. His work came to embody a new breed of politics. Machiavellian politics are clever, but some believe they lack morality. Since its publication, *The Prince* has been used as a political handbook. To this day, *The Prince* raises important questions about power and government and what it means to be a good and ethical leader.

## A True Renaissance Man

### Who was Leonardo da Vinci?

One of the philosophical views adopted during the Renaissance was that humans are fully capable of developing knowledge and skills in all areas. People believed that the ideal person was one who was well educated and knowledgeable about a variety of subjects and skill. Renaissance leaders tried their best to achieve this goal.

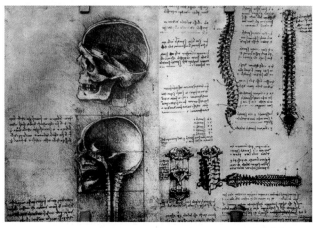

photo: Getty Images
*Sketches of human anatomy, by Leonardo da Vinci.*

Leonardo da Vinci is an example of this Renaissance ideal. He is best known as an artist. However, Leonardo was also a great thinker and inventor who made many scientific accomplishments. Leonardo was born on April 15, 1452, in Vinci, Italy, and died on May 2, 1519, in Cloux, France. He began his artistic career when he was just 12 years old, working as an apprentice in an artist's workshop in Florence. While there, Leonardo learned painting, sculpting, and technical drawing.

**Discovery** EDUCATION | SOCIAL STUDIES **TECHBOOK**

How did innovations of the Renaissance influence the development of Western society?

He would use his skills in all these areas throughout his life. Leonardo had an enormous thirst for knowledge, and in addition to his training in art, he studied astronomy, anatomy, botany, biology, architecture, engineering, and mathematics later in his life.

Although only 17 of his paintings remain, many of Leonardo's works are considered masterpieces today. Leonardo's

photo: Getty Images

The Last Supper, *15th-century mural painting in Milan created by Leonardo da Vinci for his patron Duke Ludovico Sforza and the duchess Beatrice d'Este.*

painting combined great technical skill with the ability to convey emotions in his works, what he referred to as "physical and spiritual motion." His best-known works include *The Virgin of the Rocks*, *The Last Supper*, and the *Mona Lisa*. Da Vinci also drew many accurate sketches of the human body and the way that it moves. His knowledge of anatomy helped him paint such realistic figures.

**Explore this interactive to analyze a sketchbook by Leonardo da Vinci.**

In addition to his art, Leonardo da Vinci also drew designs for hundreds of inventive machines. Although he never created working versions of his designs, many people believe that his sketches are early versions of armored tanks, airplanes, and helicopters. In addition to his artwork and inventions, Leonardo worked as an architect and engineer.

## Renaissance Artists

*What other artists made significant contributions to Renaissance art?*

Influenced by the ideas of humanism, many artists during the Renaissance began focusing on human subjects and presenting the world as realistically as possible. Their works often displayed the dignity and the power of man. The work of this time is best exemplified by the most talented and well-known artists of the era, including Michelangelo, Raphael, and Jan van Eyck.

photo: Getty Images
*Michaelangelo's painting of the Sermon on the Mount, Sistine Chapel, Italy.*

## Michelangelo

Michelangelo di Lodovico Buonarroti Simoni (1475–1564) was one of the most influential artists of the Renaissance and was widely recognized as the greatest artist of his time, even during his lifetime. Many of his works were done under the patronage of the powerful Medici family of Florence and of the Catholic Church.

Michelangelo's work is celebrated for the realistic depiction of its human subjects. This can be seen in his paintings, such as *The Holy Family* and the scenes on the ceiling of the Sistine Chapel. However, this realism is best displayed in his sculpture, including his most famous works, the *Pietà* and the *David*.

## Raphael

Raphael (1483–1520) was born in Urbino, Italy, which had become a center of culture during the Renaissance. While living in Urbino, he was exposed to humanist thought and learned the arts at an early age. He would later move to Florence, where his work was influenced by other great Renaissance artists, such as da Vinci and Michelangelo.

Like the other masters of his time, Raphael's works focused on human subjects or religious themes. His early work consisted mainly of portraits, typically of nobles and elite members of society, and several Madonnas, paintings of Jesus's mother, Mary. As his work developed, it became larger and more elaborate, as can be seen in his more famous works, *School of Athens* and the *Transfiguration*.

## Jan van Eyck

Jan van Eyck was born in what is today Belgium around 1395. Van Eyck began to work in the newly developing technique of oil painting. Oil dried more slowly than other paints, which allowed artists to work on specific sections for a longer time and create more detail. This helped van Eyck achieve the realism for which his work is known. This realism is on display in his best-known work, the *Mystic Lamb*, which is more commonly known as the Ghent Altarpiece. An inscription on this painting indicates that the work was started by Jan van Eyck's brother, Hubert. However, it is unclear how much work if any Hubert actually did on the painting. Historians today still debate which works of van Eyck's are Hubert's and which are Jan's. There is even some debate about whether they were related.

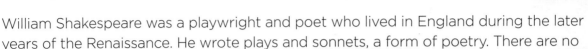

# The Bard of Avon

*What is the legacy of William Shakespeare?*

## Shakespeare's Life

William Shakespeare was a playwright and poet who lived in England during the later years of the Renaissance. He wrote plays and sonnets, a form of poetry. There are no records of Shakespeare's actual birth date, but old church documents show that he was baptized in Stratford-on-Avon on April 26, 1564. This means that his birthday was most likely near this date. Much of Shakespeare's life is shrouded in mystery. Little is known about his childhood. It is also unclear when he began to work in the theater. We do know that Shakespeare had become a managing partner in a London theater group, the Lord Chamberlain's Men (later changed to King's Men), by the 1590s and that by 1597, he had published 15 out of the eventual 37 plays that he would write in his career.

*photo: Getty Images*

*Illustration from William Shakespeare's* Romeo and Juliet.

## Shakespeare's Cultural Contributions

At the end of the 1500s, Shakespeare and his group built their own theater in which to perform. The theater was known as the Globe. Located on the banks of the Thames River in London, the circular theater was one of four important public theaters in the region. In addition to performing his plays such as *Romeo and Juliet*, *Hamlet*, *A Midsummer Night's Dream*, and *Twelfth Night* at the Globe, Shakespeare produced private shows for the royal court, performing in front of Queen Elizabeth I and her successor King James I on separate occasions.

Many of Shakespeare's plays are performed throughout the world today. Many modern stories and movies are based on Shakespeare's timeless themes of human nature: love and hate, betrayal and revenge, power and greed. These were among the conflicts and emotions he explored in his artistry as a writer. His work has been so influential that there are numerous books and college classes devoted solely to analyzing Shakespearean literature.

Shakespeare is also very well known as a poet. Shakespeare wrote in a form known as the sonnet. It contains 14 lines written in a strict rhythmic form. Shakespeare wrote 154 sonnets altogether. His sonnets became so well known that today the form of sonnets he wrote are often called "Shakespearean sonnets."

**The Real Shakespeare**

Because of the lack of information about his formal education and background, some scholars have debated whether Shakespeare actually existed, or if more than one person wrote his works. However, others are convinced that Shakespeare was who we think he was. Either way, the collected works of Shakespeare have had a lasting effect on the world.

## Spreading the Word

*How did the invention of the printing press impact culture in the Renaissance?*

One of the most important inventions of the Renaissance was the printing press. However, little is known about its inventor, Johannes Gutenberg. Historians have been able to find very few written documents from his life.

photo: Getty Images

*Illustration of Gutenberg printing press.*

Gutenberg was born in Mainz, Germany, sometime around 1400. However, some historians believe the date may be as early as 1394. Historians think that he trained as a goldsmith. By 1434, he was living in Strasbourg, Germany, working in a business that produced small metal mirrors. Gutenberg may have used the knowledge of metalwork he learned at this job to help him invent the movable type printing press.

Movable type printing had existed in China for centuries. However, that process used carved wooden blocks. This and the numerous complex symbols needed for the written Chinese language made the process cumbersome. In 1438, Gutenberg and his business partner Andreas Dritzehn began experimenting with making a metal typeset printer. It took many years before the printing press was introduced, however. By that time, Dritzehn had died and Gutenberg had a new partner, Johann Fust. It is believed that Gutenberg began work on the first printed book, the Gutenberg Bible, in 1450. The large Latin Bible was finished in 1456. That Bible, a few pamphlets, and a few other simple books would be the only ones to be printed with the name Gutenberg. In 1455, Fust sued Gutenberg for the money owed to him. Probably because the money was already used, Fust wound up owning printing press equipment instead.

Discovery EDUCATION | SOCIAL STUDIES TECHBOOK

How did innovations of the Renaissance influence the development of Western society?

Gutenberg may have continued printing smaller works after that, but Fust went on to start his own printing company and publish many other important works before his death in 1466. Even though he lost his business, Gutenberg was still recognized as the inventor of the extraordinary new machine. Gutenberg died in 1468 in Mainz, but his invention lived on.

Before Gutenberg, the text in books was hand-copied by monks using pen and ink. A single book might take months to produce, or in some cases years. The printing press made it possible to produce a large number of books in a short amount of time. Some Renaissance thinkers called this process "the art of multiplying of books." Soon, printing spread throughout Germany, Italy, and then the rest of Western Europe. Because of the printing press, ideas and literary works could be shared easily and less expensively. By the 1500s, hundreds of different book titles were being printed each year. Books were printed in different languages, and printing presses were used to create leaflets and smaller works of text that could be distributed broadly. New ideas begin to spread much more quickly. Cheaper and more numerous books also meant the monopoly on knowledge and information by Europe's social elite was over. An emerging middle class could now afford books of their own.

## The Fabric of the Human Body

*How did Andreas Vesalius change our understanding of the human body?*

The printing press helped spread new literature and ideas about art and philosophy throughout Europe. It also helped change our understanding of science. It was because of the new printing press that copies of the groundbreaking book on human anatomy, *De Humani Corporis Fabrica*, were published on a mass scale around 1543.

Andreas Vesalius was a young physician when he wrote this book. Born in Brussels, Belgium, in December 1514, Vesalius came from a family of scientists. He was interested in medicine from an early age. After studying medicine at the University of Paris in France from 1533 to 1536, he became particularly interested in anatomy, the study of the human body. Before Vesalius, medical knowledge of the human body came from Galen, an ancient physician who died in 200 CE. Galen had based much of his information about the human body on the dissection of animals. Believing Galen to be incorrect on certain points, Vesalius began conducting his own research. To do so, he dissected human bodies, a practice that was frowned upon at the time.

*De Humani Corporis Fabrica* was published in 1543. It contained the first accurate knowledge of the human body. Today, medical students commonly use cadavers to study anatomy and other aspects of medicine. In the 1500s, however, this practice was not widely accepted.

photo: Getty Images

*The second plate of the muscles, drawn by Andreas Vesalius in* De Humani Corporis Fabrica, *1543.*

Even though his was the first book to contain such accurate information, not everybody was pleased with Vesalius's use of bodies to further science. The publication led to heated debate in the scientific community and the Catholic Church. Perhaps due to the controversy, Vesalius left his professorship at the University of Padua in Italy after the book's publication and moved to Spain. He became the royal physician for the Holy Roman Emperor (and King of Spain) Charles V and later worked for Charles's son, Phillip II, when he took the throne in 1556.

Vesalius died in a shipwreck on October 15, 1564. His *De Humani Corporis Fabrica*, however, lived on to leave a lasting impact on medicine and our knowledge of human anatomy today.

## Exploration and Discovery

*How is the Renaissance related to the "Age of Exploration"?*

The Renaissance brought more than just the expansion of scientific knowledge and the arts. It was also an age of geographic exploration and discovery. It was during this time that exploration of the lands beyond Europe began. This time period is sometimes referred to as the Age of Exploration.

Europeans wanted to find new sea routes to Asia to increase trade. Until about the end of the 1300s, most people had believed that the world was flat. During the Renaissance years, the teachings of the ancient astronomer and mathematician Ptolemy were rediscovered. His theory that the world was round helped propel European interest and curiosity in exploring the world around them.

**Discovery** EDUCATION | SOCIAL STUDIES **TECHBOOK**

How did innovations of the Renaissance influence the development of Western society?

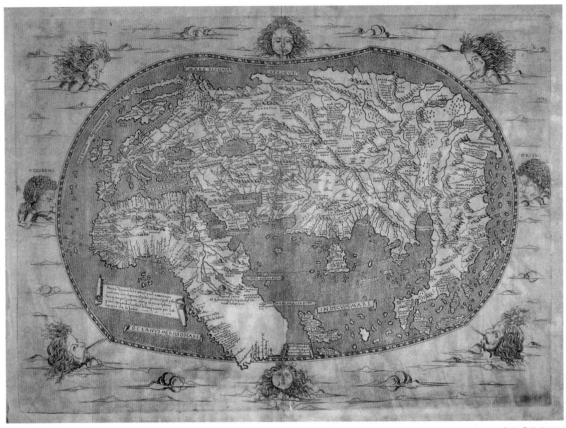

photo: Getty Images

*Renaissance scholars translated Ptolemy's* Geography *from Greek to Latin in 1406, beginning an intense boom in the study of geography during the Renaissance.*

From philosophy to art, geographical exploration to advances in science and medicine, and everything in between, the Renaissance was a time of great discovery and innovation. Many of the developments we have made in modern times, and a lot of the works of art and literature that we still hold in high regard, originated during this rich cultural era hundreds of years ago.

### Consider the Essential Question:

How did innovations of the Renaissance influence the development of Western society?

Go online to complete the Social Studies Explanation.

### Check for Understanding:

Select an innovator from the Renaissance who has influenced the modern world. How did that person's innovations affect our lives today?

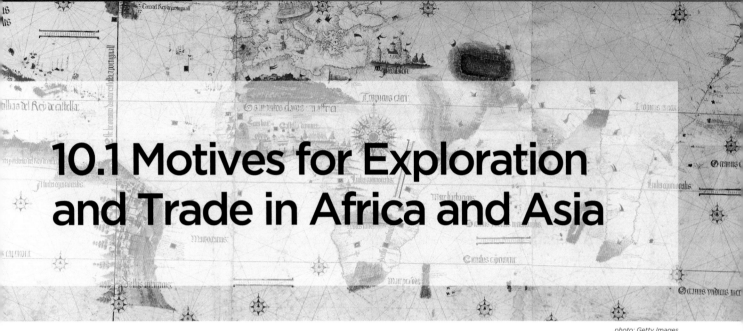

# 10.1 Motives for Exploration and Trade in Africa and Asia

photo: Getty Images

## LESSON OVERVIEW

### Introduction

In this concept, you will explore the reasons why Europeans first traveled to Africa and Asia and what happened after they arrived.

### Essential Question

Why did European leaders want to explore and conquer? What was the impact of these encounters on other regions?

### Lesson Objectives

By the end of this lesson, you should be able to:

- Analyze the motives for exploration and conquest by European nations.

- Trace the Age of Exploration and its effect on Africa.

- Explain the impact of the transatlantic slave trade on the African people.

- Trace the Age of Exploration and its effect on Asia.

### Key Vocabulary

Which terms do you already know?

- ☐ Age of Exploration
- ☐ astrolabe
- ☐ barter
- ☐ Bartolomeu Dias
- ☐ caravel
- ☐ Christianity
- ☐ colony
- ☐ compass
- ☐ Congo River
- ☐ Dutch East India Company
- ☐ Ferdinand Magellan
- ☐ Gobi Desert
- ☐ goods
- ☐ Hernán Cortés
- ☐ Hernando de Soto
- ☐ Hundred Years' War
- ☐ Ibn Battuta
- ☐ Jacques Cartier
- ☐ Johannes Gutenberg
- ☐ John Cabot
- ☐ line of demarcation

- ☐ Marco Polo
- ☐ merchant
- ☐ missionary
- ☐ Muslims
- ☐ pirates
- ☐ plantation
- ☐ Prince Henry the Navigator
- ☐ proselytizing religion/ universalizing religion
- ☐ Ptolemy
- ☐ Samuel de Champlain
- ☐ shogun
- ☐ Silk Road
- ☐ slavery
- ☐ slaves
- ☐ Tokugawa Ieyasu
- ☐ trade
- ☐ Treaty of Tordesillas
- ☐ Vasco da Gama
- ☐ Vasco Núñez de Balboa

Discovery SOCIAL STUDIES
EDUCATION TECHBOOK

Why did European leaders want to explore and conquer? What was the impact of these encounters on other regions?

# ENGAGE

**What happens when two different groups of people from different cultures interact for the first time? Visit Engage to learn more.**

## Essential Question

Why did European leaders want to explore and conquer? What was the impact of these encounters on other regions?

# EXPLORE

## Seeking New Markets

### *What led to European exploration?*

The exchange of goods between European and African empires had existed for centuries. However, the goods usually arrived after being exchanged with a third party. During the 1400s and 1500s, which is sometimes referred to as the Age of Exploration, direct trade between Europeans and Africans began to develop. Trade between Asia and Europe along the Silk Road, a network of land and sea trade routes, had declined after the fall of the Roman Empire. During the Age of Exploration, trade along this route began to greatly increase. The Age of Exploration was also a time of a great expansion of knowledge, artistic expression, and scientific discovery in Europe.

During this time, many new kingdoms throughout Europe were continuing to grow and trying to increase their power in the region. This often led to conflicts between kingdoms as they competed for land and wealth. England and France, for example, engaged in a series of conflicts throughout the 1300s and 1400s known as the Hundred Years' War. These kingdoms, as well as others, believed trade with Africa and Asia was a way to increase their wealth and gain an advantage over their rivals.

Particularly high competition for goods from China arose at this time. Europeans valued luxury goods, such as spices, tea, and silk, which China provided. In exchange, Europe sent silver to China and other parts of Asia. In the 1400s, trade along the Silk Road was tightly controlled by empires in the Middle East that would only trade directly with the Italian port cities of Venice and Genoa. This monopoly blocked trade between the rest of Europe and Asia. Europeans had to buy Asian goods from these two cities. This led to high prices and a scarcity of goods.

## Searching for New Opportunities

The European kingdoms were unhappy with the situation. They wanted to find a way to trade directly with Asia. To do this, they needed to find a way around Muslim empires. Many European leaders believed the best way to do this would be to find a sea route to Asia that would allow them to bypass traditional Mediterranean Sea routes under Ottoman control. During the Age of Exploration, European explorers began to take long voyages in search of this sea route to Asia.

The routes took these explorers around the southern tip of Africa. The journey was long and very dangerous. However, the search for a better route had unexpected results. While searching for a new route to Asia, European explorers unexpectedly came upon southern Africa, the islands of the West Indies (what is now called the Caribbean), and the continents of North America and South America.

Many people in Asia had never encountered Europeans before. For the Europeans, these lands, Asia, were a new opportunity to gain wealth. In some cases, powerful European countries conquered new lands, using those lands, called colonies, to produce gold, silver, or cash crops. This system of using colonies to enrich the "mother country" is called mercantilism. If Europeans could not conquer a region, they set up a trading port to gain access to the goods of the new region.

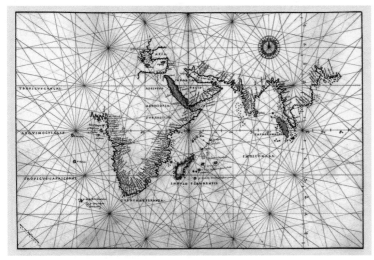

*photo: Getty Images*

*Map of Africa, the Indian Ocean, and the Indian subcontinent, 1754.*

During the 1500s and 1600s, the economic systems around the world, and especially in Europe, changed. While most Europeans were still farmers or artisans who made products at home in cottage industries, improvements in technology and an increase in goods and precious metals from around the world gave more people the opportunity to sell their goods on markets. Meanwhile, wealthy traders and trading companies could bring goods from around the world, such as tea from Asia and sugar from the Americas, and sell them at markets in Europe. This exchange of goods by private people on markets was an early form of an economic system called capitalism. This new capitalism had a strong effect on Asia, Africa, and the Americas. Just as wealthy rulers looked for gold and silver, wealthy companies and private traders looked to the outside world as a place where they could find new goods that would sell in Europe or to other lands.

Discovery EDUCATION | SOCIAL STUDIES TECHBOOK.

Why did European leaders want to explore and conquer? What was the impact of these encounters on other regions?

# Missionaries and Colonies

## What role did Christianity play in European expansion to Africa?

Although trade was the primary reason behind the initial European journeys of exploration and colonization, there was another strong motivation for continuing the expansion: spreading Christianity.

Christianity was a popular religion throughout Europe during the Age of Exploration. Christianity is a proselytizing religion, which means that some of its members try to convert others who do not believe in the same faith. As trading posts and colonies began to appear in Africa, missionaries—people on a church mission to educate and convert others—began traveling with merchants and explorers. Missionaries were often among the first to arrive in the new towns. They set to work building churches and schools and trying to convert the local populations to Christianity.

During this time, Christianity was the official religion of many European kingdoms, and many European leaders were Christians. These rulers approved of and supported the missionary work going on in Africa. They believed that establishing colonies that spread the faith in their name and the name of their kingdom showed their devotion to God and increased their power.

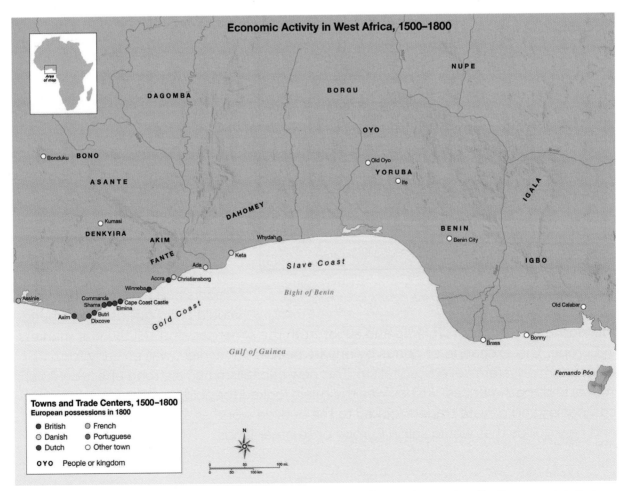

*A map shows towns and trade centers along the West African coast and uses colors to show the European state that possessed each one.*

# Innovations in Navigation

*How did advances in sailing technology impact European exploration?*

Advances in shipbuilding—such as the inclusion of rudders, or steering devices, modeled after those used on Chinese boats—improved the mobility of ships. However, the long voyages taken by the European traders and explorers were still very dangerous. They faced a variety of challenges and obstacles as they traveled, but none more important than determining where they were and where they were going. Once sailors could no longer see land, it was easy to get lost in the featureless ocean and never reach their destination.

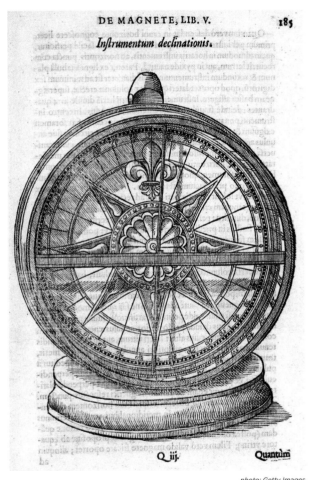

*photo: Getty Images*

*An illustration of a compass, 1600.*

In the 1300s and 1400s, navigational tools such as the quadrant and the compass allowed sailors to determine latitude, their north-south location on the globe, and direction. Although they had been used in other parts of the world, such as China, these tools were new to European sailors. European sailors could now figure out where they were, even without landmarks, as long as they had a map and knew their starting point, speed, direction, and the length of time they had been traveling.

## Direction

The compass is still used today for navigation. A compass consists of a magnetic needle that always points north. The needle floats over a disc marked with the four cardinal directions—north, east, south, and west. The device allows sailors to see what direction they are going, even in the dark or fog. The magnetic compass had been invented in China around 800 but did not become widely used in Europe until the 1100s.

## Latitude

The astrolabe was a device that sailors could use to determine a ship's latitude. An astrolabe worked by allowing sailors to measure the altitude of the sun or a nighttime star. The ideas behind the astrolabe came from ancient Greece, but the tool was developed by Muslims in the middle of the 700s.

Discovery EDUCATION | SOCIAL STUDIES TECHBOOK

Why did European leaders want to explore and conquer? What was the impact of these encounters on other regions?

The Moors, or Muslims living in what is now Spain, introduced the astrolabe to Christian monks around the early 1000s. It was widely used until the 1600s, when it was replaced by the more accurate sextant. Many astrolabes were made of brass and were very intricate and beautiful.

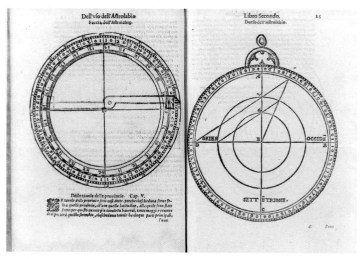

photo: Library of Congress

*An astrolabe was used to determine a ship's latitude.*

## Longitude

The key to navigating the open seas was determining longitude, or east-west position. Without an accurate clock, the key to finding longitude was finding the precise physical distance between your current location and a fixed location. The Greek astronomer Ptolemy had an idea for an instrument that could achieve this goal based on star positions. Using Ptolemy's idea, Muslim astronomers invented the quadrant around 1200. The quadrant depended on precise data of star positions. Even though Muslims had also improved astronomical measurement, locations determined by using a quadrant could still be several hundred miles off.

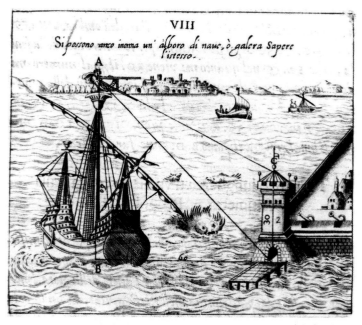

photo: Getty Images

*An illustration of sailors using a quadrant to measure distance from ship to shore.*

## The Printing Press

Johannes Gutenberg's invention of the printing press around 1450 allowed books to be printed faster and distributed farther than ever before. This meant that maps and information about new seafaring technology spread throughout Europe very quickly. Because of this, education became an important part of the success of navigators during this period.

# A School for Sailors

## *What was Prince Henry's school?*

Although the long ocean voyages were made easier by the improvement in navigation, sailors still needed to know how to use these new tools. A school was developed in Portugal to train sailors. It also contributed other important innovations to navigation and exploration.

### Prince Henry's School

Henry the Navigator (1394–1460) was a Portuguese prince. In the early 1400s, he established an observatory and a navigation school near his home in Sagres, Portugal. It was the first school of its kind in Europe. There, students learned about new shipbuilding and navigation techniques.

photo: Getty Images

*A map documenting the discoveries of Prince Henry the Navigator, 1493.*

The Portuguese were famous for the caravel, a ship with triangular sails. The caraval sailed at greater speeds than existing ships and was easier to steer. This allowed sailors to make longer journeys more quickly and easily than before.

During this time, ships were also being fitted with cannons and other large guns. This helped the sailors conquer the native peoples they encountered. It also led to an era of battles at sea between European nations competing for the conquest of the new lands.

Discovery EDUCATION | SOCIAL STUDIES TECHBOOK

Why did European leaders want to explore and conquer? What was the impact of these encounters on other regions?

## The Portuguese Expeditions

### How did Europe first encounter Africa?

The first European explorers to reach Africa during the Age of Exploration were the Portuguese. Prince Henry the Navigator did not go on any voyages himself, but he directed many important expeditions that explored the western coast of Africa. The next sections describe some of the more famous explorers from these early voyages.

### Diogo Cam (1452–1486)

Diogo Cam sailed between 1480 and 1486. He explored the western coast of Africa as far south as South Cross, near what is now Walvis Bay, Namibia. In August 1482, Cam became the first European sailor to reach the mouth of the Congo River, in what is now the Democratic Republic of the Congo. He left a pillar on the riverbank, claiming the surrounding land for Portugal.

### Bartolomeu Dias (1450–1500)

Bartolomeu Dias sailed between 1487 and 1488. He was the first European navigator to sail around the Cape of Good Hope at the southern tip of Africa. This opened the sea route to Asia for which Europe had been searching. Dias also took part in the exploration of South America. He died traveling to Brazil in 1500.

### Vasco da Gama (1469–1524)

Vasco da Gama sailed between 1497 and 1503. He established colonies for Portugal in eastern Africa at Mozambique. Da Gama was also the first European explorer to reach India by sea, but he was not able to establish a colony there.

### The First African Colony

In 1652, the first European colony in southern Africa was founded by Jan van Riebeeck (1619–1677). Van Riebeeck was a member of the Dutch East India Company, which was a trading company founded by the Dutch in 1602. Van Riebeeck's colony was called Cape Town because it was located near the Cape of Good Hope.

photo: Getty Images

*An illustration of Vasco da Gama landing near Calicut.*

The founding of Cape Town opened southern Africa for colonization by other European nations. Over the next three centuries, Britain, France, Portugal, and Spain, among other nations, would establish colonies in Africa, North America, and South America.

## Ivory, Gold, and Enslaved Africans

*How did the African slave trade begin?*

When European explorers first came to Africa, they were delighted by what they found. Africa may not have been the Far East, the destination for which they had been searching, but it was rich in gold, jewels, ivory, and exotic plants and animals.

*photo: Getty Images*

*The slave trade was an existing part of African culture before the Europeans arrived.*

Africans did not want European money, which had no value to them. Instead, the traders used a barter system, paying for their goods with cowrie shells, alcohol, and gunpowder. The traders brought back the goods they obtained in Africa to Europe. The European powers and the settlements along the African coast grew wealthy from this trade.

In addition to the trade for goods, a trade in enslaved humans also began between the European and the African kingdoms. Because of a labor shortage in Portugal, the Portuguese began buying enslaved Africans in 1444 for agricultural work. In the 1500s and 1600s, European powers began to establish colonies across the Atlantic Ocean in the West Indies and the American continents. They began buying enslaved Africans to work in the mines and on the plantations of sugarcane, cotton, and other valuable crops that were developing in these new colonies.

It was not long before the slave trade was larger than the trade for goods. As the plantations in the colonies grew, they needed more workers. Soon, these plantations could not function without slavery. In some regions, such as the British colonies in North America that later became the American South, slavery would become an intrinsic part of life.

**Explore this interactive to learn more about how increased trade affected people from four different perspectives.**

## Impact of the Slave Trade

*Where did enslaved Africans come from?*

### A Local Tradition

Although the slave trade increased with the arrival of European explorers, it was not a new concept in Africa. Long before the Europeans arrived, African kingdoms were buying and selling people (for the purpose of slavery) among themselves and with the Arab traders who moved throughout the region.

Discovery | SOCIAL STUDIES
EDUCATION | **TECHBOOK**

Why did European leaders want to explore and conquer? What was the impact of these encounters on other regions?

In Africa, enslaved people did not always remain enslaved for life and their children were not necessarily enslaved. Moreover, skin color and race were not considered signs of inferiority or markers of enslavement. These ideas of racial superiority and race-based slavery were developed by Europeans. To many African traders, the Europeans were simply a new market for the slave trade. However, the European model of race-based, permanent slavery would have enormous consequences in Africa and the Americas.

When African kingdoms went to war with each other, the winning kingdom would often take prisoners from the defeated armies and sell them as enslaved people. The captives were rounded up into groups, called coffles, and forced to march to the coast. Once there, the enslaved people were held in barracoons, or slave pens. They were forced to wait in these pens until they were sold. These pens eventually grew into huge barracks called "slave factories." Many enslaved Africans died in the factories or on the crowded boats that took them across the ocean.

Some African kingdoms attempted to fight against slavery. During the 1620s, Queen Nzinga of the Mbundu people led a war against the Portuguese, who wanted to use the Mbundu for the slave trade. Though the struggle continued after her death, Nzinga was seen as a symbol of freedom and the antislavery cause.

**Supply and Demand**

Europeans began buying large numbers of enslaved Africans to support the work that needed to be done on the plantations in their colonies. This had two major results for the Africans. First, the African kingdoms along the western coast, such as Angola, Senegambia, and Dahomey, became very wealthy.

The second result of the slave trade was that these kingdoms began to have trouble meeting the demand. The Europeans wanted more enslaved people than the kingdoms had. So, the kingdoms along the coast began to raid other kingdoms farther inland to capture more enslaved people to sell to the European traders.

The enslaved Africans that were most in demand were young men who had just become physically mature. Europeans preferred enslaved persons from African kingdoms because they believed that Africans could work harder and longer than people from other parts of the world. When the Spanish conquered South America, they tried to use the native South Americans as slave labor. However, most of them died when they were put to work for the Spanish. Many of these deaths were the result of diseases the Spanish had brought from Europe, against which the South Americans had no natural immunities. To replace the labor they had lost, the Spanish bought enslaved Africans.

photo: Getty Images

*An illustration of the arrival of a Dutch ship carrying enslaved people in Virginia.*

Because the European demand for enslaved Africans was so high, huge numbers of people were shipped out of Africa. Many of them were strong young men. This left the African kingdoms without enough people to work and fight for them. Europe, Africa, and the European colonies were all changed forever by the slave trade.

## Trading with the East

### How did Europeans establish trade in Asia?

Africa and the Americas had opened a new world of wealth and trade for Europe. However, European explorers still wanted to find a sea route to Asia so they could trade directly with China and avoid having to go through empires in the Middle East.

photo: Getty Images

*A 1733 engraving of Alfonso de Albuquerque and Hormuz Island.*

The first Europeans to reach India were the Portuguese. Vasco da Gama found a sea route to Calicut in 1498 but could not establish a colony. Muslim merchants in Calicut were suspicious and hostile, and da Gama had to fight his way out of the harbor. Another Portuguese explorer, Pedro Álvares Cabral, followed da Gama's route to Calicut. Cabral did manage to establish a trading post, but it did not last very long. The men he stationed at the post were slaughtered. Vasco da Gama was sent back to India to avenge the loss of these men. In 1503, he was finally able to establish a trading post.

After da Gama's success, other Portuguese sailors followed, expanding Portugal's trade with India and the areas surrounding it. Afonso de Albuquerque led expeditions to Goa, India, in 1510, Malaka (in modern-day Malaysia) in 1511, and the Moluccas (in modern-day Indonesia) from 1512 to 1514. The Portuguese spread their culture along with their trade. In Goa, they forced many local people to convert to Catholicism and established a religious inquisition.

The Portuguese were also the first Europeans to reach China by sea. In 1514, nearly 300 years after Marco Polo and his brother left Italy and crossed the Gobi Desert to reach China by land, Portuguese navigators successfully made the journey by sea. By 1557, the Portuguese had founded a trading station in Macao, China. In 1570, China began trading with Spanish colonies in the Philippines, and in 1619, the Dutch formed a colony in Taiwan.

## Other Europeans Follow

*How did trade increase between India, China, and the rest of the European nations?*

After Portugal's success, other explorers soon followed. Traders from the Dutch Empire banded together to form the Dutch East India Company in 1602. This organization quickly became a powerful force in Asia, establishing colonial outposts and trading centers in Indonesia, Sri Lanka, and Japan.

Throughout most of the early and mid-1600s, the Dutch fought a long conflict with Spain that included a struggle to control the increasingly valuable trade with Asia. Because Portugal was united with Spain during this period, the Dutch East India Company attacked and seized many of the Portuguese colonies in Africa and India. In the meantime, Spain increased its wealth and power by founding colonies in the Philippines as well as North and South America.

England and France soon became involved in this conflict as well, fighting against Spain, the Dutch Empire, and each other for control of trade and colonies. This tense situation, with so many players competing for the same resources, led to a rise in piracy as ship captains saw an opportunity to get rich by attacking merchant vessels carrying luxury goods home from Asia and the New World. Some pirates were supported by their governments and primarily targeted ships from enemy nations. Others freely attacked any ship they could find.

The Dutch East India Company held onto its control of European trade with Asia until the rise of the British Empire and its powerful navy in the 1700s. In 1600, Queen Elizabeth granted the English East India Company a charter to establish trade with the East Indies, and the company established several trading posts in Indian coastal cities by the mid-1600s. By the mid-1700s, after a series of British naval victories over the Dutch Empire, the East India Company greatly expanded its control over trade with Asia, extending its influence over much of India and establishing trading posts in China as well.

### Dominating India

Before Great Britain took control in the 1700s, traders from the Dutch Empire, France, and Portugal all built port cities along the Indian coastline and grew rich from the trade. These trading posts did not have much impact on the Mughal Empire, which ruled most of India at this time. By the mid-1700s, however, the Mughal Empire had dissolved into a group of small, squabbling states. As the English East India Company expanded its power in the region, it increasingly extended its influence and control over Indian rulers until it was effectively governing much of the Indian subcontinent.

Although the English East India Company remained a powerful force in India for another century, it gradually became little more than a direct representative of the British government. In the late 1700s, the company became regulated by an advisory board established by the British Parliament. In 1813, it lost its monopoly over the Indian trade with Britain. Between 1857 and 1858, after a disastrous popular uprising against company rule across much of India, the East India Company was dissolved and India became a formal British colony.

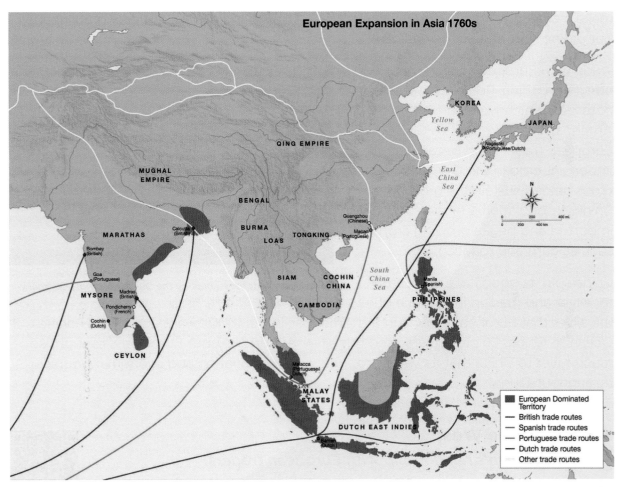

*A map of Southeast Asia uses color to highlight European-dominated territory along the east coast on India, in the Malay States, in most of the Dutch East Indies, and all of the Philippines.*

## Europe and the East

### How did China respond to European traders?

China had agreed to trade directly with Europe, but the Chinese were cautious about these newcomers. In 1656, the Chinese agreed to trade with Portugal because they were impressed with their willingness to learn Chinese customs. Despite allowing trade, the Chinese restricted Portuguese merchants to the port city of Canton.

**Discovery EDUCATION | SOCIAL STUDIES TECHBOOK**

Why did European leaders want to explore and conquer? What was the impact of these encounters on other regions?

The Portuguese tried to maintain the advantage they had gained by being the first to establish direct trade with China. They even drove away Dutch explorers, who were also trying to establish trade with China. The Dutch were eventually able to establish a colony on the island of Taiwan.

In addition to merchants, Jesuit missionaries, an order of priests in the Catholic Church, came to China in the hopes of spreading Christianity. The Chinese valued wisdom and were impressed by the scholarship of the Jesuits. However, the missionaries did not make many converts. Chinese scholars treated Christianity as an interesting philosophy but did not adopt it as their religion.

Trade with Europe had significant effects on China. Potatoes and sweet potatoes, which were native to the Americas, were brought to China by European traders and became an important crop in the 1500s. These crops helped sustain the growing Chinese population. China also imported and began growing crops such as corn and tobacco.

photo: Getty Images
*Fort Zeelandia fortress, built by the Dutch East India Company in Formosa (present-day Taiwan).*

China sold its goods to Europeans for silver and gold. In fact, much of the silver that Europeans found in the Americas in the 1600s went across the Pacific Ocean to China. Chinese rulers used this silver as currency, but Europeans brought so much silver to China that its value dropped, creating inflation and economic troubles throughout China.

## Japan and the West

### *What was Japan's relationship with European traders?*

When the Portuguese first reached Japan in 1543, the island nation was ruled by a group of powerful warlords called shoguns. The shoguns welcomed the Portuguese. Spanish and Dutch traders soon followed and were also welcomed. Jesuit missionaries also traveled to Japan. They had more success in Japan than they had in China: 300,000 Japanese converted to the new religion.

However, in 1615, a shogun named Tokugawa Ieyasu took control of Japan.

photo: Getty Images
*This folding screen depicts the siege of Osaka Castle, 1623.*

Tokugawa became suspicious of the growing influence of Christianity and other Western ideas.

He outlawed Christianity and persecuted anyone caught practicing it. He also made it illegal to own Western books. Beginning in 1639, Japan turned away all European traders except for a few Dutch ships. These ships were only allowed into Nagasaki Harbor on a nearby island, and trade was tightly regulated. Japan did not open its doors to the Western world again until 1853.

The Age of Exploration brought Europeans to Africa, the Americas, India, and Asia. When Europeans came in contact with these new places, they had a profound effect on the people they found there. Contact and trade with Europe led to dramatic changes in the culture, economy, and power balance of nations throughout the rest of the world.

**Consider the Essential Question:**

Why did European leaders want to explore and conquer? What was the impact of these encounters on other regions?

Go online to complete the Social Studies Explanation.

**Check for Understanding:**

Explain one reason Europeans increased their foreign trade during the 1400s and 1500s. Be sure to provide details and examples in your response.

**DISCOVERY EDUCATION | SOCIAL STUDIES TECHBOOK**

How did European contact and conquest in America change life in the Americas and in Europe?

# 10.2 Cultures Collide in the Americas

*photo: Library of Congress*

## LESSON OVERVIEW

### Introduction

In this concept, you will examine how European exploration of the Americas impacted the native people living there. You will also analyze how it changed the economy of Europe.

### Essential Question

How did European contact and conquest in America change life in the Americas and in Europe?

### Lesson Objective

By the end of this lesson, you should be able to:

- Analyze the causes and effects of European exploration of the Americas on the native people of the Americas and the economy of Europe.

## Key Vocabulary
Which terms do you already know?

- [ ] Amerigo Vespucci
- [ ] Atahualpa
- [ ] Atlantic Ocean
- [ ] Aztec
- [ ] Aztec Empire
- [ ] caravel
- [ ] Christianity
- [ ] Christopher Columbus
- [ ] colony
- [ ] Columbian Exchange
- [ ] conquistador
- [ ] culture
- [ ] Dutch East India Company
- [ ] Dutch West India Company
- [ ] encomienda
- [ ] epidemic
- [ ] expedition
- [ ] Ferdinand Magellan
- [ ] Francisco Pizarro
- [ ] Giovanni da Verrazzano
- [ ] Henry Hudson
- [ ] Hernán Cortés
- [ ] Hernando de Soto
- [ ] Inca
- [ ] Jacques Cartier
- [ ] John Cabot
- [ ] Juan Ponce de León
- [ ] King Louis IV
- [ ] line of demarcation
- [ ] mission
- [ ] missionary
- [ ] Montezuma
- [ ] New Spain
- [ ] population
- [ ] Queen Isabella
- [ ] Renaissance
- [ ] Tenochtitlán
- [ ] trade
- [ ] Treaty of Paris

## ENGAGE

Why did contact with Europeans have devastating consequences for Native American populations? Visit Engage to learn more.

### Essential Question

How did European contact and conquest in America change life in the Americas and in Europe?

## EXPLORE

### Reasons for Exploration

*Why did Europeans first arrive in the Americas?*

In the 1400s and 1500s, there was a rebirth of culture and scientific discovery throughout Europe known as the Renaissance. During this time, people used scientific inquiry and rational thought to explore how the natural world worked. This curiosity and spirit of discovery, which led to numerous inventions and scientific discoveries during the Renaissance, also led to a period of geographic exploration as individuals began to explore the seas and lands beyond Europe's borders.

*photo: Getty Images*

*A portrait of Prince Henry the Navigator.*

Although the ideas of the Renaissance contributed to the exploration of new lands, more practical concerns were also at play. During this period, growing European nations were in constant conflict with each other as they struggled to increase their power and wealth. Many of these nations believed trade with other countries was the best way to increase wealth. However, many of the land routes that were used for trade with Asia were controlled by Muslim countries that blocked direct trade between European and Asian nations. As a result, European leaders began to seek new sea routes to Asia in hopes of opening new trade markets.

**Discovery** | SOCIAL STUDIES
EDUCATION | **TECHBOOK**

How did European contact and conquest in America change life in the Americas and in Europe?

European leaders, such as Spain's King Ferdinand and the Portuguese prince known as Henry the Navigator, financed explorers willing to journey across the seas. Along with the idea of looking for new trade routes, they hoped to find new sources of gold, silver, and other valuables. Additionally, Europeans saw exploration as a way to bring Christianity to other cultures that lived in faraway lands.

While some explorers sailed around Africa to Asia, others thought they could find a quicker route by sailing west. These voyages led to the unexpected discovery of new lands as sailors bound for Asia came to the Caribbean islands and the continents of North America and South America.

## Europeans Arrive in the Caribbean

*What was Columbus's role in the exploration and colonization of the Caribbean and the American continents?*

On August 3, 1492, Christopher Columbus set sail from Palos, Spain, with three ships: the *Niña*, *Pinta*, and *Santa Maria*. Columbus intended to cross the Atlantic Ocean to find a quicker sea route to Asia, especially the rich lands of Japan and China. On October 12, 1492, men on the *Pinta* sighted land. Although Columbus and his crew thought they had reached Asia, they landed on what would later be known as Watlings Island in the Bahamas.

For three months, Columbus and his crews explored the islands of the Caribbean, landing on the islands of Cuba and Hispaniola (the island that contains the modern-day countries of Haiti and the Dominican Republic). Columbus and his crew also met the native peoples of these islands, the Taino. By 1494, the Spanish, led by Columbus, had established a permanent settlement on Hispaniola and begun their conquest of the island. As a result of these first encounters in the Caribbean, Europeans from different nations explored, settled, and conquered the Americas over a period of about 300 years. Competition for exploration led to a treaty between Spain and Portugal in 1494, which gave Spain the exclusive right to explore and conquer almost all of the land in the Americas. The treaty gave Portugal the right to explore and conquer lands in Africa, Asia, and the land in South America that would become Brazil. While this treaty was supported by the pope, many other countries ignored the treaty and sent their own explorers to conquer land abroad.

While Columbus may be one of the most recognizable names of the time, he was not alone in his quest. In 1497, Italian-born navigator John Cabot set out to find a sea route to Asia for the British. Instead, he discovered Canada. That same year, Italian explorer Amerigo Vespucci embarked on the first of three voyages. Looking to find a route to Cape Verde off of the coast of Africa, he instead discovered Rio de Janeiro and Rio de la Plata in South America. Assuming he had found a new continent, Vespucci called his discovery the New World. In 1507, the German cartographer Martin Waldseemüller officially named the continent "America" in honor of Vespucci.

## Deeper into the Americas

In 1513, Spanish explorer Juan Ponce de León traveled along the coast of what is now Florida. That same year, another Spanish explorer, Vasco Núñez de Balboa, crossed the Isthmus of Panama. In doing so, he became the first European explorer to cross the American continents and set eyes on the Pacific Ocean. Four hundred years later, the Panama Canal would open across the same isthmus, creating a direct route from the Atlantic Ocean to the Pacific Ocean.

Despite the discoveries in the Americas, the search for a sea route to Asia continued. In 1519, Ferdinand Magellan launched five ships from Spain and navigated around the southern tip of South America. Although he died in 1521, his expedition continued without him. The first sailors to travel around the entire globe, Magellan's expedition returned to Spain in 1522 and proved that the world was round. The sea channel that Magellan took between the Pacific Ocean and the Atlantic Ocean was aptly named the Strait of Magellan.

During this important Age of Exploration, two vastly different worlds intersected: the Americas and Europe. The exchange of people, ideas, plants, animals, technologies, and diseases between these two worlds shaped their history for the next 500 years.

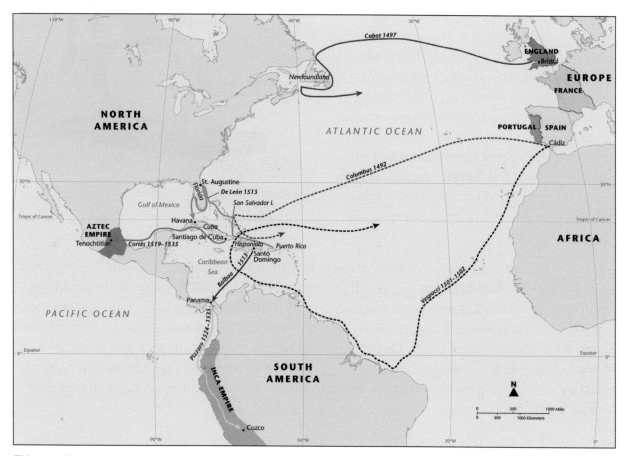

*This map shows the routes the early explorers took to the Americas.*

Discovery | SOCIAL STUDIES
EDUCATION | TECHBOOK

How did European contact and conquest in America change life
in the Americas and in Europe?

## Conquering the Americas

*How were the Spanish able to conquer Native American
populations?*

During the 100 years following Columbus's first voyage to the Americas,
Spanish conquistadors, explorers, and soldiers conquered and claimed much of the
Americas in the name of Spain. These men fought for many reasons. One reason is that
exploration and conquest could lead to great wealth, as conquistadors claimed their
share of the riches received from conquest. Other people came because they were
faithful Catholics and wanted to convert Native Americans to Christianity. Still others
thrived on the adventure of exploring new places.

Regardless of the reason for their coming
to the Americas, several factors helped the
Spanish conquer the native populations.
One factor that aided the Spanish was
their weapons. Using sophisticated, strong
weapons such as steel swords, crossbows,
and guns helped the Spanish against local
tribes, who had less powerful weaponry.
The Spanish conquistadors also had
horses, which people in the Americas had
never seen before. Fighting on horseback
gave the Spanish explorers an advantage
over the Native American populations, who
fought on foot. Lastly, the Spanish made
alliances with local peoples. Many tribes
resented the rule of larger empires in the
region, such as the Aztec Empire and the
Incan Empire. Building alliances helped
the Spanish expand their territory in the
New World.

*photo: Getty Images*

*A figure of a Spanish conquistador on horseback.*

However, one of the most important tools that the Europeans had was one they did not
even know they had brought with them to the Americas—disease. European explorers
carried over several diseases that native peoples in the Americas had never encountered
before. One such disease was smallpox, a highly contagious disease that had existed in
Europe for thousands of years. Over time, the Europeans developed some resistance to
it. Native Americans, though, had never encountered the disease and therefore had no
resistance to it. As a result, smallpox devastated the Native American populations that
encountered it.

The effects of smallpox helped two of the most famous conquistadors, Hernán Cortés
and Francisco Pizzaro. Despite commanding forces that were significantly smaller than
those of the Aztec and Incan armies, these two conquistadors were still able to conquer
the powerful empires.

## Cortés and the Aztec

### *How was Cortés able to conquer the Aztec Empire?*

In 1504, drawn by the opportunity for wealth and adventure, Hernán Cortés traveled from Spain to the island of Hispaniola. Once there, Cortés entered government and gained some power and influence. As a result, in 1511 he was chosen as part of the crew that sailed with Diego Velázquez to conquer Cuba. After the conquest of Cuba, Cortés was named clerk to the treasurer of Cuba, an important position in the government.

In 1518, because of his position and relationship with Velázquez, Cortés was appointed commander of an expedition. The expedition's purpose was to establish colonies, foreign cities controlled by Spain's government, on the mainland. After gathering more than 600 men for his 11 ships, Cortés set sail and landed in what is today known as Mexico. Cortés drilled and trained his soldiers in preparation for conquest. He was so determined to conquer new lands in pursuit of wealth that he sank his own ships to ensure there would be no turning back.

+photo: Getty Images

*An illustration of Hernán Cortés meeting the Aztec emperor Montezuma in 1519.*

As Cortés marched up the Mexican Gulf Coast, local people told him of a great empire with large quantities of gold. Cortés claimed the area as New Spain, and he and his conquistadors marched inland toward Tenochtitlán, the capital of the Aztec Empire. As they traveled, Cortés took advantage of the turmoil within the Aztec Empire. Many local tribes, especially the Tlaxcala, resented the rule of the Aztec and were in constant conflict. Cortés recruited these local tribes to be his allies. As he traveled, Cortés received two messages from the Aztec king, Montezuma II. The messages warned Cortés and his men to stay out of Tenochtitlan and offered him payments if he would go away.

Cortés ignored the warnings. His forces combined with as many as 1,000 of his Tlaxcala allies and entered Tenochtitlan on November 8, 1519. He took Montezuma hostage and ruled in his place. He and his soldiers spent nearly two years plundering the Aztec Empire while the Aztec resisted his rule. In 1520, Cortés and his forces were forced to retreat from Tenochtitlan and the Aztec retook control of the city.

**Discovery** EDUCATION | SOCIAL STUDIES **TECHBOOK**

How did European contact and conquest in America change life in the Americas and in Europe?

Cortés regrouped his forces and launched a new attack. This time, the conquistadors first conquered the areas surrounding the city and then began their assault on the city itself. They were aided in their attack not only by their superior weaponry—steel swords, firearms, and mounted cavalry—but also by the diseases they had carried over from Europe. The Aztec had no immunities against diseases such as smallpox, and the effect was devastating. It is estimated that as much as 90 percent of the Aztec population eventually died as a result of European diseases. This loss of life weakened the Aztec forces and made it easier for the smaller Spanish forces to conquer the city. In 1521, the Spanish forces destroyed Tenochtitlan and built a capital, called Mexico City, on its ruins.

## Pizarro and the Inca

### *How was Pizarro able to conquer the Inca Empire?*

Francisco Pizarro had journeyed across the Isthmus of Panama with Vasco Núñez de Balboa, a Spanish conquistador. Balboa was the first European explorer to see the Pacific. While on Balboa's expedition, Pizarro heard rumors of an empire to the south that had large amounts of gold. In the 1520s, he took two expeditions south toward the Incan Empire, centered in what is now Peru. These expeditions provided him with proof of Inca riches, including sculptures and vases of solid gold.

In 1531, Pizarro and 180 men left Panama to attempt the conquest of the Incan Empire. Taking advantage of chaos caused by years of civil war, Pizarro was able to move closer to the heart of the empire. When the conquistadors arrived at a meeting with the Incan emperor Atahualpa, they opened fire, killing thousands of unarmed men and capturing Atahualpa. The emperor tried to buy his freedom by offering vast amounts of gold and silver, but though Pizarro accepted Atahualpa's riches, he had his conquistadors kill Atahualpa. Afterward, in 1533, Pizarro established Atahualpa's brother as a ruler in name only. Pizarro retained true political power for himself. However, resistance to Spanish rule continued.

photo: Getty Images

*An illustration of Incan emperor Atalhualpa receiving a missionary.*

Due to the European presence in Central and South America, a smallpox epidemic (a disease that has spread quickly over a large area) was sweeping through the region. It had spread through the Incan empire.

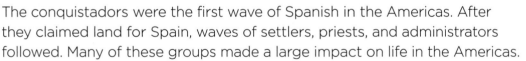

Estimates suggest smallpox killed millions of Inca. As a result, the Incan Empire was already weakened when Pizarro's conquistadors clashed with Atahualpa. In part, this allowed Pizarro to seize control of the capital and the entire Incan Empire. The spread of this new disease changed South America by devastating its population. However, the introduction of a new culture led to an exchange of goods and ideas.

Pizarro founded the city of Lima in 1535. It became Peru's capital and the center of education, power, and wealth in the region. The Spanish royal court operated from Lima, and many schools and academies were built there. In 1545, the Spanish established another South American colony, Potosí, in Bolivia. This silver-rich region became very important to the Pacific silver trade.

South America's economy depended on its ability to mine silver and trade it with the rest of the world. This silver fueled the Spanish economy and was sent across the Atlantic to Europe and across the Pacific to trading cities in East Asia. The more silver the Spanish mined, however, the more common it became in these markets, and its value began to drop. To ensure steady silver production, the Spanish enslaved native South Americans and forced them to work in silver mines. An estimated eight million indigenous people died during this time.

**Explore this interactive to learn more about how European powers were able to conquer the Americas so quickly.**

## Missions and Missionaries

*How did Spanish missionaries change life in the Americas?*

The conquistadors were the first wave of Spanish in the Americas. After they claimed land for Spain, waves of settlers, priests, and administrators followed. Many of these groups made a large impact on life in the Americas.

One of the first groups to come from Spain was the missionaries. Missionaries are people who work to spread their religion to other people. Catholic priests founded missions, a building or group of buildings used as a base for missionary work, throughout the Spanish colonies, including what is today the southwestern United States. They used these missions to spread the message of Christianity to the Native Americans.

The Spanish missions generally included a church, living quarters, workrooms, and storerooms, all within a walled enclosure. Many missions from the 1500s and 1600s are still standing, including Mission San Juan Capistrano, south of modern-day Los Angeles, California. The Alamo in San Antonio, Texas, which became a famous site during the Texas War of Independence, was also a mission chapel.

Discovery EDUCATION | SOCIAL STUDIES TECHBOOK

How did European contact and conquest in America change life in the Americas and in Europe?

The missions became the economic and religious hubs of Spanish activities. Native Americans who had converted to Christianity came to live at the missions, working in exchange for food and shelter. Some Native Americans chose to join the missions because they had truly converted to Christianity. Others came to the missions to escape Spanish exploitation outside the mission. In return for safety, converts were required to adopt Catholicism and renounce their Native American culture. Native Americans were to embrace Spanish culture, including requiring converts to speak only Spanish and to abandon their traditional clothing.

photo: Library of Congress

*The San Juan Capistrano was the 17th Spanish mission in modern-day California.*

## Encomiendas

### What was the encomienda system?

The Spanish founded colonies as a source of wealth, and they needed workers to extract that wealth—by growing valuable crops and mining gold. They developed the encomienda system to organize this labor. An encomienda was a grant by the Spanish monarch. An encomienda gave individuals the right to control a certain number of Native Americans for labor purposes. The Spanish monarch often gave encomiendas to former conquistadors or to colonial officials. In return for these grants, the *encomendero*—the person who controlled the labor—was supposed to care for and protect the Native Americans under his control.

However, in practice, Native Americans lost their lands, were treated like slaves, and suffered terrible working conditions. The encomienda system faded from use as the Native American labor force died from disease and overwork.

Both the encomienda system and the missions had negative effects on the population and cultures of the local tribes. Harsh treatment under the encomienda system led to poor health among Native Americans, and many of them died as a result. These decreased the populations of many local tribes. Missions were not as harsh as the encomienda system. However, because religious and cultural conversion were often a part of the work of a mission, many Native American beliefs, customs, and traditions were lost as members of local tribes either were forced to or willingly adopted European beliefs and culture.

## Sugar Plantations in the Caribbean and Brazil

Early on, the Spanish and Portuguese began cultivating sugar on islands off the coast of Africa. There, they used Africans as slaves to work the sugar plantations. A plantation is a farm or estate where commercial crops such as coffee, sugar, and tobacco are grown in large quantities to be sold. The sugar grown in Cape Verde and on other islands was shipped back to Europe, where demand for the sweet treat grew rapidly. As Europeans explored the Americas, they brought with them the plantation model of agriculture and more sugarcane to grow in the New World.

Sugarcane may have arrived in the Americas as early as Columbus's second voyage across the Atlantic, in 1493. By the early 1500s, sugar was being grown in Hispaniola (modern-day Haiti and the Dominican Republic). Soon, sugar cultivation spread to Jamaica and Puerto Rico. Then, in 1540, the Portuguese brought sugarcane from Madeira, off the coast of northwest Africa, to their colony in Brazil. Once production in Brazil began, the Portuguese and Dutch quickly expanded the sugar trade, and it was not long before sugar was Brazil's major export. By the 1560s, Brazil was producing about 2,500 tons of sugar each year.

photo: Getty Images

*An illustration of a French colonial sugar plantation in Martinique, West Indies, 1830. Note the quarters for enslaved people in the foreground.*

Sugar production was so profitable that other European countries wanted to get involved. France and Britain acquired islands in the Caribbean that quickly began to rival Brazil. The British established sugar colonies in Jamaica and Barbados, while France founded Saint-Domingue, Guadeloupe, and Martinique. These colonies were located close to both Africa and Europe, which made them a key part of the world sugar trade. These colonies became profitable because plantation owners paid lower shipping costs to import enslaved people and export sugar. Saint Domingue was the most profitable sugar island in the entire Caribbean. At one point, it produced 40 percent of Europe's sugar. All told, 90 percent of Europe's sugar came from the Caribbean. Coffee and tobacco were also grown on plantations in Brazil and on various Caribbean islands.

Work on the sugar plantations was hard, and eventually plantations came to rely on imported enslaved African rather than European labor or indigenous Americans. Between 1500 and 1866, more than 12 million enslaved Africans were forced to move to the Americas. Almost half of those enslaved Africans were sent to Brazil, and most others went to the sugar-producing islands of the Caribbean. About 4 percent of all enslaved Africans captured in Africa were sent to what is now the United States and Canada.

# The English in the Americas

## *What were the first British colonies in the Americas?*

Although John Cabot had explored North American shores at the end of the 1400s under the commission of British King Henry VII, English exploration of North America did not begin to increase until the mid-1500s. In 1576, Englishman Sir Martin Frobisher set sail for North America in search of the "Northwest Passage" that could lead traders to Asia. Returning to England with stories of gold and riches, he was given royal backing for two more voyages, both of which were unsuccessful.

Frobisher had not found the gold he was seeking, and his colonization attempt was unsuccessful. However, the British would not be left behind as continental Europe grew rich off of North America. In the 1580s, Queen Elizabeth I permitted Sir Walter Raleigh to create English colonies in North America. After a failed attempt, in 1587, he set up Roanoke Colony in an area of North America he named "Virginia." However, when supply ships returned to the area in 1590, the settlers had mysteriously vanished. Roanoke came to be called "The Lost Colony." Although it did not survive, Roanoke laid the groundwork for English settlement in North America. In 1606, the Virginia Company received permission from the king to open a new colony. They called this settlement "Jamestown," after King James I.

### Jamestown and Plymouth: The First Permanent Colonies

Jamestown was established on May 14, 1607. The colony was composed of men and boys—a grouping of artisans, laborers, soldiers, and wealthy gentleman looking to get rich off the new land. The organizers of the Virginia Company also hoped to grow rich off of Jamestown. The colony was supposed to help expand British trade and establish a new market for English goods, and the British hoped that the colonists would find new sources of gold and a shipping route to the Pacific Ocean. According to instructions left by the Virginia Company, the settlement was to be locally governed by a president and a group of six council members, all of whom were chosen by members of the Virginia Company before the ships had even sailed. The names were kept in a locked box, not to be opened until the site for the colony had been found.

Building an entire town from scratch was hard work, and many of Jamestown's colonists died within the first two years of its establishment due to disease and malnutrition. Food and supplies ran low, and the settlers may not have made it without the food and other gifts that local Powhatan Native Americans gave them. However, the settlers eventually created small farms, and new supplies and settlers arrived from England. When it became clear that the expected riches were not to be found, tobacco farming was introduced and, over time, the colony became economically successful.

Jamestown, like many of the American colonies that would follow, imported enslaved people from Africa. The first enslaved Africans arrived in 1619 when the English attacked a Portuguese ship that was taking them to Mexico. Many of these enslaved people were sold to settlers in Jamestown, where they worked on the tobacco farms.

photo: Getty Images

*Landing of the Pilgrims at Plymouth Colony in 1620.*

In 1620, the British established their next North American colony. The Plymouth Colony was established primarily for religious reasons rather than economic ones. A group of religious dissidents who came to be known as the Pilgrims left England to escape religious persecution. Traveling aboard the *Mayflower*, they settled in what is now Massachusetts in November 1620. Their goal was to create a farming village and practice their religion in peace.

However, because they could not afford the passage on their own, the Pilgrims entered into an agreement with a company of British merchants. In exchange for the money and supplies they needed, the Pilgrims would work for the company and send resources such as fish, animal furs, and timber back to England.

## The French and Dutch in the Americas

*What areas of the Americas did the French and Dutch colonize?*

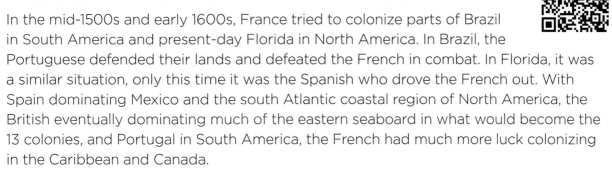

In the mid-1500s and early 1600s, France tried to colonize parts of Brazil in South America and present-day Florida in North America. In Brazil, the Portuguese defended their lands and defeated the French in combat. In Florida, it was a similar situation, only this time it was the Spanish who drove the French out. With Spain dominating Mexico and the south Atlantic coastal region of North America, the British eventually dominating much of the eastern seaboard in what would become the 13 colonies, and Portugal in South America, the French had much more luck colonizing in the Caribbean and Canada.

The first official French voyage of discovery to the Americas set sail in 1524 to find a sea route to China. Navigator Giovanni da Verrazzano explored the eastern seaboard of North America, from Cape Fear in North Carolina up to Cape Breton Island in Nova Scotia, Canada. Ten years later, Jacques Cartier explored the Gulf of Saint Lawrence, where the Saint Lawrence River meets the Atlantic Ocean in Canada, and traveled up the river to Montreal. Although an early settlement in Nova Scotia failed, the journeys brought Cartier into contact with the Iroquois and established a fur trade with the Native Americans. It also helped France take control of the river way and eventually claim the entire Mississippi River valley area. Together, Verrazzano and Cartier helped found what would become New France.

New France was composed of three separate colonies: Acadia, which was founded in 1604; Canada, which began when Samuel de Champlain founded Québec in 1608 to control the base of the Saint Lawrence River; and the territory of Louisiana, where French settlers started arriving around 1699. Over time, the boundaries of the colonies shifted—for example, by 1713, the French had lost much of Acadia to the British, and France temporarily lost control of Quebec between 1629 and 1632.

One of the reasons why French colonization was slow and difficult to defend was a lack of population. Compared with the British colonies, settlement of New France was sparse. In 1660, there were some 3,000 French colonists in total, and by 1760 that number had climbed to only around 90,000, as opposed to the roughly 1.6 million people who inhabited the British colonies. Those who came to this new land came primarily to partake in the fur trade, not to settle in a new region of the world. The French relied on relations with Native Americans to maintain control of their lands, using native peoples as guides, military allies, trade partners for food and animal hides, and the like. They lived in and among Native Americans, and indigenous peoples were welcome in their trade posts and settlements.

photo: Getty Images

*Champlain's map of the Bay of Fundy in Canada.*

Like the French, the Dutch also partook in the fur trade and were not as interested in agriculture and land domestication as the British. Controlling the Hudson River valley from the early 1600s until the mid-1660s, the Dutch built posts for the fur trade with Native Americans and towns along the river as part of their New Netherland colony. Today's New York City was then called New Amsterdam. As part of New Netherland, it was the third largest of the Dutch settlements in North America. The Dutch also established settlements on the Caribbean island of Saint Martin in 1620, eventually capturing nearby islands to form the Netherlands Antilles, also known as the Netherlands West Indies. The Dutch West India Company used these islands as a base for slave trade.

## Tomatoes for Horses

### *How did the Columbian Exchange change life in Europe and the Americas?*

The explorers and conquerors who traveled to the New World came looking for wealth and power. While they did find gold and other riches, they also opened the way for a much larger cultural exchange between the "old" and "new" worlds, which would come to be known as the Columbian Exchange. The Columbian Exchange refers to the exchange of plants, animals, diseases, technologies, and ideas between Europe and the Americas.

Consider the following. Without the Columbian Exchange, there would be no:

- tomato sauce in Italy, because tomatoes were brought to Italy from the Americas;

- orange juice in Florida, because orange trees were native to Europe and were brought to the Americas; or

- cattle ranches in Texas, because cows were also brought to the Americas by European explorers and settlers.

As demonstrated by the fall of the Aztec and Inca Empires, not all changes brought about by the Columbian Exchange were positive. Smallpox and other diseases such as malaria, influenza, and the measles devastated Native American populations that had no resistance to them. Diseases even devastated communities that did not come into contact with Europeans. Messengers and traders from other areas would unknowingly carry the disease into a town or village, and soon after many people lay sick or dying. While European explorers also suffered from living in unfamiliar conditions and being exposed to new diseases, the impact on the native population was more severe. Despite these devastating diseases, there were also several positive exchanges between Europe and the Americas.

photo: Paul Fuqua

*How does this market reflect changes caused by the Columbian Exchange?*

New plants and crops were introduced to both regions. The Europeans introduced domesticated animals such as sheep, horses, and cattle to the Americas. Farmers in the Americas learned to use oxen and horses to plow fields, increasing farm productivity and the food supply. Horses quickly became a key part of Native American culture and livelihood in the Southwest and Great Plains of the United States. Enslaved Africans brought their cultures and beliefs to the Americas, creating new and unique artistic, musical, and religious traditions in the Americas.

The Columbian Exchange also affected areas outside the Americas and Europe, particularly Africa and Asia. Key staple crops now found in West Africa, such as peanuts, maize, and cacao, originated in the Americas. Potatoes, another food from the Americas, are used often in Indian cooking. Sugarcane, which is native to the South Pacific, became a key cash crop in the Caribbean. Eventually, the rubber tree, which is native to South America, became the main source of natural rubber. By the early 1900s, it was grown on rubber plantations across West Africa and Southeast Asia.

**Discovery** SOCIAL STUDIES
EDUCATION | **TECHBOOK**

How did European contact and conquest in America change life
in the Americas and in Europe?

**Complete this activity to analyze a firsthand account of Native American experiences in the 1500s.**

The Columbian Exchange impacted lives and economies in Africa and Asia, too. Some historians argue that warfare in Africa increased so that slave-selling kingdoms could meet the demand of European slave traders. Some African regions and kingdoms lost millions of people to the slave trade. In Asia, many kingdoms and empires became increasingly focused on supplying the trade. Over time, European traders began to dominate the economies and even the political powers in China and India.

## Clash of Empires

*How did competition for land affect the relationships between empires?*

During the 1400s and 1500s, exploration and trade contributed to European empires becoming more powerful and competitive with one another. They improved their militaries by acquiring gunpowder from the East. They also began to raise standing armies, or armies that were permanently ready to be used. Previously, European countries had raised armies only when they were needed. The use of gunpowder and standing armies encouraged European rulers to attempt to expand their influence abroad, and to compete with other empires for land and colonies.

### European Conflict

Although Spain and Portugal were the first to establish colonies in the Americas, Great Britain and the Netherlands were not far behind. The struggle for influence over land and trade routes led to conflict as Europe's powers competed for the treasures of the "New World."

In 1578, King Sebastian I of Portugal died with no heir, leading King Philip II of Spain to claim the right to rule Portugal. Philip II also declared war on England and attempted to invade with his navy, leading to the destruction of many of his ships. Meanwhile, after achieving independence from Spain, the Netherlands worked to improve its navy so that it could take over Portuguese colonies. This led to the formation of the Dutch East India Company in 1602, which resulted in Dutch control of the southern Asian spice trade. In addition, the Dutch West India Company took over Portuguese colonies and colonized parts of North and South America.

Great Britain also dominated colonial trade during this time. Like the Netherlands, the British tried to expand both east, into India, and west, into North America. This competition led to a series of naval conflicts in the 1600s and 1700s called the Anglo-Dutch Wars. Great Britain emerged from these conflicts as the strongest naval power in Europe.

France expanded its empire, colonizing parts of what are now Canada and the United States. At first, France allied with Britain in its fight against the Netherlands. After the British won the Anglo-Dutch wars, France tried to become the greatest colonial empire by challenging the British. The two powers engaged in numerous global conflicts between 1688 and 1713 and again beginning in 1754. In 1763, the Treaty of Paris established Great Britain's dominance in North America and ended a struggle that became known as the Seven Years' War.

The age of increased commerce brought risks to ships carrying valuable cargo back to European powers. Piracy was common along Atlantic trade routes. Major European empires also sponsored privateers. Privateers were agents sent by governments to take the merchandise and ships of other foreign powers.

photo: Getty Images
*A battle scene from the French and Indian War.*

## Conflict in "The Gunpowder Empires"

In the 1500s and 1600s, as European powers fought for colonies, three powerful Islamic empires emerged in the Near and Middle East: the Ottoman Empire based in Constantinople, the Safavid Empire of Iran, and the Timurid/Mughal Empire of India. The empires fought for control of land in Southwest, central, and South Asia.

These three empires are often known as the "Gunpowder Empires" because of the conflicts to expand their territories, which they fought with advanced technology. This technology included cannons and guns—equipment that used gunpowder. The use of gunpowder allowed the leaders of these empires to claim more land. For example, the Ottomans used large cannons to break through the defenses of Constantinople and to claim it for themselves.

### Consider the Essential Question:

How did European contact and conquest in America change life in the Americas and in Europe?

Go online to complete the Social Studies Explanation.

### Check for Understanding:

In what ways did the Columbian Exchange impact the culture and economies of both the Americas and Europe? Be sure to provide details and examples in your response.

**Discovery** | SOCIAL STUDIES **TECHBOOK**

How did the Reformation change the balance of power in Europe?

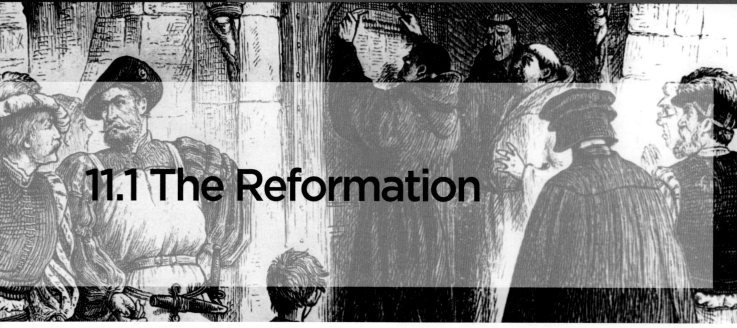

# 11.1 The Reformation

photo: Getty Images

## LESSON OVERVIEW

### Introduction

In this concept, you will learn how the Protestant Reformation began and how it spread across Europe. You will also examine how the Catholic Church responded.

### Essential Question

How did the Reformation change the balance of power in Europe?

### Lesson Objectives

By the end of this lesson, you should be able to:

- Identify the causes of the upheaval of the Catholic Church.

- Trace the spread of Protestantism across Europe.

- Identify on a world map the countries and regions that remained Catholic and those that converted to Protestantism.

- Evaluate the effectiveness of the Catholic Counter-Reformation as a response to the Reformation.

## Key Vocabulary
### Which terms do you already know?

- ☐ Calvinism
- ☐ Catholic Church
- ☐ England
- ☐ Europe
- ☐ France
- ☐ heretic
- ☐ indulgences
- ☐ Italy
- ☐ Johannes Gutenberg
- ☐ John Calvin
- ☐ King Ferdinand
- ☐ King Henry VIII
- ☐ King James Bible
- ☐ Latin
- ☐ Martin Luther
- ☐ Muslims
- ☐ New Testament
- ☐ Ninety-Five Theses
- ☐ parliament
- ☐ pope
- ☐ Protestant Church
- ☐ Protestant Reformation
- ☐ Protestantism
- ☐ Queen Isabella
- ☐ reform/social reform
- ☐ Sir Thomas More
- ☐ Spain
- ☐ taxes
- ☐ William Shakespeare
- ☐ William Tyndale

## ENGAGE

**Why did Martin Luther question the church? Visit Engage to learn more.**

> ### Essential Question
>
> How did the Reformation change the balance of power in Europe?

## EXPLORE

### The Catholic Church in the 1500s

*What was the Catholic Church like in the early 1500s?*

By the early 1500s, the Catholic Church in Europe had become very powerful. The pope, the religious head of the Catholic Church, and other Church leaders had a great deal of political power.

As the Church grew in power, some people felt that it had become too involved in worldly issues. For example, the Church collected high taxes from citizens. This made the Church very wealthy. As the wealth and power of the Church increased, some priests and Church leaders began to use the power of the Church to gain wealth and influence for themselves. These leaders lived in luxury compared with the way most ordinary people lived. This upset many of the members of the faith, as did some of the methods these leaders used to gain their wealth.

*photo: Library of Congress*

*A page from Gutenberg's Bible, written in Latin, 1455.*

Discovery SOCIAL STUDIES
EDUCATION | TECHBOOK

How did the Reformation change the balance of power in Europe?

One of the most controversial practices was the selling of indulgences. The Church had traditionally taught that sins would be forgiven if the sinner confessed, asked God for forgiveness, and did good works, such as giving to the poor. In the early 1500s, however, Church leaders began selling indulgences. This meant that people gave money to the Church in exchange for the forgiveness of their sins. To some people, this practice of selling indulgences was like letting people pay their way into heaven.

Even some of the traditional practices and structures of the Church made people feel distant from God. During this time, most Christian Bibles were written in Latin and Catholic masses were held in Latin. Most common people could not read or speak Latin. They felt disconnected from the Church. In addition, Church leaders said that only they, and not ordinary people, could interpret the Bible. This practice meant that many people felt they did not have a direct relationship with God. Some people began looking for ways to change some of these practices.

## Martin Luther

*What role did Martin Luther play in the Reformation?*

### Luther's Ninety-Five Theses

Martin Luther objected to the corrupt practices of the Church and disagreed with some of the Church's teachings. The Catholic Church taught that to get to heaven, people needed to have faith in Jesus Christ and do good works on Earth. Luther argued that faith alone, not good works, was the way for people to achieve salvation. Luther also believed people should read the Bible for themselves. Because of his beliefs and the problems in the church, he thought the Church needed to be reformed, or improved.

In 1517, Luther wrote a list of propositions for a debate about some of the practices of the Catholic Church. According to legend, Luther nailed this list of propositions to the door of a church in Wittenberg, Germany. Then, he circulated this list of ideas among his friends and sent copies to several Church leaders. Luther called this document the Ninety-Five Theses. Theses are arguments or propositions. Luther's ideas spread quickly throughout Germany, partly because of Johannes Gutenberg's recent invention of the printing press. With the printing press, information could be printed more quickly and cheaply, and pamphlets explaining Luther's ideas spread across Germany.

photo: Getty Images

*Why did Martin Luther question the Roman Catholic church?*

### Reaction to Luther's Ideas

Church leaders were angry with Luther, and the pope ordered Luther to recant, or take back, what he had written. Because Luther refused to recant, the pope excommunicated him. This meant that Luther was officially excluded from the Church. He could not attend worship services, he could not receive communion, and he could not be forgiven for his sins. Charles V, the Holy Roman Emperor and a German king, declared that Luther was an outlaw, so Luther went into hiding in the castle of a German prince. Luther had hoped to change the Church, but was now banished by both religious and political leaders.

While in hiding, Luther translated the Bible into German so that more people would be able to read it. He continued writing and trying to change the Church. His ideas gained support throughout Germany, and over time, people began forming new churches. Because they based their groups on the ideas of Martin Luther, these new churches became known as Lutheran churches. Many ordinary people followed Luther's ideas because they wanted to be closer to God or because they felt that the Catholic Church had become too corrupt. Some German princes also supported Luther's ideas. They believed the Catholic Church had become too powerful and wanted to reclaim some power for themselves.

### A New Church

People who joined Luther in protesting against the Church became known as Protestants, and the movement to change or reform the Church became known as the Protestant Reformation. Although Luther and other Protestants had initially only wanted to change the Catholic Church, they ended up creating a number of new Protestant churches.

One of the central effects of the Protestant Reformation was a shift of political power away from the Catholic Church, which many Protestants viewed as corrupt. Many common people worried that the church was more concerned with enriching itself than helping people. This shift led to

**Complete this activity to create a modern "translation" of Martin Luther's Ninety-Five Theses.**

independent, self-governing congregations. These Protestants looked to the Bible, not Catholic tradition, to guide religious and political actions. Under the Catholic Church, not all men were considered equal. Some, such as the pope, were considered to be spiritually superior. While the ideas of religious equality of the Reformation did not lead to political equality in Protestant kingdoms, the Reformation still gave common people greater power in their religious practice. It also introduced questions about why and how leaders held power.

The Reformation also benefited some powerful leaders in Europe. Kings and nobles in many parts of Western Europe sided with the Protestant Reformers because it meant they no longer had to share power with Catholic Church and the pope. They were able to seize land and other property from the Church, thereby increasing their own power. While this made individual leaders more wealthy and powerful, it decentralized power across many Protestant regions. Also, Protestant kings no longer had the blessing of a powerful, central church as a religious justification for their political power.

## Other Reformers

### How did the Reformation spread across Europe?

Luther's ideas spread quickly across Germany. Soon, they advanced beyond Germany, and reformers in other nations began following Luther's example.

### Tyndale and Zwingli

In 1520, an English scholar named William Tyndale wanted to translate the Bible into English so that everyone in England could read it, just as Luther had translated it into German. Tyndale believed the church should base its actions and teachings solely on the Bible. Church leaders in England opposed his idea of translating the Bible, so Tyndale traveled to Germany. He completed his translation of the New Testament in 1525. Because Catholic leaders opposed this action, he was captured and later executed for violating Church teachings. However, his translation became the basis for later English translations of the Bible, including the King James Bible, which is still widely used today.

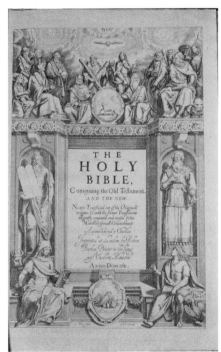

photo: Getty Images

*William Tyndale translated the Bible from Latin to English so that ordinary people could read and understand it.*

The Swiss city of Geneva became another important center of the Reformation. Around the same time that Luther posted the Ninety-Five Theses, a Swiss priest named Ulrich Zwingli preached reform ideas in Geneva. Like Luther, Zwingli believed that the Catholic Church was becoming too corrupt and that people should be allowed to interpret the Bible for themselves. Zwingli was killed in 1531 during a war fought between Catholics and Protestants, but his ideas continued to spread.

### Calvin

Another reformer who believed in many of Luther's teachings was John Calvin. Calvin was from France, but he moved to Geneva to join the reformers. Although Calvin agreed with many of Luther's teachings, he differed in one important way. Calvin believed that people's actions and faith do not determine whether or not they will be saved and go to heaven. Instead, Calvin believed that people are chosen, or predestined, to be saved.

Although he did not believe that you could change your destiny, he did believe that hard work and devotion to God were signs that an individual was chosen for salvation. Calvin's teachings gained followers, and his ideas became known as Calvinism.

Calvinism spread throughout Switzerland and then to France, England, Scotland, and the Netherlands. Calvinist churches and religious services were very plain. They had no singing. Church buildings had no images of saints or decorations like those found in Catholic cathedrals of the time. Calvinists also followed strict rules for behavior, which included no drinking of alcohol, no gambling, and no dancing. Calvin's ideas later became the basis of the Presbyterian Church. His ideas also influenced the English Puritans who would later leave England and settle in North America.

### Intolerance Among Reformed Groups

While united in their dissent against the Catholic Church, different Protestant groups did not always agree with each other. In the 1500s, both Protestants and Catholics believed that everyone in society should have the same religion. This meant that even Protestant groups such as Calvinists did not necessarily identify with other Protestant groups such as Lutherans. They had different ideas about how members of a society should worship and what they should believe.

Because each Protestant group was convinced that its view of religion was correct, the groups saw those with different beliefs—even other Reformers—as having dangerous ideas. Coexisting proved as difficult for groups such as Calvinists and Lutherans, who considered the other group "heretics," as it was for the Catholic Church and the Reformers.

Reformations in Europe showed the divisions between these groups. In Switzerland, for example, those who believed in the teachings of Calvin and Zwingli separated themselves from Catholics and Lutherans in the Zurich Consensus of 1549. In contrast, Catholicism and Lutheranism were included as options for future leaders of the Holy Roman Empire in the 1555 Peace of Augsburg, but Calvinists and other reformed groups were excluded.

## The Reformation in England
*How did the Reformation take place in England?*

In England, the Reformation began because of political arguments, not religious ones. In fact, Henry VIII initially disapproved of certain Protestant teachings. When Luther's writings reached England, a Lutheran group started to meet in Cambridge, a university town there. In the 1520s, Henry VIII had certain Lutherans killed and others exiled. He was so against the Reformation that he published a book called *Assertio Septem Sacramentorum* (Defense of the Seven Sacraments), ghostwritten by Thomas More, for which the Pope gave the king the title *Defensor Fidei*, meaning Defender of the [Catholic] Faith.

In the 1520s, King Henry VIII of England fell in love with Anne Boleyn, but he was married to Catherine of Aragon. Henry wanted to marry Anne, but before he could he had to have his current marriage annulled, or canceled. The Catholic Church did not allow divorce, and the Pope refused to grant Henry the annulment. Determined, Henry convinced Parliament to declare that England was independent of the Pope's authority. Parliament passed the Act of Supremacy, which stated that the king was the head of the new Church of England, also known as the Anglican Church.

photo: Getty Images

*The Meeting of King Henry VIII and Anne Boleyn, c. 1530.*

Henry VIII used his new role as the head of the Church of England to make the monarchy more powerful. He closed the monasteries, where monks lived and studied. He also took control of the monks' land. Henry then gave some of this land away to his political supporters. Church services were changed slightly, and a new English prayer book was written. However, the Anglican Church remained more like the Catholic Church than the Lutheran or Calvinist Churches.

Many people in England were not happy with Henry's actions and refused to accept the new Anglican Church. Even one of Henry's closest advisors, Sir Thomas More, was executed for refusing to accept the Act of Supremacy. After Henry died, his daughter Mary attempted to return the country to Catholicism. In her attempt to restore Catholicism, she punished and killed many Protestants. After Mary's death, her sister, Elizabeth, became queen and successfully returned England to Protestantism.

Despite the Anglican Church's similarities to the Catholic Church, Catholics faced intolerance in England under the new official religion. In addition to the occasionally violent destruction of monasteries, some members of the Catholic faith were also persecuted. This was particularly true under the rule of Henry VIII's successors, Elizabeth I and James I. During their reigns, being Anglican became associated with being English. Catholics became viewed as traitors to the country, and many powerful Catholics were arrested or killed. James I also sponsored a translation of the Bible into English that was published in 1611. This became the most common translation of the Bible in Protestant churches throughout the English-speaking world until the 1900s.

## The Counter-Reformation

*How did the Catholic Church respond to the Reformation?*

In response to the Reformation, leaders of the Catholic Church began a number of reforms. They hoped to strengthen and improve the Church and to stop the spread of Protestantism. They also wanted to spread the Catholic faith to new parts of the world. This movement is known as the Catholic Reformation, or the Counter-Reformation.

photo: Getty Images

*The council of Trent was made up of Catholic Church leaders who met to uphold Catholic teachings and create necessary reforms.*

Part of the reforms involved founding new orders, or special religious groups, within the Church. One of these groups was the Society of Jesus, also called the Jesuits. The Jesuits were created to serve the pope and the Church. They became known for their discipline and for teaching people about Catholic beliefs. They worked both to spread Catholicism outside Europe and to stop the spread of Protestantism. The Jesuits founded colleges throughout Europe and sent missionaries around the world. Today, a number of colleges and universities in Europe and the United States are still run by Jesuit priests.

An important aspect of the Counter-Reformation was a meeting of Church leaders that became known as the Council of Trent. The council met three times from 1545 to 1563 to discuss possible reforms for the Church. The members of the council also clarified

 **Explore this interactive to learn more about perspectives on the Reformation.**

some Church teachings to show how the Catholic Church was different from the new Protestant churches. The council members said that the Bible was still the source of God's teachings, and they reaffirmed the pope's position as the highest authority of the Church. They also said that Luther's belief that faith alone was needed for salvation was wrong. The council members said that good works and faith were both necessary.

The Council of Trent also established new rules. It limited the sale of indulgences. Later, the pope banned their sale. The council also set up rules for the training of priests and rules about where priests could live.

## The Inquisition

### *What was the Inquisition?*

In addition to these actions, the Church brought back an institution that had been created in the 1200s, known as the Inquisition. The Inquisition was a Church court that could try and punish people who were accused of being heretics, or people who do not follow Church teachings.

The Inquisition was created in the 1200s to confront a growing number of religious groups and sects, such as the Cathars in France, that were viewed as teaching heretical ideas. Initially, excommunication was the main punishment delivered during the Inquisition. In 1252, Pope Innocent IV approved imprisonment and the use of torture on those accused of heresy. Pope Innocent IV's actions would have severe consequences. They played a role in the disappearance of several dissenting religious groups throughout Europe, including Catharism. This occurred not only in France, but also in Italy. The Inquisition was spreading.

Within the next hundred years, the Inquisition operated in all of the Pope's territories, which included most of Europe. It was so widespread that the church created regional offices to make sure the Inquisition was efficient. By the 1500s, many governments had also become involved, supporting the Catholic Church's persecution of "heretics." In Spain, for example, the king and queen issued an edict expelling all Jews from Spain upon request from the head of the Spanish Inquisition, Father Torquemada.

photo: Getty Images

*Soldiers executed Protestants in the town of Haarlem, Spain, in 1567 to protect the teachings of the Catholic Church.*

During this time, inquisitors—those who presided over the trials—used common tactics to punish prisoners, but they did not coordinate with one another. However, during the Reformation, the Inquisition fell under the control of the papacy and became much more organized and widely used. Many of the trials were led by Dominicans, Franciscans, or Jesuits. The Inquisition was mostly used to convict and punish Protestants, but other groups and individuals who went against Church law were also tried.

The effects of the Inquisition were minimal in some countries, such as England and Scandinavia. Meanwhile, they intensified in others. The Inquisition spread to Spanish and Portuguese colonies in Asia and the Americas. Spain separated its Inquisition from the Pope's authority in the 1600s. This famous inquisition targeted Catholics whom it suspected of being insincere in their beliefs.

Before the Reformation, King Ferdinand and Queen Isabella of Spain had been fighting against people who were not Catholics. Spain had been controlled by Muslims for centuries. After Catholic rulers took control in 1492, the Spanish rulers forced all Jews and Muslims in Spain to convert to Catholicism. They used the Inquisition to find anyone who still held on to non-Catholic beliefs. The Spanish Inquisition became known for being ruthless and unfair in its trials and punishments. Many people were tortured or killed during this time.

## Effects of the Reformation

*How did the Reformation change Europe?*

While the Counter-Reformation succeeded in correcting some of the corruption in the Catholic Church, it did not stop the growth of Protestantism in Europe. The Reformation had the strongest effect in northern Europe. England, parts of Scotland, northern Germany, the Netherlands, and Scandinavia all became Protestant. In southern Europe, the Reformation did not grow as strong. Italy, Spain, Portugal, Switzerland, and much of France remained Catholic. The effects of the Reformation also spread to the New World. A group of Protestants, the Pilgrims, sailed to what is now the United States and established English colonies in New England. Catholics set up missions in Latin America to convert the natives of these lands to Catholicism. Today, Protestant faiths are still the most popular religions in the United States and Canada, while Catholicism is still the most popular faith in Latin America.

### Identity and Conflict in Europe

During this time, people in Europe developed national identities that were closely tied to their religion. During the early 1500s, the Holy Roman Empire ruled much of central Europe, including modern Germany, Austria, the Netherlands, and parts of France. The emperor Charles V was a Catholic king who also ruled Spain, much of Italy, and many colonies in the Americas. Charles divided his kingdom, but the empire remained in the hands of the Catholic Hapsburg family and the leaders had close ties to the pope. By the 1600s, Protestant religions had become very popular, particularly in northern parts of the empire. Many people identified with their local culture, their local leaders, and their religion more than their emperor. Many Protestant areas began to rebel against their Catholic emperor. This led to a bloody war between 1618 and 1648 called the Thirty Years' War, which drew in armies from Sweden, France, Spain, the Netherlands, and even the Ottoman Empire.

Discovery EDUCATION | SOCIAL STUDIES TECHBOOK

How did the Reformation change the balance of power in Europe?

The Thirty Years' War devastated central Europe, particularly modern Germany. In the Treaty of Westphalia at the end of the war, the Holy Roman Empire broke into many smaller pieces, each with its own national identity that was based, at least in part, on its religion. Some regions became independent states. Others remained a part of the empire but had more power to make their own decisions. Many of these national and religious identities remained important into the 1900s and 2000s. Today, Catholicism still has significant influence in southern Europe and Protestantism remains stronger in northern Europe.

In addition to effects on individual regions of Europe, the Protestant Reformation ended the domination of the Catholic Church on the continent as a whole. Not only was Europe now divided between Catholics and Protestants, but also the Protestants themselves were divided into several different groups. In addition, the Reformation weakened the power of religion. By challenging the pope's authority, it made individual rulers more powerful.

### The Reformation and the Individual

Finally, the Reformation affected ordinary people. The movement taught that individuals could have a direct relationship with God, and it created Bibles that more people could read on their own. It also allowed for more gender equality. Many Protestant groups encouraged education for middle-class women and girls. In a few cases, Protestant women were allowed to preach from the pulpit for the first time. The Reformation emphasized the importance of people's own thoughts and beliefs, not just those of church leaders. Over time, this attitude would affect how people looked at their society and their governments, not just their religion.

## Global Religious Change

*What changes to religious practice occurred outside Europe during the Reformation?*

### Catholics in the Americas

While Catholics and Protestants struggled in Europe, other religious changes took place throughout the world. The British colonies in New England were founded by English Puritans, Protestants who believed the Church of England had grown too corrupt. Spanish conquistadors and Jesuits also founded colonies in North America, including modern Mexico, Florida, Texas, and California. These Spanish colonies were entirely Catholic. Any Protestants were persecuted and driven out. However, the English colonists quickly dominated North America. Catholics did not become a large presence until the 1850s, when Irish immigrants began coming to the United States in large numbers to escape the Potato Famine.

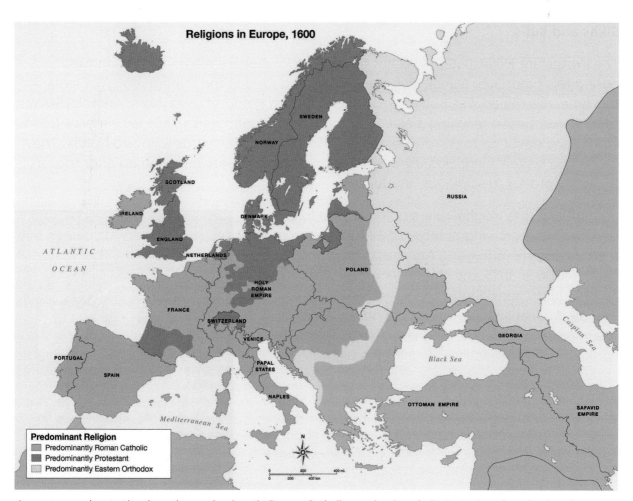

**Religions in Europe, 1600**

**Predominant Religion**
- Predominantly Roman Catholic
- Predominantly Protestant
- Predominantly Eastern Orthodox

*A map uses colors to the show the predominantly Roman Catholic, predominantly Protestant, and predominantly Eastern Orthodox regions of Europe in 1600.*

In contrast, most of the colonies in South America and Latin America were founded by Spain and Portugal. The Catholic Church established missions in these countries and converted many of the indigenous people, sometimes by force. These colonies stayed in the hands of these Catholic countries until they won their independence. As a result, most Latin American colonies developed into Catholic countries. As of 2014, nearly 40 percent of the world's Catholic population lived in Latin America.

In many of these Latin American countries, the Catholic cultures and religions mixed with native cultures and with the cultures and religions of the enslaved Africans who were brought to the Americas to work on plantations and in mines. This blending of beliefs is called "syncretism." In regions such as Haiti, Cuba, and Brazil, which had very large populations of enslaved Africans, new religions such as voodoo, santeria, and candomble emerged that blended elements of African animist religions with Catholicism. Elsewhere in Latin America, indigenous and African traditions influenced Catholic teachings creating celebrations. The Day of the Dead celebrations in Mexico that honor dead ancestors are similar to ancient Mesoamerican rituals but mark All Saints Day, a Catholic holiday. The festive dancing and costumes in Carnival parades in many Latin American cities reflect the African and indigenous roots of the people.

## Sikhs and Sufis

The Protestant Reformation was not the only revolutionary religious development during this time. Guru Nanak was a holy man who lived in the Punjab region of India. At this time, this region was home to followers of both Hinduism and Islam. Around 1500, Guru Nanak began teaching a new faith focused on monotheism, human equality, good works, and devotion to the divine name of God. Nine other gurus followed Nanak. They carried on his teachings and used them to establish the Sikh faith, named after the Punjabi word for "disciple" or "student."

In the 1600s, the Mughal rulers of India, who followed Islam, saw the growing number of Sikhs as a threat to their power. The fifth guru, Arjan, was executed for his faith in 1606. In 1675, the Mughal emporer Aurangzeb had the ninth guru, Tegh Bahadur, arrested and executed because the Sikhs would not convert to Islam. After this, the 10th and last guru, Gobind Singh, codified specific practices to unify the Sikh community, called the Khalsa. Guru Singh also established the Five "K's"—kesh (long, uncut hair, which men usually keep in a turban), kara (a steel bracelet), kanga (a wooden comb), kaccha (short cotton pants), and kirpan (a small steel dagger, kept in a sheath). These items identify Sikhs as members of the community and symbolize devotion to Sikh faith and values.

photo: Getty Images

*A portrait of Guru Nanak.*

## Sufis Expand Islam

Sufism, a mystical interpretation of Islam, appeared earlier than Sikhism and had a profound effect on the way people interpreted and practiced Islam across Asia. The ideas of Sufism could be found in Islam as early as the 800s. A poet named Rabi'a al-Adawiyya introduced the idea of a personal and intense love for God through her writing. This love would become the central idea of Sufism. In 1244, a scholar from Afghanistan named Jalaluddin Rumi met a Sufi named Shams of Tabriz. Shams inspired Rumi with divine love, and Rumi went on to recite ecstatic poetry while performing a whirling dance. Rumi's whirling dance inspired a Sufi order of dervishes, a group of worshippers who pray together through chant and movement. Rumi's poetry became famous not only among Sufi Muslims, but also across cultures.

photo: Getty Images

*A portrait of Akbar the Great, Mughal emperor.*

Sufism helped Islam gain popularity and reach new cultures. Its tradition of ecstatic love for God was similar to other mystical faiths, such as the bhakti school of Hinduism. Sufism was also a tolerant tradition, and its followers tended to embrace the traditions of other faiths instead of forbidding them. By the 1100s, Sufism had spread to India and South Asia through trade and missionaries. Sufis in these countries often included pre-Islamic traditions in their practice. For example, Sufis in Java include shadow-puppet shows in their rituals. In South Asia, the powerful Mughal emperor Akbar (1542–1605) embraced Sufi Islam and encouraged the people in his court to study Hinduism, Christianity, Zoroastrianism, and other religions. He blended practices from these religions into a new movement, but the movement was never larger than a few advisors close to Akbar.

## The Rise of Neo-Confucianism

Confucianism was yet another religion to have a "reformation." By the 1000s, Buddhism had become widespread and popular in China. However, many people began to feel that Buddhism was a "foreign" religion. This led to a revival of Confucianism, which had been the main religion in China before the coming of Buddhism. However, Confucianism had grown stale and less relevant. Under the Song dynasty (979–1279), scholars revised and updated its old ideas. The result was Neo-Confucianism, which focused on self-improvement, dedication to duties, and the importance of the family. It praised four values: benevolence (compassion for the suffering of others), righteousness (avoiding dishonorable behavior), wisdom (using good judgment to make decisions), and propriety (honoring elders and authority figures).

Neo-Confucianism emphasized the need for careful and dedicated study of texts to understand virtuous behavior. Without this study—which could be very difficult and expensive—people would not be able to act ethically. Exams to join the Chinese government required precise knowledge of specific teachings.

One of the central figures of Neo-Confucianism was Wang Yang-Ming (1472–1529). Wang was a scholar and a court official. He is best known today for his interpretation of Neo-Confucian philosophy. Wang disagreed with the main school of Neo-Confucian thought and its emphasis on studying. He argued that most people were born understanding virtuous behavior. To Wang, correct action and correct thought were the same thing. A person could recite the work of every Confucian major scholar, but unless that person acted virtuously, the knowledge was useless. Wang worried that people, especially leaders, would spend their lives studying and never act. This teaching challenged the way leaders had traditionally been trained and allowed that any person could be seen as truly virtuous. Wang's ideas were controversial at first, but soon they were accepted and spread throughout China. Today, Wang is considered one of the greatest Chinese philosophers of the past 2,000 years.

**Personal Devotion**

Sikhism, Sufism, and Wang Yang-Ming's Neo-Confucianism are very different religions. However, they do all have one thing in common. Like Protestant Christianity, these faiths turned against the traditional power structures of the religion. Like Protestant Christianity, these faiths adapted their religions and practices to focus on the personal connection between a worshipper and his or her divine being. While none of these faiths advocated political equality or democracy, they each challenged the way religious power had been organized in the past and placed more power in the hands of each individual believer.

**Consider the Essential Question:**

How did the Reformation change the balance of power in Europe?

Go online to complete the Social Studies Explanation.

**Check for Understanding:**

What effects did the Reformation have on the power of the Catholic Church? How did changes in the Catholic Church affect European governments and society?

Discovery | SOCIAL STUDIES
EDUCATION | **TECHBOOK**

*photo: Getty Images*

# 11.2 The Scientific Revolution

## LESSON OVERVIEW

### Introduction

In this concept, you will learn how the Scientific Revolution began and which individuals were most influential during this movement. You will also analyze how the Scientific Revolution affected Europe at the time and how it continues to affect the world today.

### Essential Question

How did the Scientific Revolution change the way people understood the world?

### Lesson Objectives

By the end of this lesson, you should be able to:

- Analyze the relationship between the Scientific Revolution and its predecessors, including Renaissance humanism and Greek rationalism.

- Analyze the impact of the Scientific Revolution.

- Identify important figures (Copernicus, Galileo, Kepler, and Newton) of the Scientific Revolution and their contributions.

## Key Vocabulary
Which terms do you already know?

- ☐ Amerigo Vespucci
- ☐ Aristotle
- ☐ Catholic Church
- ☐ Francis Bacon
- ☐ Galileo
- ☐ heretic
- ☐ humanism
- ☐ Isaac Newton
- ☐ Johannes Kepler
- ☐ King George III
- ☐ Leonardo da Vinci
- ☐ Machiavelli
- ☐ mercantilism
- ☐ Nicolaus Copernicus
- ☐ pope
- ☐ Protestant Church
- ☐ Renaissance
- ☐ scientific method
- ☐ Scientific Revolution

**DISCOVERY** EDUCATION | SOCIAL STUDIES **TECHBOOK**

How did the Scientific Revolution change the way people understood the world?

## ENGAGE

**How did Galileo revolutionize the way humans think?**
**Visit Engage to learn more.**

### Essential Question

How did the Scientific Revolution change the way people understood the world?

## EXPLORE

### The Influence of the Renaissance

*How did the Renaissance lead to the Scientific Revolution?*

In the 1200s, a period of cultural rebirth known as the Renaissance began in Italy and spread throughout Europe. During this time, the philosophy of humanism became popular. Humanists believe that people are rational, or able to reason clearly. This philosophy led people to believe in the potential of the human mind. Renaissance artists like Leonardo da Vinci and thinkers like Niccoló Machiavelli observed the world around them and asked questions. They challenged the accepted knowledge of their time, much of which was based on the religious teachings that had been the foundation of European society.

At first, humanism affected primarily literature and the arts, subjects that today are called the humanities. However, the ideas of humanism spread to the sciences. These ideas led to the Scientific Revolution, a period of innovation during the 1500s and 1600s.

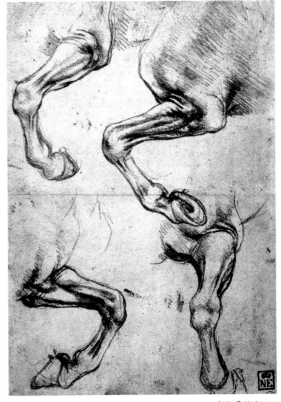

*photo: Getty Images*

*Four studies of horses' legs, by Leonardo da Vinci. How do these sketches reflect humanist thinking?*

Thinkers of the Scientific Revolution applied humanism to their work. By asking questions, making observations, and drawing conclusions based on reason, they challenged the common beliefs of the time. During this period, scientists made discoveries and innovations in many fields of science, including biology, astronomy, geography, and physics. These thinkers were influenced not only by humanism, but also by ideas from the past.

## Revolutionary Influences

*What role did ancient Greek philosophers play in the Scientific Revolution?*

J.LUYTS
PHIL.PROFES.
Institutio
ASTRONOMICA.

Apud FRANCISCUM HALMAM Acad
Typograph. cIɔIɔcLxxxxII.

photo: Getty Images

*An illustration of early astronomers: Galileo, Hevelius, Aristotle, Copernicus, and Ptolemy.*

In addition to the development of humanism, the Renaissance also led to a rediscovery of classical texts from ancient Greek thinkers such as Aristotle and Ptolemy. The works of these and other Greek thinkers had primarily been preserved and translated into Arabic in Islamic cultures. During the Renaissance, the ideas and philosophies espoused by these ancient thinkers were once again studied throughout Europe and greatly influenced art, culture, and science.

Many of these Greek thinkers had sought physical explanations for what they saw in nature rather than relying on the explanations provided by myths and religious beliefs. These scholars believed in using reason and systematically studying everything there was to know about a topic to discover concrete truths about the world. The thinkers of the Scientific Revolution used these principles of Greek rationalism to help them observe and study the world around them.

Both humanism and Greek rationalism were important foundations for the study that took place during the Scientific Revolution. These foundations encouraged the thinkers of this time to observe the universe around them and to draw new conclusions about

**Explore this interactive to learn more about key events in the advancement of scientific knowledge.**

the natural world and how it worked rather than accept the commonly held assumptions or religious doctrine as the only possible answers. However, it should also be noted that in a number of instances, the scientists and philosophers of the Scientific Revolution came into direct conflict with their Greek predecessors.

Discovery EDUCATION | SOCIAL STUDIES TECHBOOK

How did the Scientific Revolution change the way people understood the world?

Some of the new discoveries of the Scientific Revolution were criticized solely because they went against the teachings of the great Greek thinkers like Aristotle. Without the ancient Greeks and the development of humanism, scientists during this era may never have asked the questions that led to several important discoveries and innovations. By studying them, the scientists of this time period were able to develop new ways of thinking and ultimately replace the outdated thoughts of the Greeks.

## A New Way of Thinking

*How did the Scientific Revolution change the way Europeans explained the world?*

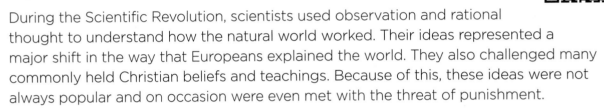

During the Scientific Revolution, scientists used observation and rational thought to understand how the natural world worked. Their ideas represented a major shift in the way that Europeans explained the world. They also challenged many commonly held Christian beliefs and teachings. Because of this, these ideas were not always popular and on occasion were even met with the threat of punishment.

### Testing Ideas

The thinkers of the Scientific Revolution challenged the commonly held ideas of the time. Many were rationalists—meaning that they believed everything in the world could be proven through argument, mathematical calculation, and observation. René Descartes (1596–1650), a French mathematician and philosopher, was one of the most influential rationalists. He believed that the universe was like a complex machine that followed patterns. Humans could use math and reason to unlock these patterns. Descartes developed many of the geometric ideas we still use today, including geometric proofs and graphing.

Francis Bacon (1561–1626), a British thinker, believed in the power of observation. Bacon also believed that people could understand the universe. Bacon observed details in the world and used those observations to form theories about how the world worked. He used experiments to test these theories and draw conclusions. This process became known as the scientific method, and it became the foundation of modern science.

Scientists and philosophers followed in the footsteps of Descartes and Bacon. They asked questions, made observations, conducted experiments, developed new theories, and tested them for accuracy. As new ideas were presented and proved, other thinkers would use this information and expand on it to make new discoveries.

photo: Getty Images

*A portrait of Francis Bacon.*

Scientists improved on existing technologies and invented new technologies, such as the telescope. They then used these technologies to observe aspects of the natural world more accurately; in the case of the telescope, they observed the night sky. Mathematicians then used the information obtained from these observations to develop theories and formulas that described phenomena such as the movement of the planets.

In one famous example, an Italian biologist named Francesco Redi challenged an idea known as the spontaneous generation of life. For centuries, people had believed that maggots and flies emerged from rotting food spontaneously—or on their own. This did not seem right to Redi. He created an experiment. He placed meat in jars to rot. He left one set of jars open and sealed the other set of jars. The jars that were open developed maggots and flies; the jars that were closed did not. He conducted similar experiments and concluded that "life comes from life." This type of experiment became known as a controlled experiment because the scientist controls one factor in the experiment— whether the jars are open or closed—to see if that factor makes a difference.

## Challenging the Church?

Most of the scientists of this time did not view themselves as antireligious. Many of them believed in God and many of the teachings of the Church. At times, they even relied upon biblical arguments to help them prove their theories or to provide historical information about the world. But they also believed that scientific observation and reasoning could help them learn more about how the things around them worked. Their teachings led to the development of the scientific method, a systematic process for determining the accuracy of scientific theories. Most scientists believed that scientific study did not go against any religious or moral codes or rules.

During this time, the Catholic Church still had a lot of power and influence throughout Europe. Members of this faith believed that the Bible and Church doctrine were the authorities on how the universe was formed and the natural history of the planet. Biblical passages were taken as proof of ideas. In addition, old theories were believed to have greater authority than new ideas; Ptolemy and Aristotle thought that the universe was geocentric, or that Earth was the center of the universe. The Church actively examined scientific ideas that did not address theological concerns or mysteries. As a result of this examination, any theories that went against the Church's teachings were considered a departure from the truth. For this reason, some scientific research was labeled heresy. Church officials also believed that scientific explanations undermined the role of God in the universe. A person who went against the Church and spread ideas about science could be tried as a heretic and, if found guilty, could be imprisoned or put to death.

## A New Theory on the Cosmos

### Who was Nicolaus Copernicus?

What do you see when you look at the night sky? When the early Europeans looked up, they saw stars and planets like we do. However, before the Scientific Revolution, Europeans thought they were watching planets circle around Earth. In 1543, Nicolaus Copernicus proposed that the sun was actually at the center of the universe.

Born in 1483 in Torun, Poland, Nicolaus Copernicus was the son of a wealthy merchant. He had been given a good education in medicine and religious law. He spent much of his professional life working as a church cleric, but one of his true passions was astronomy. During Copernicus's time, the accepted notions about astronomy were thousands of years old. They could be traced back to the Greek astronomer and mathematician Ptolemy from around 150. Ptolemy's theories put Earth at a fixed position in the center of the universe. According to Ptolemy, Earth stayed in one spot, and the sun and the rest of the planets moved in circular patterns around it. Even though the Church accepted this system, it posed many problems.

photo: Getty Images

*This sculpture stands in Krakow, Poland, as a monument to the astronomer Nicolaus Copernicus.*

In the early days of science, accurately predicting where a planet would be in the sky proved a person had knowledge of the universe. However, with Ptolemy's system, accurate predictions were difficult. This was in part because the system was incorrect. It took an incredible amount of complicated math to make reasonable predictions using Ptolemy's Earth-centered model. Also, the system could not explain things like why the planets sometimes seemed to be moving backward. Copernicus began to carefully observe the stars and planets in the night sky in the hope of finding a solution to some of these problems.

## Copernicus's New Theory

### How did Copernicus change astronomy?

After careful study and observation, Copernicus came up with new theories about the universe. He concluded it is the sun, and not Earth, that is at the center of the universe. According to Copernicus's theory, Earth and the other planets orbit around the sun. This is called a heliocentric system. It has come to be called the Copernican theory. Copernicus also said that Earth revolves on its axis once every 24 hours, giving us night and day. His explanation helped solve the problems that existed with the earlier model of the universe, including why planets sometimes appear to move backward.

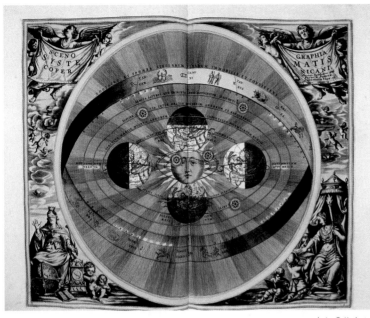

*photo: Getty Images*

*An illustration of the Copernican (solar-centered) system of the universe, 1708.*

Copernicus explained his theory in a large, six-volume work called *On the Revolution of the Celestial Spheres*. This series was mostly completed in the 1530s but was not published until just before his death in 1543. Some experts believe the delay was because Copernicus was afraid of the Church's response to his theories. Copernicus's new theory did not indicate any lack of faith; he dedicated *On the Revolution of the Celestial Spheres* to Pope Paul III. Although the Church never officially opposed the heliocentric system that Copernicus outlined in his book, *On the Revolution of the Celestial Spheres* remained on the Catholic Church's list of banned books for more than 200 years, from 1616 through 1835.

Copernicus's theories were revolutionary and changed astronomy forever. However, it would take the work of other scientists building upon his ideas over future generations to create the modern picture we have of the universe.

## An Elliptical Orbit

### How did Johannes Kepler expand upon Copernicus's work?

Although Copernicus's theory was revolutionary, it was still tied to the old model of the universe in some ways. For example, he believed the planets orbited the sun in a perfect circular motion. Today, scientists no longer think this, but it took the work of Johannes Kepler to change this concept.

Kepler was born in Germany in 1571. Even though his family was poor, he was able to attend college by earning academic scholarships. Originally, Kepler wanted to become a minister, but he was introduced to the ideas of Copernicus in school. He soon changed his focus to study mathematics and astronomy. Kepler became a math professor and first defended Copernicus's ideas in a paper published in 1596. Kepler's mathematical genius earned him respect from others, particularly Tycho Brahe, a Danish inventor and astronomer who worked as the imperial mathematician for Roman emperor Rudolph II, who held court in Prague. In 1600, Kepler moved to Prague to work as Brahe's assistant. When Brahe died the next year, Kepler took over his post.

**Discovery** EDUCATION | SOCIAL STUDIES **TECHBOOK**

How did the Scientific Revolution change the way people understood the world?

Continuing Brahe's work, Kepler calculated that Mars made an elliptical, or oval-shaped, orbit around the sun and not a circle like Copernicus had thought. With more study, Kepler came up with three theories we now call the Laws of Planetary Motion. The first, the Law of Ellipses, was that the paths of planets moving around the sun form ellipses, with the sun at one focus. The second, the Law of Equal Areas, says that a planet moves in its orbit in such a way that a line drawn between the planet and the sun will sweep over equal areas in equal times. This means that when a planet is close to the sun, it moves faster than when it is farther away. Kepler's third law, known as the Law of Harmonies, describes the relationship between a planet's average distance from the sun and the time it takes a planet to orbit the sun. According to this law, the period of time it takes a planet to orbit the sun increases as its average distance from the sun increases.

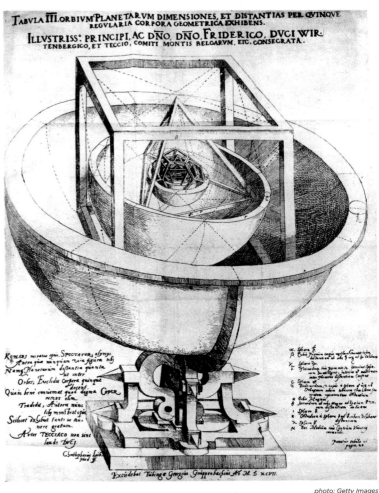

photo: Getty Images

*An illustration of Kepler's explanation of the structure of the planetary system, 1619.*

In addition to publishing books containing his work, Kepler was interested in the work of other scientists. In 1610, he published a letter supporting the research Italian scientist Galileo Galilei was doing with telescopes. The following year, he suggested a telescope design of his own in his book *Dioptrice*.

## Galileo's Fight

*How did Galileo confirm Copernicus's theories about the planets?*

### Galileo's Discoveries

Galileo Galilei was an Italian scientist born in Pisa, Italy, in 1564. He went to the University of Pisa to study medicine. While there, he took an interest in physics and math. He began experimenting with objects in motion. Galileo liked to tinker with building things, inventing devices such as a water pump and a type of balance scale that could measure small objects. However, the innovation he is most famous for is the telescope.

*Galileo Galilei was an Italian scientist born in Pisa, Italy, in 1564.*

Galileo did not develop the concept for the telescope, but he advanced it. In 1609, he learned of a handheld spyglass that had been built by Dutch eyeglass manufacturers. Interested in learning more about what this simple telescope could do, Galileo built his own version of the instrument. Galileo used the telescope to look at distant objects in the sky. Using his early telescope, Galileo could magnify distant objects by 20 times. He observed the surface of the moon and saw it was not smooth. He also saw sunspots on the sun and witnessed the moons that orbited Jupiter.

## Galileo and the Inquisition

The things that Galileo saw provided evidence to confirm Copernicus's theory that all planets orbit the sun. Because the Catholic Church still taught that Earth was the center of the universe, Galileo's findings and his vocally outspoken support for Copernicus's model angered Church leaders. In 1616, he was brought before the Inquisition. The Inquisition was an institution established by the Roman Catholic Church to investigate and suppress heresy. Galileo was told to stop defending and teaching anything about the Copernican model of the universe and sent on his way. But this did not stop Galileo!

Continuing his studies of astronomy, Galileo published a new book in 1632, *Dialogue Concerning the Two Chief World Systems*. The book was written as a conversation between three people—one person who believes in the Copernican model and argues for it, another who argues against the idea that the sun is the center of the universe, and a third person who has no opinion. Even though Galileo attempted to say that the book did not take sides, the character that argued for the Copernican model was written as an intelligent, articulate scientist and the one who argued against it was a bumbling fool. Later that year, he was once more called before the Inquisition.

## The Death of Galileo

After several months of trial, Galileo was convicted of heresy in 1633, but he was not sentenced to death. Instead, after apologizing to the Church to save his own life, he was given life imprisonment.

Discovery EDUCATION | SOCIAL STUDIES TECHBOOK

How did the Scientific Revolution change the way people understood the world?

He was placed under house arrest due to his old age and poor health. He died in 1642 while still under house arrest. It was not until the late 1700s that most of his publications on the Copernican model were dropped from the Church's banned literature list. Nearly 200 years later, in 1992, Pope John Paul II, who was the official leader of the Catholic Church at the time, issued a public apology for the way that Galileo had been treated.

## Newton and Gravity

### What scientific contributions did Isaac Newton make?

Isaac Newton, an English mathematician, astronomer, and physicist, was born in the county of Lincolnshire on January 4, 1643. Interested in mathematics from the time he was a child, Newton entered the University of Cambridge in 1661 and went on to receive both a bachelor's and a master's degree. While at Cambridge, he studied the Copernican model of the universe. He also learned about other advancements and theories proposed by philosophers, scientists, and mathematicians of the time. While still a student, Newton began making important discoveries in several fields of science and mathematics.

In 1666, Newton joined earlier mathematical ideas and laid the foundation for a new branch of mathematics: calculus. He also made several discoveries in the field of optics, the branch of science that deals with the properties of light and vision. For example, he discovered that sunlight breaks into a spectrum of rainbow colors when it passes through a prism.

Newton is perhaps best known for discovering the force of gravity. Most people have heard the story about Newton discovering gravity when an apple fell from a tree and hit him on the head. While this story cannot be proven true, historians do know that at the same time that he was working on his discoveries in calculus, Newton was also investigating celestial mechanics, or how and why the

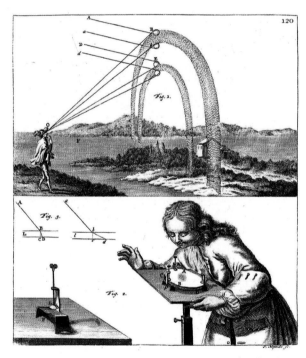

photo: Getty Images

*An illustrated explanation of principles of physics by W. J. Gravasande, a friend of Isaac Newton, 1725.*

planets and other objects in space move the way that they do. Through observation and experimentation, Newton took earlier ideas about the force of gravity and expanded upon them to explain how gravity works on objects on Earth and in space. Using Kepler's law of planetary motion, he also realized that Earth's gravitational pull extended all the way to the moon.

In 1686, Newton published what is often thought to be one of the greatest scientific books in history, the *Philosophiae Naturalis Principia Mathematica*. In it, he explained how gravity works between the sun and objects in space and how Earth's gravitational pull attracts objects to the planet's core. He also discussed other theories he had about objects in motion.

## Explaining the Laws of Motion

*What did Newton discover about the way objects move?*

*Philosophiae Naturalis Principia Mathematica* included Newton's theories on gravity and how it affected objects on Earth and in space. In the same book, Newton outlined the theories he had developed about objects in motion. These theories would come to be known as Newton's three laws of motion. The first law showed that a stopped object will stay stopped and an object in motion will remain in motion unless another force acts upon it. The second law showed what happens to a moving object when an outside force acts on it. Finally, the third law of motion showed that for every action, there is an equal and opposite reaction.

photo: Getty Images

*An illustration of a jet cart demonstrating Newton's third law of motion, 1775.*

Newton created the laws to help explain why planets traveled in elliptical, or oval, orbits rather than circular ones, but his laws of motion helped solve other problems and prove existing theories by earlier astronomers and physicists such as Galileo, Kepler, and Copernicus. For example, the laws explained why people could not feel the rotation of Earth as it spun on its axis—a problem that was used as a challenge to Galileo's work. They also solved the problem of why the planets would continue to orbit without a direct cause. Newton's laws combined existing scientific ideas into one comprehensive theory that could be used to explain and bring order to the new heliocentric universe.

In 1705, Queen Anne knighted Newton for his work and he became Sir Isaac Newton. He was the first scientist to have ever received such an honor, proving how far the world of science had come in just under two centuries. Although Newton died in 1727, his theories are still considered some of the most important ideas in modern science, and he is often remembered as the last great thinker in an era of incredible scientific discovery and innovation.

Discovery EDUCATION | SOCIAL STUDIES TECHBOOK

How did the Scientific Revolution change the way people understood the world?

Like others before him, Newton used experimentation, observation, and logical reasoning to make sense of the world around him. This approach to studying the natural world represented a shift in thinking from the Middle Ages. Rather than accepting existing ideas and beliefs, people turned to exploration, experimentation, and observation to help them learn about and understand the world around them.

**Consider the Essential Question:**

How did the Scientific Revolution change the way people understood the world?

Go online to complete the Social Studies Explanation.

**Check for Understanding:**

How did a chain of ideas lead from the ancient Greeks' thoughts about planetary motion to Newton's discoveries? What do you think was Newton's most important contribution to the Scientific Revolution?

# 11.3 The Enlightenment

*photo: Getty Images*

## LESSON OVERVIEW

### Introduction

In this concept, you will learn about how the Enlightenment developed out of the preceding movements such as the Renaissance and the Scientific Revolution. You will also analyze how the Enlightenment and its key figures affected European society.

### Essential Question

How did the philosophies of the Enlightenment influence politics and society in Europe?

### Lesson Objectives

By the end of this lesson, you should be able to:

- Analyze the relationship between the Enlightenment and its predecessors, including the Renaissance, Roman republicanism, and the Scientific Revolution.

- Analyze the impact of the Enlightenment on thought, reason, and society.

- Identify important Enlightenment thinkers (Diderot, Kant, Locke, Montesquieu, and Voltaire) and their contributions.

### Key Vocabulary
Which terms do you already know?

- [ ] autonomy
- [ ] Baron de Montesquieu
- [ ] Declaration of the Rights of Man and of the Citizen
- [ ] democracy
- [ ] Denis Diderot
- [ ] Enlightenment
- [ ] Francis Bacon
- [ ] Frederick II
- [ ] Galileo
- [ ] humanism
- [ ] Immanuel Kant
- [ ] individualism
- [ ] James Madison
- [ ] Jean-Jacques Rousseau
- [ ] John Locke
- [ ] King George III
- [ ] laissez-faire
- [ ] Nicolaus Copernicus
- [ ] parliament
- [ ] philosophy
- [ ] Rationalism
- [ ] Renaissance
- [ ] republicanism
- [ ] Scientific Revolution
- [ ] social contract
- [ ] Thomas Hobbes
- [ ] Thomas Jefferson
- [ ] unicameral
- [ ] Voltaire

DISCOVERY EDUCATION | SOCIAL STUDIES TECHBOOK.

How did the philosophies of the Enlightenment influence politics and society in Europe?

# ENGAGE

**How did Enlightenment thinkers challenge traditional ideas about power? Visit Engage to learn more.**

## Essential Question

How did the philosophies of the Enlightenment influence politics and society in Europe?

---

# EXPLORE

## The Roots of the Enlightenment

*Where did Enlightenment ideas come from?*

During the Enlightenment, also known as the Age of Reason, many people in Europe believed that they could use reason to understand and improve the world around them. The Enlightenment took place in the 1600s and 1700s. Much like the periods of social change before it, the Enlightenment was based on the ideas of earlier movements.

One source of Enlightenment ideas was the European Renaissance. Beginning in the late 1300s, the philosophy of humanism gained influence with many people. Renaissance humanists believed in the dignity of humans and what humans could accomplish. Humanists still believed that religion was important, but they also valued life on Earth. Humanism initially impacted the arts but spread to science during the Scientific Revolution and to the political sphere during the Enlightenment.

*photo: Getty Images*

*Marble stele with carving showing the people of Athens being crowned by democracy, 336 BCE.*

During the Renaissance, European humanists began to reexamine the works of the ancient Greeks and Romans. This practice carried over into the Enlightenment. Scholars studied the ideas of Greek democracy and Roman republicanism in search of ideas about how people should govern themselves. These two forms of government, which were both based on the idea that government should represent the will of the people, influenced many Enlightenment thinkers.

Another important source of the Enlightenment was the Scientific Revolution. Beginning in the 1400s, scientists began to use careful observation and rational thought to understand the natural world. Scientists such as Nicolaus Copernicus and Galileo used these techniques to discover predictable laws that governed nature and mathematics. In the 1600s, Enlightenment philosophers began to apply those methods to human behavior and government.

## Fundamental Ideas

*What were the fundamental concepts of the Enlightenment?*

The thinkers of the Enlightenment based their ideas around two fundamental concepts, rationalism and individualism.

Rationalism is the idea that people can use reason, or logical thought, to understand and improve the world. This faith in reason came partly out of the Scientific Revolution. Just as scientists such as Newton believed that they could conduct experiments and determine the laws of the universe, rationalists believed that they could analyze and understand patterns in the behaviors of people and governments. They believed that individuals and governments should make decisions based on clear reasoning rather than superstition or tradition. Individualism is the idea that individuals and their rights are important.

Rationalists drew on humanist ideas from the Renaissance and ancient philosophers. Enlightenment thinkers believed that individuals did not always need to sacrifice what they wanted or believed for the good of society or for the good of the rulers. Instead, they argued that individuals should be able to see how a government helps them and protects their interests. Using rational arguments, some enlightenment thinkers argued that the people should have a larger role in government. Many advocated for more democratic systems.

Enlightenment philosophers applied these ideas to government, society, and human behavior. They argued that by using reason and science, people could study the nature of the human individual and could understand the causes of problems facing their society. Instead of simply accepting social problems, enlightenment thinkers tried to solve them. Eventually, the Enlightenment led to conflict because it threatened important social traditions, including religious beliefs.

## Locke and Hobbes

### Who were John Locke and Thomas Hobbes?

Some of the early political philosophers of the Enlightenment came from Great Britain. Civil wars tore the country apart in the mid-1600s. One king was executed, and the country went through several governments. This turmoil led English philosophers to write about the relationship between people and their governments.

One of the earliest thinkers who tried to look at politics in a rational way was Thomas Hobbes. He believed that people were naturally aggressive and that conflict was a normal part of human nature. In his most famous book, *Leviathan*, Hobbes wrote that people could only escape war and violence by giving up their natural rights and submitting to the rule of a strong ruler. Hobbes called this agreement in which people gave up rights in exchange for law and order a social contract. Because of this negative view of human nature, Hobbes supported powerful rulers more than the rights of individuals.

photo: Getty Images

*A portrait of Thomas Hobbes.*

John Locke, another important English philosopher at this time, had a very different view of human nature. He believed that people were not born good or evil, but that their characters were determined by their life experiences. In his most well-known political work, *Two Treatises on Government*, Locke wrote that people were born free and that they naturally had certain rights. The most important of these rights were life, liberty, and property.

Locke agreed with Hobbes that governments were formed through a social contract, but he saw the purpose of government differently. Locke wrote that the purpose of government was to protect natural rights. The only reason people should give up any of these rights was in exchange for a just, or fair, government. According to Locke's idea of a social contract, if a government did not rule justly or did not protect people's rights, the people had a right to overthrow their leaders.

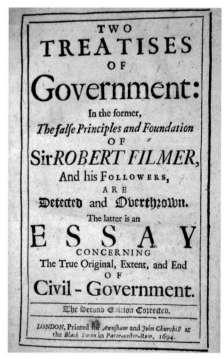

photo: Getty Images

*According to Locke's writings, what is the primary responsibility of governments?*

**Explore this interactive to learn more about the enduring debate between Hobbes and Locke.**

## The Enlightenment in France and Germany

*Who were some of the other important thinkers of the Enlightenment?*

In the mid-1700s, the most important Enlightenment thinkers lived in Paris, France. This group of thinkers is known as the *philosophes*, which is the French word for philosophers.

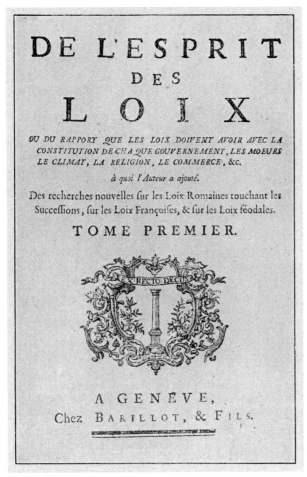

photo: Getty Images

*Original edition of Montesquieu's* The Spirit of the Laws, *1748. How did Montesquieu's writings influence the Framers of the U.S. Constitution?*

### Voltaire

One of the most influential *philosophes* was François Marie Arouet, who wrote using the name Voltaire. Voltaire's written works included plays, poems, and historical and philosophical essays. He was well known for using humor to make his political points. Voltaire wrote in favor of religious tolerance and free speech, and he often criticized important people in society. As a young man, Voltaire was arrested and put in jail for writing verses that made fun of government leaders. He also criticized church leaders and supported the separation of church and state. Voltaire's most famous work is a humorous novel called *Candide*, in which he made fun of the attitudes of other philosophers of his day.

### Montesquieu

Like John Locke, Charles-Louis de Secondat, the Baron de Montesquieu, wrote extensively about politics. In *The Spirit of the Laws*, Montesquieu wrote about factors that would create a fair, uncorrupt government that protected people's rights. He believed that the way to achieve this goal was to separate power so that no one person had too much influence. Montesquieu wanted governments divided into three different branches: a legislative branch, an executive branch, and a judicial branch. Each branch should have different responsibilities. The authors of the U.S. Constitution used this model for the U.S. government.

Discovery | SOCIAL STUDIES.
EDUCATION | TECHBOOK

How did the philosophies of the Enlightenment influence politics and society in Europe?

## Rousseau and Diderot

### *What were the contributions of Rousseau and Diderot?*

Another French *philosophe*, Jean-Jacques Rousseau, wrote about politics in a work called *The Social Contract*. In Rousseau's ideal society, people would be able to vote on the laws they must follow rather than merely obeying laws imposed on them by a ruler or rulers. While Rousseau supported democracy, he also wrote about other topics. These included how children should be educated and the benefits of spending time in nature.

The *philosophes* in Paris shared many of their ideas with one another. One of them, Denis Diderot, spent much of his career spreading their ideas even further. Diderot was the editor of the *Encyclopédie*, a collection of articles on many different topics in art and science. Diderot worked on the *Encyclopédie* for nearly 20 years and published 28 different volumes of it, which contained articles by writers such as Voltaire and Montesquieu. Both the government and the church criticized the *Encyclopédie*, however, and attempted to ban it. They said it was too radical and could lead to revolution.

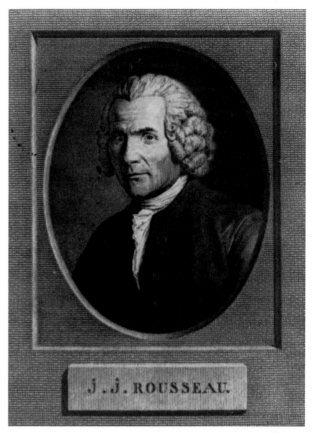

photo: Library of Congress

*The French philosopher Rousseau believed that people should be able to vote on issues in their society.*

### A German Thinker

Immanuel Kant, a German philosopher, was the source of influential ideas about politics, language, history, mathematics, psychology, morals, religion, and other subjects. Kant wrote about how it is possible for people to understand the world around us. At the time, some philosophers believed that human knowledge and understanding could only come from experience. Others stressed rationalism, the idea that people were endowed by God or nature with the capacity for reason and logical thought. Kant tried to bring these ideas together. He said that people's understanding had to come partly from their experience but also from their reason. Kant also wrote that people's moral decisions also needed to be based on rational thought.

## The Influence of the Enlightenment

*How did Enlightenment thinkers affect society and government in Europe and America?*

### Enlightened Despots

Although some European rulers opposed Enlightenment ideas and tried to censor these writers, others tried to put their ideas into practice. Frederick II, ruler of Prussia, a German state, even invited Voltaire to stay with him at court for a time. Frederick II—known also as Frederick the Great because of his military victories—was considered an "enlightened despot." This term means that he used enlightenment ideas to create some legal reforms but never took actions that threatened his own power or significantly changed the structure of his society. A despot is someone who rules with unlimited power.

photo: Getty Images

*A portrait of Catherine the Great.*

Frederick II did bring about some improvements for the people of Prussia. He increased religious tolerance, and he attempted to create a system of universal primary education. Frederick also reformed Prussia's judicial system and required judges to pass an exam before serving on a court. He attempted to improve the lives of peasants by introducing new industries and crops and by changing some land policies, although these changes were not long-lasting.

Joseph II of Austria and Catherine the Great of Russia were two other European rulers at the time who were known as enlightened despots. They also adopted some of the ideals of the Enlightenment but did not significantly change the way people ruled and lived in their countries.

## The Enlightenment Spreads

*What role did Enlightenment ideas play in the American Revolution?*

Enlightenment ideas affected politics more significantly in a location farther away: the British colonies in North America. In the mid-1700s, the American colonists were angry about tax policies and other actions taken by the English lawmaking body, or Parliament, and King George III, the ruler of England during that time. Colonial leaders used ideas of the Enlightenment, especially those of John Locke, to justify their decision to declare independence.

**Discovery** SOCIAL STUDIES
EDUCATION **TECHBOOK**

How did the philosophies of the Enlightenment influence politics and society in Europe?

The Declaration of Independence also included Locke's idea that a ruler who violates the rights of the people breaks the social contract. In that case, the people have a right to overthrow that government and create a new one.

In 1787, leaders of the new nation wrote the U.S. Constitution. That document created the existing structure of the U.S. federal government, using many ideas from the Enlightenment. One of

photo: Getty Images

*The first public reading of the Declaration of Independence, 1776.*

the most important of these ideas was the separation of powers, the idea that the Baron de Montesquieu had described in *The Spirit of the Laws*. James Madison, an American who is known today as "the father of the Constitution," adopted Montesquieu's idea that the government should have three separate branches so that no one person or group would become too powerful. The U.S. legislative, judicial, and executive branches, and the system of checks and balances that allows each branch to limit the others' powers, directly reflect Montesquieu's ideas.

## Revolution Spreads

*What role did Enlightenment ideas play in the French Revolution?*

Enlightenment ideals also contributed to the French Revolution, which began in 1789. The French Revolution was partly caused by unfair tax practices. The nobles and the clergy paid few taxes while the common people paid most of the taxes that the government needed to function. Another cause of the

revolution, however, was the changing attitudes of the French common people. Enlightenment ideas had begun to spread through the nation. In particular, Jean-Jacques Rousseau's idea that ordinary people should have a say in their government gained influence with many people in France.

In 1789, the people of France overthrew their king and created a new Assembly in which the common people had more rights.

PRISE DE LA BASTILLE le 14 Juillet 1789.
Par les Citoyens et les ci-devant Gardes Françaises.

photo: Getty Images

*The Storming of the Bastille, Paris, 1789.*

The Assembly wrote a new constitution, which included the Declaration of the Rights of Man and of the Citizen. This document was heavily influenced by the ideas of Rousseau and other Enlightenment thinkers. It said that "Men are born free and remain free and equal in rights" and it listed the natural rights that people are born with.

Over the next few years, the French Revolution grew increasingly violent. The king and queen of France were executed in 1793, and the revolutionaries divided into factions. This led to the imprisonment and execution of thousands of people. This period, known as the Reign of Terror, ended when General Napoléon Bonaparte took control of the government in 1799.

Although the violence of the French Revolution was excessive and is rejected by most people today, its original ideals of equality and rights remain important to people all over the world today. The Enlightenment, which was the origin of those ideals, is seen as a time when people's belief in rational thought led to important historical changes.

## Consider the Essential Question:

How did the philosophies of the Enlightenment influence politics and society in Europe?

Go online to complete the Social Studies Explanation.

## Check for Understanding:

What were the three basic principles of the Enlightenment? How did these ideas shape government and society?